Kafka Comes to America

KAFKA COMES TO AMERICA

FIGHTING FOR JUSTICE
IN THE WAR ON TERROR

STEVEN T. WAX

OTHER PRESS · NEW YORK

Production Editor: Yvonne E. Cárdenas

Text Designer: Rachel Reiss

This book was set in 10.5 pt Celeste Regular by Alpha Graphics of Pittsfield, New Hampshire.

10 9 8 7 6 5 4 3 2 1

Library of Congress Cataloging-in-Publication Data

Wax, Steven T.
  Kafka comes to America : fighting for justice in the war on terror / Steven T. Wax.
      p. cm.
  Includes bibliographical references and index.
    ISBN 978-1-59051-295-1
  1. Detention of persons—United States.   2. War on Terrorism, 2001—Law and legislation—United States.   3. Civil rights—Government policy—United States.   4. Due process of law—United States.   5. Terrorists—Legal status, laws, etc.,—United States.   6. Prisoners of war—Legal status, laws, etc.—Cuba—Guantánamo Bay Naval Base.   I. Title.

  KF9625.W39 2008
  345.73'056—dc22

                                                              2007045437

For Jack and Julius

Our government is the potent, the omnipresent teacher. For good or for ill, it teaches the whole people by its example. Crime is contagious. If the government becomes a lawbreaker, it breeds contempt for law.

—Justice Louis Brandeis, *Olmstead
v. United States*, 1928

———————————

Whenever I despair, I remember that all through history the way of truth and love has always won. There have always been tyrants and murderers, and for a time, they may seem invincible, but in the end, they always fall.

—Mahatma Gandhi

Contents

Kafka Comes to America

Prologue

We cannot defend freedom abroad by deserting it at home.

—Edward R. Murrow[1]

IN JANUARY 2002, THE GATES OF HELL opened in Guantánamo Bay, Cuba. The first prisoners from the U.S. incursion in Afghanistan and the hunt for Osama Bin Laden were brought trussed, blindfolded, earmuffed, and muzzled to what has become the United States' most notorious prison. Two years later, terrorist bombs blasted the morning commute in Madrid, Spain, into a scene of carnage, killing 191 people, including three Americans, and wounding more than two thousand. In May of 2004, Brandon Mayfield, a lawyer in my hometown of Portland, Oregon, was arrested as a material witness to the bombings in Madrid based on a mistaken fingerprint identification by the FBI. I was assigned to represent Brandon on the night of his arrest and to represent seven of the men held in the prison in Guantánamo Bay a year and a half later.

Early in my career, I wielded the power of our law enforcers as an assistant district attorney in Brooklyn, New York, prosecuting robbers, kidnappers, and mass murderers, including the notorious Son of Sam. I worked side by side with dedicated public servants but also dealt with rogue cops who laughed as they ran roughshod over the rights of the Brooklynites they had sworn to serve. Usually the people abused were poor and black.

Before getting into the trenches, first as a prosecutor, then later as a defense attorney, I had learned about executive power, and executive abuse, on a grander scale as a law student from Archibald Cox, who was just back to teaching after the "Saturday night massacre," the night President Nixon's attorney general, Elliot Richardson, and his deputy resigned rather than follow the president's order to fire Cox from his job as special Watergate prosecutor before Solicitor General Robert Bork did the job.[2] After a month of prodding from his students, Cox shared his experiences as the special prosecutor investigating the Watergate scandal, the burglary and cover-up that eventually led to Nixon's impeachment and resignation. Cox's gangly and stooped body belied the strength of his character as he led a heady discussion about personal responsibility, the importance of the rule of law, and the abuse of presidential power.

Cox's lecture stirred memories of my family's history, the stories I had grown up with about dangerous despots, my grandfather's conscription into and flight from the czar's army in Russia shortly after the turn of the century, and my great-grandfather's murder in a pogrom. This history had burned into me as a child, and I had been drawn to the law as an instrument of justice to protect the weak and oppressed. When I first headed off to law school, I thought I would be what was then called a "poverty lawyer" and work on civil cases to help bring about social change. My constitutional and criminal procedure classes showed me that it is in enforcing the criminal law that our government continually encroaches on our freedoms. Cox's lecture underscored how important it is to have people of integrity, who understand the limits under which they must work, wielding the government's police powers and moved me in a different direction.

After several years exercising the executive's power, I realized that I was drawn into the lives of the people I was prosecuting and was too often uncomfortable with my role in taking away their freedom. I could have continued as a prosecutor in political and corruption cases, but the defense side of the bar beckoned and I left the district attorney to lead the county public defender's office in Binghamton, New York.

As much as I like helping the little guy and am fascinated and titillated by the drama of the human condition revealed in criminal cases, I have always been more interested in the big issues in these cases—liberty versus security, when the police can stop us on the street, enter our homes, intercept our telephone calls or e-mails, or monitor our Internet use. For most of my career, these issues have often been obscured by the emotion of the crime and the miserable reality of the defendants' lives.

In the wake of the fear spreading across the country following the attacks of September 11, 2001, on the World Trade Center and the Pentagon, the focus has shifted. The "big issues" at stake in the courtroom are now clearly visible as the dialogue about freedom and security has shifted to the forefront and top government officials and their lawyers openly argue that the president needs unchecked power of the kind not seen in America or England in hundreds of years in order to keep us safe. In designing and executing the "war on terror," the Bush administration has argued for these expanded powers in court, worked with its friends in Congress to rewrite the law, and grabbed power through executive orders and presidential fiat. While I was comfortable wielding the executive's power as a prosecutor in Brooklyn in the 1970s, I could never assist in the current efforts: They go too far and are based on too many half-truths and outright misstatements.

I have spent much of the last six years fighting against the administration's assault on civil liberties and the corrosive effect of fear. This has not been an abstract battle for justice or the concept of freedom, it has been a fight for the lives of the individuals caught in fear's wake. This book tells the story of my work for Brandon Mayfield, a United States citizen and lawyer, and Adel Hamad, a Sudanese relief worker, both falsely accused in the war on terror.

1 | Footprints in the Carpet

You're not paranoid if they are after you.

—Anon.

AROUND FOUR IN THE AFTERNOON ON April 8, 2004, Brandon Mayfield's wife, Mona, walked up the front steps onto the porch of their two-story wooden home in Beaverton, on the west slope of the hills that circle Oregon's largest city, Portland. Since Brandon had opened his own law practice the year before, Mona spent most days working as his paralegal and office manager, but she had taken this Thursday off to catch up on chores around the house. Juggling her purse and a bag of groceries, Mona put the key in the lock and turned it the way she had hundreds of times. But the door didn't budge. The dead bolt had been thrown, a dead bolt she and Brandon never used. Unlocking the door, she peered inside, then called out, but no one answered.

Looking around, Mona walked in slowly and went into the kitchen, where she put her purse and groceries on the counter. Then she went into the living room. As she stepped on the carpet, she stopped. She can't say why, but something just didn't feel right. Was one of the pictures on the mantel out of place? No. Well, maybe. Were the blinds on one of the windows ajar? Was that a footprint she saw in the deep-pile white carpet? Mona had vacuumed that morning and there shouldn't have been any footprints; Brandon had been in the office all day, and their children, Shane, Sharia, and

Samir, had been in school. Nothing had been taken; the television and computer were where they should have been. She stood there a while, shook her head, then went back into the kitchen to prepare dinner.

When Brandon got home that night, Mona checked with him. "Did you use the dead bolt when you left for work today?"

"No," he answered. "Why?"

Mona told Brandon what had happened. They looked around together, but nothing was missing and they could not be sure anything was out of place. Brandon checked with the kids, but none of them remembered using the dead bolt and none had come home from school during the day. The whole family went to bed that night with a lingering sense of unease, though Mona and Brandon wondered if they were just imagining things.

Returning from work a week later, Mona got out of her car, walked up the drive, and put the key in the lock. Again, the dead bolt was thrown. Mona stood there a while, then unlocked the door and walked into the living room. Just like the week before, something was not right. But this time she was sure; the digital clock on the VCR was blinking and so was the one in the kitchen. Someone had been in her home.

Mona called Brandon. "You need to come home. It's happened again."

"Are you sure someone's been there?"

"How can I be sure of anything, Brandon? Please come home."

Mona and Brandon searched carefully, from living room to dining room, from the den to the upstairs bedrooms. The digital clocks and clock radios were blinking. Also, it looked like someone had rummaged through some of the drawers in their bedroom. But, again, nothing appeared to be missing. Brandon checked the circuit breakers in the basement, but they had not been tripped. Mona called PGE, their electric company, to see if there had been any outages in their neighborhood that day—there had not been.

Brandon and Mona sat up half the night trying to figure out what could be going on. What kind of burglary was this? Who would invade their home? Until then, everything was looking good for Brandon. His children were all doing well in school, his law practice was growing, and Mona was happy helping out at the office and running their home.

Born in the southern Oregon fishing and logging port of Coos Bay, Brandon had grown up in the small Kansas communities of Halstead and Buhler where his father, Bill, worked as a custom harvester and his mother, AvNell, worked as an art teacher. These were conservative Christian communities where the fact that Brandon's family, though nominally Christian, did not attend church made them stand out as a little leftist.

Brandon graduated from Halstead High School in 1984 and joined the army reserves the next spring, signing up for a full tour. He met Mona on a blind date one night in 1987 while stationed in Fort Lewis, Washington. The daughter of an Egyptian professor at St. Martin's University, in Olympia, Mona and her father had left Egypt when she was five, and they lived in Paris and Massachusetts before he was offered the professorship at St. Martin's. While Mona was raised as a Muslim, and her faith continued to be important to her after moving to the United States, she was a westernized Muslim.

Brandon re-upped for another year in 1988, then left the army to attend college in Oregon. Returning to his roots, he enrolled at Portland State University and graduated in 1992. When Brandon and Mona fell in love and decided to marry, Brandon, for whom his Christianity had never been particularly deep, converted to Islam. After graduation, he rejoined the army, qualifying for officer training, and soon became a lieutenant. Brandon was then stationed in Bitburg, Germany, where he served with distinction in the fifth battalion, seventh division Air Artillery until his commitment ended in 1995. Among other jobs during his service, Brandon worked with a Patriot missile battery. That posting would later haunt him.

After discharge from the army, Brandon and Mona moved to Kansas, where he enrolled in the law school at Washburn University. Even though Brandon's family was nearby, they felt isolated there and decided to move back to the Northwest where they had found the people to be more tolerant and progressive. Brandon completed his degree requirements at the Northwestern School of Law at Lewis and Clark College in Portland and received his law degree on his thirty-third birthday, July 15, 1999.

Brandon had been an average law student, and the coveted judicial clerkship and large firm positions appeared out of reach and not of particular interest. He was happy to be hired as an associate with Macpherson, Gintner, Gordon, & Diaz, a small firm in Newport on the Oregon coast, midway between the California and Washington borders. Most of the cases Brandon worked on involved divorce and custody issues, but he also handled a couple of simple criminal matters.

After two years of small-town life, the Mayfields decided they wanted to be closer to Portland, where there was more of a Muslim community, and Brandon set up his own practice. While continuing to handle domestic relations cases, Brandon branched out into immigration law and attracted a growing number of Middle Eastern and Muslim clients. He was also involved as a volunteer with the Oregon State Bar's Modest Means Program, providing legal services to the poor at greatly reduced rates.

The year before his arrest, one of Brandon's domestic relations clients was Jeffrey Battle, one of seven homegrown Portland jihadists who had attempted to join the cause in Afghanistan after the U.S. incursion in the fall of 2001. Battle hired Brandon to help arrange for custody of his son when it became apparent that he was going to be sentenced to prison for his effort to join the fight against the United States. Brandon had no way of knowing at the time, but his brief professional connection to Battle would be used against him in court a little more than a year later.

In the years after September 11, 2001, Brandon and Mona had been troubled by the rise in anti-Muslim sentiment in the country. This affected them personally in the increasingly hostile stares directed at Mona and Sharia, who followed Muslim custom and covered their heads when they were out in public. Although Brandon had converted to Islam, he and his family were moderate in their practice. Brandon attended mosque on Fridays but did not stop his work to pray five times a day as orthodox Muslims do. Politically, he believed strongly in the Constitution but was in the minority in democratic Portland, having voted for George W. Bush in the 2000 election.

In several late-night phone calls, Brandon and Mona told his parents about the disturbances in their home and their suspicion that they were somehow being targeted because Mona was Egyptian and the family was Muslim. AvNell and Bill counseled the best they could, but Brandon and Mona were so traumatized that the conversations eventually turned to what his parents should do with the kids if something happened to them.

Before the break-ins, Brandon and Mona often kept large sums of cash, up to $10,000, in a small safe in their house. Following the teachings of the Koran, they tried not to engage in banking transactions that would bring them interest. But after the unexplainable intrusions, Mona was spooked enough to take a safe-deposit box at a local bank and put in their passports, birth and marriage certificates, and her naturalization papers, along with their cash. Within a month, this innocent act would also come back to haunt the Mayfields.

Brandon and Mona just could not shake the feeling that something terribly wrong was happening, and they started acting erratically. While driving, Brandon would pull into a driveway or cul-de-sac, then suddenly turn around, looking to see if he was being followed. He would sometimes drive away from his home, only to circle the block, searching for watchers. Even Mona and the kids thought they saw a suspicious-looking white van that kept cruising the neighborhood. One time, Brandon spotted a van and, recalling countless scenes from spy movies, called the phone number printed on the side to see if it was legitimate. It seemed to be.

Once the fear set in, even prospective clients were suspect. Late in April, Mona took a routine call at the office from a man who said he was calling from San Francisco and had heard from someone named Walid that Brandon did immigration law. While he spoke in English, the caller had an accent and said he knew Arabic. Mona didn't recall anyone named Walid, but that wasn't unusual. Maybe the man had heard of Brandon from a client; maybe he had seen an ad they had taken in an Internet yellow page aimed at the Muslim community; maybe he had seen Brandon's name in the newspaper from the one publicized case he had been peripherally involved in, his representation of Jeffrey Battle in the custody dispute while Battle was being prosecuted as a terrorist. Whatever the source, at first this seemed to Mona to be the type of word-of-mouth referral that all lawyers hope for and that builds a practice.

She set up an appointment and took a call-back number. When the man didn't show up for their meeting, she called the number he had given her and got no tone or message. A month before, Mona would have shrugged this off, but not now. She told Brandon about the "situation," and he agreed that it was "odd." A couple of days later, the man called back, apologized for missing his appointment, and told a story about being questioned by the FBI. Now Brandon and Mona were worried and started speculating: Had the FBI tapped the office phone? Was the caller an FBI agent? From immigration? Did this have something to do with one of Brandon's cases?

. . .

Brandon and Mona had learned about the Madrid bombings while they were watching the Disney Channel with their children the night of March 11, 2004. Brandon's immediate reaction had been disgust: "How can terrorists do such things to innocent people?" Although Brandon was not an activist, he was more interested in human rights issues than most people. He read widely, used the Internet to study world events, and had spoken up a few times about issues that bothered him, including the treatment of the Palestinians in the Middle East, where he felt the United States, with its support for Israel, was not evenhanded in the conflict. When he learned about the bombings in Madrid, Brandon wanted to understand what had happened and spent time searching the Internet for information on the circumstances and the terrorists. This would turn out to be another innocent act that would later cause him trouble. The attacks did not involve him personally, and like most Oregonians, Brandon never drew any connection between them and what looked like strange intrusions into his home.

■　■　■

Two more weeks passed after the initial break-ins, weeks in which the fear and worry began to dissipate as no more incidents occurred. Then it happened—a knock on the door around 9:30 in the morning on Thursday, May 6. People living under a host of dictatorships around the world, from Russia to Latin America to North Korea, have learned to dread the "knock on the door" from the KGB, Cheka, or Stasi. But here in America it is not something we have had to fear since the "visits" from government agents and recruitment of informers during the Communist witch hunts in the late 1940s and early 1950s by Senator Joseph McCarthy and the House Un-American Activities Committee. Even then, the fear was never widespread. When Brandon answered the knock on his office door in Beaverton that day, his worst nightmare turned real.

2 | "Portland Lawyer Arrested!"

A too confident sense of justice always leads to injustice.
—Reinhold Niebuhr[1]

I FIRST MET BRANDON MAYFIELD IN THE Multnomah county jail on Friday morning, May 7, 2004. When the door opened into the eight-foot-square institutional green visiting room, I saw a man around my height, five ten, but slight and studious looking, with stringy brown hair, wearing metal-framed glasses and dressed in jail blues. I thought he looked overwhelmed and in need of reassurance. His life had been turned upside down the day before when he was arrested by the FBI.

As Brandon described it, the day of his arrest had been unfolding like any other until he heard a knock. He got up from his computer to open the door of his office on the ground floor of a strip mall near his home.

"Good morning, Mr. Mayfield. I'm Special Agent David Carroll with the Federal Bureau of Investigation, and we'd like to ask you a few questions. May we come in?"

"What's this about?" he asked Carroll and his partner, who were standing side by side blocking his exit.

"We'd rather talk about this inside."

"I don't want you in my office. I have client files here and I don't want you coming in."

"I am sorry, Mr. Mayfield. We can't stay out here."

Brandon and the agents will never agree on whether he eventually invited the agents in or they just entered. But he is certain he made it clear to them that they had no business being in his office anywhere near his client files, which were in the reception area visible from the doorway. The reality is that Brandon had no choice—they had guns and an arrest warrant.

Once inside, Carroll told Brandon that he wanted to talk to him about Spain. Brandon, who was in the midst of preparing for a federal trial for a client in a personal injury case, politely but firmly told the agents that he did not want to talk to them. He just did not understand the gravity of the situation.

Brandon told them again, "I don't want you here with my client files and I don't want to talk to you. I don't want you in my office. I have client files here."[2]

Apparently realizing that they weren't getting anywhere with Brandon, Agent Carroll shifted gears and told Brandon that he was under arrest. He then proceeded to read two warrants that had been issued by Senior Federal Judge Robert E. Jones earlier that morning: a warrant authorizing a search of Brandon's law office and a warrant for his arrest. Shocked by what he had just heard, Brandon has no memory of being told why he was being arrested or being questioned about Spain.

Following standard procedure, the agents started to handcuff Brandon. Concerned about his reputation and his practice, Brandon asked them to stop.

"There's no need to handcuff me." When they did not stop, Brandon repeated, "Please don't put the handcuffs on here. I don't want my neighbors to see me in that state."

The cuffs went on and one of the agents told Brandon, "They'll know soon enough. The media is right behind us."[3]

How was that possible? Grand jury proceedings are supposed to be conducted in secret. Police, including the FBI, and prosecutors have an obligation to protect their witnesses. Yet someone had told the media, and not just the local outlets; Michael Isikoff, of *Newsweek*, broke the story before anyone else and knew of Brandon's friend, fellow Muslim, and attorney Tom Nelson's involvement in the case within minutes of Nelson's learning of Brandon's arrest.[4] When Brandon first told me about the "media" conversation in the county jail that Friday morning, it immediately reinforced my concern that he was being held not as a witness but as a suspect in the bombings.

The agents led Brandon to their dark blue car for the trip to the FBI offices in downtown Portland. During the brief stop there, Brandon asked one of the agents to call Nelson to come to the courthouse to represent him at the arraignment on the arrest warrant. He was then driven to the new Mark O. Hatfield Federal Courthouse three blocks away.

The Hatfield Courthouse is a sixteen-story behemoth with a Statue of Liberty crown that dwarfs the columned, Depression-era county courthouse across the street. The United States marshal has his offices on the fourth floor, along with a small day jail to hold prisoners with court appearances. Brandon was taken there while arrangements were made for his first appearance in court. Tom Nelson, who had stopped at the United States Attorney's offices on the sixth floor of the courthouse and gotten a copy of the warrant and the affidavit the FBI had filed with the court to get the warrant, met Brandon in the marshal's lockup.

It was only when he read the affidavit with Nelson that Brandon realized he was being connected to the Madrid train bombings by a fingerprint identification. Sealed from public view, but with the key points leaked to the media, the affidavit provided a very condensed version of Spain's investigation of the bombings. In particular it pointed to the lifting of a fingerprint labeled "latent print #17" from a bag of unexploded detonators that had been found in a van and Spain's request for help through Interpol in trying to identify the print. The affidavit told the judge that the FBI had declared with 100 percent certainty that latent print #17 matched Brandon's.

Later that day, in midafternoon, Judge Robert E. Jones arraigned Brandon on the material witness warrant. For the protection of the witness, the arraignment was held behind the closed doors of his wood-paneled courtroom. Based on the "100 percent" fingerprint identification, Judge Jones, an austere-looking man in his fortieth year on the bench and known in legal circles as "the Ice Man," held Brandon without bail.

Under the law, prosecutors are allowed to have a person arrested as a "material witness" if they don't believe he committed a crime but believe he knows about it and will flee if they ask for his testimony voluntarily.[5] In theory, that's why Brandon was arrested. But when Nelson saw the "100 percent" identification and that the material witness warrant described terrorism charges carrying the death penalty, he realized that Brandon could actually be charged with the bombings and needed lawyers expert in federal criminal defense. He arranged with Judge Jones to call my office, where he reached assistant defender Chris Schatz, the duty attorney responsible for new case intake that day. Chris set out to get the arrest warrant and the supporting affidavit from Nelson, then went for a brief visit with Brandon in the county jail next door to the courthouse.

That night, headlines around the world announced, "FBI Connects Lawyer with 'Portland 7' Tie to Madrid Bombings."[6] Soon, the banner headline in Oregon's largest newspaper, the *Oregonian*, blared leaked information, "Fingerprint Links Oregon with Spain." The story went on to state that Brandon was "linked to the attack" by a "fingerprint on a bag containing detonating devices."[7]

. . .

After the first team of agents had arrested Brandon, a second team spent the rest of the morning conducting a thorough search of his law office, taking Brandon's computers, many of his client files, and miscellaneous papers.[8] As Brandon told me later with some bitterness, one thing the agents did not take was a framed copy of the Bill of Rights that hung next to his office door.

At the same time as Brandon's office was being searched, a separate team of FBI agents was at his home with another search warrant, going through it room by room, drawer by drawer, and paper by paper. They left with numerous documents, some books, and his home computer. Mona described the FBI's approach as anything but gentle, their home looking like it had been "ransacked," like they "had been robbed."[9]

The agents also took Brandon and Mona's credit cards and the key to the safe-deposit box Mona had opened just weeks before. Later in the day, the FBI froze the Mayfields' bank accounts. Mona, who was home that morning, obviously knew something was terribly wrong. But what? With the court proceedings closed to the public, Mona did not know what had happened to Brandon. As far as she was concerned, Brandon had disappeared.

The seizure of the law office and their home computer and papers made it difficult for Mona to carry on with her life and keep Brandon's law practice afloat. But as devastating as this was, it was nothing compared to the conversation she had with the children. As Mona put it weeks later, "The most difficult part was telling our children that their father had been arrested. You can't imagine what it did to me to hear little Samir say, 'They took our daddy away.'"

. . .

The night Brandon was jailed, Chris had called, interrupting me at home where I was trying to help my son Michael catch up on homework missed the day before when we celebrated his thirteenth birthday. Chris, only two years younger than I am, is an intense and incredibly well-read man whose office is lined with books on philosophy and religion rather than law. Five ten, barrel-chested, with salt-and-pepper hair and small hands, Chris had left behind a thriving private practice in Southern California for Oregon and the federal defender office in 1991. Chris had taken the call late in the day from Tom Nelson and thought that I, as head of the office, should know that we were about to get into a huge case.

In May 2004, I had seventy employees, including twenty-one assistant federal defenders and eighteen investigators, in three locations. My office represents people in criminal and habeas corpus cases in federal court, handling between 60 and 70 percent of all federal cases filed in Oregon. The office headquarters is in Portland, with branches in Eugene, 110 miles south in the Willamette Valley, and Medford, 15 miles from the California border. As the head of the office, I wear many hats. While I went to law school to become a lawyer, I am also now a manager, teacher, and supervisor. Believing that the best way to lead is by example, I keep an active caseload and often get involved in the more complex cases that come our way. Hence, the call from Chris.

When Brandon's case hit the office, I had just been appointed to my sixth four-year term as the federal public defender for the District of Oregon by the United States Court of Appeals for the Ninth Circuit, the body charged by Congress with appointing the federal defenders on the West Coast. Twenty-one years earlier, when I started my first term after eight action-packed years in the state system in New York, I was the youngest federal defender in the country and by 2004, I was one of the longest-serving office heads.

When Chris and I checked in with the deputy sheriff in the Multnomah County Justice Center to see Brandon that first time Friday morning, we did not use the name Mayfield. Instead, we asked for a visit with "Randy Taylor," the name the United States marshal for Oregon told us he had made up when he booked Brandon into the jail the night before. The marshal's intention was to hide Brandon's identity, to protect him from the other inmates and to keep his arrest as a grand jury witness secret. But the only thing the false name accomplished was to slow down our visit as the deputy and I sorted out in whispers who we really wanted to see. In Portland, and around the world, anyone reading a newspaper or watching television knew that Brandon Mayfield, Portland lawyer, Muslim convert, and husband of an Egyptian, had been arrested and lodged in the county jail.[10]

When the deputy brought Brandon into the meeting room and locked the door behind him, we shook hands tentatively and then sat down in the off-white plastic chairs encircling the round table that took up most of the room. Chris and I had brought yellow pads, the arrest warrant, and the affidavit. We knew we would have to address the "100 percent" identification, but I wanted to start the conversation by building rapport, talking about the grand jury witness process, and our roles as Brandon's lawyers and his as a client. Even as a lawyer himself with some familiarity with the criminal justice system and the pressures of the courtroom, the appearance in court on Thursday had been overwhelming for Brandon. Being taken from his office in handcuffs and separated from his family had shaken him profoundly. As he later described it, "It was pretty dark for me those first couple of days—being treated like I'm public enemy number one and knowing there's a capital punishment penalty at the end of all this."

Lawyers make notoriously difficult clients. We are used to giving advice, not taking it, so we all felt our way slowly for the first half hour as Brandon got used his new role. Brandon told us what he had said to Judge Jones in court the previous day.

MR. MAYFIELD: That's not my fingerprint your honor.
THE COURT: . . . What were you going to say? It wasn't your fingerprint?
MR. MAYFIELD: If it is, I don't know how it got there. It is not my fingerprint.[11]

The United States attorney, Karin Immergut, was represented in court that first day, and throughout the case, by three assistants: Charles Gorder, chief terrorism prosecutor in Oregon; Pam Holsinger; and David Atkinson. In keeping with the practice that had held in Oregon for decades, Immergut was a professional prosecutor rather than a purely political appointee, having served as an assistant U.S. attorney in Los Angeles and as both an assistant U.S. attorney and assistant district attorney in Portland. Immergut's only political hook was five months spent working for Special Prosecutor Kenneth Starr on the investigation into the Monica Lewinsky scandal involving President Clinton.

Gorder and I had gotten to know each other a bit outside the courtroom when we were both adjunct professors at the Northwestern School of Law at Lewis and Clark College. A low-key and straightforward man in his mid-fifties, Gorder can listen carefully at a meeting of chiefs and work them toward consensus. While he and I had not always agreed on how a case should be resolved, I always felt that Gorder acted out of a sense of justice and had understood the limits on his role as prosecutor.

Atkinson, a stocky, deep-voiced man with a bristling mustache, was all business. A good lawyer, Atkinson has a rigidity that sometimes makes it difficult for him to see beyond the immensity of his responsibility as a terrorism prosecutor charged by the attorney general with doing whatever he can to ensure that America is not attacked again. He had been trained in the Lane County district attorney's office in Eugene in the late 1970s and served a stint as an assistant U.S. attorney in St. Croix in the Virgin Islands before settling in the United States attorney's office in Portland.

Holsinger fell somewhere between the two in her approach. In her mid-forties, she had been working as an assistant U.S. attorney in the drug unit in Portland since moving west from Washington, D.C., in the early '90s, where she had worked in the drug division in the Department of Justice. True to her Marine roots as a JAG officer, Holsinger had always been a tough advocate, but she did occasionally see the defense side of things.

In addition to the three assistant U.S. attorneys, looming in the background in court on May 6 and throughout the case was the presence of "Washington" in the form of the FBI and of Attorney General John Ashcroft —the former Missouri senator who was appointed by President Bush after he lost his bid for re-election to Mel Carnahan, whose name remained on the ballot even though he was killed in an airplane crash just a month before the election. Ashcroft's conservatism and inflexibility were frequently on display, including his order to hide the statue of Lady Justice that had graced the attorney general's office for decades behind a blue curtain because he found her bare breasts offensive.[12]

When Brandon interrupted Judge Jones at his arraignment to tell him that it was not his fingerprint, the judge, having heard protestations of innocence countless times during his career, reminded Brandon not only that he had the right to remain silent and that any response could be used against him if he was charged with the crime, but that his statements could also be used against him "even to the extent they might consist of an inconsistent or false statement." Meaning, if the prosecutors thought Brandon lied in his testimony, those lies could form the basis for a perjury prosecution even if he was innocent of the bombings.

As a material witness, Brandon was supposed to tell the grand jury what he knew about the Madrid bombings. At the first court appearance, the judge told Brandon that if the prosecutor agreed, he didn't actually have to appear in front of the grand jury but could talk directly to the prosecutors less formally in a deposition. But, like the statements the judge had just warned him about, whatever he revealed to the prosecutors or the grand jury could later be used to prosecute him—for capital murder. The only way Brandon could refuse to testify was if he took the Fifth, that is, asserted his right under the Fifth Amendment to the Constitution not to incriminate himself.

At the arraignment, true to his style, Judge Jones pushed to get things moving and scheduled the grand jury to meet the following Tuesday, only four days away. He also told Brandon that if he agreed, an informal deposition could take place sooner. And, what Brandon heard most clearly from the judge that first day was that he could "be released upon giving sworn testimony under oath in a deposition." Only if he talked, the judge said, would the court be in a "position to release you."

To help Brandon understand his options, Judge Jones gave him a copy of a decision by the United States Court of Appeals for the Second Circuit involving a college student named Osama Awadallah.[13] Awadallah had been arrested on a material witness warrant in San Diego shortly after the attacks of September 11. The prosecutors thought Awadallah knew something about the attacks even though he said he did not. Like Brandon, Awadallah protested his innocence and wanted to get out of jail. Given the same choices Judge Jones gave Brandon, Awadallah agreed to talk to the prosecutors in a deposition. Even though Awadallah was never charged in the September 11 attacks, the prosecutors believed he lied in the deposition and he was then charged with perjury. Awadallah had to suffer through years of litigation before a jury acquitted him of the charge.

By the time I sat down with Brandon on Friday morning, he had read the entire eighty-three-page Awadallah decision. He wanted out of jail and had understood the judge to mean that he could get out as soon as he talked. He had not been told that there was a catch to giving a deposition. Unlike the grand jury, where a person can't be forced to testify unless he is given immunity, if Brandon agreed to talk in an informal deposition, there was no requirement of immunity. Awadallah had found this out the hard way, and Chris and I were not about to let it happen to Brandon. We also had to tell him the prosecutors would probably not believe anything he said as long as they had the 100 percent fingerprint identification.

Early in our meeting, Chris told Brandon, "We need to assume that you really are a defendant, not just a witness. You may be in the witness basket now and we want to keep you there, but we have to plan as though the government is going to make you a defendant."

After a second long day in the jail with Brandon on Saturday, I saw that day's *Oregonian* when I got home, and the story on Brandon confirmed our fears about what was really going on. Government officials were reported to have said that they didn't intend to take Brandon before the grand jury because they knew he would not talk and they were not going to grant him immunity. The real purpose of the arrest was clear: It "gives the FBI time to finish its investigation."[14]

My instincts that we should move slowly were reinforced by the *Oregonian* article, but even with the ultimate penalty looming, the thought of going slowly was difficult for Brandon to hear. He was angry; he felt violated by what had happened to him and used by the fact that the FBI had told him the media was there at the arrest. As he had told the judge in court, "I have got clients I have got to assist . . . I am an officer of this court. To me it is embarrassing. It is humiliating. . . . If *Newsweek* and so forth is going to be here and I'm detained, I have zero credibility with my clients."

When he raised the same concerns with us, Chris and I told him that grand jury proceedings are indeed supposed to be held in secret and we would bring up the leaks. The secrecy is supposed to be for the protection of grand jury witnesses, Chris added.

Brandon's anger was clearly visible in the jail, fueled by much more than the leaks. References to his religion in the warrant affidavit cut him deeply; he felt that he had been singled out because he was a Muslim. As Tom Nelson had politely told Judge Jones, "I'm very troubled by the innuendo in the affidavit regarding Islam. I think that's something we will ultimately have to think about, but the damage is done for Mr. Mayfield."

We needed to make the critical decision very quickly about whether Brandon should testify in the grand jury. But before we could answer that, Chris and I were convinced we had to start figuring out the details of the fingerprint identification. If the identification was correct, we needed to assume that the material witness notion would be dropped and Brandon would be charged with capital murder. While my first impression of Brandon made the idea of him being involved in the bombings ridiculous, that impression foundered on the apparent rock of the fingerprint identification and, like Judge Jones, I had heard protestations of innocence melt away any number of times during my career. Periodically surfacing from its presence in the background of our discussions about the fingerprint over the next days was the possibility that Brandon would be charged with a capital crime.

. . .

It was tough to talk to Brandon about the possibility of a death penalty charge. It's like a doctor telling a patient with what he thinks is a routine stomachache that he has pancreatic cancer. While the death penalty hovered over our discussions, as long as Brandon was in the witness basket it stayed somewhere off in the distance. But more immediate, and even more difficult to talk about, was the possibility that we might not ever get to see Brandon again—a possibility made real by the policies of the Bush administration.

On April 20 and 28, less than two weeks before Brandon's arrest, Solicitor General Ted Olson and his chief deputy, Paul Clement, had argued to the Supreme Court on behalf of the president and his administration that the president had the power to take or order anyone, including U.S. citizens arrested in the United States, out of the federal court system and hold them indefinitely in military detention without charges or trial.[15] Of the three cases in which the solicitors made their arguments, two involved U.S. citizens who had been arrested on suspicion of terrorist activities and links to Al Qaeda. José Padilla, who had been arrested at the Chicago airport on a material witness warrant related to the attacks of September 11, and Yaser Hamdi, who had been picked up in northern Afghanistan, were taken away to the navy brig in Charleston, South Carolina, where they were still being held without charges and without trial. Though arrested as a material witness to the September 11 attacks, Padilla was actually being held on suspicion of plotting to blow up a radioactive bomb.

The other case involved two British citizens who had been captured in Afghanistan after the United States joined the fight against the Taliban in the months after September 11. These men, Shafiq Rasul and Asif Iqbal, had been taken out of Afghanistan and flown to the U.S. military prison at Guantánamo Bay, Cuba, where they languished for more than two years.

There was nothing subtle about the administration's position. In Padilla's case, Deputy Solicitor Clement told the Supreme Court that the president "might well have" the authority, even "in the absence" of congressional authorization, to take and hold someone rather than just try to punish him for a war crime, if the president thought the person had valuable information.[16] Expressing some skepticism about this assertion, the justices asked Clement why the administration believed it had to jettison the criminal justice system and even the system of military trials.

When I read the transcript of the argument and Clement's response, I thought the deputy solicitor had read *Henry the VI, Part II*, where Shakespeare has anarchist and criminal Dick the Butcher explain how to get away with their plots: "The first thing we do, let's kill all the lawyers." Understanding the power of lawyers in enforcing the rule of law, the deputy solicitor told the justices that the administration wanted to keep people out of the justice system, military or civilian, because in either system there would be a right to "counsel who likely is going to say you shouldn't talk."

I told Brandon about the argument and that, "It's possible you won't be here tomorrow." In light of the administration's stance, I had to add, "Brandon, this is real; they've actually done it. Hamdi and Padilla are in the naval brig."

Trained in the law and believing in American justice, Brandon could not accept what I had said. "But I'm a United States citizen."

"So are they. It doesn't matter."

His voice rising, he barked back, "I'm a lawyer! I have cases pending in the federal court next door!"

"I understand. This is the new reality. We have to deal with it, Brandon. We need a plan. If anyone comes to take you out of the jail, ask who they are and where they are taking you. They probably won't tell you, but try, politely but firmly. Try to call us."

Periodically in its history, the United States had turned on aliens and foreigners. Just after the Russian Revolution, the government had orchestrated mass deportations of "reds." Once, during World War II, the victims even included citizens, when 112,000 Japanese Americans living on the West Coast were locked up in "internment camps." Now the attorney general had declared that the official policy of the Bush administration was that citizens could be stripped of their rights merely on the president's word. No process, no grand juries, no district attorneys, no nothing, and I had to tell my client, an attorney himself, that it could happen to him.

The position taken in the Supreme Court by the nation's highest lawyer about the reach of the president's power was consistent with the overall strategic decisions the Bush administration had taken in the days after the attacks of September 11. America's response to the terrorist attacks was going to be a war, a war fought abroad and at home, a war fought with soldiers but also in the shadows "using any means at our disposal," as Vice President Cheney stated.[17] The United States was not going after only Bin Laden, the architect of the September 11 attacks, or his minions to bring them to justice in a courtroom. Rather, as Cofer Black, head of the Central Intelligence Agency's Counterterrorism Center declared in 2001, "We locate the enemy wherever they are across the planet. We find them and we kill them."[18]

Sitting in that jail cell, all we could do was promise Brandon that if he disappeared, we would fight like hell through the courts and in Congress. Everyone in the world would know about it. But our words were not terribly reassuring.

I had read Solzhenitzyn's *Gulag Archipelago* with its description of the nighttime arrests of Soviet dissidents and the rough life in the Soviet labor camps. I had taken a course in law school on comparative law that described the sham of the Soviet legal system. Now I was sitting in the county jail in Portland, Oregon, actually telling a client that he might disappear and we were even planning for the possibility. I had to question what was going on in my country. Were the president and attorney general that afraid? Did they have such little faith in the strength of our legal system? I could not have guessed, sitting there with Brandon, that two years later I would be in an American gulag in Guantánamo Bay representing men who had been "disappeared" and held without charges or trial for more than four years.

3 | A Cry for Help from Guantánamo

The choices we make in the grip of fear are the truest test of our humanity.

—Stephen Kyle[1]

EARLY IN THE EVENING OF MARCH 3, 2006, I stepped out of a fifteen-passenger twin-propeller plane onto the airfield of the United States Naval Base in Guantánamo Bay, Cuba. Nonmilitary personnel could get to Guantánamo only out of Ft. Lauderdale, Florida, on Lynx Air, which ran the fifteen-passenger planes, or Sunshine Air, whose planes were even smaller and noisier. If the Lynx flight was bringing in supplies as well as people, as mine was, you had to stop on the tiny Bahama island of Exuma to refuel because Cuban Premier Castro would not let flights to Guantánamo cross Cuban airspace on the way to the base. Our flight had to go all the way to the eastern end of the island and then double back along the southern shore where the airport sits right on the coastline on the leeward side of the base.

The sun had set by the time we landed and the plane pulled up to the airport building, a small room attached to a large hangar. Walking across the tarmac to picnic tables under a walless roof, where two soldiers waited to search our suitcases, I was excited finally to be in Guantánamo to meet one of the four clients my office was then representing—Adel Hassan Hamad, a Sudanese man who had been a prisoner there for forty-four months.[2] It had been a long road for me but a much longer one for Adel.

It was one year to the day since Adel had handed a one-paragraph hand-written habeas corpus petition to the guards in Guantánamo and asked them to send the paper to the United States District Court in Washington, DC. Adel's petition, like those of nearly fifty other prisoners who filed petitions at the same time, is poignant in its brevity and clarity. He proclaimed his innocence and asked for help, concluding deferentially, "With my appreciation and my respect to you and my trust you will do me justice." Unlike the other three petitions my office had received, Adel's did not reveal anything about himself, including why he thought his imprisonment was unjust.

Habeas corpus, Latin for "bring the body forward," is one of those seemingly arcane legal writs that were brought to America from England. Unlike many of the other ancient English writs with Latin names—like *audita querela* or *assisa de morte antecessoris*—that sound like they should be incantations uttered by one of Harry Potter's teachers and whose meaning is known today only to scholars of legal history, habeas corpus has remained a fundamental part of both Anglo and American law.[3] It dates back to 1215, to the Magna Carta, when the barons reined in King John at Runnymede. As Justice Sandra Day O'Connor described the writ, it is the most powerful tool in Anglo-American law for guarding against executive abuse, allowing our independent judiciary to act as a "critical check on the Executive, ensuring that it does not detain individuals except in accordance with law."[4]

The Founding Fathers were so concerned about the abuses of the English kings that they enshrined habeas corpus in the Constitution in what is called the Suspension Clause.[5] The writ is so important that neither the president nor Congress can get rid of habeas except in times of "rebellion or invasion," and even then only temporarily. So sacrosanct is the writ that it has been suspended only four times in our history: during the Civil War, briefly in 1871 during the height of the Reconstruction battles, in the Philippines during the Spanish-American War, and in the territory of Hawaii after Pearl Harbor.[6]

Five months before landing at the naval base, I had been assigned by the federal district court in Washington, DC to represent Adel and three other men imprisoned in Guantánamo, Mr. Chaman and Mr. Nazar Gul from Afghanistan, and Mr. Shabaan from Syria. I was a relative latecomer to the habeas corpus litigation, which had begun in 2002 shortly after the first twenty prisoners were flown to Guantánamo from Afghanistan in chains, muzzles, earmuffs, and blindfolds by U.S. forces. The legal challenges to imprisonment in Guantánamo had been started through the Center for Constitutional Rights (CCR), a public interest law firm in New York City that has specialized in civil and human rights work since 1966.[7] CCR was founded by lawyers William Kuntsler, Leonard Kinoy, Morton Stavis, and Ben Smith, then prominent in the antiwar and civil rights movements, who were deeply concerned about the threat to civil liberties they had experienced while working in the South. The lawyers' anti–Vietnam War and pro–civil rights activism brought them in conflict with President Johnson and the FBI shortly after CCR opened its doors. As the Johnson administration's spying and use of undercover agents to infiltrate anti–Vietnam War organizations surfaced, CCR took them on. The organization survived the early battles, and in the forty years since it opened its doors, has flourished, keeping its political focus while becoming heavily involved in international human rights issues as well.

CCR's first Guantánamo habeas clients were the children of English-speaking British citizens, including Rasul and Iqbal, and an Australian, David Hicks. The petitions were complex documents that had to be written by the lawyers without any contact with the clients because the Bush administration refused attorney access to Guantánamo. The core of the arguments, though, was straightforward: The detainees should be released because the government was violating our Constitution and the Geneva Conventions, the treaties entered in 1949 to curb the abuses against civilians and prisoners of war that were endemic in World War II, by holding the men without charges or trial, civilian or military.

The attorney general's response was just as straightforward, telling the court the prisoners did not have a right even to ask the court for help because Guantánamo is outside the geographic boundaries of the United States and the jurisdiction of the federal courts. The attorney general went on to say that the petitions had to be dismissed since all the men in Guantánamo were aliens so could not assert any rights under our Constitution while they were outside the United States. As the litigation went on, the attorney general added that the prisoners could not ask the U.S. courts to enforce the rights our country had ratified in the Geneva Conventions because they were not considered prisoners of war.

In addition to the Rasul, Iqbal, and Hicks petitions filed by CCR, habeas petitions were filed in February 2002 on behalf of twelve Kuwaiti nationals imprisoned in Guantánamo.[8] Unlike the vast majority of the cases, which have been handled on a pro bono basis with the lawyers arranged by CCR, the attorneys working on behalf of the Kuwaitis, led by Tom Wilner, managing partner of the International Trade and Practice group at the multinational law firm Shearman & Sterling, were retained. The families of the prisoners and the Kuwaiti government joined together to get them representation from a firm they were familiar with through ordinary business dealings. Also in the fight from the beginning were cocounsel with CCR on *Rasul*, Professor Joe Margulies of the MacArthur Justice Center at Northwestern Law School in Chicago and Clive Stafford Smith, a lawyer and director of the British-based human rights organization Reprieve. Smith, a dual citizen of Great Britain and the United States, became the lawyer for thirty-six men imprisoned in Guantánamo.

Eventually, CCR, which had filed the first petitions on behalf of prisoners whose families had contacted them, tried to file on behalf of all of the prisoners in Guantánamo in a case called *570 John Does v. Bush*—calling them John Does because the administration would not release the names of the men being held. The Department of Defense objected to those petitions and moved to dismiss them, but that fight, started when the suit was filed in 2005, is still in progress.

After getting the litigation moving in 2002, CCR found that its small staff could not handle all of the petitions and turned to some of the large law firms on the East Coast for help. Initially, about a dozen answered the call and, in the best traditions of the legal profession, took on cases. Later, more firms volunteered, swelling the ranks to scores of mainly large firms in New York, Boston, Washington, and other cities across the country, including three in Portland. The firms have donated thousands of hours and many hundreds of thousands of dollars in out-of-pocket expenses. A three-day trip to Guantánamo runs around $5,000 in airfare, hotel, expenses, and interpreter fees. Few solo practitioners and criminal defense attorneys from small firms can afford to fund the cases themselves.

When Adel, my three other clients, and forty-four more detainees filed habeas petitions in March 2005, Chief Judge Thomas Hogan of the DC district court contacted CCR to see if they could take on the cases. Given the complexity and the logistical issues involving prisoners in Guantánamo and classified information, the DC district court did not want the cases to proceed without attorneys. Unfortunately, CCR told the judge that they were pretty much tapped out and that the well of pro bono attorneys had run dry. Judge Hogan, who had the authority under the federal Criminal Justice

Act to assign attorneys in the habeas cases, faced a political dilemma. He could have started assigning the cases to lawyers in private practice in the District of Columbia, but there were few, if any, lawyers there who had any experience with habeas cases remotely like the ones filed by the Guantánamo prisoners. He also recognized that assigning private lawyers would pose substantial risks. The Bush administration and Republican Congress had been taking potshots at the judiciary for years over a host of issues and had been telling the judges in DC for three years that they had no jurisdiction at all over Guantánamo.[9] If lawyers in private practice were assigned to represent the prisoners and started submitting bills, the administration could have made an issue out of tax dollars being spent on the "worst of the worst," as then Secretary of Defense Donald Rumsfeld called the prisoners in Guantánamo.

So Judge Hogan turned to my counterpart in the District of Columbia, A. J. Kramer, head of one of the eighty-three other federal defender offices that provide representation in nearly every state in the country. It was a natural move, since the defender offices are supposed to handle 75 percent of all assigned cases according to judiciary guidelines. Kramer told Judge Hogan that he would love to help but that his office could handle only a couple of cases—not fifty. Over the summer, Judge Hogan, Kramer, the Administrative Office of the United States Courts, and CCR discussed an alternative plan and put out a call to federal defender offices across the country asking for volunteers who could fund the representation out of our existing budgets.

The danger of the administration's arguments for unchecked executive power had been driven home for me in a very real way when I had told Brandon about the solicitor's statements in Rasul's case, and ever since, I had been following their moves in Guantánamo. So, when Kramer sent an e-mail to all the federal defenders, I jumped at the chance to get involved in the fight, along with approximately thirty other defenders who volunteered. I then put out the word in my office that we might be getting into the Guantánamo cases and I needed to figure out how many cases we could handle. More than half of my staff said they wanted to be included if any assignments were made.

■   ■   ■

The caseload I have built for my office in Oregon is different from the caseloads in most federal defender offices. Decades ago, the Oregon judges recognized that federal habeas corpus challenges to state convictions are so complex that state prisoners can't effectively represent themselves and started assigning my office to represent them, something few of their counterparts around the country are willing to do as a matter of routine. As a result, my office has had the largest noncapital habeas corpus caseload in the country since the 1970s. But it is extremely difficult to win a habeas corpus petition for a state prisoner who says his conviction was obtained in violation of his federal constitutional rights because a case cannot even reach the federal court for review until it has been through multiple layers in the state courts. Nationwide, the success rate on state prisoner habeas cases is around 1 percent. In Oregon, the success rate is around 5 percent—still low, but five times the national rate.[10] We like to think our work accounts for at least part of the difference.

Since the federal prison opened in Sheridan, Oregon, in 1989, my office, led by my chief deputy of twenty-four years and good friend, Steve Sady, has also been a leader in habeas corpus challenges for federal prisoners. We have taken on the Federal Bureau of Prisons in a series of habeas cases for the inmates housed there, challenging how they calculate good time credits, give inmates benefits under the federal sentencing statutes for participating in intensive drug treatment, and place people in the federal boot camp program. Sady, one of the most brilliant and energetic lawyers not only in the federal defender system but anywhere in the country, calculated a year ago that our work had saved the federal government hundreds of millions of dollars by forcing the Bureau of Prisons to properly calculate our clients' sentences.

Perhaps because of our success in habeas work, the lawyers who handle civil immigration cases and a number of private groups that work with immigrants had sought us out in 2000 to see if we could help with the people who became our first group of indefinite detainees. These clients were in the country illegally but could not be deported because of political turmoil in their home countries for fear that they would be tortured if they were sent back, or due to bad relations between their home countries and the United States. Although many of these clients had never committed a crime (other than being here illegally), and those who had committed crimes had long since completed their sentences, our government would not let them go free. Their detention, a polite word for imprisonment, was indefinite with no way out.

Worse yet, they were being held in county jails across the country, mostly alongside convicted criminals. Because these jails are not built to house people for long periods, they often have minimal, if any, recreational or educational facilities; at some, the inmates never even get to go outside. By 2005, we had won release from our Oregon judges and the Court of Appeals for the Ninth Circuit for nearly one hundred of these immigration detainees. The judges told the Bush administration that it could not detain these people indefinitely but had to release them on conditions if they could not be repatriated within six months of their arrest. The attorney general resisted the most intensely on our Cuban clients, and we did not win their release until we had taken one of their cases all the way to the Supreme Court.[11]

The victory that touched my staff the most was for a Chinese teenager who had run away from an arranged marriage in northern China only to find herself locked up by our government for more than a year and a half. When we finally won her release, she literally fell to her knees and kissed the sidewalk outside the INS building in downtown Portland. The Bush administration's treatment of these detainees was a precursor to its treatment of the prisoners at Guantánamo.

· · ·

When I volunteered to participate in the Guantánamo cases, I did not know if the clients the court would assign us would be terrorists or innocents. What I did know was that the rule of law was under siege and that the fight for the rule of law was the most important legal battle there could be. For years, when people have asked how I can do defense work, I have referred to *A Man for All Seasons*, Robert Bolt's play about Sir Thomas More's defiance of Henry VIII. More and his daughter's fiancé and aspiring lawyer, Will Roper, get into a debate over the law, and More speaks up for "the devil himself."

ROPER: So now you'd give the Devil benefit of law!

MORE: Yes. What would you do? Cut a great road through the law to get after the Devil?

ROPER: I'd cut down every law in England to do that!

MORE: Oh? And when the last law was down, and the Devil turned round on you—where would you hide, Roper, the laws all being flat? This country's planted thick with laws from coast

to coast—man's laws, not God's—and if you cut them down—
and you're just the man to do it—d'you really think you could
stand upright in the winds that would blow then? Yes, I'd give
the Devil benefit of law, for my own safety's sake.

Whether defending alleged terrorists, drug dealers, or white-collar criminals, criminal defense attorneys know that most of their clients have done
something. While it is often easier to represent people who are innocent—
though scarier because of the risks if you mess up—you can't do the type
of work I do unless you are willing to give the same effort to every client—
whether he "done it" or not. As More told Roper, when you are representing a person accused of a crime, you are also representing a principle—the
rule of law. You are keeping the police, prosecutor, and king (or president)
honest, making sure they follow the rules and, in doing so, you are keeping everyone safe. I knew when we got into the Guantánamo cases that if
we were assigned prisoners who were, indeed, "the worst of the worst," I
would still be fighting a worthy battle for the rule of law.

· · ·

I was notified in September 2005 that cases would be assigned to my office.
I was also told I would be able to obtain only a limited number of security
clearances for the office, something the Departments of Defense and Justice
required for visits to Guantánamo and review of classified material. I put
together a team of eight lawyers, seven investigators, and a legal assistant as
the core group who would apply for security clearances. Terry Henry and
Andrew Warden, the lawyers who were our point of contact in the terrorism section at the Department of Justice, which was handling the cases for
the Bush administration, told me that sixteen clearances was a lot and we
might not get that many. Expecting that we might be assigned more cases
and wanting to include as many people in the office as I could, I did not cut
my request.

Lawyers Chris Schatz and Amy Baggio and investigators William Teesdale and Janan Stoll from the Mayfield team were eager to get involved
again. The other lawyers included Steve Sady; Bryan Lessley from my Eugene branch, who has been with the office for more than fifteen years and
handled more than his share of complex white-collar cases; Ruben Iniguez,

a consummate professional and all-around lawyer who is as comfortable in trial as he is in the more cerebral appellate courts; and Chris Dahl, who has since become a war crimes prosecutor in The Hague. Cocounsel with me on Adel's case was Pat Ehlers, at age thirty-seven one of the younger assistant defenders in the office but a lawyer who had seen it all, including the execution of two of his clients. Pat moved to Oregon to join the office from Oklahoma, where he had spent eight years defending capital cases, first as an assistant state defender trying cases in the state courts, then as an assistant federal defender working on capital habeas corpus cases for my counterpart in Oklahoma City.

The investigators on the team included Bruce Daily, a savvy former newspaper reporter; Rod Saiki and Maia Godet, longtime investigators in the Portland office and law school graduates who were great on complex cases; Martin Caballero, one of our hardest-working investigators; and Toni Pisani, a tenacious investigator and former police officer. Senior legal assistant Lisa Powell rounded out the team that would get security clearances. Even though they were not going to get security clearances in the first round, research and writing assistants Lynn Deffebach and Michelle Sweet, and chief investigator Don Grant were included in the work as much as possible.

When I got on the plane in Oregon before dawn at the end of February 2006 to fly to Guantánamo, I knew virtually nothing about Adel. Since calls to the prison were not allowed, I had not been able to speak with him. Nor had I received any mail from him, so I did not know if he knew that his handwritten petition had even reached Washington and that help was on the way.

Although I had asked repeatedly, Henry and Warden had refused to provide us with any information about Adel. The prosecutors have remained a mystery to me throughout. Because the administration has been so successful in avoiding court appearances in the Guantánamo cases, I met Henry, a thin, controlled man with a calm voice who has been a prosecutor for decades, only once. I never met Warden.

The intransigence of the administration was so great that Henry and Warden would not even tell me what country Adel was from until three months after my assignment to represent him. It was not until late February, after raising the issue at the one court hearing I ever had on his case, a hearing that dealt only with some basic procedures, that Henry told me Adel was from Sudan and spoke Arabic. But even then, after my security clearance had come through and I had been approved for my first visit to Guantánamo, he would not tell me why Adel was in prison, what he was alleged to have done, or whether he was classified as an "enemy combatant"—the status defined by President Bush in an order he issued on November 13, 2001, that gave the secretary of defense authority to seize and detain Taliban and Al Qaeda fighters in Afghanistan.

Desperate to learn something about Adel and Shabaan, our other Arabic-speaking client, so we could figure out what we should be doing for them in court, I hired Dirgham Sbait, a professor of Arabic at Portland State University, to look at the petitions and tell us whatever he could. It wasn't much. Professor Sbait told us that Adel's petition was written in standard Arabic and that he was clearly an educated man, but there was no clue in the writing as to his native country. Shabaan's petition was also in standard Arabic, though Sbait believed Shabaan was less educated and his petition included the fact that he was from Syria.

The petitions for our other two clients, Chaman and Nazar Gul, were written in Pashto, one of the languages of Afghanistan. For Chaman, we had some brief information because the judge assigned to his case had ordered the Justice Department to file a "return," the legal document that the habeas corpus rules require the person holding a habeas corpus petitioner to file explaining why he believes the imprisonment is legal. In the Guantánamo cases, this meant the evidence the administration believed showed they were Al Qaeda or Taliban fighters or supporters. As we got farther into the cases, we learned that there was no pattern to the decisions to order or deny returns; it was the personal preference of each judge and had nothing to do with the merits of the cases. While all the judges had agreed to coordinate their decisions on some issues, on others, including whether the administration should be required to answer the petitions, they went their individual ways. In violation of the habeas corpus rules, returns were ordered in very few cases. The unclassified portion of Chaman's return that we were able to get from the court in the fall of 2005 told us that the Defense Department believed Chaman had worked closely with a top Taliban official, Gulbuddin Hekmatyar, who had been funded by the United States, had briefly been leader of Afghanistan in 1992, and had met clandestinely with Al Qaeda operatives. The papers that had been filed with the court also included Chaman's denial that he ever supported the Taliban.[12]

As for our other clients, we did not just sit back when Henry and Warden refused to give us information; we turned to the Internet. While there was a wealth of information on Al Qaeda, the Taliban, the Afghan wars, and Guantánamo, we found references to only one of our four clients, "Commander Chaman," and that only duplicated what was in the return.

I was uncomfortable heading for Guantánamo without any information about Adel. I had flown from Portland to Ft. Lauderdale, the jumping-off point for the flight to Guantánamo, ahead of the other members of my team, so I could visit with my eighty-five-year-old mother. Around noon on Friday, March 3, I drove my rental car down to the Ft. Lauderdale airport. It took me a while on that first trip to find the Lynx Air counter, tucked downstairs in a side wing of terminal four. Already waiting there were the two security-cleared interpreters we had hired, Felice Bezri, a midforties professional Arabic interpreter, half Lebanese and half Italian, who had been to Guantánamo more than twenty times with CCR and pro bono counsel; and Mavish Khan, a third-year law student in Miami who was of Afghan descent and spoke Pashto. Assistant defenders Chris Schatz and Bryan Lessley, who were going to see Chaman with Mavish, were also there, along with my cocounsel on Adel's case, Pat Ehlers.

We caught each other up. Pat had great news. On Thursday, bowing to an order from Judge Jed Rakoff in New York in a Freedom of Information Act lawsuit filed by the Associated Press, the Department of Defense had released unclassified records on hundreds of the prisoners in Guantánamo.

The records consisted of portions of the unclassified transcripts of the Combatant Status Review Tribunal (CSRT) and Administrative Review Board (ARB) hearings. In July 2004, after holding hundreds of men in the prison for more than two years with no hearings of any kind by either civilian or military personnel, the Bush administration had responded to the Supreme Court's decision in Rasul's case with a directive from Deputy Secretary of Defense Paul Wolfowitz that each prisoner should be given a CSRT hearing on his status as an "enemy combatant."[13] Every year after that, the Department of Defense was supposed to hold an ARB to see if the prisoner still presented a threat to the United States. The little bits of information we had been able to get on these hearings suggested that the both the CSRT and ARB proceedings were a sham. The men were not allowed to see the evidence or even hear the specific charges against them, and they had no right to lawyers or to call any witnesses. Under the procedures defined in

Wolfowitz's memorandum, the military officers presiding over the hearings had to presume that the detentions were lawful.[14] As we would find out, some of the prisoners, including Adel and one of my later Afghan clients, Amin Ullah, were given only one ARB hearing and the process appeared meaningless.

The material produced in response to Judge Rakoff's order was released without any index or discernible order. One of our investigators, William Teesdale, had spent much of Thursday night and Friday morning searching the thousands of pages the Department of Defense had posted on its Web site for our clients' names. When William finally found the records on Adel, he e-mailed them to Pat.

While we waited to board our plane, I got my first glimpse of who Adel might be—an innocent charity worker and hospital administrator who had never been near a battlefield. I combed the seventeen pages that William had downloaded for something more substantive, but there was nothing. The charges I read were all guilt by association. Some of the directors of the charities Adel worked for had taken anti-American positions, and in the late '80s or early '90s he might have seen two of them at refugee camps where he delivered food. After dealing with the allegations in the arrest warrant in Brandon's case, I was not surprised to see a client once again tarred with someone else's political beliefs.

■ ■ ■

After the soldiers at the airport at Guantánamo finished their perfunctory search of our luggage, we passed through a revolving gate and were met by a military escort who directed us to board the public bus, an old school bus painted white. It was a five-minute ride to the Combined Bachelors Quarters (CBQ) on the leeward, or western, side of the base, our home for the next four days. Our escort told us that we could walk around on most of the leeward side but that our movements would be restricted the next morning once we got to the windward side, where the heart of the base and prison are located.

The CBQ resembles a college dormitory. Each room has two areas divided by the bathroom and a kitchenette with microwave, two burners, and a sink. Each side has its own door off the corridor and two twin beds, offering the possibility of a different bed each night on a four-night stay. The first time

I went into the bathroom I thought that someone had used the toilet and forgotten to flush. I pushed the handle and watched the yellow water fill the bowl again. The water coming out of the tap was the same yellow color. I learned the next day that the water on the base comes from a large desalination plant that was built in the early 1960s after Castro cut off the water supply from Cuba proper in a fit of pique.

Up at 7 A.M. to catch the 7:40 bus driven by a Jamaican contract worker, we caught the 8 A.M. ferry for the twenty-minute trip across the bay to the windward side. The water was blue and clear, the spray of the water was warm, and the sun was already fulfilling the promise of a hot day. As we disembarked, our "escort" of the day, Martin,* a fifteen-year veteran who was sick of "Gitmo," as he not so affectionately called it, greeted us. It was Sunday and the main part of the base was closed, including the ID card processing office, so Martin handed us temporary badges with no photos or numbers and drove us toward the prison.

I was struck by the ordinariness of the place. The base looks pretty much like any small town or army post in the southwestern United States, a shopping mall with a combination grocery and soft goods store with low prices, Subway, A & W Root Beer, Kentucky Fried Chicken, and McDonald's. The big debate on the bus that morning, as it was nearly every morning I was at the base, was whether to stop for breakfast at Subway, McDonald's, or an ersatz Starbucks that had real coffee but no croissants or scones. Felice loved the real coffee, I usually wanted food, and Pat didn't really care, but a stop was necessary because the only place to get food on the leeward side was the Clipper Club, a bar a half mile from the CBQ that served frozen chicken bits and pizza for dinner, with equally unappealing breakfasts. That first morning, we followed Felice's lead and went to Starbucks.

Past the heart of the town we passed subdivisions with names like Iguana Terrace and Caribbean Circle that sit off Hillside Beach Road, the winding two-lane blacktop that ends with a view of the Caribbean that would be breathtaking if it were not marred by the razor wire of the prison. Guantánamo Bay is on the dry side of Cuba, so the roads are dusty and the golf course brown, with electric wind turbines stalking the hills that surround it. The predominant vegetation is a scrubby cactus that looks like a stunted version of the majestic saguaro of the Arizona deserts.

---

* The escorts' names and road names have been changed for security reasons.

Around a last bend in the road, we could see the fences of the prison maybe a half mile away. A couple of hundred yards from the first fence was a guard post with three or four young soldiers, one of whom got on the bus and perfunctorily looked at our nondescript badges. Before we knew it, we were at the gate cut into the chain-link fence with its razor wire top that surrounded Camp Echo, the portion of the prison where we were going to visit our clients. The sandy ground and temporary shacks surrounded by double fences of razor wire evoked the Middle East more than a Caribbean island.

We were handed off by our affable escort to the military prison guards, prototypical peach fuzz–faced men and stoic women, some of whom did not know how to deal with the lawyers for the "terrorists." Of the five guards we dealt with that morning, two would not even acknowledge my hello. Unlike our escort, Martin, the names on their uniforms were covered with tape.

Following the advice of the CCR lawyers, we carried Arabic and Afghan food from Portland for Adel and Chaman: figs, nuts, dates, and baklava baked by one of the team's investigators, Janan Stoll, from her Palestinian grandmother's recipe. We had also brought along heavy metal thermoses filled with tea and coffee from McDonald's. While the guards had no problem with our food and the thermoses, the plastic spoon we had picked up with a Styrofoam container of eggs from McDonald's was a problem. The guards were adamant that it could not come in. Instead, we were told that the guards would bring a "spork" to the visiting room, a plastic spoon with forklike tines. We learned on subsequent visits that the rules about what can and cannot go into the camp are constantly changing, as are the rules for the prisoners—changes that needlessly increase tensions within the prison. The guards would probably not have been amused to learn that the sporks were known among the lawyers, in our gallows humor reaction to some of the absurdity we encountered at the base, as "Guantánamo Kalashnikovs" because, unlike the flimsy plastic McDonald's spoons and forks that we could not bring in, it looked like the tines of the sporks could be whittled into a weapon.

Once through the inner fence and gate, we were in a quadrangle with individual little buildings on the perimeter. Chris, Bryan, and Mavish split off to building 1 to meet Chaman, while Pat, Felice, and I walked around a concrete path to building 12. The path bordered a nicely manicured gravel quadrangle that I made sure not to step on; we had been told by some of the pro bono lawyers that the gravel field was mined to prevent any attempted escapes. No one on the base would ever answer my question about the mines and I never tested the fields.

Our guard unlocked the door to number 12, and we walked into a twenty-by-eight-foot cell with a table two-thirds of the way in. A thick metal eye hook in the floor anchored a chain that was attached to leg irons on a man who was sitting behind the table. He was officially prisoner 940 in the government lexicon, but he is the man I have come to know as a caring and happy human being: Adel Hassan Hamad, a handsome, dark-skinned forty-four-year-old with close-cropped black hair, a short but full beard, and smiling eyes.

4 | Innocence Is Irrelevant

*We must execute not only the guilty. Execution of the innocent
will impress the masses even more.*

—Attributed to N. V. Krylenko[1]

AFTER GETTING SOME SENSE OF WHAT we would need to do to help Brandon by studying the affidavit and reviewing the details of our first meeting in the county jail, I put together a team of six to work on his case. Unlike
most state and locally funded public defender offices, we are fortunate to
be adequately funded. My office in Oregon is also one of the largest in the
country for a variety of reasons. Oregon, unlike many states, is not divided
into multiple federal judicial districts each having its own defender. We
are also assigned in more habeas cases than most offices, and the United
States attorney in Oregon has historically been more active and filed more
cases than many of her counterparts. The size of the office allows me to
shift staff and money when we are hit with something huge, like Brandon's
case. In addition to Chris, I pulled Amy Baggio, a truly gifted young lawyer, onto the case. At the time she was one of our research and writing attorneys, but by the time we got into the Guantánamo cases, she was already,
thanks to her dedicated work ethic and talent, an assistant defender.

The lawyers were not going to work the case alone. In my opinion, a good
lawyer needs a good investigator to effectively represent his clients. While
some defender offices often hire ex-cops to do their investigative work, I
generally do not. Ex-cops tend to be good at gathering records and finding

people, but they often have a difficult time pushing for the guilty clients. Most of my office's investigators come from the county public defender office and some even have law degrees. I want people who will challenge the lawyers, and our investigators do.

In consultation with my chief investigator, Don Grant, I assigned William Teesdale, Janan Stoll, and Jim Strupp to work on Brandon's case. William, whose crisp British accent gives away his roots, loves the investigation side of law even though he is a licensed attorney in Oregon and a British barrister as well. Great in dealing with issues requiring an analytic mind, William took the lead on the fingerprint and immediately started looking for experts and gathering material so Chris and I could take on the FBI lab.

Janan Stoll, who had come to us from the county public defender office, is brilliant at pulling together what we usually call mitigation, the aspects of a client's life that can help explain how he got to us and might lead to a lesser sentence. She began collecting background on Brandon and his family.

Jim Strupp had started working at the office on a temporary basis straight out of college, thinking he might go to law school in a few years. Jim was a New Jersey boy (about as close in spirit to my birthplace, Brooklyn, as one can get), and I loved his energy and soon found a permanent slot for him. He started in on the money issues we faced, tracing the sources of Brandon's few assets that we knew Gorder and crew would worry about.

After assembling the team and getting everyone going, Chris and I went back to the jail, where we spent the rest of the weekend with Brandon.

. . .

Although the impetus for Brandon's arrest came from Washington and centered on the fingerprint identification made in the FBI lab in Quantico, Virginia, the affidavit Gorder helped the FBI file with Judge Jones for Brandon's arrest warrant was actually prepared by a local special agent, Richard K. Werder, an FBI agent since 1983 and a member of the Portland Joint Terrorism Task Force. What Werder wrote went far beyond the fingerprint, to Brandon's religion. He told the judge that the FBI had observed Brandon attending a mosque and monitored a call to a Muslim man the FBI was watching in southern Oregon, and that Brandon had advertised as a lawyer in an Internet Muslim yellow pages. Werder thought the advertisement was important because the person who ran the yellow pages, a resident of Portland, had once had dealings with another person, and that person, whom Brandon had no connection with, had worked for Osama Bin Laden.[2]

The affidavit then went on to tell the judge about the religious views of Brandon's child custody client, Jeffrey Battle, recounting Battle's recent conviction on terrorism charges and his anti-American and anti-Semitic vitriol. Apparently, Werder thought that Battle's problems and views supported Brandon's arrest. When I talked to Judge Jones about the case years later, he told me that his forty years of experience with fingerprints convinced him that the print was Brandon's and that he believed it had most likely gotten to Spain through some contact with Battle while Brandon was representing him.

I have fought against racial profiling for decades in representing African-American and Hispanic clients—black men pulled over for driving in all kinds of neighborhoods, just for being there, and clients stopped and searched on Interstate 5 for going 67 in a 65 mph zone or, as the clients put it, "driving while Hispanic." In most of these cases, the police deny any racial motive for the arrests, swearing that they didn't know the race of the driver until after they pulled the car over even when their log books show an overwhelming number of minority arrests in predominantly white Oregon.

But the arrest warrant for Brandon was different. The FBI was telling a federal judge that there was probable cause to arrest a lawyer because he had provided representation to a "bad guy" who was a Muslim. As we reviewed the affidavit's references to religion with Brandon that first weekend, he asked, "What does this have to do with anything? Is this what my arrest is really about?"

Many of the original settlers in this country fled religious persecution in Europe, or came seeking greater religious freedom in new colonies here: the Pilgrim separatists and the Puritans, from England; the Huguenots from France; Roger Williams in Rhode Island; the Amish, Mennonites, and Quakers in Pennsylvania.[3] The right to religious freedom was so fundamental to our nation's founding that it was given the place of honor as the First Amendment in the Bill of Rights. Yet, here was a man's religion being used to justify his arrest. Chris and I were deeply troubled by the FBI's repeated references to Brandon's Muslim religion in the affidavit. It struck especially close to home for me as a Jew whose family had fled state-sanctioned religious persecution in Russia less than a century ago.

Just as I saw the mentions of Brandon's religion crossing the First Amendment line, I saw the full paragraph in the affidavit about Battle's beliefs undermining one of the fundamental premises of our justice system—that everyone is entitled to representation. My clients, very few of whom are lawyers, are rarely popular; some have espoused extreme and violent causes. If the government was going to start justifying lawyers' arrests based on the views of their clients, the entire justice system would be weakened. While criminal defense work is never for the faint of heart, the reality is that good men and women would stay even farther from the work if they had to worry about being arrested for whom they represented. Of course, that first weekend I didn't know, as I sat in the Multnomah County Jail cell with Brandon, that in two years' time I would find out that guilt by association was the only thing that put Adel in prison.

Troubling as the profiling and guilt by association were, my answer to Brandon's question, "Is this what my arrest is really about?" had to be no.

"Brandon, you were arrested because of the fingerprint."

"It's not my print."

"Okay. Then how did it get there?"

"I don't know."

"Have you been to Spain?"

"When I was in the army in the early 1990s."

"In the affidavit, the FBI says they think you traveled under an assumed name."

"No way. I haven't been out of the country for at least ten years."

"Then how did it get there? We need to consider every possibility. Let's think about it. Could someone have taken it from your house?"

"What do you mean?"

"Well, have you ever had a blue plastic bag in your house?"

"How would I know?" Brandon was getting angry at what seemed like absurd questions.

"Sure, it's possible," he went on. "You go shopping, you get bags, some could have been blue."

"Okay. Did you ever take a bag to the mosque where you might have left it and someone picked it up?" Chris chimed in.

"Why are you asking about the mosque?"

This was a tough subject. For the first couple of days, every time Chris or I asked about his mosque, Brandon bristled.

"Look, Brandon, the FBI says your fingerprint was found on a blue bag in Spain, and we know that some of the members of your mosque have been convicted of trying to join the jihad in Afghanistan. Maybe someone else at the mosque had a tie to Spain?"

"I'm not aware of anything like that. I've never heard people talking about terrorism except how awful 9/11 was. I don't really remember people talking about the Madrid bombings."

"Have you ever had any guests at your house?" I asked.

"Ever?" Brandon asked back, looking at me like I had slipped a gear somewhere.

"Yes, ever," I repeated. "Did you ever have anyone over who might have picked up a bag that somehow ended up in Spain?"

"How can I answer that? Sure, we sometimes have people over. I don't remember anyone asking to borrow a bag or bringing a blue one over. But I doubt I'd even remember something like that."

We were getting nowhere. Brandon was right: How could he remember? Nothing out of the ordinary had happened. All he could say was that he wasn't there, it wasn't his print. But if it was, he had no idea how it got to Spain and did not have anything to do with the bombings.

"It must be a mistake," Brandon added.

"Brandon, that's not likely. Fingerprints are one of the most reliable forensic tests. If this was a hair or footprint match, maybe. The FBI says they have never made a mistake with a fingerprint."

Chris and I told Brandon that in our collective fifty years of lawyering in New York, California, and Oregon, the only fingerprint mistakes we had dealt with involved corrupt cops who had manufactured prints or simply lied about identifications.

"Well, that must be what happened here," Brandon said.

"That's a possibility we'll explore, but we can't operate under that assumption. We have to assume that it is your print," I said.

"Why?" Brandon just could not accept, or admit, the possibility that it was his print.

"Because this is what the government assumes," I said.

"Huh? I had nothing to do with the bombing."

"Sorry, Brandon, but at this point your innocence is irrelevant."

We were sitting in the marshal's lockup in the federal courthouse when I said that. Unlike our visits in the county jail where we were face-to-face and could shake hands and look at papers together, in the lockup we were separated by a wire mesh screen that blurred facial expressions. But there was no mistaking Brandon's expression when I said "innocence is irrelevant." The words cut into him. He was hurt. We all sat there looking at each other. Then, his voice edged with distrust, Brandon said, "Do you mean you don't believe me?"

The words had just come out of me. As I looked at Brandon, I was seeing the fences in Manzanar, Tule Lake, Jerome, and the two dozen other large and small "detention centers" where our government had imprisoned the Japanese Americans in the months after Pearl Harbor.[4] They were innocent, but it did not matter. The fear of the "yellow peril" led to their imprisonment by presidential decree under the euphemistic term "internment."[5]

Fear is a corrupting force in government, distorting and being used to distort, the decision-making process. In the criminal justice system, I have seen fearful witnesses and victims identify the wrong person and the certainty with which they make their mistaken identifications lead their champions in police forces and prosecutors offices forward with disastrous results. When I was teaching Constitutional Criminal Procedure at the Northwestern School of Law, one of my favorite articles for the section on identification was an op-ed from the New York Times, "I was certain, but I was wrong," written by a courageous rape victim. Fourteen years after testifying that she was 100 percent certain that the suspect the police had brought to her for identification was her attacker, DNA evidence had exonerated him.[6] That case had been run like so many others, with blinders on. So sure that they were correct, the investigators could only follow her lead down one track, like a horse at Churchill Downs, never even considering the possibility that the rapist might be someone else. An innocent man spent eleven years in prison as a result.

I tried to explain this to Brandon. "Whatever you say, the government is going to see it through the fingerprint. That's their perspective. The print. It's you."

"What do you mean by that?" he asked. There was some hostility in his voice.

"Brandon, they have the print. They believe in it. Whatever you say is going to run into that and become an excuse, cover-up, lie."

We all sat there not speaking. It was Chris who finally broke the silence. "Brandon, look me in the eye. I tell you man to man, I believe you. You are innocent."

Brandon looked at me. He didn't say anything, just looked. Was I going to give him the same reassurance? For a moment, the attorney-client relationship, Brandon's willingness to work with and trust me, hung in the balance.

As Chris and Brandon waited for me to say something about his innocence, I was thinking about how we each brought something different to defense work. Chris and I saw the attorney-client relationship differently. He deeply felt Brandon's need for reassurance and responded to that. Even though I knew what Brandon wanted to hear, I also knew that I had to tell him what I honestly felt. I believed we needed cold objectivity in making the decisions that were looming over us.

"Look, Brandon," I said, "whether or not I believe you are innocent is *not* the issue. I'm going to fight just as hard for you whether you are involved or not. The truth matters in deciding what we do, not whether I fight."

That a good defense attorney fights just as hard for a guilty client as an innocent one is something many clients, people in general, and even lawyers have a hard time understanding. Brandon was no exception. While he agreed intellectually with what I said, in his predicament, he couldn't feel it. What he heard was that I doubted his innocence.

"Are you telling me you think I had something to do with this?" he asked.

The easiest answer would have been to say no and try to move on, but that's not how I practice law.

During our very first meeting I had given Brandon the same speech I give all my clients: "We need to deal with reality and be honest with each other. I will never pull any punches with you. You're going to know exactly what I know about the case. There are some tough decisions that you will have to make, and my job is to help you make them, armed with the best and most complete advice I can give you. You may not always like what I say and, when you don't, remember this conversation and that I can serve you best with complete honesty between us."

That's what I returned to in that moment. "Brandon, I don't know." I looked at Chris and went on. "With all respect to Chris, he doesn't know either. Only you know what you have been doing this spring. Only you know who you've been with and where you've been. I hear you say you are innocent, but I can't act on that because the government won't. We have to help you decide whether to testify in the grand jury. The advice I give is going to be based on the existence of the fingerprint."

Having given Brandon his personal assurance, Chris was able to nod in agreement. There were issues that Brandon, Chris, and I still had to work out, but Brandon now understood that I was trying to help him.

Most important, Chris and I were there in the cell with Brandon as his counsel and he was in his hometown. As Brandon described his situation to a reporter a few weeks later, "I'm fortunate because I have these legal friends and I'm from the Midwest and know the language and I'm an attorney, but there are others who aren't as familiar with the process and the language who are undergoing this type of thing."

5 | Seized and Disappeared

In war, truth is the first casualty.

—Aeschylus

As Pat, Felice, and I walked into cell 12 in Guantánamo's Camp Echo, Adel stood up to greet us. Stocky in build, he was a little shorter than I am, about five seven, his face open and curious, yet wary. He was dressed in a white short-sleeved shirt and white loose-fitting pants, his head covered by a knitted kufi, or skullcap. There was no wall or screen between us, but he was chained to the floor. Pat, always the go-getter, strode right up and said hello. Both men reached for each other and shook hands while Felice struggled to catch up and start interpreting. A few paces behind Pat, and trying to take in as much as I could from my first impression, I stepped up to Adel. He turned from Pat, we shook hands, and he smiled tentatively.

We all sat down at the small table, Felice in the middle, directly across from Adel. Pat and I, on the flanks, started unpacking our bags, taking out our legal pads as well as the figs, nuts, packaged Arabian cookies, and Janan's baklava. Adel thanked us but did not dig in. Although our greeting had been moderately friendly, I could see the tension in Adel's face, checking out these supposed allies after being locked away for more than three years.

Pat started in, asking Adel how he was doing and whether he had any health problems. Adel assured us he was well, his words matching his healthy appearance.

Pat then shifted to an explanation of who we were and what we hoped to accomplish during our visit. Adel nodded politely, listening for a while, then asked, "Where is the interrogator?"

Pat and I were taken aback. We had been warned that some of the men imprisoned in Guantánamo were so distrustful of Americans after the lies and ruses they had suffered at the hands of the FBI, CIA, and Department of Defense interrogators that they refused to come out for visits with habeas counsel or else cut them short after a few minutes. "Interrogator?" I wondered what Adel meant. Was he about to stop the meeting?

"No," I assured Adel, "there are no interrogators with us."

Adel then pulled out the Arabic translation of a letter of introduction we had written to him while we were waiting for our security clearances and pointed to a word Felice translated for us as "interrogator." This was the first we knew that he had received our letter. Felice looked up from the page and told us that our Portland translator had used an Arabic word for our staff investigators that translated for Adel as interrogator.

Shaking my head with relief, I explained to Adel, through Felice, the misunderstanding. "Adel, Pat and I are lawyers, but in my office we don't work alone. We have people on our staff, called investigators, who help us with our clients. They work for us, for you. They don't work for the military or the FBI. They don't interrogate you."

Adel clearly understood what we meant about the confusion over the translation and we all laughed, the wariness evaporating. We could then get down to the business at hand: learning how Adel had come to be in Guantánamo and starting to figure out how we could help him.

.   .   .

Adel's nightmare began at 1:30 in the early morning hours of July 18, 2002. He was asleep in his second-floor apartment in the University District in Peshawar, Pakistan, when he was startled awake by scraping noises outside. Getting out of bed, he looked out the front window to see a stream of Pakistani security police dropping into the yard from ladders they had placed against the wall that separated the house from the street.

In 1986, Adel had left his native Sudan for Pakistan when he had obtained a job with Lajnat Al Daawa Al Islamiya (LDI), an international Kuwaiti charity that ran camps in Afghanistan and Pakistan for refugees of the Afghan war with the Soviets.[1] At home on vacation a year later, Adel married, then went back to Pakistan. Adel and his wife Salwa's decision to leave their families in Sudan had not been easy, but even with a degree in air-conditioning engineering from the technical university in Alexandria, Egypt, Adel had found it difficult to make a reasonable living in Sudan. The civil wars that had racked his country over the past twenty-five years had taken their toll. The Kuwaitis offered an opportunity for Adel to earn a living wage while helping people, and he took it. The benefits of his job with LDI included a month-long trip home every year to see family.

Adel left LDI for a job with a Saudi-funded charity in Pakistan, the World Assembly for Muslim Youth (WAMY), in 2000, and trips home were again part of the benefit package. Adel, his wife, and daughters reunited with their relatives in Sudan each year.[2] But when Adel and his family left for Khartoum in June of 2002, they were not sure if Salwa and the girls would return to Pakistan this time. Their oldest daughter, Zaynab, had outgrown the Arabic-language school in Peshawar, and Adel and Salwa wanted her to go to university. On top of that, Salwa's father was sick and she had been thinking of staying in Khartoum to help her mother.

Two weeks into their vacation, Salwa's father died, finalizing the family's decision about Pakistan. Adel would go back alone, pack up for his wife and daughters, and see if he could get a transfer to the WAMY office in Khartoum. They knew it would not be easy for Salwa and the girls, who would be staying initially in one small room. In 1996, Adel, with money he had saved from his job at LDI, had bought a piece of land in the Haj Yusef neighborhood on the outskirts of Khartoum, where he and Salwa planned to build a home for their family. By 2002, Adel, with help from Salwa's brother, had laid the foundation for the home but had finished only one rough room.

The decision for Salwa and the girls to stay in Sudan was also prompted by the hostile situation in Pakistan toward Arabs. A week before he was scheduled to leave on the flight from Khartoum to Islamabad, Adel had called his supervisor, Abu Hadifa, an Iraqi who was director of WAMY's charitable activities in Pakistan. Adel wanted to be sure that it was safe to return. He had reason to be worried because he knew that some Arab aid workers for RIHS (the Revival of Islamic Heritage Society) had been arrested in Peshawar in the spring.[3] The rumor mill in Pakistan had been churning with tales of more anti-Arab treatment. While most Pakistanis and

Arabs are Muslim, the decision of Pakistani President Pervez Musharraf to bow to American pressure and shift his support from the Taliban had led to anti-Arab sentiment. The official government line in Pakistan now paralleled the American view that Arab terrorists were heavily involved in the Afghan wars.

Adel also had a more personal concern about his safety. A few months earlier, he had refused to go along with Pakistani security men who were pressuring him to divert some food, clothing, and other supplies that he was responsible for getting to refugee camps for WAMY. He knew the security men were not happy that he had stood his ground. Abu Hadifa assured Adel it was safe to come back, as there had been no more arrests since the RIHS men had been seized, the border between Pakistan and Afghanistan, near Peshawar, had been quiet, and WAMY was a respected international charity with more than two thousand employees in fifty-five countries.[4]

On the morning of July 14, Adel said good-bye to Salwa and his daughters and left for the Khartoum airport. It was the last they would hear from him for eight months—Adel simply disappeared. When I spoke with Salwa by phone in April 2006, she told me bitterly how she had gone to the Sudanese Foreign Ministry and the WAMY office in Khartoum, but neither could answer her increasingly frantic inquiries.

I had sometimes thought of the people who had been "disappeared" in Central and South America in the 1970s and 1980s. When Salwa had told us about her attempts to find out about Adel and her fears, her tale was chillingly similar to the 1982 movie *Missing*, in which Jack Lemmon portrayed a conservative American who ran into a stone wall everywhere he turned as he tried to find his son, who had been "disappeared" by the Argentine dictatorship. As a defense attorney, I have experienced firsthand how our state and federal governments "bury" people with sentences so long that they mean death in prison for an increasing number of nonviolent offenders. But until I met Adel, I had never had a case where our government made someone disappear.

Early in the morning of July 18, when the Pakistan Inter-Services Intelligence Police stormed into his apartment, Adel was, of course, concerned but not terribly worried. He had done nothing wrong, and his passport, visa, and work permit were properly stamped. He took some comfort in the fact that he was not isolated, having talked regularly with United Nations, World Health Organization, and other international officials at the hospital in

Chamkani, Afghanistan, and in Pakistan. And, while he had crossed the men who had wanted some of WAMY's supplies, he had worked closely with Pakistani government officials on distribution of food and medical supplies at Afghan refugee camps throughout Pakistan. Yet Adel's life was about to be devastated by a blond American man who led the Pakistani security team.

The heavily armed Pakistanis came over the wall in waves from the front and back of the house. The front wave of security police split when they entered the duplex. One group of around ten men broke into the apartment of Adel's down stairs neighbor, Ammeur Mammar, an Algerian who had lived on the ground floor of the duplex for eight years with his wife and three children. Ammeur had worked in the oil industry in Algeria for a number of years in the 1980s, then moved to Kenya, where he ended up working for a Saudi-funded charity. In the mid-'90s, the Algerian government had called passport holders home, and Ammeur, concerned about the political situation there, had moved to Pakistan. When the Algerian government refused to reissue his passport after it expired in 1996, Ammeur sought and gained refugee status from the United Nations. For the past six years he and his family had been living in Peshawar as officially documented refugees. Adel and Ammeur met when Adel and his family moved into the apartment upstairs. As Arabs in Pakistan, the two men had a common bond, even though they were from different cultures and were in Pakistan for different reasons. Their relationship was friendly but nothing more.

A second group of security police bolted up the stairs to Adel's apartment. Just out of bed when they burst through his door, Adel was wearing an ankle-length jallabiyah as a nightshirt. Six or eight men carrying machine guns and sidearms fanned out in the apartment. The man who seemed to be the leader, a Pakistani intelligence officer speaking Pashto—a language Adel had learned while working in Pakistan—demanded Adel's passport. When he started to move to his closet to get it, the leader barked at him to stay put. Adel sat on the bed and pointed to a shirt hanging in his closet. "My papers are in the pocket."

The lead Pakistani crossed the room to get the papers. Adel was then grabbed by the upper arm and pulled from his bed. He was roughly searched and then dragged into the living room, where he was pushed down on the couch.

"Are there any guns?" This time the question was asked in both Arabic and Pashto.

"I have no guns," Adel assured him.

Indeed, none were found.

"You have my passport and visa," Adel said, "and they are all in order."

One of the other Pakistanis, who was holding Adel's passport and work visa, laid them on the coffee table in front of the couch.

The group that had broken into Ammeur's apartment appeared upstairs with Ammeur in tow. One of them was holding his United Nations refugee card and handed it to the leader of the team that had taken Adel. The leader looked it over, then put it down on the coffee table next to Adel's papers. That simple act would haunt Adel years later when he was finally able to see some of the charges against him, charges that included possession of a UN refugee card.

The man who seemed to be in charge of the Pakistanis started talking to a blond American who had been lurking in the background.

"He has proper papers. Should we still take him?"

In butchered Pashto, the American answered in the affirmative.

"But here is his passport and work visa. He just came back to Pakistan yesterday."

"Take him," the American said.

"What about the Algerian? He has papers from the United Nations."

"Take them both."

Adel was sure from his accent that the man was an American but never heard a name and was not able to tell if he was FBI, CIA, military intelligence, or something else. It was clear to Adel, from the way the Pakistanis looked to the American for guidance and deferred to his decision, that he was in charge of the operation.

Adel and Ammeur were then handcuffed by the Pakistanis and taken in the same car to a local police station. The American was not traveling with them and, on the way, the Pakistanis told them that they were sure they would be released the next day.

Adel and Ammeur sat in the local jail overnight, and on the following day, July 19, new security officers came and took them out of the cell.

"We are taking you to Islamabad for a couple of days. You will be questioned and then sent home," the security man told Adel and Ammeur.

They were indeed taken to a security station in Islamabad. True to their word, the Pakistani security men questioned Adel and Ammeur. For both men the questioning was perfunctory; Adel recalled no more than twenty to thirty minutes of interrogation.

"Why are you in Pakistan?"

"I work for the World Assembly for Muslim Youth in administration. I have spent most of the last two years working in the WAMY hospital in Chamkani, Afghanistan."

"What do you do there?"

"Administration. I work with the supplies. Getting food and medicine from the United Nations. I was in Islamabad in June working with the Ministry of Health arranging warehousing for a shipment of supplies we were expecting. You can speak with them."

"Why were there boxes in your apartment?"

"My wife and daughters did not come back with me from Sudan. I will be shipping the boxes home."

The interrogation ended with the same reassurance Adel had been given the day before. "Your papers are in order, you should be sent home soon."

Adel and Ammeur slept better that night. But for the next two days, no one came. No food, no water, no interrogation. No Pakistanis. No Americans. Nothing. Then, on the twenty-second, the door to the cell opened. This time, the treatment was different. There was nothing polite about the way the new team of Pakistanis hooded Adel then chained him with heavy metal links and old-fashioned padlocks, and took him out to a van. Rather than being sent home, he and Ammeur were taken to an ancient, dank prison in Islamabad, probably something left over from the British colonial days.

For the next six months, Adel and Ammeur suffered in the misery of the Pakistani prison. The food was often rotten and spiced beyond recognition. The men were given a half liter of murky water each day. Their clothes had been taken when they were first brought in and replaced with one shirt and one pair of pants, which had to be washed in rotation if Adel wanted anything clean and did not want to go naked. They were given filthy mattresses and no sheets. For the first few months, as the Pakistani summer dragged on, the prison was a sweltering, fetid hell. Once the winter winds reached Islamabad from the Himalayas, the stench froze on the walls.

In the third month of his imprisonment, an infected tooth that Adel had put off treating began to fester, but there was no medication. Soon, dysentery hit hard. Adel's weight began dropping. When he'd come into the prison in July, he weighed in at a robust 200 pounds. By December, he was down to 135 pounds.

As Adel told us how sick he had been, there was no pathos in his recounting the story. This man, who had been through so much, gestured to himself with a smile, now showing off his solid physique. "Thanks to Allah, I could afford to lose weight."

In the Pakistani prison, there was nothing to pass the time. Adel and Ammeur could not write letters home. They could not see anyone from the Sudanese or Algerian consulates. There were no lawyers and no charges against them, and no interrogations. During the entire time that he was there, Adel was questioned only once, about Afghan mujahideen fighters he did not know. He does not even remember the names the interrogator threw at him during the session. It lasted only two hours at most, and that was it. Back in the cell he shared with Ammeur and staring at the walls, Adel could only speculate about why they were there. Neither had ever had any contacts with Al Qaeda, the Taliban, or any mujahideen.

In early January, the Pakistani phase of Adel's imprisonment ended when the security police returned with their hoods and chains. This time there were no promises that he would go home soon, and Adel and Ammeur were taken to a van for a ride that Adel remembers lasting little more than an hour. When the van stopped, he could not see where they had been taken, but the language he was hearing was English and the accent American. Peeking through the bottom of their hoods, Adel and Ammeur could make out a tarmac and the shape of airplanes. The Pakistanis removed the heavy metal chains and Adel heard their voices receding into the distance.

While in the Pakistani prison, neither the security forces nor the guards had ever beaten either Adel or Ammeur, but that changed on the tarmac. Adel was thrown on the ground, kicked roughly, and retrussed with something lighter than the chains the Pakistanis had used, some of it plastic. Although he could not understand the words his new captors were saying, Adel clearly understood the hostile tone of voice. He was pulled, half walking and half dragged, onto a waiting airplane. He could not see through the hood on his head, but he could tell that it was not a commercial plane because the seats lined the walls of the fuselage, facing in. Chained to the seats by their captors, no one told them where they were going, or why.

Adel's best guess is that the flight lasted two hours. When the plane landed, the chains that held Adel and Ammeur to their seats were taken off and they were pushed and dragged again, out into a freezing night and thrown on the ground. All the voices were now American. They did not know it at the time, but Adel and Ammeur were at the United States Air Force base in Baghram, Afghanistan. For a few minutes, no one asked or told them to do anything while they lay shivering on the ground. Eventually, someone kicked Adel, then jerked him up. Still outside on the tarmac, someone with a knife cut off his clothes, leaving him naked on the ground. After a time, Adel was pulled up off the ground and taken inside a large converted hangar that he later learned served as a prison and interrogation area. Inside, Adel was given a set of rough clothes with a number sewn on the sleeve and thrown into a bare cell where, for the first time since he was taken from his home, Adel was separated from Ammeur.

There was no furniture in the cell and Adel propped himself in one of the corners. That was when he was given his first instructions. A guard, who had apparently remained at the door, barked, "Stand up!" While Adel did not understand the words at first, there was no mistaking the instruction. Every time he began to sit down, there was a bang on the door and the order, "Stand up!" For three days and three nights this continued. After a day, Adel would start to nod off to sleep while standing, but every time a guard would bang on the door to keep him awake. Several times a guard brought some water into the cell, but no food. Adel was not being singled out for this treatment. It was the same routine he became aware was being used on his fellow prisoners.

For some, this "softening-up period" lasted even longer. In March 2003, the *New York Times* interviewed two Afghans who had recently been released from Baghram, Mr. Jabar and Mr. Shah. Jabar described being forced to stand, "hooded," "arms raised and chained to the ceiling," and with his "feet shackled: for thirteen days."[5] Shah described similar treatment in a freezing room for ten days and guards who, like Adel's, kept him awake by shouting at and kicking him to stop him from falling.

After three days, two guards entered Adel's cell and he was again hooded and chained, this time with handcuffs and leg shackles. Turning corners several times, probably down different corridors, eventually the little procession came to a halt in a spot where Adel was told to stand. He now understands that this was the interrogation room. As he stood with the hood covering his entire head, the questioning, in Arabic, began. The essence, as Adel remembered it four years later, had to do with Al Qaeda and his work for LDI.

"What were you doing for Al Qaeda?"

"I am not Al Qaeda."

"Who were your contacts?"

"I have no ties to Al Qaeda."

"What did you do for Khalid al Sheikh? You met him at the Jelazee Camp in 1988."

"Yes, I did some work at the Jelazee refugee camp in the 1980s when I worked for LDI. We were helping Afghan refugees from the wars with the Russians. The director of the camp was Mohammed al Sheikh. I understand his brother is Khalid al Sheikh. Maybe he came to the camp once or twice to visit his brother. I never met him."

"What have you done for the Taliban?"

"I never supported the Taliban."

"What about Gulbuddin Hekmatyar? You delivered food to his camp?"

"I delivered food for LDI to refugees at the Shamshatoo camp around 1990. I never met Hekmatyar and have no idea if he ever came to the camp. I do know he became president of Afghanistan in 1992 after the Russians left."[6]

The first session lasted several hours. Although Adel was not beaten after the first night on the tarmac, every time he was moved for interrogation, he was jerked, pushed, and insulted. For three days this went on, several times a day. Adel was hooded, handcuffed, placed in leg shackles, and taken from his cell. In the interrogation room, he was questioned, yelled at, and berated. Three sessions, four sessions, five sessions. Sometimes the voices were the same. Sometimes they were different.

Each time Adel told his interrogators the same thing. The interrogators were never satisfied; they never varied the questions. Six times, seven times, maybe more. Then Adel collapsed. Weakened from his ordeal in the prison in Pakistan, the lack of sleep, the lack of food, and the cold in the prison in Afghanistan, Adel's body just gave out.

.   .   .

It was disturbing to hear Adel describe being treated this way by my countrymen. Notions of common decency as well as studies on interrogation techniques have led our police and military away from torture and coercion as instruments of investigation. In the criminal justice system, police interrogators abandoned the third degree in the 1950s and '60s. The Supreme Court also spurred more changes in a series of decisions during those decades that culminated with the *Miranda* decision in 1966, with its now familiar warnings about the right to silence and counsel.[7] Few, if any, people suggest that a Miranda-type warning is appropriate in a military setting, but too many studies have shown that torture is not an effective interrogation tool. One reason is that it simply does not get reliable information. In his autobiography, *Faith of My Fathers*, Senator John McCain, a victim of torture by the North Vietnamese in the 1960s, says everyone has a breaking point and will say anything to get the torture to stop, leading to as many false confessions as valuable information. But the Bush administration took a different view and ignored these warnings.

In late 2001, as the Afghan war was beginning, staff in the White House and the Department of Justice engaged in extensive discussions about the legality of harsh treatment and interrogation as a tool in the war on terror. These discussions culminated in a series of memoranda prepared by the Department of Justice's Office of Legal Counsel under the direction of Attorney General Ashcroft and White House legal counsel, Alberto Gonzales.[8] The memoranda provided what the administration viewed as legal justification to ignore the requirements in the Geneva Conventions regarding the treatment of prisoners of war, and they authorized military commanders and interrogators to use their own discretion on treatment.

Known as the "torture memos," these papers were prepared by Deputy Assistant Attorney General John Yoo, White House Counsel Alberto Gonzales, and Jay Bybee, a top lawyer in the White House Office of Legal Counsel and now a judge on the United States Court of Appeals for the Ninth Circuit. The memoranda justified harsh treatment of the men seized in the war on terror by saying that they were not prisoners of war entitled to the protections of the Geneva Conventions. In addition, they said, extreme measures were justified under the president's power as commander in chief in order to extract information that could be useful in protecting the United States. The memoranda had to deal with the fact that the conventions prohibit not only "torture" but also "violence," "cruel treatment," and "humiliating and degrading treatment."[9]

While the memoranda were still warm from the copy machines, they were answered with stinging criticism from attorneys in the State Department and by Secretary of State Colin Powell himself. In a memo dated January 26, 2002, Secretary Powell argued that the United States was required, and that it was right, to comply with international norms.[10] President Bush, as reflected in an order he issued on February 7, ignored Secretary Powell's cautions and accepted the reasoning of Yoo and Gonzales that prisoners taken in the war with the Taliban and Al Qaeda would not receive the protections of the Geneva Conventions.[11] Although he did not directly endorse torture, the president clearly set a tone that eventually led to the abuse of thousands of prisoners in Baghram, Guantánamo, and the American-run prison at Abu Ghraib in Iraq. For the president and vice president, it was more important to get information that might lead to Bin Laden or prevent a future attack than to comply with international norms and treat its prisoners humanely.

Even after the president's February directives, apparently some people in the administration were not sure how far they could go, and Gonzales sought clarification. On August 1, 2002, he was given a fifty-page memo by Jay Bybee. Torture, the memo said, is only action that "inflict[s] pain that is difficult to endure." That meant it must be so intense it is like the pain that accompanies "organ failure" "or even death." If the pain from treatment was only mental, it would have to last "for months or even years" to be considered torture.[12]

In June 2007, Barton Gellman and Jo Becker wrote in the *Washington Post* that, even though the memos written in January and February of 2002 had been circulated within the upper levels of the administration, it wasn't until 2004 that Secretary Powell and National Security Adviser Condoleezza Rice learned about the August 2002 memo. They described Rice dressing down Gonzales.[13] When I read the newspaper report, I thought about Archibald Cox and his pursuit of justice in the Watergate scandal and how Attorney General Richardson had resigned rather than follow President Nixon's directive that he fire Cox. Powell and Rice spoke up in 2002 and 2004 but, unlike Cox, soldiered on when they were ignored. I wonder whether the harm done to thousands of victims of harsh treatment over the next several years, including Adel and my other clients, and the extreme damage done to our country around the world could have been avoided if

Powell and Rice had struck the balance differently between the competing values of loyalty and justice.

.   .   .

When Adel had collapsed, the interrogators took him to the prison hospital, where his dehydrated and malnourished body began the slow process of recovery. But other inmates at the prison in Baghram were not as resilient. On March 4, 2003, under the headline "U.S. Military Investigating Death of Afghan in Custody," Carlotta Gall of the *New York Times* reported on three deaths from similar mistreatment that had just come to light. The death certificate for one, a twenty-two-year-old farmer named Dilawar, pronounced the cause of death as "blunt force injuries to lower extremities complicating coronary artery disease."

Two weeks after his body gave out, Adel was discharged from the prison hospital. He was taken to a different section of the prison, where he had furniture in his cell and was allowed rest and sleep. In early March, Adel was allowed his first contact with people outside the prison, a visit by a team from the International Red Cross. By then, his condition had begun to improve and he had started gaining back some of the weight he had lost in captivity. Through the Red Cross, Adel was permitted to write a letter to his wife, a letter he was told would pass through U.S. military censors. Knowing that Salwa would be sick with worry about him and not knowing how much more she could take, Adel wrote a simple letter telling her that he was well and in a United States prison in Baghram, Afghanistan. When we later spoke with Salwa about the letter, she described the relief mingled with fear that she felt when word that Adel was alive finally arrived. She did not know when, or if, she would ever see her husband again.

Adel's letter had arrived in Khartoum a month after being written, just as he was being chained and hooded yet again by the Americans—for transfer to the U.S. military prison at Guantánamo Bay. This time, instead of a hood to block his sight, the guards used a blindfold and earmuffs. Perhaps to ensure that their chained prisoners could not bite their way to freedom, or perhaps just to prevent any communication, a full muzzle was strapped on Adel's face and on those of the other men on the plane. The chains, muzzle, blindfold, and earmuffs were kept in place for the entire thirty-hour flight. Adel told us that he did all right with the sensory deprivation, but that some of the prisoners could not handle being cut off from all sight, sound, and smell. When Adel needed to relieve himself on the plane, he was led in chains and full headgear to the toilet, where he was told to sit. No hands and no toilet paper.

Adel arrived at the prison in Guantánamo around March 15, 2003. When the guards finally removed his blindfold, he saw the chain-link fence and razor wire surrounding the barrackslike cells of his new prison home. And he also saw the sun. For a man brought up under the bright African sun, that, at least, was a welcome sight. It was the first time Adel had seen it since his seizure the previous summer.

Adel joined approximately five hundred other prisoners who had been brought to Guantánamo over the previous year (because of the administration's secrecy, the precise number may never be known). Among the men in Guantánamo when Adel arrived were an unknown number of British citizens of Arab, Afghan, and Middle Eastern descent, including Shafiq Rasul, Asif Iqbal, and Rahul Ahmed. Although Adel never met these men, it was the Supreme Court case involving Rasul and Iqbal that played an important role in bringing Adel and me together and that I had described to Brandon.

6 | From September 11 to Guantánamo Bay

[The] concept of "national defense" cannot be deemed an end in itself, justifying any exercise of legislative power designed to promote such a goal. Implicit in the term "national defense" is the notion of defending those values and ideals which set this nation apart. For almost two centuries, our country has taken singular pride in the democratic ideals enshrined in its Constitution. . . . It would indeed be ironic if, in the name of national defense, we would sanction the subversion of . . . those liberties . . . which make the defense of the nation worthwhile.

—Chief Justice Earl Warren, *United States v. Robel*[1]

WHEN ADEL WAS BROUGHT TRUSSED AND blindfolded to Guantánamo, more than a year after the prison was opened, the first twenty prisoners were still being held virtually incommunicado and without having been charged in any way in any type of proceeding, military or civilian. The existence of the isolated prison, the often abusive treatment its prisoners have endured, and the lack of any meaningful process to challenge their detention are no accident. They are a key part of the Bush administration's strategy in response to the attacks of September 11, as are the decisions that led to Brandon's arrest on the material witness warrant. In order to understand how innocent people like Brandon and Adel can be thrown in prison and held up by the U.S. government before the world as terrorists, it is necessary to take a detour back to September 11 and explore the forces the president, secretary of defense, and attorney general put in motion after the attacks. The policies of the administration were intended to—and did—make far-reaching changes in our legal and governmental structures.

.   .   .

September 11, 2001, began like any other day. Our son, Michael, had started fifth grade the week before, and my wife, Kathleen, and I got up a little before 6 A.M. to the usual news of the day on NPR and started getting ready for work before we woke up Mike. Kathleen went downstairs to let out our dog, Scottie, and put the kettle on, but minutes later she burst into the bathroom to tell me that Steve Sady had called saying a plane had hit one of the 110-story towers of the World Trade Center in New York. We knew this had to be big, since Sady, an inveterate newshound, had called before at odd hours with news flashes, which usually involved people who were soon to become our clients.

Kathleen had the television on when I came downstairs. The first minutes were maddening for us, as they were for so many people that day. We watched with disbelief as the mighty symbols of U.S. capitalism billowed smoke. But the towers had personal meaning for us as well. In 1979, Kathleen had had her first legal job interview there with New York Attorney General Robert Abrams. The next year, my parents had hosted a dinner in the fabulous Windows on the World restaurant on the 107th floor of the North Tower for my mother's cousin Volodzha and his wife, Rita, who were visiting from their home in the far north of the Soviet Union. They were the first members of my mother's family that had stayed in Russia after 1920 who had been permitted to travel to America. The dinner was the high point, literally and figuratively, of the visit.

When Kathleen and I tuned in to the news, neither tower had yet collapsed and we did not know that a plane would hit the Pentagon or that another one would be taken down in a Pennsylvania field. Wandering in and out of the den as we continued getting ready for work, we knew we were witnessing a horrible event, but all reports as to the cause were still just wild speculation. Then, at 6:30 A.M. Pacific time, President Bush made the first announcement that we had experienced "an apparent terrorist attack." But the towers were still standing, and the collapse of the mighty pillars was not even a possibility on anyone's radar screens so we decided to wake Mike for school. Then, at 7:05 A.M. our time, the South Tower collapsed. All 110 stories and 625,000 tons of steel and concrete just dropped. It took only ten seconds for life to change forever.[2]

Twenty-three minutes later, as all three of us watched, the North Tower followed its twin into history. Our thoughts and feelings were twisted like the melted steel of the towers as we started to grapple with the emotions of our son. You can't tell a ten-year-old that the world is no longer a safe place, that terrorists have struck the heart of the incredible city we had visited the previous Christmas, and that they could strike again anywhere in this great country. But Michael already knew that something fundamental had changed. He, like so many children that day, needed reassurance that his parents and the adult world would do all we could to keep him safe. I never imagined that I would be spending so much time over the next few years talking to Michael about the tactics our government would say it was using to make us safe and the difference between safety and a false sense of security.

. . .

When I walked into my office around 8:30, there were knots of people everywhere listening to radios and talking in hushed voices of disbelief. A few people were in Wendell Williams' office, a veteran investigator in charge of our audiovisual equipment, including a television we usually used for viewing police videos of drug deals. That morning, however, we were watching the scenes of devastation in New York and Washington.

The caseload my staff and I should have been focusing on included our usual drugs, guns, fraud, and immigration clients charged by the United States attorney and cases of state prisoners who were asking the federal court to order their release based on violations of their rights in the state courts. As the head of the office, I carry a reduced caseload that includes the same mix. A few assistant defenders had to be in court for scheduled hearings and the daily duty attorney had to meet new arrests in the marshal's lockup in the courthouse, but no one else had the energy to focus on work.

Around 9:30, I called a meeting in the library for those who wanted to share their feelings and for all of us to be together as a team so we could process what had happened. Everyone who was in the Portland office that day came in. With phones conferencing in the staff in our Eugene and

Medford branches, there were nearly sixty people in the library, physically and virtually. I started off by thanking everyone for being there, and then, although we are a federal agency in which overt religious action is not appropriate and I am not particularly religious myself, I asked everyone to take a minute to reflect, calling on God or whatever power or philosophy they believe in for those who had died. I reminded everyone of the importance of compassion for the victims, their families, and also for each other. I also talked about the importance of reason. As terrible as the events were, we needed to remember why we worked in the defender office and the dangers that lay ahead, not just from terrorists but also from the domestic fear and anger their acts would undoubtedly spawn.

My colleagues shared their thoughts and feelings. There were tears, questions, disbelief; people wondered about the who and why; they talked about the victims and their families. There was a great deal of sadness but very little anger in the room, which I found reflected the tremendous compassion and forgiveness typical of the type of people who want to work in a public defender office.

Every day we are pushing against prosecutors, police, judges, and probation officers, often for clients who have committed violent and unpleasant acts, telling the other players in the system that they are wrong, they have the wrong person, they violated our clients' rights, overcharged them, or are seeking sentences that are too long. The constant pushing, no matter how politely phrased, inevitably causes tension that sometimes bubbles up from our adversaries and also from the public when we do win and our clients are acquitted, evidence is thrown out, or shorter sentences are imposed. Then when we lose, or win only on some points, our clients and their families are not happy.

I have often been asked why people do criminal defense work and particularly in a public defender office. Most of us are fascinated by people and the complexities of the human condition; we like working with other people. Most also have tremendous empathy, feeling deeply the injustices suffered by those less fortunate. Also, most of my staff and colleagues, like me, believe firmly in the rule of law. We want to heed the call to action implicit in the letter Martin Luther King Jr. sent from the Birmingham City Jail, on April 16, 1963: "Injustice anywhere is a threat to justice everywhere."[3] The need for compassion and desire to fight injustice were huge before 9/11. They are more needed now.

A little after ten o'clock, most of the staff had returned to their casework. We had a reason to keep going—continuing the fight for justice. While our clients' problems had been put on hold for a few hours, their futures were in our hands, and we quickly turned back to them with our usual intensity.

·   ·   ·

President Bush was in Sarasota, Florida, visiting the Emma Booker Elementary School on September 11. Although he inexplicably continued to read *The Pet Goat* to the second-grade class he was in when he was given the news,[4] his address to the nation that night was powerful, and it moved me.

> A great people has been moved to defend a great nation. Terrorist attacks can shake the foundations of our biggest buildings, but they cannot touch the foundation of America. . . . America was targeted for attack because we're the brightest beacon for freedom and opportunity in the world. And no one will keep that light from shining. Today, our nation saw evil, the very worst of human nature. And we responded with the best of America—with the daring of our rescue workers, with the caring for strangers and neighbors who came to give blood and help in any way they could.[5]

Looking back years later, I am still drawn to his message but angry at the way the positive energy of that time has been squandered. The president's intentions soon focused on revenge and a military response to the terrorists and made it clear he was going to cast a wide net that would include anyone he believed helped or harbored the attackers in any way—a strategy that would quickly ensnare innocent people such as Adel.

On September 14, Congress responded to the president's call to arms. Even though the president is the commander in chief of the armed forces, under the Constitution, only Congress can declare war and only Congress can authorize the federal government's expenditure of money.[6] Since the founding of our republic, presidents have committed troops overseas nearly three hundred times with only a handful of actual declarations of war. But public reaction to the deadly but undeclared wars in Korea and Vietnam in the 1950s and 1960s led to the War Powers Act of 1973 that requires the president to consult with Congress if he or she wants to send troops overseas, although the president is allowed to do so for up to sixty days without congressional authorization.[7] Under the War Powers Act, Congress can either make a formal declaration of war or pass a resolution authorizing the use of force.

At the time, President Bush could not ask for a formal declaration of war because there was no nation to retaliate against. But immediately after the attacks, the president sought, and Congress passed, a resolution that he signed into law on September 18. Known as the Authorization for the Use of Military Force (AUMF), it authorized the use of "all necessary and appropriate force against those nations, organizations, or persons he determines planned, authorized, committed, or aided the terrorist attacks that occurred on September 11, 2001, or harbored such organizations or persons, in order to prevent any future acts of international terrorism against the United States by such nations, organizations or persons."[8]

The AUMF clearly authorized the president to send troops to Afghanistan. But in the years since 2001, he has interpreted it far more broadly than was originally intended, even saying it allows him to dispense with court authorization and warrants for domestic surveillance on people he suspects of terrorist ties. Those loose interpretations took center stage five years after the AUMF was passed, during the national debates over the administration's actions, when it was disclosed that President Bush had ignored the Foreign Intelligence Surveillance Act and authorized domestic wiretapping without any court approval.

On September 20, President Bush addressed a joint session of Congress. Again, he spoke like a strong leader, reassuring the country that we would be all right. He reminded the world that we are a strong nation and that we would deal harshly with the terrorists who had attacked us. While the president did not use the word "crusade," a word he would use three days later, the discordant note of crusade was implied in the speech, and he introduced a new concept to the nation: a Department of Homeland Security.

> We will take defensive measures against terrorism to protect Americans. Today, dozens of federal departments and agencies, as well as state and local governments, have responsibilities affecting homeland security. These efforts must be coordinated at the highest level. So tonight I announce the creation of a Cabinet-level position reporting directly to me—the Office of Homeland Security.[9]

Kathleen and I listened to the president's speech with George Saslow, the beloved "dean" of psychiatry in Oregon and one of the founding fathers of Oregon's Psychiatric Security Review Board, an innovative parole board–like body that oversees supervision of the criminally insane in Oregon. We met George when Kathleen was the director of the board, and their friendship continued after she left to become the director of the State Board of Medical Examiners. Born in 1906, George had studied and lived in Germany and England and still subscribed to the London *Times, Frankfurter Allgemeine,* and the *New York Times.* He was still practicing at ninety-five years of age.

The stridency of the president's speech made me uncomfortable, and while thunderous applause was still cascading down to the House floor after the president finished his address, I asked George what he made of this new Department of Homeland Security. Without even a slight pause, George reached back sixty-eight years to Adolf Hitler's speeches in 1933 when he first came to power, and said, "Hitler and the Homeland. This is what we need to fear." The hair stood on the back of my neck as I took this in. George had lived through every war of the twentieth century, had seen the red scares and deportations under Attorney General Palmer in 1919–1921, Hitler's and Stalin's fascism, the Cheka and the Stasi, the Soviet and East German secret police agencies, J. Edgar Hoover, and the Communist baiting under Senator McCarthy in the 1950s. George's reaction to this new department crystallized the discomfort I had felt and the notion that our system of checks and balances was at risk. It was as if a lid had been removed from a genie's bottle and the escaping presence would not be benign.

In that speech, the president also invoked "the war on terror" directly for the first time. "Our war on terror begins with al-Qaida," he said, "but it does not end there. It will not end until every terrorist group of global reach has been found, stopped, and defeated." That phrase, which the president has repeated so many times since September 11, had been used numerous times in the past century and a half, including in the late 1800s in Britain when there was a wave of anarchist bombings and again in the 1940s in describing Zionist terror bombings in Palestine.[10] As President Bush uses it, however, it becomes a war without end and a war that sometimes sweeps far too broadly.

∎ ∎ ∎

The September attacks were unprecedented—the first successful attacks on United States soil by foreign agents since Pearl Harbor. Although, unlike most terrorist actions, they were not accompanied by any boasts of success or demands, the assumption around the world was that they were the work of the Al Qaeda network of Osama Bin Laden, which was then based in Afghanistan under the protection of the fundamentalist Taliban regime.

Bin Laden, whose anti-Soviet actions were welcomed by the United States in the chaotic scene in Afghanistan in the 1980s, had become persona non grata with our government when his anti-Western positions focused exclusively on the United States after the Soviets were thrown out of Afghanistan in 1989.[11] When intelligence sources quickly confirmed the assumption that he had been behind the September 11 attacks, the Bush administration made the decision to go after Bin Laden in earnest.

This was not the first time the United States had gone after him. After intelligence sources pinned the blame for the August 7, 1998, bombings of the United States embassies in Nairobi, Kenya, and Dar es Salaam, Tanzania, on Bin Laden, President Clinton had ordered bombing attacks on suspected Bin Laden bases in Afghanistan and Sudan.[12]

The United States, which was funneling money and supplies to Afghan forces called the Northern Alliance, which had been fighting the Taliban for some time, increased its support and, on October 7, 2001, began its own armed incursion in Afghanistan with bombing campaigns in Kabul, Kandahar, and Jalalabad. The first U.S. troops hit the ground on October 19 and soon started capturing prisoners.[13]

Needing legal justification to hold those prisoners, President Bush issued an order on November 13 authorizing Secretary of Defense Rumsfeld to detain members of Al Qaeda or any other person who committed, planned to commit, or assisted in any terrorist act against the United States. The order authorized the secretary to hold these people at any location either within or outside the United States.[14] This was part of the Bush administration's strategic plan to take Al Qaeda and other fighters out of the war—not just the war in Afghanistan but also the broader war on terror—and to put them in a place where they could be mined as intelligence assets; that is, interrogated, for as long as the administration wanted. It is ostensibly under the authority granted by the November 13, 2001, presidential order that my clients in Guantánamo, including Adel, were soon seized.

It took just over a month for the Northern Alliance forces to take Kabul, and in late November, the United Nations convened a meeting of Afghan leaders to discuss the shape of a postwar government. By December, the last Taliban stronghold had fallen, and Hamid Karzai was sworn in as interim president of the country.[15]

The allied effort then shifted its focus to Bin Laden in particular, and the hunt was on in earnest in the northeastern mountains of Afghanistan near the Pakistani border. The search dragged on unsuccessfully throughout the next year, with more than ten thousand U.S. troops remaining in Afghanistan. The Taliban receded in power, the warlords united briefly behind Karzai as permanent president, and while the chaos and intertribal fights continued in the background, the incursion in Afghanistan seemed to be a success.

Late in 2001, the U.S. forces began to receive prisoners from Afghans and Pakistanis—a few had been captured on the battlefields; most had not. The U.S. commanders unquestionably had the authority under widely accepted international laws of war to detain men they picked up on the battlefields. But the Bush administration had given them broader authority as well, and others were arrested after the battles had waned. Some were turned over to U.S. forces in response to bounty posters and leaflets posted and dropped from airplanes by our military as part of the campaign to win hearts and minds in Afghanistan.[16]

"Get wealth and power beyond your dreams," read one.[17]

The posters offered payments of $5,000 for regular Al Qaeda members and up to $25,000,000 for Bin Laden.[18] While some of the men handed over were Al Qaeda and Taliban fighters, others were nothing but victims of greed and the opportunity to settle old scores.

Most of the men picked up by U.S. forces or turned in by Afghans or Pakistanis were initially held in prisons at the U.S. bases in Baghram and Kandahar or in prisons in Pakistan before their transfer to Guantánamo. Secretary Rumsfeld said it was "the least worst place" to hold the worst of the worst, the "most dangerous, best-trained, vicious killers on the face of the earth."[19] The administration has been quite open about the fact that it chose Guantánamo because it was not part of the United States and so believed its actions there would not be subject to scrutiny by the federal courts.

Where to hold the prisoners was only one piece of the equation the Bush administration had to solve. The president and his staff had to decide whether to treat them as prisoners of war with the rights of access, humane treatment, and process required by the Geneva Conventions of 1949 to which the United States was a party, or whether they should be treated as unlawful belligerents or guerrilla warriors without rights. The administration also had to determine how far to go in mining its prisoners as intelligence assets—what types of interrogation techniques would be permitted.

Lawyers in the White House, Department of Justice, Department of Defense, and State Department were kept busy throughout the fall of 2001 and winter of 2002 working on these issues. As memos on these subjects began to surface years later with arguments about the need for virtually unlimited executive power, it became apparent that more than the twin towers had fallen in the September 11 attacks.

The administration came out of the box with a memo on January 9, 2002, from Justice Department lawyers, led by Deputy Assistant Attorney General Yoo, that told Secretary of Defense Rumsfeld, the custodian of the prisoners, that neither the laws of war nor international law, including the Geneva Conventions, had any "binding legal effect on either the President or the military."[20] In Yoo's view, the president's power as commander in chief was virtually unlimited. Colin Powell's State Department was incensed by these assertions, and it took only two days before its legal adviser, William Taft IV, fired back that Yoo's memo was "seriously flawed." State wanted to follow the Geneva Conventions.

On January 25, the president's confidant, White House Counsel Alberto Gonzales, dismissed State's complaints as based on a view of the world that had become obsolete. Adding weight to Gonzales's memo was its coauthor, David Addington, Vice President Cheney's legal adviser. They argued that there was a "new paradigm" for describing the conflict in Afghanistan and with Al Qaeda and other terrorist organizations that "renders obsolete Geneva's strict limitations on questioning of enemy prisoners and renders quaint some of its provisions." Their view also "eliminate[d] any argument regarding the need for case-by-case determinations of POW status." Individual determinations of culpability, the hallmark of our system of justice, could be thrown out the window. The Gonzales/Addington view was adopted by Rumsfeld, and for two and a half years no hearings were held to determine what—if anything—the prisoners at Guantánamo had done. For men such as Adel, throwing out the need for case-by-case determination meant that they could be held based on collective guilt ascribed even to employers for whom they worked.

Undoubtedly anticipating that not everyone was going to agree with their opinions of how prisoners should be treated, Gonzales and Addington discussed a solution to the problem of potential prosecution of U.S. personnel responsible for seizing, detaining, and interrogating the men taken in Afghanistan and elsewhere in the war on terror. Their memo discussed a new paradigm for rejection of international law that "substantially reduces the threat of domestic criminal prosecution under the War Crimes Act."

The White House/Cheney memo on the new paradigm, authored by Gonzales and Addington, did not go over any better with Secretary Powell than the memo from the Justice Department he had objected to three weeks earlier. This time Powell personally opposed the views espoused in the "paradigm" memo, but his was a lonely voice in an administration that knew it was pushing the legal and political envelope to the breaking point. A week after Powell spoke up, Attorney General Ashcroft weighed in with a letter to the president, dated February 1, explaining how the administration could minimize the "various legal risks or liability, litigation, and criminal prosecution" it was taking with the imprisonment and treatment of its prisoners. The solution Ashcroft proposed was to declare Afghanistan under the Taliban a "failed state."

On February 7, the president made that call, following Gonzales and Ashcroft's advice and concluding that very few of the protections of the Geneva Conventions needed to be given to the prisoners. Under this umbrella, possible fighters and anyone who aided them could be seized on the flimsiest of hunches, held in prison indefinitely, and subjected to interrogations that much of the world would consider torture.

The policies the Bush administration adopted toward its captives in the war on terror were a reversion to a much earlier time. The question of how to treat prisoners of war is as old as war itself. The Egyptians, Greeks, and Romans often enslaved entire enemy populations, and distinctions were drawn among high- and lowborn captives.[21] What we consider brutal torture today was commonplace.

In the United States, however, the norm has been humane treatment of prisoners from the beginning. During the Revolutionary War, as early as the first Battle of Trenton in late December 1776, General George Washington captured hundreds of Hessian mercenaries who were fighting with the British. While he had been literally weeping only months earlier as he watched the British slaughter his own troops who had been captured after the colonial defeat in the Battle of New York, Washington ordered that the Hessians be treated decently. The legacy of Washington's belief that our enemies are human beings worthy of respect and decent treatment is carried on today by war heroes such as Senator McCain, who has argued, based on his own experiences in North Vietnamese tiger cages, that we should treat our prisoners fairly not only because it is the moral thing to do but also because it is in our self-interest, increasing the likelihood that captured Americans will be treated decently.[22]

The administration's decisions to deny applicability of the Geneva Conventions and the Laws of War were in line with its overall response to the September 11 attacks as acts of war calling for a military response—not crimes to be handled with prosecutions in the criminal justice system. And in this war, the administration determined that it would take virtually no risks. Ron Susskind called this the administration's "one percent doctrine" in his recent book that detailed the development of the Bush administration's policies in the war on terror. If there was even a 1 percent chance that America could be attacked again, that someone was engaged in, or thinking about, terrorism, the administration was going to act first.[23]

.   .   .

Shortly after the Karzai government was in place in Afghanistan and the main Taliban forces had been defeated, the Bush administration set its sights on Iraq. The war begun there by the United States in March of 2003 also generated a host of prisoners, many of whom were locked up by the American military at Abu Ghraib, the refurbished former Hussein regime prison. Only a few months after the United States began housing prisoners there, stories started emerging about torture.[24] It wasn't long before there was a full-blown scandal around the inhumane treatment of Iraqi prisoners documented in numerous investigations by Congress, international organizations, and the military itself.[25]

Many of the horrific stories from Abu Ghraib about abuse of Iraqi prisoners that came to light in early 2004 involved techniques that were used first in Guantánamo in 2002 and 2003. There was a direct link between the two prisons: Major General Geoffrey D. Miller, who had been the commander in Guantánamo when the harshest treatment of prisoners was in vogue there in late 2002 and 2003, was detailed to Iraq on August 31, 2003, to assist in the start-up of the Abu Ghraib prison.[26] Miller had sent in what were called "tiger teams" of Guantánamo Bay interrogators and analysts to help train the personnel there.

As with many of the prisoners at Guantánamo, like Adel, a fair number of the men who were thrown into the prison at Abu Ghraib were innocent victims of the incredibly broad brush the administration used to sweep the streets and its manipulation of and disregard for the truth about who they were. Given the distortions about Iraq that were used by the administration to justify its large-scale invasion of a sovereign nation—the supposed links between Saddam Hussein and Al Qaeda; the presence of weapons of mass destruction; and the tales about the purchase of aluminum tubes, nuclear weapons, and Niger that were revealed as lies when the administration leaked the identity of CIA agent Valerie Plame to discredit her husband, Ambassador Joseph Wilson, who had debunked the alleged Niger/Iraq transaction in aluminum tubes—its willingness to hold thousands of Iraqis for months and years on end without any evidence that they were a danger to Americans or part of the insurgency that followed Saddam's fall is not surprising.[27]

It appears that in the view of the Bush administration, trampling on the rights of a few individuals, including my clients, was a small price to pay to protect the nation from another terrorist attack. Of course there is no question that terrorists and suicide bombers pose a real threat around the world, but one of the fundamental differences between the United States and other countries has been our commitment to the dignity of all people and a belief in the importance of the rule of law. The Bush administration has shifted the balance and placed the ends before the means.

How far the administration was willing to go was seen in 2002 with the sellout of some of the men imprisoned with Adel in Guantánamo, the Chinese Uighurs.[28] Xinjiang province, bordering Pakistan, Kyrgystan, and Kazakhstan in northwestern China, is the home to tens of millions of Muslims. While the world has focused a great deal of attention on the Han Chinese suppression of Tibet and its Buddhist population, the Chinese government's efforts to suppress the desire of the Muslims for more political and cultural freedom in Xinjiang has proceeded out of the spotlight.

In the late 1990s, a number of Uighurs left China, some to avoid political repression, others on trading missions. By the summer of 2001 a small Uighur village had sprung up by chance in the White Mountains region of Afghanistan near Jalalabad and the Pakistani border, an area that was targeted for reasons having nothing to do with the Uighurs when the United States began its bombing campaign in Afghanistan in October of that year. The Uighurs fled along with many local villagers and, in the confusion, a group of eighteen Uighurs who had headed toward the border were captured by Pakistanis. These men were eventually turned over to the Americans as terrorists in return for bounty payments, and they were shipped to Guantánamo. However, their U.S. interrogators soon realized that these men were not combatants.

When it became clear to Saddam Hussein in the summer of 2002 that he was in the crosshairs of the Bush administration's gunsights, he figured that his best hope of averting disaster lay with the Chinese. On August 24, Saddam dispatched his foreign minister, Naji Sabri, on a mission in Beijing to ask the Chinese to tell the Americans that they would not be happy if the United States invaded Iraq. His trump card was the vast reservoirs of Iraqi oil that the Chinese economy desperately needed.

The Bush administration got wind of Saddam's plan and moved into high gear—the race for Beijing was on. Deputy Secretary of State Richard Armitage was dispatched on an urgent mission to get the Chinese to stay on the sidelines. Beating the Iraqi Sabri to Beijing by one day, Armitage met with senior Chinese officials on August 26.

The Chinese expressed understanding of our concern regarding Saddam but raised some concerns of their own about the Uighurs and reminded Armitage that the United States was holding a group of them in Guantánamo. The Chinese asked for access to the Uighurs, to have the United States declare them terrorists, and to place the East Turkestan Islamic Movement, one of the main Uighur political movements, on our terrorist watch lists.

Given the administration's prior dealings with the Uighurs, the Chinese demand should have been rejected. When the terrorism watch lists compiled by the U.S. intelligence community were reviewed after September 11, the Uighurs had not been included and, while we were holding them in Guantánamo even as early as the summer of 2002, our military and political leaders knew that their seizure and imprisonment had been a mistake. They had not been fighting in Afghanistan but had been living there quietly as refugees. Indeed, many were staunchly pro-American, but Armitage and the administration were not deterred.

The need to keep the Chinese on the sidelines in the event of an invasion of Iraq was too strong, and the administration wasn't going to let the
fate of a handful of Uighurs interfere with its plans. Armitage acceded to
the Chinese demands, and in late August, the Uighurs were added to the
official government list of terrorist groups. But the concessions did not stop
there. In September, Chinese agents were permitted to visit the otherwise
inaccessible and highly secure facility in Guantánamo and were even permitted to interrogate the Uighur prisoners. More than half are still there.

Our government will not let the Uighurs into the United States, and although our allies loudly and repeatedly condemn our policies in Guantánamo,
for years none of them were willing to give the Uighurs a home. In the divide between public outcries and action and the indifference of much of the
world to the Uighurs' plight and refusal to take them in, history is repeating itself. When Jews tried to flee the Nazis shortly before and during World
War II, they were often unable to find a country to take them in. In July 1938,
a conference was called at Evian, France, to discuss the plight of Jews who
were seeking refuge from Germany. After a great deal of hand-wringing and
expressions of sympathy, none of the thirty-two countries that attended took
any significant action to allow Jews to immigrate.[29]

Doors remained closed even after the destruction of Jewish communities throughout Germany on Kristallnacht in November 1938 and the start
of World War II. The official British policy during the war to prevent Jewish immigration to Palestine was even enforced by gunfire. On the very day
Hitler invaded Poland, the British ship *Lorna* opened fire on the refugee
boat *Tiger Hill* as it tried to make its way to Palestine.[30] Other boats were
turned away from country after country in Central and South America.[31]

It took more than two years before a home was found for five of the innocent Uighurs. In an ironic postscript to their story, the Uighurs who were
finally freed in 2006 were sent to a refugee camp in China's old client state,
Albania. Eager to curry favor with the West, the Albanians decided to risk
the wrath of their former patron. It was not long in coming. Shortly after
the five arrived, the Chinese demanded their return to Beijing for prosecution.[32] Fortunately for the Uighurs, Albania's eye on membership in the EU
is strong and they have refused. Five of the Uighurs live in a refugee camp
surrounded by barbed wire in one of Europe's poorest countries. The rest
are still in Guantánamo with Adel.

7 | The Matching of Latent Print #17

The wise man, even when he holds his tongue, says more than the fool when he speaks.

—Yiddish proverb

AROUND 6:30 ON THE MORNING OF MARCH 11, 2004, three electric trains in Spain's extensive rail network pulled out of the busy station in Alcalá de Henares, a suburb eight miles east of Madrid, carrying commuters and students into and around the cosmopolitan capital of three and a half million people. Before each train pulled out of the station, terrorists blended in with the regular riders and carried or loaded backpacks on board. Each pack contained ten kilograms of explosives. Terrorists also boarded a fourth train that originated farther out in the city of Guadalajara and stopped briefly in Alcalá de Henares at roughly the same time.[1]

At 6:40 A.M., one of the trains reached the huge Atocha interchange, just a few blocks from the world-famous Prado Museum in the heart of Madrid. As the electric train pulled into the station, the morning calm was shattered by bombs detonating in the third, fourth, and fifth carriages. The train was cut in two; pieces of metal were flung high in the air. At least thirty-four people were killed by the blasts; some bloody victims were able to crawl from the mangled cars; others were trapped and burned to death in their seats.

The shock waves that cascaded out of the station echoed back one minute later with renewed force as the terrorists, again using cell phones as timers, set off a second set of backpacks laden with explosives in the first, fourth, and sixth carriages in the second train that had left Alcalá de Henares as it passed Tellez Street, just outside the Atocha interchange. Those explosions left shards of twisted metal scattered over the rails and platforms around the now severed train. Later that morning at Atocha, the Spanish police found and safely detonated three more packs full of explosives, detonators, and cell phones.

Within a minute of the second set of explosions at Atocha, blasts in the fourth and fifth carriages of a double-decker train ripped it apart at the El Pozo station, six miles from Atocha, where panic quickly ensued. When the rubble was finally cleared at El Pozo, the death toll reached seventy. Then, barely a minute after the devastation on the double-decker, a fourth round of explosions at the Santa Eugenia station killed at least seventeen people.

News reports described "carriages totally torn apart," "people scattered all over the platforms," arms here, legs there.[2] City buses were requisitioned as emergency ambulances as regular ambulance services were backed up. Those less severely injured sat on curbs, blood dripping off their faces, calling on cell phones to tell family and friends that they were alive. The carnage was overwhelming. Veteran ambulance driver Enrique Sanchez told the Spanish media, "I've seen horror. I won't forget this, ever."[3] One of the commuters who miraculously escaped, Luz Elena Bustos, described "pieces of flesh and ribs all over the road . . . ribs and brains all over . . . people running all over, crying."[4]

The terrorists had managed to detonate a total of ten bombs that morning. They used copper detonators to explode Goma-2 explosives, and cell phones were used to set off the devices, modified with holes drilled near the power uptakes.

Traumatized by the attacks, the Spanish put virtually their entire national police force on the case. As so often happens in major investigations, it was a chance observation that gave the police their first big break. A doorman at a building near the Alcalá de Henares station, Luis Garrudo, told the police that he had seen several "suspicious-looking" men get out of a gray van a couple of blocks from the station. Garrudo was able to show police where the van had been parked and, luckily for the investigation, it was still there.[5] The police ran the license plate of the Kangoo van and found that it had been reported stolen on February 28. A search of the van produced a backpack with a blue plastic bag inside filled with unexploded detonators, traces of explosives, and a tape with verses from the Koran. The detonators matched those found on the bombs that had not exploded at the Atocha station. Within a day, the Forensic Science Division of the Spanish National Police had lifted two usable fingerprints from the blue bag, one labeled Latent Print #17 and the other Latent Print #20. Other usable latent fingerprints were also lifted from material found at the stations where the bombs had exploded.

Lifting a fingerprint? How did the Spanish obtain the prints, and did it matter? Defending people accused of crimes requires knowledge about much more than the law and human nature. A defense attorney also needs to learn science, engineering, chemistry, real estate, forestry, and psychiatry. Depending on the subject matter of the charge or the nature of the defense, I have had to become a temporary expert in many different disciplines—one of the most fascinating and challenging parts of the job. During the second week in May 2004, along with several other members of Brandon's team, I took a crash course in fingerprinting.

The pattern of loops, whorls, and ridges on each person's fingertips is unique, or at least relatively so. No matter how clean our hands feel, they contain oil or grease that we leave behind when we touch a surface. We can all see such marks easily on windows or television and computer screens. Sometimes when a finger touches a surface, it leaves a mark that isn't visible to the naked eye. These are called latent prints. Over the past century, forensic police have found a number of ways of developing latent prints, including the "dusting" method most people are familiar with. In dusting, depending on the color and composition of the surface, different types of powder are dusted on. If a person has touched the surface hard enough to leave grease or oil from the fingertips, the dust will adhere where the ridge lines on the finger touched the surface but not where there are valleys in between. The pattern of the print then becomes visible in the dust. Depending on their location and the conditions, latent prints can remain on a surface for a long time.

Because of the nature of the surface of the blue plastic bag, the Spanish Forensic Sciences Division used the cyanoacrylate method to lift the latent prints, a much more sophisticated method that can reveal prints the dusting method cannot. Cyanoacrylate, the basic ingredient in super glue, produces fumes that eventually leave a white residue in the pattern of the fingerprint and is then treated by placement in a humid container, or in a vacuum, or heated.

Once a latent print has been found through dusting, it must be "lifted" from the surface and transferred to a slide or card for comparative analysis in a laboratory. It is often accomplished by carefully placing tape over the dust, then lifting the tape and placing it on a paper card. With the cyanoacrylate method, the latent print is not transferred but is photographed in place. This second process was used by the Spanish with the latent prints developed on the blue bag.

Because of a spate of bombings in Spain in recent years by the Euskadi Ta Askatasuna (ETA), a group that had been seeking autonomy for the Basque region in the Pyrenees mountains of northern Spain for years, the immediate reaction of the Spanish was to blame the ETA for the bombings. Within hours, however, suspicion shifted to Muslim extremists from Morocco and Algeria when the forensic police determined that the explosive used in the blasts was Goma-2, a type that had been identified with Al Qaeda attacks, while the Basques typically used an explosive called Titadine.[6] Moreover, the Basques were not known to use telephones as timers for their bombs.

The Madrid bombings were one of the worst terrorist attacks in the world since September 11 and drew international attention and media coverage. In Portland, the headline in the *Oregonian* on Friday, March 12, 2004, screamed "Mass Murder in Spain." For the Spanish, the bombings were a national trauma, and 11.4 million people, more than a quarter of Spain's population, demonstrated in cities across the country the day after the bombs wreaked their havoc.

National elections were scheduled in Spain for Sunday, March 14, just three days after the blasts. While the government of Prime Minister José María Aznar called for a period of national mourning and canceled all campaign activities, postponing the elections would have given the terrorists a tremendous victory. The decision was made to hold the elections as scheduled. With the nation still in shock, the Spaniards voted Aznar out of office in favor of José Luis Rodríguez Zapatero, who was less friendly to the war in Iraq.[7] Whether or not the change in government was a direct result of the blasts, one thing is certain—the new government quickly pulled out of what the Bush administration called the "coalition of the willing" in Iraq and called home the twelve hundred soldiers Spain had contributed to the war effort.[8] On a very different scale, the change in government in Spain would also soon play a major role in Brandon's life.

．　．　．

Spurred by the initial forensic work, the shift in focus from Basque separatists to Muslim extremists as the perpetrators of the bombings was solidified two days later when cell phones that had been recovered in the unexploded packs led the Spanish police to a telephone store. On March 13, seven suspects, the first of more than twenty eventually taken in, were arrested; two Spanish citizens of Indian origin, two other Indians, and three Moroccans, including Jamal Zougam, were identified as the primary suspects. Zougam, who had been under surveillance for previous terrorist acts in Spain, was linked to a group suspected of Al Qaeda connections. On March 18, five more men were arrested, including four Moroccans and one Spaniard. Again, the Spanish police announced significant ties to Al Qaeda.[9]

The first formal charges were filed in Spain on the 19th against Zougam and two other Moroccans. The strength of the Moroccan connection to the bombings was then confirmed on March 31 when the Spanish issued international arrest warrants for five more men. Then, on April 3, Spain was rocked by another explosion when Spanish police moved in on suspects in an apartment building in Leganés, twelve miles southwest of Madrid. The suspects blew themselves up rather than face capture, and took one Spanish special forces officer with them and wounded eleven more.

Although the Spanish National Police had quickly made significant progress on the case, they did not find a match on latent print #17. On March 13, Interpol Madrid had submitted to their counterparts in a number of friendly countries, including the United States, digital photographs of fourteen prints that had been recovered during the investigation, including latent prints #17 and #20 from the blue bag. As soon as the photographs were received in Washington, DC, they were forwarded to the FBI forensic laboratory in Quantico, Virginia, for analysis.

．　．　．

During my first two weeks representing Brandon, everything I learned about the investigation came from the affidavit Agent Werder had submitted to

Judge Jones for the arrest warrant. Werder had told Judge Jones about the Spanish request for help in their examination of the fourteen prints and how, on March 17, FBI senior fingerprint examiner Terry Green, an agent with thirty years' experience, found fifteen "points of identification" between latent print #17 and Brandon's right index finger.

Green's statement hit me hard. Having challenged fingerprint analysis a number of times in my career, I knew that fifteen points generally meant that the identification was unassailable. Things got even worse in the next part of the affidavit where Green reported he had made a "100% identification" and that his work had been "verified" by a supervisor and a retired thirty-year analyst, John Massey, whom the FBI had brought back specially to look at these prints. I had never before heard any experts offer an opinion with 100 percent certainty. They will testify to "a reasonable degree of scientific accuracy," but not complete certainty.

As confident as the "100%" identification made Green sound, Agent Werder included something else in the affidavit that made me wonder whether I was dealing with a truly unique match or a man who had succumbed to the sin of pride. Werder told Judge Jones that the Spanish were not quite as sure as the FBI that latent print #17 was Brandon's.

"In mid-April it became apparent that the preliminary findings of the Forensic Science Division of the SNP concerning the fingerprint were not consistent with those of the FBI laboratory," Werder admitted.

It was good that Werder mentioned the Spanish opinion, but what did he mean by "not consistent"? Had the Spanish actually identified the print as belonging to someone else? Or were they just not convinced it was Brandon's print? Either way, I did not understand how one team could be 100 percent certain and another team be in disagreement and wondered whether Werder had shaded the truth in the affidavit.

One thing was definite: Someone in the FBI was sufficiently troubled by the Spanish position on the print that they sent a team to Madrid to meet with the Spanish forensic team. Werder briefly described a meeting that took place on April 21 between the FBI and "ten members of the Forensic Science Division of the SNP." The brief description of the meeting that followed downplayed the differences between the FBI and the Spanish. The FBI reported that the Spanish examination was only "preliminary," and the Spanish admitted that they had not gone into "level three characteristics" as had the FBI.

There are three basic levels of analysis in fingerprint comparisons. First, the examiner tries to understand the orientation of the print on the object, for example, are the fingers pointing up or down. He notes the flow of the ridges, the observable lines and grooves, to see if they share the same basic pattern. At that point, he is also seeking to exclude prints that do not share a basic pattern. At the second level, the examiner is looking for a match through an aggregate comparison of the ridges, loops, and whorls, for location, type, direction, and relationship. Are the ridges in the same place on the latent print and a known exemplar? Are they the same length? Do they butt up against whorls in the same place?

The third level of analysis that the FBI used in Brandon's case, and that the Spanish did not, involves comparison of individual friction ridge characteristics and the sweat pores in each friction ridge. One reason the Spanish had not used ridge comparison is that there is an ongoing debate in the forensic community about the reliability of "ridgeology." While the FBI and many other examiners believe it is reliable, there is a significant group that believes it is not because it moves away from the counting of matching points to a more subjective analysis.[10]

The outcome of the April 21 meeting, as Werder reported it, was that, "At the conclusion of the meeting it was believed that the SNP felt satisfied with the FBI Laboratory's identification of LFP#17 and indicated that the Forensic Science Division intended to continue its analysis of the latent print comparison." The FBI "believed" that the Spanish "felt satisfied." What on earth did that mean? Did the Spanish agree with the FBI or not?

My team and I could speculate all we wanted about the fingerprint, but it was clear to me that Chris and I could not offer Brandon any meaningful advice unless we knew more clearly what the Spanish work had produced and what had happened at the meeting in Madrid. We knew from Werder's statement in the affidavit that the "FBI lab stands by their conclusion of a 100% positive identification that LFP#17 as [sic] the fingerprint of BRANDON BIERI MAYFIELD." But with the references to the "inconsistent" Spanish position, the affidavit just didn't add up. The words were too clever and too vague. We were convinced that the FBI had not told Judge Jones the whole story.

8 | A Lonely Battle

You can't control the wind, but you can adjust your sails.
—Yiddish proverb

As my Mayfield team began our investigation for Brandon, we quickly learned that it was going to be a lonely battle. Somehow Portland, the laid-back City of Roses, whose homogeneous population, 90 percent Caucasian, was a bastion of environmentalists and liberal Democrats, had produced a steady stream of terrorism prosecutions of Muslims since September 11, 2001. The attacks had prompted the broadest change in law enforcement priorities and strategy that I have seen since first setting foot in a federal court as a law clerk thirty-four years ago. The impact of these changes and the terrorism prosecutions in Portland had left many in the local Muslim community uneasy.

. . .

After September 11, fighting terrorism suddenly became the primary focus of federal law enforcement. Over the following years, their ranks swelled considerably with dollars reallocated by the government. The Department of Justice had added hundreds of new assistant United States attorneys and one thousand new and "redirected" FBI agents, and set up one hundred new Joint Terrorism Task Forces (JTTF). The United States attorney in Oregon added five assistants specially designated to handle terrorism cases and the local FBI office received its share of new agents.

The "redirection" by the attorney general meant that investigation of the usual federal crimes—drug conspiracy, fraud, bank robbery, regular immigration, tax crimes, counterfeiting, and environmental—was cut back as agents were shifted to investigate terrorism. The FBI, the primary federal law enforcement agency, which had encroached on the turf of the Drug Enforcement Administration (DEA) by greatly expanding its investigation of drug cases in the 1980s, drastically scaled back its drug shop.

The task forces are groups of law enforcement agents drawn from a variety of federal agencies and state and local police forces.[1] Their job is to prevent and investigate terrorist activities and suspected terrorists and terrorist groups. They had done this with traditional law enforcement techniques such as visual surveillance, infiltration, and use of informers. Since September 11, they have also used the new tools for electronic surveillance and searches given to them by the Patriot Act.

There have been several hundred arrests and prosecutions around the country by the new terrorism agents and prosecutors since 2001, relatively few considering the number of agents and attorneys and amount of money earmarked for terrorism work. The attorney general and local United States attorney say that most of the antiterrorism work has been preventative, involving surveillance and disrupting terror groups.[2] There is, of course, no way to verify this claim.

And just what preventative surveillance and disruption mean is not clear. Shortly after the 9/11 attacks, JTTFs in Portland and across the country had sent agents out to speak with as many Muslims and Middle Easterners as they could find.[3] While the JTTF in Portland had tried to be friendly and nonthreatening in its approach, to many Muslims here the fact that the knock on the door came at all was frightening. The reaction of one man of Egyptian descent whom I tried to help was typical. He was so upset when he came home to find an FBI agent's business card in his door a week after the FBI had been at his home and spoken with him that he called a federal judge, a soccer friend of his, for advice. The judge, in turn, had asked me to speak to him and try to help him figure out if he had anything to worry about—other than his heritage. We could not figure out any reason for a repeat visit, so I called the agent and asked what was going on and why they wanted to speak with him again. The agent wouldn't tell me anything other than what had been said publicly about the interviews, that they were trying to see if anyone knew anything that could help in the war on terror.

Many in Portland's Muslim community and its supporters in the city felt the visits were more sinister. They asked why a third-generation American of Syrian or Somali descent would be any more likely to have information about terrorism than a third-generation Italian. Some were sure the FBI was creating a database so it could keep tabs on millions of innocent people based on the accident of birth or religion.

.   .   .

While Portland's JTTF was starting its canvass of the Muslim community, it also dove into the first of Oregon's terrorism prosecutions.

In 1993, Ali Khalid Steitiye, a Palestinian refugee from Lebanon who had moved to Oregon in the 1980s and who had never been particularly religious, moved within several blocks of the Masjed As-Saber (Islamic Center of Portland) in southwest Portland. He divorced his first wife, an American, traveled to Lebanon to visit his family, and soon came back with a new Lebanese bride.[4]

Eight years later, Steitiye tried to buy a gun at the Gun Broker in Tigard, Oregon. He was turned down because he had a decades-old felony record for theft and illegal weapons possession.[5]

Then, shortly after, came September 11 and, in the first major push in the Bush administration's redirection of federal law enforcement priorities, nearly all federal agents were pulled off ongoing investigations and assigned to find out anything they could about the Trade Center and Pentagon attacks and if any other attacks were planned. In their efforts to turn over every possible stone, agents were sent to as many gun dealers in the country as possible. Detectives dread these types of investigations; they are tedious and painstaking. But it is this kind of detail work that can break a case.

I knew it from my days as an assistant district attorney when I worked on the Son of Sam case, the prosecution of David Berkowitz for the murders of white couples in New York City during the summers of 1976 and 1977 (the subject of the Spike Lee movie *Summer of Sam*). It was plodding thoroughness that ultimately broke the case. When the killer struck in Brooklyn on July 30, 1977, for what turned out to be the last time, several policemen were assigned to investigate all parking tickets that were written within twenty blocks of the crime scene. One turned out to have been written for a car parked illegally at a fire hydrant a few blocks away. The car was registered to a David Berkowitz, a name that meant nothing to the police at the time. But it was the routine follow-up trip to the address in Yonkers that led to the connection between the ticket and the murderer and Berkowitz's arrest.[6]

As part of the gun dealer canvass after September 11, Special Agent Shawn Alexander of the DEA's Portland office visited the Gun Broker and learned about Steitiye's attempt to buy a gun several weeks earlier. This was precisely the type of information that the government was hoping to find. DEA agent Alexander turned his information over to the Bureau of Alcohol, Tobacco and Firearms, the federal agency that has primary responsibility for investigating gun crimes. During the investigation that followed, the agents confirmed that Steitiye had a criminal record he should have reported on the purchase form. But they also mistakenly read his record as showing that he was still married to an American.

Soon after, the canvass revealed that ten days after Steitiye had tried to buy a gun, a Middle Eastern man had tried to buy an AK-47—a legal weapon in most states—at the Rose City Gun Show. When the dealer refused to do business with the man, an American woman who was with him became irate, arguing loudly that the dealer would not make the sale because the man was from the Middle East. The JTTF agents immediately, but mistakenly, jumped to the conclusion that Steitiye was the Middle Eastern man who had been refused a gun at the Rose City show.[7]

By mid-October, the agents were ready to move in and obtained federal arrest and search warrants. Steitiye was arrested on October 24. The agents searched his home and found $20,000 in cash, fraudulent credit cards and other financial documents, false immigration documents, several guns, and a sign of some sort with the word "Hamas."[8]

Assistant Federal Defender Dennis Balske was on our duty rotation when Steitiye was brought into court. Dennis, like Chris Schatz, had left a successful private practice in the early 1990s to come to Portland and join the office, though Dennis had come from Alabama rather than California. Given Steitiye's Middle Eastern origin and the anti-Muslim climate in the country in the fall of 2001, I asked Dennis to keep me closely informed even though it was a straightforward case involving charges of felon-in-possession of a gun and fraud.

Steitiye's case remained routine until December 12, when Portland police chief Mark Kroeker held a press conference and announced that it was the local JTTF that had made the arrest.[9] Chief Kroeker described finding the guns in Steitiye's car, the one thousand rounds of ammunition, and the Hamas plaque. But he did not stop there. He announced that a calendar had been found in Steitiye's home with the date of September 11 circled, and added that there was a "connection to other activity" that "is not to be talked about."[10] This leap, which posited a direct link between Steitiye and the attacks of September 11 based on a date on a calendar, was precisely the type of fear-driven assumption I had been worried about ever since I had listened to the president's speeches in September.

From the moment Chief Kroeker held his press conference, Steitiye's case was observed under a microscope, which is not a good position for any defendant to be in, particularly a Middle Easterner post–September 11. The government wanted to know what Steitiye knew about the attacks. But our job is to represent our clients to the fullest, regardless of public opinion or government desire. World Trade Center or not, Steitiye was going to get a zealous defense. Our investigation had revealed that the government agents, perhaps blinded by the attacks and the involvement of men from the Middle East, had jumped to a terribly wrong conclusion.

When the ATF agents had interviewed the dealer at the Rose City Gun Show, they were so sure of the link between the aborted gun purchases there and at the Gun Broker several weeks before that they brought with them photographs of Steitiye, who looks like he is from the Middle East, and the woman they believed was his wife, the European-looking Rebecca Lynn Smith. Then, violating standard identification procedures, they showed the witnesses only the single photographs, not a photo lineup as law enforcement manuals require.[11] Not surprisingly, they got positive identifications. But they were dead wrong on two counts. Steitiye had not been married to or associated with Ms. Smith for years, and neither of them had been anywhere near the Rose City Gun Show on September 7, 8, or 9.

How does this happen? In 1948, Supreme Court Justice Robert Jackson, who had recently returned to the Court from his duties as chief prosecutor at the Nuremburg trials of Nazi war criminals, wrote an opinion about the importance of search warrants and a judicial check on police officers. He described how police get caught up "in the often competitive enterprise of ferreting out crime" and how that can affect their judgment.[12] As Rutgers

University Law School professor Sherry F. Colb has said, "a police officer['s] job is to be suspicious," to have a bias in favor of searching or conducting surveillance.[13] It is precisely because the suspicious nature and competitive aspects of police work can skew judgment that our system has built in checks and balances and requires neutral judges to approve when law enforcers want to intrude on our privacy. That balance has been revised by the Bush administration's policies for the war on terror.

Given its view of Steitiye, the government would not engage in any plea negotiations and, given the evidence found during the search of his home, there wasn't much Dennis could do about the crimes of which he truly was guilty. Under the Federal Rules of Criminal Procedure, Steitiye could not plead guilty and still appeal certain pretrial motions that Dennis had filed and lost without the prosecutor's permission, something he would not give. So on June 24, 2002, Steitiye entered what are called stipulations to the evidence and allowed the judge to find him guilty, preserving his right to appeal.[14]

Following standard procedure when a person is found guilty in federal court, the trial Judge, Anna Brown, ordered the probation office to prepare a presentence report, a document that gives some information on the defendant's background and identifies the sentencing factors for the judge under the federal guideline system that limits judges' sentencing discretion. Steitiye's sentencing was set for mid-September.

▪   ▪   ▪

While we were waiting for the probation office to file its final version of Steitiye's presentence report, Portland was rocked by another press release about the JTTF, this time from the FBI. On Sunday, September 8, 2002, three days before the first anniversary of the 9/11 attacks and ten days before the date set for Steitiye's sentencing, the FBI announced that when Sheik Mohammed Kariye, the imam at the Islamic Center of Portland, the mosque Steitiye attended, had tried to board a plane at the Portland International Airport earlier that day, traces of explosives had been found in his luggage. The imam was arrested and the FBI announced that he would be brought into the federal court on Monday.[15]

All sorts of stories began appearing purportedly linking the imam, who had come to the United States in 1983 to avoid conscription into the Somali army, to a number of charities and activities that smacked of terrorism and Al Qaeda.[16] Notwithstanding the fanfare at Chief Kroeker's press conference nine months before, Steitiye's case had never moved beyond the routine, but with the news about the imam's arrest, it looked like Portland was about to experience a real terrorism case.

The media was having a field day with the testimony about explosives that came out at the bail hearing where the imam was ordered held in jail. But the actual charges filed against the imam had nothing to do with terrorism or anything resembling explosives. They were, rather, minor fraud charges dating back a decade based on some false information the imam had provided on some Social Security forms.[17] The disconnect among the FBI's statements, the prosecutors' arguments in court, and the actual charges caused many people in Portland to be outraged by what they saw as a racially and religiously based arrest. Hundreds of the imam's supporters rallied on September 22 and heard his lawyer, New York civil rights attorney Stanley Cohen, decry the imam's arrest and urge Portlanders not to cooperate with the police in the terror probe unless they had an attorney present.[18] This was the type of support we could not get at the outset of Brandon's case as a result of the events that soon followed.

While the imam was languishing in the same county jail Brandon would sit in two years later, Steitiye's case came up for sentencing. The courtroom was packed: The prosecutors were all fired up, arguing that Steitiye should be given a lengthy sentence.[19] Why? Because, they said, Steitiye was a terrorist. But they would not produce any evidence to back up their claims. Dennis argued vociferously that the prosecutors should put up or shut up. If they had evidence that Steitiye was connected to the September 11 attacks, or any other terrorist activity, they needed to disclose it so he could respond and the judge could sentence Steitiye based on facts, not innuendo. If they had enough, indict him; otherwise, Dennis told the judge, Steitiye should be sentenced only for the fraud and gun charges the government had brought against him.

Judge Brown quickly cut in, asking the prosecutors, "Do you have any evidence?" They did not. Judge Brown held firm and told the prosecutors that without evidence she could not consider their arguments. "Mere political thought cannot be the basis for sentencing someone," she said. "That's not the country we believe in." Even though given ample opportunity, the prosecutors produced no witnesses, so Judge Brown sentenced Steitiye according to the sentencing guidelines to thirty months in prison for fraud and gun possession. Later, in Brandon's and Adel's cases, we needed judges to follow Judge Brown's example and hold firm in the face of the prosecutors' words.

. . .

Within a week of Judge Brown's refusal to accept the prosecutors' urgings at Steitiye's sentencing and less than two weeks after all the media about the explosive residue and the imam's arrest, the roller coaster of terrorism charges in Portland took another dramatic turn. On September 21, Stanley Cohen, the imam's lawyer, announced at a press conference that the airport tests were wrong; there had been no explosive residue on the imam's luggage at all.[20] Before speculation about Cohen's source could get very far, the United States attorney confirmed that the imam's luggage had been clean, there had been no explosive residue.

The United States attorney and JTTF were wiping another very messy egg off their faces. But for Portland's Muslim community, this new turn was about more than embarrassment. The arrest of a respected imam had cut deeply. The September 29 Oregonian featured a meeting of "faith leaders," including "Jews, Muslims, and Christians," quoting one area resident who summed up the concerns: "Everyone's very upset because it was such a big show—there's TNT—and then nothing came out of it. It's very disturbing to see what happened to (Imam Kariye) because it's like, who's next."[21]

Many Portlanders may have been upset at the local police and FBI, but dripping egg or not, Portland's law enforcers were not deterred. While the preventative work they were now engaged in meant that they were moving more quickly than in the past, increasing the risk that they would make mistakes that would harm innocent people like my clients Brandon and Adel, they had a job to do—protecting the country—and they were going to do it.

On October 4, 2002, an important day for the Bush administration's war on terror not just in Portland but around the country, Portland's FBI chief, Charles Mathews, and Oregon's United States attorney Mike Mossman (now a federal judge) flew to Washington to make an announcement alongside Attorney General Ashcroft himself. The attorney general called the fourth "a defining day in America's war on terrorism," discussing a number of developments in terrorism cases across the country.[22] In the Portland piece of the press conference, the attorney general announced the indictment of five men and one woman—Jeffrey Leon Battle, Patrice Lumumba Ford, Ahmed Ibrahim Bilal, Muhammad Ibrahim Bilal, Abdulla Al Saoub, and October Monique Lewis—in a multicount indictment that alleged a conspiracy to levy war against the United States and conspiracies to provide material support to Al Qaeda and the Taliban.[23]

Of the six in the Portland indictment, Ford's background was the most interesting.[24] His father has been a well-known political activist in Portland since the 1960s, when he headed the Portland branch of the Black Panther organization, a group that was on the cutting edge of black political activism in that turbulent decade. Named after Patrice Lumumba, the first elected president of the Congo when it gained freedom from Belgium in 1960, Ford was a good student at Portland's Lincoln High School, where he gave an address on Martin Luthur King Jr. in his junior year and served an internship in the Portland mayor's office. As a student at Portland State University in the early 1990s, he spent three semesters in an overseas study program in China. After he returned, he interned again in the mayor's office.

Battle, the man Brandon represented in the custody dispute, was born in Florida and raised as a Jehovah's Witness before converting to Islam when he was in his twenties. An elder care worker in nursing homes for much of his adult life, Battle joined the army reserves in the late 1990s and was working as a security guard in Portland shortly before the abortive jihad. He and Monique Lewis married while they were both living in Houston and raised Battle's son, Geoffrey, from a previous marriage. When it became clear that both Battle and Lewis were going to spend time in prison, Battle retained Brandon to help him with custody of Geoffrey.

The Bilal brothers were born in the United States but spent time in Saudi Arabia as kids. Al Saoub, a Jordanian refugee who had fought against the Soviets in Afghanistan, was called "Emir" by the others and seemed to be the leader of the group.[25]

The Portland Six case, as it was called in the media, was originally assigned to Oregon's chief federal judge, Ancer Haggerty, but Judge Jones, with his reduced caseload as a senior judge, volunteered to take the case and it was reassigned to him in early November. This reassignment set the stage for Jones to become Portland's "terrorism" judge and take Brandon's case when it was filed.

The indictment against the Portland Six spun out a detailed plot by the conspirators to join an Islamic jihad against the West. The conspiracy began in the spring of 2001, when the Bilal brothers started target practice with firearms and Ford then joined them in "physical training to fight a jihad."

Although the men of the Portland Six had started thinking about Jihad before September 11, it was the events of that day that seemed to energize them and serve as the catalyst for the travels that followed. It seems that Ford, Battle, and the Bilal brothers saw the towers collapse and wanted to join the fight against America.

On September 14, the indictment said, Ford purchased a shotgun to further his training in anticipation of actually going to Afghanistan to help the Taliban and Al Qaeda in their struggle against the Northern Alliance and the United States. The indictment alleged that the men went target shooting a number of times, including in a gravel pit in Skamania, Washington, on September 29 where a sheriff's deputy spotted them. He passed his observations on to the JTTF, giving them a major boost in their investigation.

By October, the men were ready and left the United States for China, where they started the twenty-five-hundred-mile trek from Hong Kong, on the southeastern Chinese coast, across to Xinjiang province, the home of the Uighurs, that borders on Afghanistan. They made it to Xinjiang, but they failed to find a way into Afghanistan. The Chinese, unhappy about the strength of Islam, fundamentalist or not, in Xinjiang province, did not want their territory used as a jumping-off place for fighters joining the Taliban in Afghanistan and had secured their border.

By mid-November, the would-be jihadists abandoned their efforts to get to Afghanistan through China and headed back to Hong Kong. Ford returned home, but the others tried alternate routes through Indonesia and Bangladesh for several more months. Battle was the last of the Portlanders to give up, finally coming home in early February 2002. Al Saoub never returned to Oregon.

As startling as it was for Portlanders to learn that there had been a terrorism cell in their midst, the most shocking part of the indictment for my office had nothing to do with the six named defendants. It was, rather, the naming of the recently sentenced Steitiye as an unindicted coconspirator and one of the men identified by the deputy sheriff as target shooting in late September. We learned that this was some of what Steitiye's prosecutors had been referring to during his sentencing. It was apparent now that they were not ready when he was sentenced to reveal what they had on Steitiye because it would have short-circuited the larger investigation.

The Steitiye references, though, did not add up. What did the prosecutors mean by calling him an "unindicted coconspirator"? If they had enough evidence, surely they would have charged him. There were only two reasons we could think of for the prosecutors' decision: a weakness in evidence, or the prosecutors' desire to try to turn Steitiye into a government witness by holding out the threat of prosecution. Although they could have tried to get Steitiye's cooperation after indicting him, naming him as an unindicted coconspirator signaled more clearly to all of the conspirators that it was Steitiye's assistance they really wanted. This is a standard prosecutorial technique in conspiracy cases.

As the facts of the aborted jihad emerged after the arrests in October 2002, it became clear that the JTTF had infiltrated the Portland Six in 2002 and had kept detailed watch on the conspirators over the year until their arrest. The infiltrating informer, Khalid Mustafa, who had worked as an informer for the DEA in 2000, was arrested on new charges in 2002 and had started cooperating with the agents as soon as he had been picked up. When the Portland Six returned in the spring of 2002, Mustafa was sent to deal with them wearing a body wire.[26]

Based in part on information obtained from Mustafa, the JTTF obtained warrants for electronic surveillance of the telephones, computers, and homes of the Portland Six. When the JTTF investigation in the case became public, it seemed as though bugs had been placed everywhere, producing a treasure trove of information—more than forty-five hundred telephone calls on at least four telephones, nearly one thousand e-mail messages, and over one thousand hours of recordings from bugs placed in Battle's home. Ford, Battle, and Lewis were heard discussing the trip to China, efforts to get into Afghanistan through Pakistan, and domestic and political things such as how much easier it was to get money to go to Afghanistan when the Soviets were there and complaints about the Patriot Act's interference with jihadist-type activities.[27]

The case of the Portland Six had all the earmarks of a protracted and complex factual and legal battle. Because Steitiye was named in the indictment, my office could not represent any of those who were actually charged. Since none of the defendants had the money to hire counsel, I asked some of the most prominent criminal defense attorneys in Portland who take assigned cases to help out. Behind the scenes, I consulted with the lawyers as they put together the first major attacks in the nation on the use of the new post-9/11 antiterrorism statutes to prosecute people who never actually fought against the United States but had tried to help a group on the government's terrorism watch list by providing "expert advice and assistance." The lawyers challenged the statute as overbroad and vague, allowing prosecution for mere words, something the free speech clause of the First Amendment usually protects. With thousands of hours of taped conversations, the case also presented issues of fundamental importance about the government's power to engage in electronic surveillance under the Foreign Intelligence Surveillance and Patriot acts.

Through the late fall and winter, many in Portland watched patiently for some court action on the Portland Six case to see whether the three prosecutors on the case, Gorder, Holsinger, and Atkinson, the same trio who would handle Brandon's case two years later, had evidence to back up the charges in the indictment or whether the United States attorney's office and JTTF would be embarrassed, as they had been with Steitiye and Imam Kariye. At our office, Dennis and I waited nervously for Gorder to file an expanded or superseding indictment that would make Steitiye a defendant.

Then came March 20 and the arrest of Maher "Mike" Hawash in connection with the Portland Six case. Hawash's case started in almost the same way as Brandon's did a year later—the arrest of a respected middle-class member of Portland's Muslim community as a material witness. He was taken down by a score of JTTF agents in flak jackets and armed with assault weapons as he arrived for work at the suburban campus of Intel, the huge microchip manufacturer where Hawash had worked as a software engineer since 1992.[28] The agents used the same multiteam approach as they would later with Brandon, one team arrested Hawash at work while another team descended on his home. The search team found Hawash's wife, Lisa, and their three children in bed, rousted them, and meticulously searched the house for four hours, carting away numerous records and computer equipment.[29]

Hawash's arrest brought storms of protest about racial profiling and abuse of the material witness statute, and was greeted with particular outrage at Intel where Hawash was a highly respected engineer and known to be a coach for his stepson's soccer team.[30] While the fact that Hawash had been seized by federal agents was obvious to anyone who had been there, the federal authorities refused to confirm or deny that Hawash was in custody, a position that lent an even greater aura of mystery and, for some, increased the level of outrage.[31]

A trio of Hawash's closest colleagues, Rohan Coelho, Debbie Burke, and Steven McGeady, set up a Free Mike Hawash movement and created a Web site—www.freemikehawash.org—and solicited donations to help defray the costs of his defense.[32] The arrest and community response drew national attention with frequent stories in the *New York Times, Newsweek,* and the *Wall Street Journal,* and on CNN.[33] Because Hawash was being treated as a grand jury witness, there was very little news emanating from the FBI (there were far fewer leaks than in Brandon's case) and most of the stories were about the community's support for Hawash and belief in his innocence.

On April 28, a little more than a month after Hawash was arrested on the material witness warrant, the support he had enjoyed turned to stunned disbelief when he was brought back to court by Gorder and company on a criminal complaint naming him as a defendant in the Portland Six conspiracy.[34] On May 3, Gorder filed a superseding indictment to the one filed against the Portland Six in October, formally adding Hawash to the conspiracy. The new indictment tracked the one filed in October except now it included a detailed account of Hawash's travels with the other men and his financial dealings, including transferring the title of his house to his wife and signing a power of attorney giving her the right to act in all his affairs. Hawash had been right alongside Battle, Ford, the Bilal brothers, and Al Saoub as they traveled from Portland to Hong Kong, to Xinjiang, back to Beijing, and then home to the United States.

While the May charges against Hawash caused many Portlanders to stop their protests against the JTTF, the protests picked up steam at the end of the month when Imam Kariye was sentenced to probation and a $1,000 fine on minor fraud charges, all that had been filed after the "explosives" arrest. Shortly after the imam's sentencing, more than one hundred people picketed the offices of the *Oregonian* to protest its earlier strident coverage of the imam as a terrorist.[35]

Some in liberal Portland realized, however, that this time it was not the FBI or JTTF that had egg on its face. Chastened, the Free Hawash group offered to return the $25,000 they had gathered in the month after Hawash's arrest.[36] The national media, which had been helping beat the drums for Hawash, quietly decamped.

Unlike his coconspirators, Hawash was chastened, or as he put it later, he emerged from the state of "confusion" into which he had wandered. Born in Nablus in what was then part of Jordan, Hawash was three when Israel defeated the Arab countries that had invaded it during the Six-Day War and annexed what became known as the West Bank. His family, along with thousands of others, fled to refugee camps. After a number of years in a camp in Kuwait, the Hawashes returned to Nablus, where Hawash excelled in school and won a scholarship to the University of Texas. Mike, as he had started calling himself, had a mind for computers and was offered a job with the computer manufacturer Compaq after graduation.[37]

In 1992, he switched companies to Intel and moved to Portland. By then he was a naturalized U.S. citizen, and people who knew Mike in the 1990s describe him as a secular Muslim. Mike met Lisa, a native Oregonian, and they were married in 1995.

But those same friends say that they saw a change in Mike in 2000, the year his father died. He apparently sought solace in his religion, went on the obligatory Muslim hajj to Mecca, grew a beard as do religious Muslim men, started wearing a prayer cap, asked his friends to call him Maher, the Muslim name of his birth, and started attending the Islamic Center of Portland, more orthodox than the Bilal Mosque that he had previously attended and where the Portland Six worshipped.[38]

Over the late spring and summer of 2003, Hawash cooperated fully with Gorder and the JTTF. He provided whatever pieces were missing from the prosecutors' case. On August 5, in a closed courtroom and unbeknownst to his coconspirators, Hawash entered a cooperation agreement with the prosecutors and pleaded guilty in exchange for a reduced sentence. The plea was publicly announced on September 12. Whenever the prosecution offers a plea deal to one defendant in a multidefendant case, it has several goals. One is to secure evidence to use against the other defendants. A second, and perhaps more important, goal is to induce the other defendants to give up their right to a jury trial and admit guilt as well. Hawash's plea had the desired effect. On September 18, the Bilal brothers threw in the towel and pleaded guilty, followed in short order by Lewis on September 26 and finally Battle and Ford on October 16.

Although they were the last to plead guilty, Ford and Battle were the first to be sentenced, appearing in court on November 24 and taking full advantage of their opportunity to speak. At their sentencings, they made no apologies for their actions, instead explaining why U.S. actions toward Muslims justified what they had tried to do. A letter that Battle wrote Judge Jones noted that "many Muslims throughout the world" saw the American action in Afghanistan in the fall of 2001 "as an attack on Islam itself." After describing the callous American view of the loss of innocent Muslim lives, he explained why he tried to get to Afghanistan. "I refused to stand passively in the face of policies which inflicted such tremendous injustice, death, and destruction on Muslims." In the courtroom, Battle broke into song, repeating the refrain, "Free is the only way to be," five times.[39]

Ford also talked about the principles that led him on the jihad, expressing the hope that one day his son would "understand the value of the principles for which I went to prison." Judge Jones blasted back, calling Ford "an insult to the Muslim religion."[40] Ford and Battle were each sentenced to eighteen years in prison.

One week later, in a much more subdued proceeding, Monique Lewis, the only female member of the conspiracy, and whose only role was to wire money to the jihadists overseas, was sentenced to three years. The remaining conspirators were sentenced on February 9, 2004. At his sentencing, Hawash was introspective, talking about how his renewed belief in his duty to Allah had been the force behind his joining the conspiracy. In a letter he wrote to Judge Jones, Hawash described "a suppressed sense of fear" creeping in as "the initial speculations" about 9/11 "began pointing to Muslims." While he "had all the reasons not to go" to Afghanistan, he continued, "I had felt the tension grow towards my duty in front of Allah. . . . I was torn, and had never felt such pressure in my life." Judge Jones told Hawash that he had been a mystery to him from the beginning and that he had hurt his "religion very deeply."[41] The sentence Judge Jones imposed, six years and ten months in prison, gave Hawash only a small break for his cooperation in comparison with the Bilal brothers, who were seen by all the participants as less culpable than Ford and Battle, and received eight- and ten-year sentences.

As for Al Saoub and Steitiye, Al Saoub was the only one of the Portland Seven who made it to Afghanistan. It is believed he joined up with Al Qaeda fighters and was killed by Pakistani forces in a border battle in 2004.[42] Steitiye was never indicted in the Portland Seven case. Instead, his case took a stranger turn as the thirty-month sentence handed down by Judge Brown on the fraud and handgun charges was ending and he was being readied for deportation. The United States attorney filed a new weapons indictment in March 2004, this time by the terrorism team of Gorder, Holsinger, and Atkinson.[43] The weapon Steitiye was alleged to have possessed was a Chinese-made assault rifle, charged in the indictment as a machine gun.

Although the indictment was filed in 2004, the charge was not new— the assault rifle was alleged to have been possessed in the gravel pit in Skamania in September 2001. If convicted as charged, Steitiye faced a twenty-five year sentence. Our best guess was that Gorder and the JTTF still believed that Steitiye had information on terrorism and they were still try-ing to squeeze it out of him. After more than a year of wrangling and behind-the-scenes work by a new lawyer from outside my office, Steitiye finally pleaded guilty to possessing the machine gun and was sentenced to five more years in prison.

■　　■　　■

When Brandon was arrested less than three months after Hawash and his coconspirators had been sentenced, very few people in Portland were pre-pared to assume that he was innocent. Too many in the Muslim commu-nity had been burned by their initial support of the Portland Six and their even stronger support of Hawash, and they were hesitant to stick their necks out again. Many people had also read about the use of informers and ex-tensive wiretapping in the Portland Six/Seven case and were afraid that they could get in trouble if they spoke out. Others had been approached by JTTF agents during the investigation and felt that they were being watched.

This type of fear combined with admissions by the Portland Seven and FBI statements of 100 percent certainty about Brandon's fingerprint had a chilling effect on our investigation for Brandon. Some people we needed to talk to were hesitant to cooperate at all, leery of any contact that might put them in a bad light, afraid that cooperating with a terrorist, as Bran-don was being portrayed, would come back to haunt them. The battle for Brandon's freedom was, indeed, a lonely one.

9 | Feeding Refugees and Teaching Orphans

If you want peace, work for justice.
—Pope Paul VI[1]

AS PRESSURE PACKED AS MY TIME WITH Brandon had been two years earlier, I knew that as long as he was not whisked away to a military brig, I could see him in the county jail any time I wanted. Because of the logistics of getting to Guantánamo, we did not have that option with Adel and needed to cover as much ground as possible in our visits. Pat and I would need to prove that Adel's presence in Pakistan and Afghanistan was completely innocent if we were to have any chance of winning his release. On our first visit, we pushed not only ourselves but also Adel and our interpreter, Felice, as hard as we could to get the measure of the man and learn Adel's life history—how he ended up as an aid worker in Afghanistan and Pakistan, and what he had to say about the accusations the military had made against him.

· · ·

Adel was born in the Dunkala region of northern Sudan in 1958.

"When?" I asked. "What's your birthday?"

"You might as well write down January 1," Adel replied. "We do not keep track of birthdays. I don't know the day."

Adel's grandfather, Abdul Mutaleb, later moved the family from Dunkala to the village of Jubate, near Port Sudan on the Red Sea, where he found a job on the docks. Adel's father, Hassan Hamad Abd al-Mutaleb, was able to get training as a nurse there and took courses throughout his career as a physician's assistant. It was clear from Adel's description that Hassan was the closest thing to a doctor many of the people in the rural areas outside Port Sudan ever saw.

"He was not a doctor from medical school, but he was a doctor. My father would sometimes take me along with him as he went from village to village."

"How did he get around?" Pat asked.

"Sometimes on foot, or on a mule, and for a while in an old car," he told us.

Adel deeply loved and respected his father. While he was telling us about his childhood, connecting it to his own life's work, tears welled up in his eyes.

"My father and mother put the seeds of mercy in me," he said.

While they were poor by Western standards, Adel never wanted for anything growing up. His parents were loving and happy people who wanted their children to have an even better life. They believed in education as a path to that better life and kept Adel in school, sending him to secondary school outside Port Sudan. When he graduated, they helped him through the Institute Wabera Al-Meyah, a trade school in Alexandria, Egypt, where he studied air conditioning. This black Sudanese Arab's story was very similar to the American immigrant experience I knew so well—the belief that a better life can be obtained through education, hard work, and compassion.

After graduating from the university in Egypt, Adel moved back to Sudan and got a job working on the air conditioning in a textile plant, where he stayed for two years.

"I liked the job well enough. The engineering was interesting," Adel told us. "But I was restless. Sudan was poor, and even with my education, I wasn't making enough money for a family."

"Is that why you ended up in Pakistan?" I asked.

"That was part of it. Also this wasn't how I wanted to spend my life. The air conditioning was fine, but I wanted to work with people."

"What else was going on in your life then?" Pat asked. "What do you mean by restless. How did you feel about the situation in Sudan?"

"I don't know. Life was good, but could have been better for more people. I went to a few meetings of the brotherhood when I was back in Port Sudan."

Since the 1970s, the Muslim Brotherhood had been growing in Sudan, and in 1984, Adel joined. For more than thirty years now, the brotherhood has been a thorn in the side of many of the autocratic regimes in the Arab world.[2] Some view it as a political and charitable organization, distributing aid among the poor. Others view it as a political organization (today the brotherhood holds many seats in parliaments throughout the Arab world). Still others view the brotherhood as a terrorist organization and have linked it to bombings and assassinations in a number of countries. In the 1980s, as now, what the brotherhood represented depends on whom you ask.

By 1986, Adel was disenchanted with the group and stopped attending meetings. Shortly after, he got the job with LDI and moved to Pakistan to work with Afghan refugees from the ongoing war with the Soviet Union.

The Soviet invasion of Afghanistan on Christmas Eve 1979 was the culmination of a complicated history of Russian/Soviet-Afghan relations.[3] For centuries, the Russian czars had been interested in Afghanistan as they spread their empire south and east. Eventually the predominantly Muslim regions bordering Afghanistan became the republics of Turkmenistan, Tadjikistan, and Uzbekistan in the Soviet Union. After King Mohammed Zahir Shah was deposed in a coup in 1973, the Soviets significantly increased their entanglement with the new Afghan government. Then, in 1978, the cold war activities led to a second coup that installed a pro-Soviet government headed by Noor Mohammed Taraki. In December of that year, the two countries signed a mutual assistance pact in which the Soviets agreed to send troops to aid the Afghans upon request. Over the next year they significantly increased the number of "advisers" in Afghanistan to help Taraki deal with ongoing resistance to his regime.

The Iranian revolution in February 1979 that deposed the U.S.-backed shah and brought radical Islamic clerics to power rattled the Soviets. When Taraki was overthrown in yet another Afghan coup in September 1979, the Soviets had had enough. The United States and Iran were rattling sabers at each other. The Muslim population in the southern Soviet republics was growing restive, and their client state was crumbling into anarchy. On that Christmas Eve, the Soviets moved into Afghanistan in force, but they were not met with open arms. Instead, their presence seemed to draw the Afghans together; they put aside their tribal differences to fight the invaders.

By 1986, when Adel was hired by LDI, the Afghan-Soviet war had claimed the lives of nearly one million Afghans and turned nearly five million into refugees. The conflict finally ended with the withdrawal of the Soviet soldiers in February 1989, but the humanitarian disaster had spilled across the impoverished region of the Afghan-Pakistani border—just the place for Adel to nourish the "seeds of mercy" his parents had planted in him.

LDI is a quasi-governmental Kuwaiti organization that continues to operate throughout the Muslim world to this day. It was added to the U.S. government's terrorism watch list in 2003, but in the 1980s, the help LDI was giving victims of the war with the Soviets was fully aligned with U.S. interests in Afghanistan, where the U.S. government was funding many of the mujahideen who were giving the Soviets so much trouble.[4]

"Adel, what about LDI?" I asked. "Was it political? Extremist? Working with terrorists?"

"I don't know. I did not. I never met any of the directors and do not know what they do. I never saw or heard anything like Al Qaeda."

Adel never had any idea whether LDI was fighting the United States, if anyone in LDI was working both sides of the war, or if the United States was funding LDI in some way.

"Were there meetings where people tried to get you to join the jihad?" Pat pushed on.

"Nothing like that. We would meet and discuss our work. I would be asked to deliver food to a camp or help with a class."

Adel was interesting. Unlike many of my clients, he never overstated his case. He never said "that could not be" about the heads of the charity. Instead, he told us what he knew, what he saw, what he heard.

"So, what did you do for them?"

"Well, at first I was a teacher at the Hira Institute."

Adel went on to tell us that he spent his first six years with LDI working primarily as a teacher at a school in a refugee camp in the village of Babi about an hour outside of Peshawar, Pakistan. He taught orphans of the wars and kids whose parents had taken them out of range of the fighting basic reading, writing, arithmetic, and religion, and about life in general. While he spent most of his time teaching during his first years in Pakistan, Adel also helped with administration and some food deliveries. It was this work that his interrogators in Baghram and Guantánamo had focused in on.

"What about religion? Anything extreme in the classes?"

"You keep asking this. What is extreme? I am a Muslim. It is part of my life and what I taught."

Even while he pushed back in reponse to our question, there was no anger in Adel's voice. He was trying to bridge the cultural divide, to find out if I thought any mention of the merciful Allah was a sign of fundamentalism. I assured Adel that I did not and did not compare a belief in Allah to Bin Laden and the Wahhabists and those Muslims who turned into suicide bombers killing innocent women and children.

"No. There was nothing like that. I taught the children life."

When Pat and I talked with Adel about the orphans he had taught, his smile was warm and wide, his pride radiating. He had kept track of some of them and knew that a few had been able to finish high school and that several had even gone on to medical school. Adel gave us the names of some of the kids he had taught. We hoped to connect with them during our investigation.

On his leave home in 1987, Adel went with his father to the home of Salwa Othman, a young woman from the Al Jaris East section of Khartoum. Adel asked Salwa's father for her hand in marriage. They were distant cousins who had known each other as children and, as cousins, had been able to continue socializing into adulthood—something that would otherwise have been prohibited in Islamic Sudan. They were married that summer.

Salwa's parents had supported her staying in school until she was nineteen. Now married at twenty, although she was anxious about leaving her family for Pakistan, she was also excited about the adventure. In July, Salwa and Adel were off to Pakistan and his job at the Hira Institute. Within a year, the first of their five daughers, Zaynab, was born. Tasneem followed in January 1990, Maryam in August 1994, and Rahmah in 2001. We did not learn about Adel's fifth daughter, Fida, born after his arrest, until our second visit to Guantánamo in May.

Life was good for Adel and his family. They made a nice home in Babi; Adel enjoyed teaching; Salwa was happy with the girls and they were able to get home each year to see their families.

When Adel started working with LDI, its director in Peshawar was Zahid Al-Sheikh, whom Adel knew casually as the top man in the front office. Ever since he was seized, Adel's problem has been that Zahid's brother, Khalid Sheikh Mohammed, had taken a different path and had become a mujahideen leader in the 1980s, fighting against the Soviets. Whether he was funded by the United States in those efforts is left to be known. But what we do know is that Khalid Sheikh Mohammed, or KSM as he is referred to in government documents and the media, did not stop fighting after the Soviets were defeated. In 2001, he was one of the masterminds behind the World Trade Center and Pentagon attacks.[5] Shortly after the attacks he disappeared, not to resurface until September 2006 when the Bush administration was finally forced to admit that it had been holding men it believed to be top Al Qaeda operatives in black hole prisons in Europe and Asia. KSM was one of fourteen men the Bush administration flew to Guantánamo from a black hole in early September 2006.[6] How long he had been in custody has not been revealed.

It was, of course, no secret that KSM's brother Zahid had been employed by LDI in the late 1980s and had spent some time working at the Jelazee refugee camp outside Peshawar, a camp that LDI helped fund. U.S. intelligence sources determined that KSM had visited his brother at the camp a couple of times. The problem for Adel was that his interrogators believed that he had been delivering food to the Jelazee camp when KSM had visited his brother there. I picked up on that thread.

"What about KSM? Did you meet him?"

No matter how many times I asked Adel, he answered me as he had his interrogators. "It is possible. I was never introduced to the director's brother, but I cannot say that he was not at the camp at the same time I was there."

More important for our work, Adel told us that he abhorred what KSM had apparently become.

Adel was just as open when we asked him about his trips to Shamshatoo, a refugee camp run by the mujahadeen leader, Gulbuddin Hekmatyar. Adel told us that he knew his name and even what he looked like. "Why not?" he asked. "He served as Afghanistan's president in the early 1990s."

Before our first trip to Guantánamo, Pat and I had not known Hekmatyar would be an issue for us. We had focused on learning about Sudan, Islam, and how to deal with victims of torture. Back at the CBQ the evening after our first day with Adel, Chris and Bryan filled us in on Hekmatyar. They had studied the Afghan wars and shifting alliances among the warlords and had learned a fair amount about Hekmatyar in preparation for their visit with Chaman, our client who had been an Afghan mujahideen fighter against the Soviets and an associate of Hekmatyar's in the 1990s. They confirmed what Adel had told us: Hekmatyar had been an important mujahideen commander and leader of the Afghan government for several years after the Soviets left and before the Taliban came to power. But those facts were not a problem for Adel.[7]

What made the references to Hekmatyar difficult was that around 2000 he became a supporter of the Taliban and Bin Laden. Adel never met Hekmatyar or had any direct dealings with him, but he believed Hekmatyar had been at the Shamshatoo camp one of the times he had delivered food there. Of course, that was long before Hekmatyar switched sides, and it may well have taken place while he was still receiving U.S. support.

In early 1993, Adel was promoted from his teaching position to more administrative work and the family moved from Babi to Peshawar near the LDI office on Arbab Road in the University District. Adel did some bookkeeping, helped with general administration, and helped out at some LDI sites in other parts of Pakistan. He had some more time for himself and was able to pursue his lifelong interest in education and, in 1995, completed a master's degree in Peshawar. When my staff and I were able to make contact with Adel's family later on in the summer of 2006, we learned that Adel's brother-in-law, Adil Al Tayeb, had visited Adel in Pakistan around the time he got his master's degree. Al Tayeb confirmed that there was nothing political about Adel's work or studies.

Adel continued doing administrative work for LDI. After the first Gulf War, the Kuwaiti funding for LDI slowly dried up, and in 1999, Adel was laid off.

"That must have been difficult for you. How did you live?"

"We had a little money from LDI, but I had to work. I talked with some of the people I knew at other NGOs [nongovernmental organizations]. There were other Sudanese in Peshawar, but nothing happened for a while."

"Why not go home? Did you think about that?"

"Yes. I talked to my brother, but the economy in Sudan was still worse than in Pakistan. Then a man I had met who ran a small import/export business said he needed some help."

"What did you do?" Pat asked.

"I made two trips to China, Xinjiang province. I brought back small electronic equipment—cell phones, pagers, and calculators. And women's and children's clothes."

Pat and I were not happy to hear that. The clothing part was acceptable, but going to the Muslim part of China and bringing back electronics bothered me. After all, cell phones had been used to detonate the bombs in Madrid.

"Are there any records of the trips?" I asked.

"Of course. These were business trips. I had all the necessary papers from Pakistan and China. Your government should have records in my passport and all the receipts are in Peshawar."

It was another piece to add to the investigation list.

But these business trips were not the type of work Adel wanted, and after several months his efforts paid off when he was hired to be the administrator of a hospital in Chamkani, Afghanistan, run by the World Assembly for Muslim Youth, a Saudi-based charity.

Chamkani sits in the middle of Paktia province, part of the eastern border region of Afghanistan and Pakistan. The rugged mountain area is home to Pashtun tribesmen whose homeland was divided by an artifical border drawn by the colonial rulers more than a century ago. In 2000, Paktia's rugged mountain tribesmen were still hosting thousands of refugees of the Afghan wars that had been raging and receding for thirty years.

The area's only true medical facility, the hospital in Chamkani, serves roughly three hundred thousand people who live within automobile, donkey, and walking distance. From the mid-1990s to 2004, the Chamkani hospital was a first-class operation, funded by WAMY and inspected regularly by the World Health Organization. It received food from the United Nations Food for Peace Program, used U.S. equipment and supplies, and coexisted with the Afghan government, both the Taliban and later the U.S.-backed Karzai regime.[8] The Taliban influence in Chamkani was much weaker than in many parts of Afghanistan and the hospital attracted doctors who had left positions in Kabul and even spent time in exile in Pakistan before finding that they could practice good medicine without political or religious interference in Chamkani.

Adel loved his new job at the hospital. Its reputation for excellence spread beyond Paktia province, and people came from as far away as Kabul and from across the border in Pakistan. The staff, medical and administrative, worked and lived together serving the sick and injured, and played games in their time off. Most worked twenty-two to twenty-five days on with six to eight days off. While Chamkani is not far from the border with Pakistan, there was no direct route over the rugged mountains, so non-Afghans like Adel spent two of their days off on an arduous trek back toward Kabul, around to the border crossing, and on to Peshawar to spend a few days with their families.

"You were the administrator at the hospital, but what did you do?"

"I paid the bills. Made sure the patients had enough food. Worked with the supplies."

Later, when we were able to speak with some of the doctors from the hospital, it was clear that Adel was the main administrator and kept the place running. But Adel's modesty would never allow him to say that.

After the World Trade Center and Pentagon were attacked, anticipating a U.S. response, the Taliban advised all charitable organizations working in the country that it could not guarantee the safety of their employees, and WAMY directed its foreign employees at the hospital in Chamkani to get out of the country. Adel stayed as long as he could and was the last non-Afghan to leave the hospital, being driven in the hospital ambulance to the Torkham Gate border station that leads from the Khyber Pass road into the Peshawar area of Pakistan. He passed through the gate around September 16 and was interviewed by local television and news outlets that were there covering the exodus.

Back in Peshawar, Adel went to work in the WAMY offices, handling budgeting and public relations projects, and helping with supplies. He stayed in touch with his Afghan colleagues at the hospital but could not go back. In his new position, Adel traveled to Islamabad, Pakistan's capital, a number of times to meet with government officials about stalled medical shipments and tried to put an end to the corruption that was siphoning off supplies before they could reach WAMY camps and schools.

Many Arabic speakers left Pakistan over the next six months, and the Sudanese government soon closed the school Adel's children had been attending. Adel and Salwa wanted the girls to continue their education; their two choices were to move to the WAMY offices in Islamabad where Arabic-language schooling was still available or return to Sudan. They were still undecided when they left for their annual trip to Sudan in June.

It was one month later, when he returned alone to Peshawar, that Adel's nightmare began.

When I made my third visit to Guantánamo months later, I questioned Adel about the corruption in Pakistan more intensively than I had the first time.

"We had our supplies in a warehouse and I was asked to move them," Adel explained.

"By whom?"

"The Pakistani security police. Some of them had a connection to another warehouse and wanted us to move the supplies there."

"So what was the problem?" I asked.

"I knew that some of our supplies had been diverted from the other warehouse and I said there was no need to move."

When I pushed him about the warehouse and supplies issue as a possible explanation for his seizure, Adel would not blame the men he had been dealing with, saying he did not know why he was arrested.

During research in Sudan in April 2007, William, my investigator, and I tracked down a man who had worked in Pakistan coordinating charitable activities for a number of NGOs from 1992 to 2004. He confirmed the rampant corruption and pressure that Adel had resisted. He did not have any firsthand information about Adel but, based on his dealings with the Pakistani security police, he believed Adel's resistance to their demands was the reason he was taken.

.   .   .

Adel told us during our first meeting in March that after the nightmare of the Pakistani prison and Baghram, he had been treated reasonably well in Guantánamo. While many of the interrogation techniques used in Abu Ghraib were first used in Guantánamo, by the time Adel arrived there in the spring of 2003, they had stopped.

"The first month was not easy, but it bore no relation to what I had experienced in Pakistan or the air base at Baghram. I was in a cell in isolation. I was given no extra clothes to have in my cell and a blanket was handed to me each night and taken away in the morning when the guards woke me."

"Could you have anything in the cell with you?" I asked.

"No. Nothing. We were not allowed any personal items."

"How were you treated? Beaten? Interrogated? Yelled at?"

"There was nothing like that. The only time I was hit at all by Americans was on the airfield in Baghram. I was taken for interrogations daily for the first weeks, then it began to taper off."

"How long did you stay in the isolation cell?" Pat asked.

"It was about one month. Then I was moved to a dormitory in Camp Delta where I have been ever since."

"Adel, we keep hearing there was torture here. What do you hear from the other prisoners?"

"I have not heard of anyone being tortured since I have been here. There is no torture or beatings except the ERF and the psychologic of not knowing why you are here or when you will ever get home."

We had heard about ERFing from some of the other lawyers. ERF is an emergency response force of six guards dressed in riot gear that resembles a superpadded hockey uniform.[9] They march into a cell area led by a guard armed with a large padded shield and another armed with a very unpadded baton. Depending on the reason for the call and the response of the inmate, ERFings can get brutal.

While Adel had seen ERF beatings, he had never been ERFed himself, although one of my other clients has, and he described being terrified the first time the team busted into his cell in a dispute over whether he could keep a blanket. He resisted and was badly beaten. He said when it happened a second time, he was able to stay relaxed and was barely bruised as the team piled on top of his unresisting body.

Adel's treatment in Guantánamo mirrored what I had heard from the attorneys who had been handling cases over a longer stretch of time. No one had reported overt physical torture at Guantánamo since 2003. The torture now lies in the isolation, the indefinite nature of the imprisonment, the absence of any process or hope, and the unrelenting petty indignities and arbitrary rules.

Although the interrogators still take Adel out for a session every few weeks, he said that since the summer of 2003, "It is like a game, ridiculously the same. Even the interrogators know this. Each time I tell them I worked for the charities and helped the Afghan refugees. I have taught the orphans, delivered supplies to the hospitals and camps, and worked in the administration. They know I am not a fighter. I have no idea of anyone in Al Queda or the Taliban."

At one point, we directly discussed the attacks of September 11, and Adel told me the same thing he had told his interrogators. "I feel sorry for the innocents killed in September. The Muslims who did it are perverted with no moral or human character."

.   .   .

During the afternoon of our first day with Adel, he had told us that he had been given some paperwork by the Administrative Review Board that looked at his case at the beginning of August 2005. Pat told him we were very interested in seeing it and to bring it to our meeting the next day.

As we walked into the cell the next morning, we saw a manila envelope on the table alongside a small stack of papers. Eagerly, Pat dove in and immediately realized that they had not been included in the material that William had downloaded from the Associated Press lawsuit. The download had included seventeen pages from the Combatant Status Review Tribunal and seven from the ARB. Adel had five more pages, including a list of the ARB's assessment of his situation.

The list was broken down into four sections: "factors favoring detention," "commitment," "association," and "factors favoring release or transfer." It was all guilt by association. Just as with the material William had downloaded, nothing in the pages Adel gave us accused him of ever being on a battlefield, being a terrorist, or harming anyone. He was never accused of financing terrorism or being an arms runner. All the "factors," "commitment," and "association" in the government's documents were from Adel's life and work, matching what he had been telling us. The papers said that Adel was a prisoner because he had worked as a relief worker for LDI and WAMY, which "may" be affiliated with Al Qaeda, and that WAMY supported the Palestinians.

William's Internet searches had revealed that WAMY was not even listed on our government's antiterrorism watch lists. When we asked Adel again about his employers' views, he philosophically explained that he did not agree with all their positions. "All fingers are not similar," he said.

As for Khalid Sheikh Mohammed, the ARB papers said that he had been at the Jelazee refugee camp in the 1980s when Adel had delivered food there and had been recruiting Afghan refugees to return and fight the Soviets.

Pat and I were mystified. Was this really why Adel was in prison? What could our government be thinking? We had been funding the mujahideen to fight the Soviets during the 1980s. How could that be a reason for the United States to put a man in prison? Worse yet, the papers did not even allege that Adel had met, let alone worked with, KSM.

As Pat and I vented our anger at the unfairness of this type of charge, Adel broke in, "Yes, the entire plague was not there yet." Adel reminded us that when he started working with LDI there was no Al Qaeda as we know it today—Bin Laden was fighting the Soviets and there was no U.S. war on terror.

As we finished reviewing the papers, there were only two pieces that Adel disputed. Factor twelve favoring detention was the allegation that some identification cards showing United Nations refugee status had been found in his apartment when he was arrested. Adel said there may have been, but they were not his, they must have belonged to his downstairs neighbor, Ammeur and his family, the registered UN refugees. Adel could only speculate that when the security police brought Ammeur upstairs to his apartment on the night of the arrest, they had put the two men's documents together. He thought the same must be true regarding factor eleven favoring detention, which said that a copy of a Muslim Brotherhood newsletter had been found in his apartment. There was no question that Adel had briefly been a member of the brotherhood in the 1980s, but he had no contact with them in two decades. Ammeur, on the other hand, had.

What kind of process was the Department of Defense using? The more we talked with Adel and learned about the CSRT and ARB, the more my suspicions that it was a complete sham were realized. While Adel was fortunate that the "charges" against him actually contained some detail, as with most of the prisoners he was shown no facts to back them up. But unlike most of the detainees, there never could be anything to back them up because nothing was based on secret information, nothing had been obtained on a battlefield, or from informers the government did not want to disclose. Also, nothing in the papers even hinted that the military, FBI, or CIA in Pakistan, Afghanistan, or Cuba had bothered even to try to verify Adel's statements. Adel told us that the "personal representative" he was given for the CSRT had done nothing for him. The person was not a lawyer and was not allowed to argue on his behalf, and neither Adel nor his "representative" could call any witnesses to confirm his account. Adel told us that his representative was a nice enough person but did little more than read the vague charges to him.

In the winter of 2006, a team at Seton Hall Law School led by Professor Mark Denbeaux published an analysis of the public information on 517 of the detainees in Guantánamo, including the information that the Department of Defense had released. Denbeaux's study confirmed what Adel had told us.[10] Not only did the DOD refuse to call witnesses who were outside the prison, but in 74 percent of the cases, the DOD even refused requests to call witnesses who were in the prison. In at least three cases, Denbeaux reported, when a CSRT found that a person was not an enemy combatant, new tribunals were ordered that later that changed the ruling. Court filings in 2007 revealed that the number of times new CSRTs were ordered for people who were found not to be enemy combatants was significantly greater than three. One was a declaration William and I obtained from a member of Adel's CSRT. He personally sat on six CSRTs where "do overs" were ordered.[11]

The papers Adel showed us focused our discussion and took us through the morning and well into the afternoon. Around 3:00, Pat and I switched gears and engaged him in planning our work for the coming months. We agreed that Adel should continue to be cooperative with the interrogators and prison administrators. Armed with the contact information Adel was able to give us for his wife and brother-in-law in Khartoum, and older brother Hashem in Port Sudan, Pat and I would let them know Adel was doing okay. We would start investigating with his family and anyone else we could find to confirm Adel's account, which the FBI, CIA, and military had not done. Assuming our investigation gave us material to work with, we would push hard in court and try to get Judge Bates, the judge in Washington assigned to Adel's case, to look seriously into his plight.

■   ■   ■

It was difficult when Pat and I had to leave at the end of the second day of our visit. Pat and I were about to go back to the larger world, but Adel was headed back to the loneliness of Camp Delta. Pat said his good-bye and shook Adel's hand. I said good-bye, in English and Arabic, "*Salaam Alechem*," and shook Adel's hand.

I turned to get my papers, but before I could pick them up, Adel asked, "When will I go home?"

"We can only promise that we will fight for you in every way we can," I told him.

Adel's eyes, which had been so calm for most of the meeting, started to darken. He reached out again and took my right hand, at first with his right hand but then with both. Tears welled up in his eyes. He could see the ray of hope that had entered the cell with us beginning to die with our leaving. I put my left hand over our joined hands and we stood there looking at each other. There was no sound in the cell; I am not sure anyone was even breathing.

"*Inshallah* [God willing] it will be soon," he said, "and I will welcome you in my home."

10 | The Unconscionable Detention of Adel Hamad

We can't solve problems by using the same kind of thinking we used when we created them.

—Albert Einstein

AT OUR FIRST MEETING WITH ADEL IN March, everything was new, every step filled with anticipation. My anxiety had been heightened by the pro bono lawyer's descriptions of guards who took twenty minutes to look through a half-inch stack of papers, rules about food and clothes that changed on every visit, and being dressed down for trying to talk to the guards. When we went back to Guantánamo at the end of May, I already knew Adel as a pleasant man and, after all, my experiences at the prison had been very familiar. Unlike most of the pro bono lawyers who were used to the walnut paneled world of business law, in my decades of visiting jails and prisons, I had grown accustomed to the petty indignities of security, standing spread eagled while a guard passed a wand over my body; having to take off my blue dress shirt when I forgot that visitors can't wear blue in the Oregon State Penitentiary; having my files searched and questioned; and helping the women attorneys in the office deal with the Federal of Prisons when they set their magnetic screens so high that they had to take off their brassieres to go visit their clients.

In March we had all felt the intensity of first contact. Borrowing from Robert Heinlein, we were all "Stranger[s] meeting in a strange land." Our second visit with Adel in May was a reunion filled with warmth and affection, handshakes that extended into hugs. Pat and I started emptying our bags, putting papers and food on the table.

Adel shifted in his chair, leaned forward, and took a piece of baklava. "This is good. Not too sweet."

Pat and I smiled. Of all the food we had brought with us to Guantánamo that first week in March, the biggest hit was our investigator Janan Stoll's baklava. Baked with her Palestinian grandmother's "less sweet" recipe, it turned out to be a hit not just with Adel but with people from all over the Middle East: our Lebanese interpreter Felice, our Palestinian interpreter Dr. Sbait, and, later, our clients from Afghanistan, Yemen, Syria, and Algeria.

Before we were even settled in our seats, Adel asked, "Does the little sister who baked the baklava still work with you?"

That question spoke volumes to me as a measure of the man I was seeing, someone whose caring for others hadn't dried up even after four years in prison. As we learned more about Adel during that visit, the repercussions for him and his family of the war on terror, and the reality of life in the prison in Guantánamo, the absurdity of his imprisonment became even more clear.

After settling down to our day's work, Pat and I started filling Adel in on our progress since March. I was struck by his calmness as we told him that we had been able to get through to his brother Hashem and brother-in-law Al Tayeb and conveyed greetings from them both, and from his wife Salwa and his oldest daughter Zaynab. Adel's calmness broke only when he asked about Rahmah, the daughter who was born just a few months before his arrest.

In many ways, speaking with Adel about his family was the most important part of that visit. However far from him they were, talking about his wife, his four daughters—Zayneb, Tasneen, Maryam, and Rahmah—and brothers with people who cared, brought them closer. Later that afternoon, after we had finished going over further details of Adel's work and possible witnesses and were beginning to relax a little before the guards came to take us out, I was asking Adel about his family when he shared with us for the first time that he had a son and a fifth daughter.

In 1996, after three daughters, Adel and Salwa were blessed with a son, Mohammed. But the baby was born with massive birth defects and died after only ten months. There was no pathos in the telling, no search for pity.

Adel could not have known that this piece of his life touched a deep chord in me.

I rarely share personal aspects of my life with my clients. In order to maintain the objectivity needed to offer difficult assessments and hard advice, it is important to keep a clear divide between my clients and myself. That divide is also important to my mental health. Day in and day out I hear horrific stories about abuse and ruined lives, which is one of the reasons there is so much burnout among criminal defense attorneys. If you let the clients' lives enter your psyche, after a while you're filled with their pain and need to stop that line of work, or start burying the pain with alcohol or drugs, or tune out and lose your ability to push for each client regardless of what he or she has done.

But when Adel told me about Mohammed, I felt inclined to share something very personal with him. Michael was my second child. In 1990, my first son, Danny, like Adel's Mohammed, had died at ten months. Adel and I had both longed for a son; it's the desire many men have to carry on their family name. For Adel, this was compounded by his religion, even though he had been blessed with three daughters. For me, Danny's arrival in Kathleen's and my life through adoption was the culmination of years of pain and frustration with infertility. While we were fortunate to adopt Michael a year later, the pain of Danny's loss will always be with me. Adel and I shared a special grief that only fathers who have lost their sons can know.

In addition, Adel told us that he had lost a daughter. Almost two years after his imprisonment, a letter came from Salwa through the International Red Cross, telling him that she had been pregnant when he left for Pakistan in July 2002 and that Allah had blessed them with a fifth daughter, whom she had named Fida. Like Mohammed, Fida had been born sickly. Adel did not know any details but knew she had needed extra care and medicine. With Adel locked up, Salwa simply could not afford it. The family tried to help, but it was not enough. Before she turned two, Fida died. Locked away in Guantánamo, Adel never saw her, never held her, could not help her.

That night was the most difficult I have had in Guantánamo. Walking outside the CBQ, looking up at the star-filled May night, my thoughts kept returning to the children in both Adel's life and my own. I replayed Danny's life and death over in my mind and the sad path Pat and I had wandered with Adel in hearing about his son Mohammed's death and the anger I felt about the death of Fida. My mind wandered from Adel's and my children to Kenny Leisten, whose mother, Lisa was then my office administrator. The rest of my staff and I got to know Kenny when he would come by the office after school or just hung out there. He grew into a strapping but somewhat troubled teen, and when he was seventeen, he joined the Army National Guard. It was the most positive experience he had had in years. Then, in 2004 he was shipped out to Iraq, and on July 28, while driving a Humvee in Taji, the vehicle struck an IED, improvised explosive device, killing Kenny instantly.[1] While Adel's Fida had not been hit by an IED, a suicide bomber, or a bomb from an F-15, his baby girl, like Kenny, had been a casualty of the war on terror.

. . .

The harshness of Adel's life at Guantánamo was much more visible in May than it had been when Pat and I visited in March. We arrived ten days after the prison had been buffeted by what the Gitmo command called a coordinated attack and what the prisoners called a spontaneous response to the guards once again disrespecting the Koran.[2] Two weeks before our trip, I had heard about the incident from some of the pro bono lawyers and knew that the prison had been locked down. I did not know for precisely how long, but visits were canceled and prisoners moved to different sections of the camp. Adel told us the problem started in Camp Delta, the largest section of the prison that housed more than 140 of the men and the part of the prison where most of the men were getting along. The guards had decided to conduct a sweep, something done periodically in all prisons, to search for weapons and other contraband. The team was searching in one of the units and demanded to look through the prisoners' Korans and, as seen by the men, disrespecting them in the process.

Whatever the reality of the initial confrontation, things turned ugly when the ERF was called in to deal with some of the prisoners who refused to hand over their Korans for inspection. Some of the prisoners reacted with whatever was at hand, something that rarely happened there. Books, pieces of furniture, toothpaste, feces, and fans torn off the wall were thrown at guards. The problem quickly spread throughout Camp Delta.

The prison authorities dealt with the disturbance by moving nearly every-one out. Adel had been moved from the reasonably open environment of Camp 4 in Delta—where the men lived in dormitories, could interact through-out the day, and move freely within the camp fences—to Camp 1, where the men were kept in single-person cells, locked up for twenty-two to twenty-three hours a day, without the "privilege" of mattresses, blankets, regular showers, and unrationed toilet paper. Adel wasn't angry that he had been moved to Camp 1, even though he had been a peacemaker during the dis-turbance, encouraging the angry prisoners to roll with a compromise on the guards' search: All prisoners give their Korans to an elder in the sec-tion, who would then cooperate during the search with the guards.

"Do you know the game chutes and ladders?" he asked. "Three moves forward then slide back down a chute?"

I could only shake my head and laugh at yet another glimpse of the sur-real. There I was in Guantánamo prison talking to a Sudanese Arab who was chained to the floor like a mad dog, being asked about a board game I had played fifty years ago with my childhood friends and, more recently, with my own son.

Adel returned to Camp 4 after about a month, when the prison authori-ties had sorted out the troublemakers. Trying to be a peacemaker during the disturbance was not the first time that Adel had put himself at risk with some of his fellow detainees in an attempt to calm a tense situation.

"Last summer," Adel told us, "three other Sudanese detainees went on a hunger strike. The prison wardens must have known that they were not fundamentalist and asked if I would talk to them."

For years, hunger strikes have periodically swept the prison. Some men stop eating out of despair and loss of hope. For some, to stop eating is the only thing in their lives over which they have any control. For others, the strikes are pure political protest.[3] There seems to be some recognition by the prison administrators that different reactions are appropriate for dif-ferent strikers. Some men are treated roughly and force-fed. For others, there is a little more understanding. The Sudanese strikers in the summer of 2005 were lucky.

"It was very unusual for anyone in the prison to talk to me like that and I told them, 'yes,' and was moved into their section of the prison. I talked with my brothers about the strike and what they were doing to themselves.

They had no hope. I was there for about a week before they agreed to start eating again. After a couple of weeks I was moved back to Camp 4. While I was happy to help my brothers, it was good to get back to Camp 4."

.   .   .

Adel's family and the situation in the prison consumed a large part of our May visit, but Pat and I also had a lot we needed to go over with Adel about the legal aspects of his case. At the beginning of May I had traveled to what is called the secure facility in Crystal City Virginia, to read the government's official and classified version of the evidence that it said justified keeping Adel in prison. I was eager to talk to Adel about it, but I had been required to sign what is called a Protective Order demanded by the Department of Defense and issued by the court and enforced by a Memorandum of Understanding, which placed severe limits on what I could tell my client.

In the CSRTs that were held during the summer and fall of 2004, the Department of Defense refused to allow the prisoners access to the classified information they presented. This meant that they rarely showed the prisoners any of the evidence on which the enemy combatant decisions were made. After the Supreme Court decided the *Rasul* case[4] and it was clear that the habeas attorneys would have access to their clients and it appeared that the habeas cases would move forward, the Department of Defense and CCR worked out a compromise on access to classified information. The lawyers would be able to see the evidence but could not tell their clients what they had seen or even question them about it. The limitations were incorporated in Protective Orders entered in all the cases, which included the establishment of a location run by the Department of Justice in Crystal City where the habeas lawyers could go to read the classified material and prepare classified pleadings for the courts.

For a lawyer, this is like representing a client blindfolded. You read, hypothetically, that a soldier mentioned that an Afghan said a client/prisoner was seen in Tora Bora with Bin Laden in December. You need to be able to ask the client if he knew the Afghan, if he had been in Tora Bora, if he had seen Bin Laden. But under the Protective Order, you can't.

There was material for me to read about Adel in the secure facility because one of the motions I had filed over the winter had actually been granted. In December, just after we had filed amended habeas petitions for our clients, we had asked the judges in three of our cases, including Judge Bates, the District of Columbia district judge assigned to Adel's case, to order the Department of Defense to file returns to their habeas petitions and tell us why the government believed it had the right to keep our clients in prison. Much to our surprise, given the small number of returns that had been ordered, Judge Bates directed the return. In fact, even as late as 2007, my office had received returns in only three cases.

On May 1, two versions of the return had been filed. One was a declassified version in the public record, which was based on the CSRT proceeding that William had downloaded from the Internet after the order in the AP lawsuit in February. The second version was classified and locked up in the secure facility.

In preparation for the filing of the return, I had booked a flight to Washington for May 2 and, not knowing how much material would be filed, I had arranged with the security officers at the secure facility to let me in early, at 7:30. Walking the two blocks from the hotel, the anticipation built. Would there actually be some evidence against Adel? Would I see a "smoking gun"? Would the image I had formed of this peaceful man be shattered?

The facility was in a nondescript office tower, at the end of a windowless hallway pockmarked with a myriad of nail and screw holes where different locking mechanisms had once been. I pushed the office's buzzer, and a security officer asked my name, I assume checked it against a sheet of visitors for the day, and let me in. He checked my Federal Defender ID, had me sign in, and then disappeared for a minute, returning with a manila envelope barely one quarter inch thick. I signed for the envelope and the officer said I could use any of the rooms or desks.

The secure facility suite was a warren of rooms and cubicles, filled with desks and computers—but none with access to the Internet. There was no one else around, just the officer and me. Wandering through what felt like a movie set, I chose a cubicle at random, sat, and opened the envelope. It took me less than an hour to read the classified return. The Protective Order precludes me from disclosing its contents, as it did with Adel, but I can say that I was both relieved and disgusted. Relieved, because there was nothing I needed to worry about; disgusted because it reinforced my belief that Adel's imprisonment was wrong.

During my visit at the end of May, I told Adel, "I have been to the secure facility and read the classified return. I am not worried about anything we have discussed or I might want to say for you."

I was sure that if I had been allowed to tell him what I had read and ask some questions, Adel would have been able to give me direction for more investigation of facts that would help prove his innocence. But I could say nothing more than I had.

It made sense that Adel was not surprised by my report. He knew he was innocent and that many of the release and detention decisions were irrational. Adel told Pat and me that earlier in May a group of Saudis had been sent home. He had lived with some of them in Camp Delta for several years. "Three or four of the Saudis, like me, never got an answer from the ARB. They never did anything against your country. But I know two who were fighters. All the principles of democracy and freedom and justice, I am not sure they exist now."

Pat and I shared Adel's disillusionment about the irrationality and unfairness of the situation in Guantánamo. While it did not surprise either of us that Adel knew some of the people our government had sent home were fighters, it did increase my belief that too many of the decisions that our government was making about Guantánamo had little or nothing to do with the danger any of the men it had seized actually presented.

However, in the midst of the absurdity, there was one piece that made perfect sense. One person in an official position who had reviewed Adel's situation had understood the immorality of his imprisonment. Several pages of the CSRT that were included in the unclassified portion of the return not released to the AP but filed on May 1 included the actual decision of the tribunal that heard Adel's case. Of the hundreds of records released by the Department of Defense and discussed on the CCR Web site by the habeas counsel, Adel's was the only one that was not unanimous. While the decision of the two-person majority tracked the charges, the third member, an army major, could not accept Adel's imprisonment. Since nearly all of the decision was unclassified, I was able to read it to Adel.

The dissenting major had reached his "conclusions" considering "both classified and unclassified information." This was significant, I told Adel, because even though I could not discuss the classified material, I could tell him that the major had found nothing incriminating in it and we could all proclaim that the dissent was based on the classified material.

The major rejected the notion of guilt by association. Even if it was true, he wrote, that Adel had "associated with al Qaida [*sic*]," "this allegation is insufficient to show that the detainee should be classified as an enemy combatant." The major pointed out that Adel did not dispute the fact of his work for LDI and WAMY. Even if both organizations had "provided some support to 'terrorist ideals and causes,' this fact does not incriminate the detainee. . . . These NGO's presumably have numerous employees and volunteer workers who have been working in legitimate humanitarian roles. The mere fact that some elements of these NGO's provide support to 'terrorist ideals and causes' is insufficient to declare one of the employees an enemy combatant."

Under this theory, the major went on, "all physicians, nurses, and aid workers employed by alleged terrorist connected NGO's would also be declared enemy combatants." Similarly, the majority's view would require declaring all "local merchants" who "came in contact" with an Al Qaeda member to be enemy combatants. The dissenting major rejected these notions of guilt by association. "Absent any allegations that the Detainee himself 'directly supported hostilities in aid of enemy forces,'" the definition of enemy combatant promulgated by Deputy Secretary of Defense Wolfowitz on July 7, 2004, forces the conclusion that there was no basis to detain Adel. "Even assuming all the allegations in Exhibit R1 are accurate, the Detainee does not meet the definition of an enemy combatant.

"To reach such a conclusion would provide for unconscionable results."

"Unconscionable." It was what Pat and William and I and everyone in the office who had looked at Adel's case had felt so strongly. The imprisonment of this peaceful aid worker was shockingly wrong.

11 | The Seeds of Mercy

You can only protect your liberties in this world by protecting the other man's freedom.

—Clarence Darrow[1]

ADEL WAS IMPRISONED IN GUANTÁNAMO because the seeds of mercy his parents had sown in him as a child had led him to social work in Pakistan and Afghanistan, where he was eventually seized by the U.S. government. Why was *I* there? What were the seeds that had led me, a Jewish kid raised in a small community outside of New York City, to fight for the Muslim Mayfield and the Arab Hamad? My parents had not been lawyers or political activists, but they had given me a sense of justice and the belief that I should try to do something positive in the world. Looking back at those first emotional meetings with Adel led me to reflect on my roots and the path that took me to the prison in Guantánamo.

The Hyatt senior residence in Lantana, Florida, where I visited my mother before each trip to Guantánamo, was a far cry from the vibrant community where I had grown up. In 1950, two years after I was born, my parents had bought into a unique cooperative in what was then the wilds of northern Westchester County—forty miles north of their apartment in Brooklyn, New York. Founded by architect Frank Lloyd Wright, two of his students, and a group of politically and socially progressive people from Brooklyn, Usonia Homes was an experiment in cooperative living and architecture.[2] It had been an interesting place to grow up. Everyone's door was always open; if you needed an adult to talk to other than your parents, someone was there to listen. Most of the forty-five homeowners were businessmen who kept in touch with their leftist and sometimes Socialist roots even as most of them became highly successful.

While we talked politics a lot at home, my parents were not politically involved like many of their neighbors who were active in the liberal wing of the Democratic Party, the Committee for a Sane Nuclear Policy, and civil rights organizations. When my mother's father, Julius, visited from Brooklyn, he and my father often fell into heated yelling matches about politics and current events. Julius was more than a little deaf, but they probably would have raised their voices much of the time anyway. That ferment, their questioning the status quo and willingness to challenge the powers that be, was important to my developing sense of the world, but the forces that led me to Guantánamo sprang from something deeper.

When I was six or seven years old, my grandfather told me the story of how he came to America. He wasn't more than five feet tall, and when I was old enough to remember him, he had shrunk to even less. Yet after hearing his story he became a giant in my eyes. A Jew conscripted into the czar's army in 1910, he had a miserable time, particularly with one lieutenant whose favorite pastime was Jew-baiting. Little twenty-year-old Julius took it and took it, until one day in the chow line, he could take the abuse no more. He had just gotten to the front of the line when the lieutenant ordered him out to clean the latrines. In one swift move, Julius turned on him with his mess kit, drawing on all the strength his short but compact body could muster. The lieutenant went down and Julius took off. His friends helped him get out of the army compound and hid him in the countryside until his father, Alkona, could come with a wagon. Passed from family to family, he was smuggled out of Russia. Somehow, my great-grandfather got Julius the necessary papers and he shipped out to America.

It was 1913 when Julius settled in New York City. Even though he was far from danger, he knew his family was still near to it. Six years later, a roving band of Cossacks rampaged through the village of Loisk, where his father had taken the family after Julius had left for America. It was a small village in the section of the Ukraine that was known as the Pale of Settlement, the area in greater Russia in which Jews were allowed to live. In the pogrom, my great-grandfather Alkona Strauss was murdered. The murderers placed the gun in his wife's hand and squeezed the trigger while two of my great-uncles were forced to watch. The younger, Nat, would not stop screaming, so they ripped up Alkona's prayer books and stuffed his mouth with the paper. As a boy, I remember Nat had a nervous habit of pushing his tongue out of his mouth. Only years later when I was told the story of my great-grandfather's murder did I finally understand that he was trying to push the prayer pages out so he could breathe.

It wasn't only my mother's family that had felt the sting of state terror. In 1907, Sam Wax and his sister Eda left another village in Eastern Europe, Lusk, also in the Pale of Settlement but nearer to what is now Poland than the part of Ukraine where Julius had been raised. Sam and Eda settled in New York, where Sam got married a year later and Eda became "engaged" to a left-leaning Russian/German émigré named Novikoff. His first name is lost in the shadows of history. Ahead of their time, Eda and Novikoff lived together but never married.

Less than a year after my great-grandfather Alkona was murdered in the pogrom, great-uncle Novikoff was deported in the Palmer Raids, the mass arrests and deportations orchestrated by Attorney General A. Mitchell Palmer—a staunch anti-Communist—in response to the red scare that followed the Russian Revolution.[3]

The victory of the Bolsheviks in Russia had encouraged unionists and Socialists throughout the world, including the United States. It also spread fear throughout the United States that workingmen and -women would demand a larger share of the capitalist pie. The year 1919 had been filled with labor unrest in this country.[4] On February 6, commerce in Seattle was stopped cold by a general strike of more than sixty-five thousand workers who walked off their jobs in solidarity with thirty-five thousand longshoremen who had been on strike since January 21. The strike ended five days later, but only after army units, including machine guns and tanks, had been moved onto the streets from Fort Lewis, the sprawling army base forty miles to the south.

On May Day 1919, tanks filled the streets of Cleveland, Ohio, where there was a scene of bloody clashes between labor activists protesting the arrest of Socialist leader Eugene V. Debs. Then, on June 2, the country was rocked by bomb blasts in eight cities, one damaging the home of President Wilson's recently appointed attorney general, Mitchell Palmer. Later in the year, the country was shaken again by the Great Steel Strike of 1919, a three-month strike by 350,000 steelworkers throughout the Midwest.

The government did not stand by passively as this wave of terror crossed the nation. Throughout 1919, the brand-new General Intelligence Division of the Justice Department's Bureau of Investigation gathered "intelligence" on radicals, anarchists, Socialists, and Communists. The division was the forerunner of the FBI, and it was helmed by J. Edgar Hoover, the bureau's first and longest-serving director. On November 7, Hoover started a series of raids, rounding up, often without any warrant, people on his lists. Most of these people were aliens, here legally but not yet citizens. The small raids of November and December were just a prelude to a coordinated series of raids that started on January 2, 1920, and resulted in the arrest and deportation of ten thousand people. Most were simply arrested by federal agents and sent packing without charges, hearings, or trials. Great uncle Novikoff was one of them.

Novikoff's troubles did not reach Eda or Sam or his children, including my father, Jack, who grew up in New York City. Meanwhile, Julius and his bride had settled in Brooklyn and their daughter, Anne, my mother, grew up there. Barely six months after meeting on a blind date in 1941, Anne and Jack were married. I was born in Brooklyn seven years later, and we moved to Westchester county when I was two.

It was there that I learned what it was like to be the "other," the "commie Jews" living on the hill outside the mainly Christian and Republican bedroom community of Pleasantville. It didn't matter that not everyone in Usonia was Jewish and none were Communists; everyone was colored with the same two strokes. There were swastikas carved into the desks in school and anti-Semitic comments were a staple of my childhood. Though not a big kid, I was the largest of the six or seven Jews in my class through junior high school and I was the one who occasionally fought back physically.

While there may have been a black family or two in Pleasantville, no black kids attended my school. It was sometime in the early 1960s that actor Sidney Poitier bought a large house on seven acres between the village and the hill where Usonia sat three miles to the east. While I was too young to appreciate his fame, it was still a thrill getting a ride from a famous actor one day while hitchhiking home from the town. That brief contact became a little more personal when a cross was burned on his lawn the following

year and I heard the fear in the voices of some of the Holocaust survivors in Usonia as they talked about the incident. Even a decade and a
half after the end of World War II, their scars of racism and terror were
still raw.

1963, the summer I turned fifteen, I learned firsthand about the responsibility we all have for what goes on around us. The nonviolent protests
and demonstrations of the civil rights movement were in full swing throughout the South. While the freedom riders abjured violence, the communities they passed through sometimes did not, and fire hoses, police dogs, and
beatings were common. The nation watched on television as Birmingham
Alabama police chief Bull Connor turned police dogs on marchers. Civil
rights leaders, like Medgar Evers, the field secretary for the NAACP, were
murdered. On June 21, President Kennedy convened a meeting in the White
House with 250 leading attorneys and used the prestige of his office to urge
the legal profession to mobilize, join the civil rights movement, and help
stem the tide of violence.[5]

Roland and Faye Watts, two members of Usonia who worked for a non-
profit organization helping rural sharecroppers, were among the idealists
who answered the president's call. They helped organize a group of people
in their early twenties, including a number of Usonians, to go on the freedom rides to integrate lunch counters and register voters. Because of the
violence that surrounded these visits and marchers, the teenagers in the
community were not allowed to go. But on my birthday that year, a sweltering July day, I ran straight into the wall of racism while on a bicycle trip,
not in the South, but in nearby Pennsylvania.

I was one of ten teenagers in a group led by Walter Lawton, the director
of the Northern Westchester Ethical Culture Society, pedaling through the
Pennsylvania Dutch country. As we sweated our way into a small town one
afternoon, our faces brightened as we first heard, then saw, a deliciously in-
viting municipal swimming pool. We rode our loaded bikes up to it and,
pushing each other aside, headed for the gate where we were met by the pool
director. Our anticipation of the cooling water mounted with his friendly
greeting, but then he asked, "Are there any niggers in your group?"

Someone yelled out no.

Walter called us aside. "We can swim," he said, "but should we?"

We caucused in a sweaty silence under an ancient maple tree ponder-
ing his question.

After a minute someone in our group said, "What difference does it make that we are all white? Won't we be supporting their views if we go in?" Walter asked for consensus, and while there was a little grumbling at first, the decision was unanimous. We told the pool director that we appreciated his hospitality but could not accept it if it would exclude colored people. We mounted up and rode away, sweat dripping as hard as before, but it was much easier to bear the heat knowing that we had taken a moral stand. The lesson Walter helped us learn that hot July day is the kind you never forget.

Two years later, I ran into another wall of racism—just down the road from my house. The violent side of anti-Semitism came burning home one night in Usonia in the same way as it had been directed toward Sidney Poitier, when a cross was burned on the lawn of my Jewish neighbors Murray and Gertrude Gabel. Back then I don't think I connected the two sets of cross burnings—the targeting of black people and Jews—but I see it clearly now as I speak out against hate crimes and discrimination against Muslims. The evils of racism and discrimination know no bounds; we are all at risk of being labeled "the other." When asked now how I can defend Muslim terrorists, the answer is easy for me. I am defending a principle that protects all of us, the rule of law that keeps us safe.

The seeds planted in me as I grew up in Usonia, the awareness of injustice, the sense that none of us are immune from its worst excesses, the idea that we have a responsibility to do something about it, started to sprout when I was a sophomore in college in 1968. It was a year of upheaval. The Vietnam War was raging overseas, spawning angry protests throughout the country; the promises of the civil rights movement of the early and mid-1960s had not been fulfilled. Then in April, Martin Luther King Jr. was assassinated, triggering riots in major cities across the country. King's assassination was also the trigger for college students, riled by antiwar protests, to take over administration buildings on campuses from Columbia University to the University of Washington to the University of Hawaii and my own alma mater, Colgate.[6] The unrest continued to grow with the assassination in June of Robert Kennedy in Los Angeles after he had won California's Democratic Party primary.

In college, I was active in student politics and had participated in several antiwar demonstrations and a sit-in at the administration building. But it wasn't until I stood face-to-face with bayoneted national guardsmen on

Michigan Avenue in Chicago, the night Hubert Humphrey won the Democratic Party nomination, that my real political awakening took shape.

My trip to Chicago had begun innocently enough. During the summer of 1968, I invited a Czech exchange student, Michal Kosta, to see American freedom and democracy in action. Michal's parents were top officials in the government of Alexander Dubček, who had breathed a little freedom into Communist Czechoslovakia, as the country existed then, with the Prague Spring.[7] A neighbor of mine who had been elected as a delegate to the Democratic National Convention had offered to get Michal and me tickets to the International Amphitheater gallery. Though one year shy of the twenty-one-year-old voting age, I had been eagerly leafleting in the Democratic primaries since "Clean Gene" McCarthy's antiwar position had driven President Johnson from the race.

Michal had come to the United States in June in anticipation of the start of the fall semester at Colgate. When he left home, the Prague Spring was in full bloom and Michal's parents were helping push the democratization of the Czech Communist Party. But by the time we got to Chicago in late August, Michal was a refugee. On August 21, Russian tanks had rolled into Prague. The only resistance came from Czech students and a few workers, and within days, Dubček was driven from power and thrown into prison. Fortunately, Michal's father was on a business trip in Italy when the Russians invaded; his mother escaped with his sister two days after the invasion through a mountain border crossing still manned by soldiers loyal to Dubček.

Michal and I never made it to the convention. Instead we were caught up in what the Walker Commission, a group put together by former President Eisenhower's brother Milton and chaired by Daniel Walker, vice president and general counsel of Montgomery Ward, called a "police riot."[8] Michal and I were prevented from getting near the amphitheater because of orders from Mayor Richard Daley to the Chicago police to keep all unauthorized people miles from the site. We wandered back toward Grant Park on the beautiful Lake Michigan shore. We listened to protest songs and speeches about the Vietnam War on a steamy August afternoon. Later in the day, comedian and political activist Dick Gregory energized the crowd. He even invited everyone in the park, fifteen thousand to twenty thousand protesters, observers, and police informants, to dinner at his house, conveniently located on the South Side of Chicago on the far side of the amphitheater.

Not expecting actually to have dinner with Gregory, Michal and I joined in the protest walk and were near the front of the long line of invited guests. Less than a half mile from the park, we could see the front of the pack stop and then start to waver. We could feel the energy lift, then heard the noise level rising and the people in front start to jumble together, some falling, some being pushed off into doorways and the cross streets. We were propelled forward by the people behind us until we could see what had stopped the marchers. The police were driving jeeps into the crowd of peaceful marchers—jeeps whose hoods were covered with chain-link fencing edged with barbed wire.

Then we saw more barbed-wire-covered jeeps driving into the crowd from the side streets with phalanxes of baton-and-shield-carrying policemen right behind. The entire march unraveled, with people screaming, running, jumping over the backs of the jeeps, scrambling across vacant lots, and getting away any way they could. Michal and I were part of that chaos. My memory is filled with images of jeeps, bodies, and police; being buffeted by bodies moving in every direction; the noise of the tumult; and then open space and silence. Somehow we had gotten off the main street and away from the jeeps. Hours later, drenched with sweat from running, Michal and I were on Michigan Avenue, across from the Hilton Hotel, the official site of the presidential candidates. By then, the National Guard had been called in and soldiers lined the avenue, bayonets fixed ahead of them.[9] Angry, confused, and sad, we walked right up to one of the National Guardsmen and Michal asked, "How can you do this to your own people while the Russian soldiers are in Prague?"

Decades later, that question still resonated in my head as I worked with Brandon and later Adel. Once again my country was responding out of fear and without understanding, flexing its muscles and striking out like a bully without precision, and innocent civilians were getting hurt.

Late in August 1970, fifty years after my great-grandfather was murdered, I headed north from the suburbs of New York City to Harvard Law School in Cambridge. The first stop on the trip was at the nursing home where my grandparents had just moved following a stroke that took part of my grandmother's mind. Shuffling with a cane to greet me at the front counter, my grandfather Julius was bursting with pride. I was proof to this Russian immigrant that the American dream was real, and he was one of the reasons I was going to law school. The story of Julius's life in the Pale of

Settlement in Russia, the poverty and lawlessness that ran rampant through-out that country and took my great-grandfather's life in a pogrom, had burrowed deep into my psyche. I viewed law as an instrument of social change and the rule of law as a fundamental protection for minorities and the oppressed.

In my last year of law school, Professor Cox's discussion about the Watergate scandal and his subsequent dismissal from the Nixon administration helped cement the connection for me among the abuse of power, personal responsibility, and public service. That same semester I tried my first case as a criminal defense attorney in the law school's clinical program. The seeds that had traveled across the ocean from Russia had taken root, but their growth was not yet assured. That would happen during my first years in practice as a judicial law clerk, then prosecutor, and finally as a defense attorney.

In the spring of 1981, two years after leaving the Brooklyn district attorney's office for the other side of the scales of justice, as the head of the Broome County Public Defender's Office in Binghamton, New York, I went to a New York State Defenders Association board meeting at Grossinger's, one of the decaying hotels in the Catskill Mountains. In Grossinger's glory days, the often jeans-clad and long-haired defenders would have been out of place and unwelcome in the midst of the leisure suits, fur coats, and buffet tables piled high with bagels, blintzes, and several kinds of lox. But by the early '80s, Grossinger's was hungry for business, and our less than affluent crowd of defenders blended in nicely with the chipped paint and frayed carpet.

I was exhausted when I checked in, having just completed a grueling trial for a Vietnam veteran who had been convicted of murdering his own children. Our defense had been built on a flashback to Chet's experiences in Vietnam, where he had been a body bagger along the insecure front lines. When the jury returned to the courtroom after two days of deliberations and announced its guilty verdict, one of the jurors, an older woman, was crying. She later called me to say that the jury had believed everything I had argued about Chet but could not forgive him for killing his children. I knew exactly how she felt. As much as I believed in Chet and the harm done to him by the Vietnam War, I could not get the images of his children out of my head. The trial had left me shaken and wondering how much more I could take.

It was at the board meeting that I talked to Milton Adler. Adler was in his early seventies and still working as a line assistant in the New York Legal Aid office side by side in the trenches with the kids who had just gotten out of law school. Milton had risen through the ranks at Legal Aid, and in the mid-1960s he became the chief of the Criminal Division, responsible for the hundreds of assistant defenders in the five boroughs of New York City. After a decade, he had tired of the political infighting and bureaucracy and gone back to what he loved best—representing the poor and downtrodden in trouble.

I was in awe of Adler, and mystified. I was feeling tired after only two years of defending and wondered how he had been doing it for nearly fifty. I asked him how had he kept his fight. And why. He fixed me with his dark eyes, set under bushy eyebrows and a head still full of wavy but graying hair. Part quizzical, part pity, part full of a wisdom that said if you stick with it, you will know, his answer has kept me going ever since whenever my energy has flagged. "If not me kid, who?"

Thirty years and thousands of clients later, the seeds planted in me by my family and nourished by Milton's words put me shoulder to shoulder with the alleged Muslim terrorists Mayfield and Hamad.

12 | A Life Exposed

Civilization is the progress toward a society of privacy. The savage's whole existence is public, ruled by the laws of his tribe. Civilization is the process of setting man free from men.

—Ayn Rand, *The Fountainhead*

"All right, Brandon. What are the problem areas?"

"What do you mean?"

"Look, it's difficult to prove a negative, that you had nothing to do with the bombing and don't know anything about it. So we need to assume the government thinks it has more on you than is in the affidavit. We need to figure out what they might be looking at or thinking about so we can try to explain what it really means."

Everyone on Brandon's team had read about FBI abuses under J. Edgar Hoover, the spying on Martin Luther King Jr. and infiltrating anti–Vietnam War groups.[1] We had even experienced out-of-control agents in some of our own cases. I had just finished a fraud case involving a group of Russian and Slavic émigrés where the main informer had taken his FBI handler for a ride and gotten more than $200,000 in cash out of the deals before he ran off to Canada.[2] But most of the agents we had dealt with over the years were intelligent, level-headed, and honest men and women. So we had to assume they had seen something more that worried them. All day Friday and over that first weekend, Brandon, Chris, and I kept returning to the question of problem areas. Over those three days, Brandon's life was laid bare and the list of possible issues kept growing.

We started with the basics. I asked Brandon, "Have you ever been arrested?"

"Yes, but nothing ever came of it."

Brandon went on to tell us how he had been driving home late one night when he was a teenager and his car went off the road. He broke a window of a car parked nearby and borrowed the jack to get his car going again. Nearby neighbors heard the noise and called the police. Even though he was taken to the police station, Brandon was never convicted and he paid for the damage he had done. Soon after, he entered the army. Nothing to worry about there, I thought, except, as I heard the story, it occurred to me his arrest and military service were both ways Brandon's fingerprints might have gotten into the AIFIS database.

"What was your discharge?" I asked.

"Honorable. Both times."

"*Both* times?"

"Yes. I was in for three or four years, separated, went to college then to Officer Candidate School, and then spent four more years as a lieutenant."

"What about protests, politics, people you see at the mosque?" I asked.

"Nothing. I've never been in a protest. I don't know any radicals. I'm mainstream. I'm struggling to support my family and raise my kids. I have cases pending in this courthouse. Look, Steve, I'm so mainstream, I voted for George Bush in 2000."

A George Bush supporter. Brandon would have had to undergo a 180-degree conversion to have any involvement in terrorism, I thought. Of course, that might also be the profile the FBI would suspect Bin Laden or others of his ilk would try to create for "sleeper cell" members—terrorists who looked like normal Americans until called upon to act. We kept talking, pushing Brandon, looking at what he had said under a high-powered microscope.

"What did you do in the army?" I asked.

"The first time I was pretty much a clerk and ran a teletype. The second time was much more interesting. I was stationed in Germany most of the time."

"What was your job on the second tour?"

"Air Defense Artillery," Brandon answered. "I worked on a Patriot missile unit."

Maybe this was something. My mind reverted back to my time as a prosecutor, as it often does when I am trying to figure out how the United States attorneys are assessing facts or evaluating a case. I was reaching back twenty-five years, but my training in Brooklyn had been intense. There were no easy cases in the DA's office when I was there in the 1970s. New York City was in the throes of a financial crisis, the office was even more underfunded than usual, and Brooklyn had not pulled out of the downward spiral that saw many of its neighborhoods change from vibrant middle class to crime quagmires in just thirty years.

As a prosecutor, I had cut my teeth on armed robberies, ransom kidnappings, and mass murders. I learned a lot in Brooklyn but never more than the year I spent at the side of a true master, Harold Rosenbaum, in the prosecution of Doc LeGrande for the murder of two teenage Puerto Rican girls.[3] Doc was a self-proclaimed minister with a cultlike following whose "nuns" worked the streets for donations during the day and worked the factories with their bodies at night. When anyone crossed Doc, he would kill them, and the DA figured his victims numbered in the twenties by 1975. There had been several prosecutions involving Doc and his sons over the years, but the DA's office had never been able to win a case and have it stand up on appeal, which was when Rosenbaum was brought in. He had been in the office for thirty years but had crossed the DA years before and was not assigned to any of the trial bureaus. Rosenbaum loved the work, though, and would not leave. Whenever there was a case that just had to be won, the DA grudgingly called on him to handle it.

The year I worked with Rosenbaum, I watched and learned how he put the LeGrande case together, then spun it out in a three-month trial. The case could have been scripted in Hollywood. The two teenage victims were murdered in the basement of Doc's "church," their bodies chopped up, driven upstate to Doc's "farm," burned, and the remaining bone fragments thrown in a lake. The girls would probably have been written off as missing runaways except one of Doc's henchmen had a falling out with Doc over one of the "nuns," and told the police what had happened. The DA's office rented a gold dredge to search the lake and pulled up hundreds of bone fragments, which were assembled into skeletons by the head of the anthropology department at New York's Museum of Natural History.

The drama continued throughout the trial, when one of Doc's "wives" broke out of the protective custody she had asked for to run back to the house where sixty of the cult members lived. A different "wife" was murdered during the trial, and one of Doc's sons testified for the defense that he was the murderer and brought a saw into the courtroom with him saying it was the very same one he had used to cut up the girls' bodies. Throughout the case, Rosenbaum took seemingly innocuous facts and made something of them, fitting them into his theory of the case.

Prosecutors are expected to be different from other lawyers and seek "to do justice," not just win.[4] In my experience, most prosecutors try hard to do that. But watching Rosenbaum in the LeGrande case, I saw one of the weaknesses of our adversarial legal system, how the roles its players are assigned shape how they view the facts. However objective we try to be, we understand and assess the facts we see from the perspective of our roles and our theory of a case.

This understanding of perspective and the prosecutorial skills I learned at Rosenbaum's side have helped me to avoid (as much as possible) the "self-hypnosis" of defense attorneys. I try to see the weaknesses in a case, and sometimes how to overcome them, how to take a bad fact, embrace it, and make it my own or gently push it aside. At this early stage of Brandon's case, I was conscious of the need to identify the weaknesses that the prosecutors might seize upon, and working on a Patriot missile battery was a distinct possibility. I recognized how the FBI and Gorder and his team of prosecutors could see that fact and believe Brandon was someone to worry about—knowing information about our nation's weapons systems and missile defense would certainly appear to make someone more dangerous.

What made Brandon's missile work even more of a problem was that he had done what so many soldiers do—brought home a souvenir from his time in the service. We knew that his souvenir was going to catch the eye of the FBI, if they had found it, which we had to assume they had. Brandon had brought home one of the books he had been issued describing the Patriot system. He couldn't remember it exactly and whether it was one he had been allowed to take out of the missile battery with him. There was no question in my mind that Gorder and the FBI were going to be suspicious, even though our own investigator, Jim Strupp, was able to download detailed information about the Patriot missile from the Internet.

When I talked with Judge Jones about Brandon's case years later, he confirmed how much of a problem the Patriot missile had been. The government had told him that they had found something about missiles, but when he asked to see it he was told it had been "shipped to Washington." Gorder was not able to tell him anything more about it. This "mystery document," as Judge Jones referred to it, hung over his decision on whether to release Brandon. He never did see it.

The Patriot missile connection wasn't the only suspicious piece. When Brandon was in the army the second time, he took over a platoon from Lieutenant Yee. At first, the name meant nothing to Chris or me. Brandon explained, "Captain Yee, the chaplain who got in trouble at Guantánamo earlier this year. He left the platoon to go to chaplain school."[5]

The fact that Brandon had crossed paths with Yee, who had been charged with violating the security at Guantánamo by transmitting messages from the prisoners, was bad because the FBI was likely to view it as something more than just a coincidence. Then Brandon added, "I researched Yee on the Internet."

The FBI was certainly going to have noted the Internet work on Yee and Guantánamo, and I was even more concerned that they would not have passed it off as a benign coincidence.

"What else might the FBI have found in the house during the searches?" I asked.

Brandon thought for a minute and said, "Well, Mona had a book on Osama Bin Laden a while ago. I can't remember if it was from a college course or someone gave it to her. It was probably in the house."

Great! Now the FBI was going to be thinking Brandon was a devotee of Bin Laden armed with Patriot missile technology.

"Anything else like that?" Chris asked.

"I owned a gun. Legal and all, but I have never used it," Brandon replied. Gorder had mentioned the gun to us and to Judge Jones, although he had described it as a stolen weapon. It turned out that the gun was perfectly legal, but at the time a supposedly stolen gun in his house weighed heavily against him.

Getting a clearer sense of how the government would likely be looking at him, Brandon put the icing on the cake. "I had a private pilot's license for a while, and I am sure there were books and papers in the house on flying."

To the mind of an investigator steeped in the belief that there were sleeper cells of Muslim terrorists all around the country, I could see the hairs rising on the back of any FBI agent's neck.

"All right, what about your computers. Is there anything on them we need to worry about?" I asked.

"This is getting offensive," Brandon said. "We use our computers. I looked up a number of sites after the bombings in Madrid. I have been on other sites that give an Islamic perspective on the news. Sharia [Brandon's twelve-year-old daughter] had a homework assignment this spring on a trip to Spain, so I am sure there are lots of travel sites."

He stopped.

"Oh, yeah, Shane [Brandon's fifteen-year-old son] is taking a class in Middle Eastern studies. He's been online, too."

From our conversations with Mona, Chris and I knew there was still another fact that the FBI would find highly suspicious—the $10,000 and passports neatly tucked away in a safe-deposit box that was opened in April.

"Brandon, where did the money in the safe-deposit box come from?" I asked.

He wasn't sure but believed it was left over from the sale of their house in Newport and said we would have to talk to Mona about it. I would have been much happier if Brandon had been able to give a direct and simple answer. Of course, when we spoke with Mona on Monday, she gave us the details of the sale of their house in Newport and the cash they were able to save even after buying their house in Portland. I then asked Jim Strupp to get all available financial records and start putting together a spreadsheet with exhibits. But the FBI wasn't going to look at the money in the same way.

Over the weekend Mona had brought us a list of Brandon's clients, and we spent several hours in the jail on Monday going over the list with Brandon. He had been reluctant to discuss their cases with us, concerned about breaching the attorney-client relationship by telling a third party, even his own lawyer. I spoke with the disciplinary counsel at the Oregon State Bar Monday morning, and they agreed that since the FBI had seized Brandon's client files, which could potentially be used as evidence against him, it would not violate his obligation to maintain client confidences if he discussed the cases with his attorneys. Many of Brandon's clients had Middle Eastern or Muslim-sounding names and many of the cases involved immigration issues. I could see how the prosecutors and FBI could view the names as suspicious.

Even without my prosecutorial training, it was apparent that there were strong reasons for the FBI and United States attorney to be suspicious of Brandon that went far beyond the facts set out in the arrest warrant affidavit: an arrest record, military training, a pilot's license, a supposedly stolen gun, a book on Bin Laden, Internet hits all over Spain, a safe-deposit box with $10,000 and passports. By noon Monday, my team knew that however much Brandon protested his innocence, Gorder and the FBI would test not only his statements against the fingerprint but also the facts set out in the affidavit about his religion and representation of a convicted terrorist. We also had to assume they had seen and seized everything Brandon had told us about in our meetings. As angry as I was that Gorder had presented Judge Jones with the FBI's affidavit referring to Brandon's religion, making it look like his arrest was based on a religious profile, I had to recognize that there were far more suspicious facts not included in the affidavit that we would have to deal with. Over the next week, we would hear about them in every discussion with Gorder and his colleagues.

13 | The Ice Man

*The person who strays away from the source is unrooted and is
like dust blown about by the wind.*

—Molefi Kente Asante[1]

THE MONIKER THE "ICE MAN" WAS FIRST whispered in the halls of the Multnomah County Courthouse when Judge Jones was in his first or second year
on the county bench. When the nickname caught up to the judge, it turned
out he didn't mind, and it has stuck with him ever since. Seventy-seven
years old at the time of Brandon's arrest, Judge Jones had been sitting on
one bench or another for forty years. As a young lawyer in the days before
the Oregon Republican Party was taken over by the religious right, Robert
Jones joined a group of progressive Republicans that later spawned gover-
nors, United States senators, state representatives, and state and federal
judges. Appointed to the Multnomah County Circuit Court Bench by Republican governor Mark Hatfield in 1963, Judge Jones served in the rough-
and-tumble county trial court for twenty years before being appointed to
the State Supreme Court in 1982. Judge Jones had wanted an appointment
to the federal bench in 1980 but was passed over even though President
Carter did end up putting a Republican and an independent on the bench
along with one Democrat. In 1990, Hatfield, then a United States senator,
finally got Judge Jones his turn with an appointment to the federal bench
by President Bush senior.[2]

The "Ice Man" described Judge Jones to a T. A midsized man at five eight, you'd never know it walking into his courtroom. Judge Jones "sat tall" on the bench, his back ramrod straight from his days in the navy and navy reserve as a captain, his large head rising from between his square shoulders, his face rigid, without a hint of a smile. As a county trial judge, Robert E. Jones was known as a terror. When you got to his courtroom, you needed to be prepared, and your client needed to expect to be glared at and grilled about why he should take the deal the prosecutor was offering. But unlike some of his counterparts, Judge Jones did not just coerce pleas from defendants. He would make up his own mind about what a case was "worth" and get the deal he thought should be offered from the assistant district attorneys.

When I met the Judge after his appointment to the federal bench, he told me about the time in the mid-'70s when the Multnomah County Court was so backlogged that the civil lawyers, whose cases had to follow the criminal cases, couldn't get anything to trial for years. The presiding judge at the time assigned Judge Jones to try his hand at getting rid of the backlog, and he rammed through more than one thousand pleas in three months. On the federal bench, the judge had proved to be just as practical and evenhanded.

When Judge Jones moved to the federal bench, he confronted the new federal sentencing guidelines, a bane to attorneys. The assistant United States attorneys and defense attorneys too often worked out a plea deal only to have the federal probation office, which prepares presentence reports for the court, rework the lawyers' guideline calculations and gum up the case. With Judge Jones, you did not have to worry about that. He understood that the professional prosecutors and defenders often had very good reasons for working out a plea bargain. Maybe the case wasn't as strong as it looked, maybe the police had messed up, or maybe the prosecutor understood the human problems of the defendant. In his court, all pleas were "contract" pleas. Judge Jones would tell the parties up front that they would get what they had bargained for. Sometimes he infuriated the probation staff, like the time he took a plea in a drug case where there was a question about whether the defendant had had a gun with him when he'd sold drugs to an undercover policeman. Judge Jones told the probation officer who was assigned to write up the case flat-out, "I don't want to see a gun in the presentence report."

When Brandon's case began, outward appearances suggested that the fourteen years Judge Jones had served since his lifetime appointment to the federal bench had not mellowed him much. He still sat ramrod straight, looked austere, and walked with the same carriage of authority. But I had gotten to know the judge off the bench over the years. Part of my job is to be a lawyer, but another part is to run the federal defender office, which includes developing and maintaining relationships with all the players in the criminal justice system in Oregon. Every year I attended the Ninth Circuit judicial conference, a meeting of all the judges on the West Coast, federal defenders, United States attorneys, and private lawyer delegates from each district. I have eaten my share of rubber chicken and overcooked steak at bar association dinners.

I had gotten to know Judge Jones as a man, a devoted father (his son is following in his footsteps as a judge), and a grandfather. I had often seen him with his high school sweetheart and bride of more than fifty years, doting Pearl. From functions and through work on a number of cases in his court, we had developed a mutual respect. I appreciated not only his evenhanded practicality but also his keen legal mind. The judge was a student of the rules of evidence, author of a treatise on evidence, and a frequent lecturer to other judges on the subject. He had even gone out of his way to compliment me publicly at some of the conferences and dinners over the years, and, while I certainly lost my share of arguments in his courtroom, it was clear that he appreciated that I was ready to go toe to toe with him on the law, facts, or procedure, but always with respect for his position.

In my first meetings with Brandon, I had told him that I thought we were lucky to get Judge Jones on the case. While he was not as moderate in his political views as some of the other judges we could have drawn, he wouldn't be cowed by the local prosecutors or the higher-ups in the Department of Justice and the FBI, which was probably the most important thing. We needed a judge who would not be swayed by pressure or public opinion, the magnitude of the Madrid horror, or international media frenzy.

Two years earlier, the Ice Man had shown his mettle in deciding *Oregon v. Ashcroft*, which was brought to court by Attorney General Ashcroft against Oregon's Death With Dignity Act—the law that authorized doctors in Oregon to assist the terminally ill in ending their lives with dignity. Due to the Bush administration's championing of states' rights, one might have thought they would have accepted a law passed directly by Oregon's voters in two referenda. But assisted suicide was not something they could leave alone. The attorney general filed a lawsuit to enjoin the suicide law's enforcement, arguing that the use of sedatives would violate federal narcotics laws.

In what was the first case ever to address these issues, and one that was watched around the world and upheld four years later by the Supreme Court, Judge Jones rejected the attorney general's arguments, placing clear limits on his power. He said, "To allow an Attorney General to determine the legitimacy of a particular medical practice . . . would be unprecedented and extraordinary."[3]

The Ice Man's practical side always influenced his rulings and had been apparent on that first day in court when the judge tried to cut through legal formalities and get Brandon to talk informally to the United States attorney in an Awadallah-like deposition. On Monday, May 10, after Chris and I had spent the weekend familiarizing ourselves with some of the issues in the case, Judge Jones was eager to keep the momentum going. He scheduled a conference in chambers for the lawyers early in the afternoon.

I had spent the morning with Brandon and the state bar professional liability lawyers trying to figure out how to handle Brandon's cases, and Chris had been in conference with Gorder and Atkinson about the media leaks and our need to know more about the FBI investigation. Meanwhile, Amy had hit the books to research a number of issues including the law on gag orders, whether we could get the judge to order the prosecutors to give us any information in a grand jury matter, and release issues for material witnesses.

Around 1:30, my team and I walked out the back entrance of our building onto Second Avenue to the private doorway of the courthouse a half block away, accessible to us with key cards, and traveled up the elevator to Judge Jones's fourteenth-floor chambers.

The judge's judicial assistant, Cindy Schultz, buzzed us in and we continued down the almost block-long hallway lined with photos of old Portland to the spacious waiting area. Gorder and Atkinson had already arrived, and Schultz waved all of us into the judge's work area, with its heavy maroon leather furnishings. Filling the bookshelves behind his oversized desk were copies of the evidence books he has authored during his long career on the bench.

The judge was steaming mad. Over the weekend he had seen the media coverage, and on Monday morning his chambers had been deluged with calls. The Ice Man started right in on Gorder and Atkinson.

"Let's get all of this business of putting all of this stuff out in the news in violation of what I consider to be professional restriction that people were obligated not to discuss the case."[4]

The judge then started to read aloud some of the news clippings his law clerks had pulled together that morning. The leaks had come from the very top. "A White House Bulletin" said, "Investigators found a perfectly formed fingerprint they couldn't identify . . . Federal officials told *Newsweek* that they doubt Mayfield has been innocently swept up in the case of international intrigue." Sifting through the pile of clippings, the judge went on, "Senior law enforcement officials in Washington said Mayfield had been under FBI surveillance for several weeks." The articles went on and on, and Judge Jones wanted to get his point across that the local prosecutors had better do something about the higher-ups in Washington. Then the judge turned toward me and read a couple of quotes from Tom Nelson, the lawyer who had been with Brandon at his first court appearance. Finally, he stopped reading and looked around the room, his gaze briefly falling on each of us.

"So, I guess what I'm emphasizing is that there's been leakage on both sides, and I understand that you want, both of you, all of you want this stopped. Is that right?

"Mr. Schatz."

"That's right, Your Honor," agreed Chris.

"Mr. Gorder."

"That's right, Your Honor," added Gorder.

We all did agree, but there was no way any of us could have said anything different given the look in the judge's eyes.

Gorder then told the judge that we had been working on a gag order that morning and he was embarrassed by the leaks. "I think it's time to do something along those lines because, frankly, it's compromising both our investigation and our integrity."[5]

But Gorder couldn't act without "input from Washington." Perhaps it was his reference to Washington that got the judge going again, prompting him to remind Gorder of problems the Justice Department had recently had with a terrorism prosecution in Detroit.

"I can just tell you that our co-author on our book here, Judge Rosen in Detroit, held the U.S. Attorney General Ashcroft in contempt and gave him a public reprimand for commenting on that litigation." He finished, "Of course since then that litigation was blown all up with all sorts of Brady violations and the like."[6]

The reference to the Detroit case was an admonition to Gorder. The prosecution of four men arrested in Detroit shortly after September 11, 2001, known as the "Sleeper Cell" case, had been trumpeted by the attorney general as a major breakthrough on the domestic side of the war on terror. While the case was ongoing, Ashcroft had publicly praised the government's key witness, calling him a "critical tool."[7] Judge Jones knew all about the case from his friend Judge Gerald Rosen. They were about as unlikely a pair of friends as one could find. Jones, a septuagenarian, grandson of a Congregationalist minister, Republican, and decorated veteran from the hinterlands of Oregon; Rosen, a midforties Jewish Democrat from one of the most urbanized areas in the country. But they shared a love of the rules of evidence and an abiding belief in the importance of a strong and independent federal judiciary as a check on the executive and legislative branches—particularly when those branches overreached their constitutional prerogatives.

Judge Rosen had been incensed by the attorney general's deliberate indifference to the rights of the alleged terrorists in the "Sleeper Cell" case. He had tried to deal with the leaks informally and through a gag order. But when the stories kept pouring out of Washington and the attorney general himself spoke out about the case, the judge had had enough. He personally and publicly rebuked Attorney General Ashcroft, saying that he had "exhibited a distressing lack of care" for the rights of the defendants.[8]

Judge Jones's reference to *Brady* was another reminder to Gorder about the prosecution's obligations in a criminal case. In addition to the ethical rules that govern all lawyers, prosecutors, with their unique power as representatives of "the people," are held to a higher standard. *Brady*, a case decided by the Supreme Court in the 1960s, made clear that prosecutors are obligated to give defendants information that could be helpful to their defense, such as evidence that a star witness has a record of perjury or if there is disagreement about a scientific test like a fingerprint.[9]

In the spring of 2004, the convictions in Detroit had been threatened when the defense learned that the prosecutors had withheld two key pieces of *Brady* material. The first was an admission by the star witness, about whom Ashcroft had spoken so flatteringly, that he had lied to his FBI handlers about the defendants' involvement in any plot. The second was the prosecution's denial that they had any photographs of a key piece of evidence, when in fact they did and the photographs showed that a supposed map of a defense installation was just an idle doodle. The Detroit terrorism fiasco had turned into an embarrassment not only for the Department of Justice but also for the country as a whole. Eventually the convictions were thrown out and the assistant United States attorney who had prosecuted the case was indicted on conspiracy and obstruction of justice charges.[10]

Judge Jones did not want any problems in his case, either with the prosecutors withholding evidence from my team or with leaks that would prejudice Brandon and threaten any potential prosecution. Fashioning a gag order, however, wasn't a simple matter. Most such orders tell the parties not to discuss a case with anyone, not just the media, and that if they do, they face a contempt of court citation. A broad order like that would have been devastating, preventing us from discussing what we had learned from the affidavit and from Brandon with potential witnesses. We would not have been able to ask about the secret grand jury matters, the detonator bag, the fingerprint, Brandon's alleged travel to Spain, the intrusions into the Mayfield home, his clients, what had been going on at the Bilal mosque, or anything about his background.

The judge was not going to leave the leaks issue open any longer than necessary or spend any more of his time on it. At the end of the hearing, he took control as only a federal judge can and urged us to come to some agreement and "provide a joint order" by the next morning.[11] The judicial encouragement worked, and we were able to present the judge with an order that barred any further dissemination of information to the press but authorized defense disclosures "as necessitated by legitimate defense investigation activity." It also allowed any disclosures necessary for us to deal with the Oregon Bar on Brandon's cases and practice.

After having made it clear at the outset that the leaks issue needed to be resolved, the judge then turned to the question of Brandon's testimony. He wanted to revisit the prior week's discussion of the Awadallah deposition procedure as an alternative to testimony in the grand jury. But we had to tell him there was no way Brandon could appear before the grand jury on the following day as scheduled. Nor was Brandon prepared to speak with the prosecutors in any other way. We simply did not have enough information available to us in order to advise Brandon to talk in any setting.

Even though Brandon, Chris, and I had spent many hours together over the past four days, our progress was slow and there was so much to cover: Brandon's law practice and clients, many of whom were originally from Middle Eastern and Southeast Asian countries; his time in the army; his friends, acquaintances, and contacts in Portland; Mona's family, Internet sites he and his children had visited; his representation of the convicted terrorist Jeffrey Battle and people he had come in contact with then. My investigators had just begun interviews with Brandon's family members and were reaching out to his friends, acquaintances, and business associates. Until we had a clearer picture of Brandon's life and corroboration of what he had been telling us, we told Judge Jones he was not going to talk to anyone. Acknowledging our position, the judge reset the grand jury appearance from May 11 to May 21.

The hearing then turned to the question of Brandon's law practice. When the FBI had searched Brandon's office, they had taken away scores of his client files. The search warrant had not directed the FBI to any particular files or put any limits on what they could remove. The only pattern we could see in the file seizures was that many had Middle Eastern or Muslim-sounding names. The seizure of privileged files is generally frowned upon, but in this instance it was even worse, as many of the cases involved immigration matters and other lawsuits against the United States—cases in which the seizure of the files put them in the hands of the defendants in the cases. Whether he was going to remain a witness or become a defendant, it was clear that Brandon was not going to be released from custody in the next couple of days and that something needed to be done to protect his clients.

We asked Judge Jones to order Gorder to return all the files to Brandon or at least deliver them to the court. Gorder objected strenuously, arguing that the FBI needed to review the files to see if they contained any information relevant to the investigation of the bombings and that Mayfield and his clients were protected because the United States attorney had set up what is called a "taint procedure," where only prosecutors who were not involved in the Mayfield matter would review the files beforehand and remove anything that they thought was privileged. My response to that was, "No, thanks." Everyone on the defense team felt that the "trust us, we're from the government" line just did not work. I asked the judge to appoint a special master, someone who worked directly for the court, to review the files instead. Judge Jones's answer was music to my ears: "I have time to do the evaluations myself."[12] This was one of the other things about the Ice Man—he loved to be involved in and informed about everything that was going on in his cases. Sometimes this took him a little beyond a strictly neutral judicial role, but now it worked to our advantage.

At 3:30 that Monday afternoon, the judge ordered Gorder to have the two bankers' boxes of law office files delivered to his chambers. By mid-afternoon the next day, he had finished his review and we had caught our first big break in the case. The judge had seen that Brandon operated a normal law practice and found no evidence of involvement in terrorist activities.

Judge Jones was now willing to work with us to get Brandon's law practice up and running again. I called his chambers late on Tuesday to discuss the logistics. Since Brandon's law practice did not involve issues related to the grand jury matter, the call I placed was ex parte, that is, without the prosecutors present. I pointed out that Brandon could not work on the files in the county jail as there was no space, no privacy, and no phone. Ever practical, the judge volunteered one of the empty law clerk offices in his chambers and said he would have the marshal bring Brandon to the court-house Wednesday morning and for however many days were necessary.

The next day, Brandon and I got an early start in the judge's chambers. Midmorning, Judge Jones wandered in to check on how we were doing. Seeing us huddled in that cramped interior space, the judge suggested we move to a nice conference room with a window—ironically, one whose view of Mt. Hood and the Willamette River was blocked by my office building and that looked out directly into the western side of the federal defender offices. The deputy marshal, who had been posted outside the law clerk office, realized there was no real security risk and had no problem with the move.

Brandon started going through his files, figuring out what needed his attention first. The Oregon Bar sent over lawyers to help him with court filings and client contact. As we worked, Judge Jones just could not stay away. His chambers business seemed to bring him past our conference room every half hour or so, and he would pop his head in and ask how things were going. Around one o'clock, the judge came by again and must have seen Brandon looking stressed and tired.

"Did the marshal bring you lunch?" he asked.

A couple of minutes later the Ice Man came back with a yogurt from his chambers refrigerator.

"Here, you look like you could use this." Whatever the flavor was, the judge seemed a little embarrassed by it and joked that he hoped it was all right.

This was our second big break of the day. Judge Jones had seen Brandon as a human being. In nearly every criminal case, one of the defense attorney's goals is to humanize the client, to get the judge, prosecutor, and jury to see him or her as just a fellow member of the human race rather than as the object "defendant," "rapist," or "terrorist." However much we try to treat everyone by the same standards in the criminal justice system, the same laws of human nature that cause us to dehumanize an enemy in war as the "other"—to make killing him easier—are at work in the courtroom. It is much easier to treat a "rapist" or "terrorist" more harshly than someone you see as your neighbor. Judge Jones had now seen Brandon as just another lawyer, and a tired and hungry one at that.

Brandon and I were back in the chambers Thursday morning when the judge wandered by again.

"Steve, do you have a minute?" he asked me. I stepped out into the hall where the judge was practically ready to burst, his ice mask completely melted.

"I just chewed Comey's ass."

I looked puzzled. The judge explained that Deputy Attorney General James Comey was in the building visiting the United States attorney that day and the judge had asked him to come up to chambers where, he said, "I personally served the gag order on him." He went on to tell me that he had told Comey that he better give the order to his boss, Attorney General Aschcroft, when he got back to DC. Apparently the deputy AG took offense and asked whether the judge was impugning the attorney general's integrity. That's when the "ass chewing" took place. I couldn't stop the smile that crept across my face as the Ice Man described the brief conversation. He told me he had warned Comey that the leaks were going to stop and that he would hold the attorney general personally responsible if they did not.

Brandon, my team, and I had been fortunate to have a couple of good days. We were nearly ready to turn to the bigger issues: the fingerprint and Brandon's release.

Adel and his daughters Zaynab and Tasneem, circa 1998. Source: Salwa Othman.

William Teesdale and the author greeting a local politician during Ana Sudan volunteer construction of another room at Adel's house. April 2007. Source: Steven T. Wax and William Teesdale.

Interviewing Adel's brother Hashem under the colored cloths brought in for the day at Adel's home. From left to right, William, Dr. Osman, the author, and Hashem. April 2007. Source: Steven T. Wax and William Teesdale.

Adel's house at 5 Bilal Lane, Peshawar, Pakistan. August 2006. Source: William Teesdale.

NOTIFICATIONS

1. A Combatant Status Review Tribunal (CSRT) has determined that you are an enemy combatant. Because you are an enemy combatant, the United States may continue to detain you.

2. In addition, you have been notified that you may challenge the lawfulness of your detention in a United States court. The following procedures are available if you want to challenge your detention in a U.S. court.

3. You may ask a civilian judge to look at the lawfulness of your detention through a process called a *petition for a writ of habeas corpus*. You may ask a friend or family member or a lawyer to file such a petition with the court. If you do not have a lawyer or a family member or friend who could file this petition for you, you may file your own petition. According to prior court rulings, petitions may be sent to:

United States District Court for the District of Columbia
333 Constitution Avenue, N.W.
Washington, DC 20001

If you do not wish to file a petition, you do not have to do so. However, a court will only consider your case if you file a petition.

Detainee ISN: _____   Date: _____

Signature of Officer Serving Notice: _____

Printed Name of Officer Serving Notice: _____

Notice that detainees can petition for habeas corpus.

Staff at the WAMY hospital including Adel and Dr. Najib.

PETITIONER: (DETAINEE'S NAME)

عادل حسن حمد

ألتمس من محكمتكم الموقرة النظر في طلبي هذا بعين
الإعتبار وكون أنني أعترض على إحتجازي بمعسكر الـ ٢ تحتجاز
بجوانتانامو باي بكوبا كقتلي عدو.
فإذن أريد أن أقدم عريضة دعوى it of Habeus

مع تقديري و إحترامي لكم و ثقتي بأنكم ستنصفة بني

Signed: _____   Date: 23 . 3 . 2005

ATCH 1

ISN 940

Adel Hamad's March 2005 handwritten petition for a writ of habeas corpus. Source: Mitzi Miller.

1	identified in excess of 15 points of identification during his comparison and has advised the
2	affiant that he considers the match to be a 100% identification of **BRANDON BIERI**
3	**MAYFIELD**.

7	8. In mid-April it became apparent that the preliminary findings of the Forensic
8	Science Division of the SNP concerning the fingerprint were not consistent with those of the
9	FBI Laboratory. As a result, a meeting was held between a representative of the FBI's

14	had not been rendered. The SNP also indicated that they had not gone into the level three
15	characteristics (ridge edges, ridge breaks, pores, and incipient ridge events) utilized by the
16	FBI when making their initial comparison. At the conclusion of the meeting it was believed

| 19 | comparison. I have been advised that the FBI lab stands by their conclusion of a 100% |
| 20 | positive identification that LFP#17 as the fingerprint of **BRANDON BIERI MAYFIELD**. |

Paragraphs from affidavit submitted to Judge Jones to secure Brandon's arrest. May 2004. Source: Mitzi Miller.

Latent fingerprint #17 lifted from the blue bag by the
Spanish National Forensic Police. March 2004. Source:
Mitzi Miller.

2. ANALYSIS

The enlargements consisted of latent 17 and a copy of the left index fingerprint taken from Mr. Brandon Mayfield. The enlargements had been marked by means of red dots placed on certain ridge characteristics. There were sixteen dots on each enlargement (see figure 1).

The expert failed to notice the difference in the core area, open delta in the latent mark and a closed delta in the known. In the known print, all the characteristics had been illustrated, but in the latent mark there was a gap with unmarked characteristics (see figure 2).

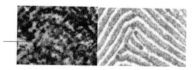

Figure 2, Core areas of latent 17 and the known print

At the top of the enlargements there were four ridge characteristics marked up in both impressions. These had no bearing to the other characteristics, (see blue arrows) which surrounded this formation (see figure 3).

Figure 3, Areas showing four dots at the top of the impressions.

The platform ridges below the deltas had been marked incorrectly, for example, there were characteristics shown in the latent mark, which were not in the known print.

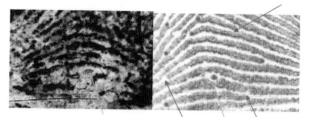

Figure 4, Areas showing platform ridges below the delta.

Excerpt from fingerprint expert Allen Bayle's report showing discrepancies between latent fingerprint #17 and Brandon's fingerprint. May 2004. Source: Allen Bayle and Mitzi Miller.

JAN-04-2005 13:09   CDRJ-OGC-FBI

                                                                    POLICE
     MINISTRY   HEADQUARTERS
     OF THE INTERIOR   FORENSIC SCIENCE
                                            REOCION   DIVISION

OFFICIAL LETTER

Your reference: Reg. Sda. N°001 N° 200400010480
                     POLICE REPORT 8470 DATED 3/17/04
                     FILE 20/04 COURT 6 NATIONAL HIGH COURT

Our reference: 57-IT-04

Madrid, 13 April, 2004

SUBJECT: __ANALYSIS AND COMPARISON OF FINGERPRINTS__

   In response to your document of reference, in which you requested the analysis and
comparison of three deca-dactylar cards belonging to BRANDON BIERI MAYFIELD, from the
FBI Laboratory in the United States, we inform you that the Special Proceedings Sections[1]
performed the appropriate studies[2] of the above mentioned, with the latent prints discovered
during the different crime scene inspections carried out as a result of the 11 March, 2004 terrorist
attacks investigations, as well as the deca-dactylar cards of the varied suspects that were given to
this Police Precinct. The result was NEGATIVE. We also report that the fingerprints have been
entered in our Automatic Dactylar Identification System for their respective study regarding
matters connected to the 11 March, 2004 attacks, as well as any other criminal activity. The
result was also NEGATIVE.

   The study of the deca-dactylar impressions is ongoing. If the results are positive, you will
be notified accordingly.

                         CHIEF SUPERINTENDENT

                         (SIGNATURE)

                     Signed: ████████████████████   O-1

   [1]TN: Section within the Forensic Sciences Division that works with the National High
Court in cases of terrorism, major disasters, etc.

   [2]TN: When the writer refers to the "appropriate studies" he/she means the analysis and
comparison of the deca-dactylar cards   DOCUMENT

April 13, 2004 letter from the Spanish government to the FBI telling them that the result of their comparison of latent fingerprint #17 with Brandon's fingerprint was "negative." Source: Mitzi Miller.

STEELE, ELIZABETH A. (PD) (FBI)
_____
From: (P), (S)   LA) (FBI)
Sent: Wednesday, May 05, 2004 10:12 AM
To: STEELE, ELIZABETH A. (PD) (FBI)
Subject: RE: LA Times

SENSITIVE BUT UNCLASSIFIED
NON-RECORD

Beth Anne,
No problem. No, I haven't received any inquiries but will play dumb and glean what I can if I do. I'll let you know immediately should I get a call. By the way, are you going to Quantico in June?
Take care (P), (S)

-----Original Message-----
From: STEELE, ELIZABETH A. (PD) (FBI)
Sent: Wednesday, May 05, 2004 9:16 AM
To (P), (S)   (LA) (FBI)
Subject: LA Times

SENSITIVE BUT UNCLASSIFIED
NON-RECORD

(P), (S)

I left you a voice mail this morning, but I figured this was a more secure way to leave the details for you.

There is a man living in the Portland area who has been tied to the Madrid bombings by a fingerprint found at the scene. His name is Brandon Mayfield, Muslim convert and attorney.

Earlier this week, an LA Times reporter in the Paris Bureau called the Legat in Spain, Ed Sanchez, to ask about information the reporter had heard that there was an American tied to the Madrid bombings. At that time, we don't think he had the name or location or the fact that the evidence is a fingerprint.

The problem is there is not enough other evidence to arrest him on a criminal charge. There is a plan to arrest him as a material witness if and when he gets outed by the media.

Neither the National Press Office nor the Portland Division has received any media calls as of this morning, and (P), (S)   thought is that, at some point, LA may receive a call from the Times trying to nail this down. If you do receive this call, we would just ask that you confirm nothing and try to get out of them how much they have and whether or not publication is imminent. The powers that be are trying to hold off as long as possible on any arrest, but they want to make sure an arrest happens before anything hits the media.

To complicate things, the Legat just notified Portland that he received an inquiry from a Spanish publication about the same thing, and it had the details about the evidence that it said it planned to publish "soon".

Thanks for your help,
Beth Anne Steele/FBI Portland
(503) 552-5238

SENSITIVE BUT UNCLASSIFIED

FBI 00093

L INFORMATION C (P), (S)
...REIN IS UNCLASSI...

E-mail from Beth Steel, Portland FBI office to Los Angeles FBI office, telling them they do not have enough evidence to charge Brandon so plan to arrest him as a material witness. Source: Mitzi Miller.

Brandon at the press conference, the author, AFPD Chris Schatz, and Brandon's children in the background. May 2004. Source: Federal Defender staff.

Brandon and the author at the press conference. May 2004. Source: Federal Defender staff.

14 | Something to Hide

What you don't see with your eyes, don't invent with your mouth.
— Yiddish proverb

GUANTÁNAMO HAS BEEN HOME TO U.S. Navy personnel since our fleet rode out the hurricane season in the beautiful bay in 1898 during the Spanish-American War. In 1903, Cuba granted the United States a perpetual lease for coaling and a naval station. The lease payments were set at $4,085 per year in 1934, but since Fidel Castro came to power in 1959, he has, symbolically, refused to cash the checks the U.S. government sends once a year.[1]

My clients and the other prisoners of the war on terror are not the first people to be held at Guantánamo. In the early 1990s, when our coast guard and navy picked up thousands of Haitian boat refugees trying to make their way to Florida, they were initially taken to Guantánamo while the Clinton administration decided what to do with them.[2] So there were already some facilities in place when the Bush administration decided to bring prisoners there from Afghanistan. But the Bush administration's intention to make use of Guantánamo as a more permanent facility was made visible in April 2002, within months of the arrival of the first prisoners, when a larger prison, Camp Delta, was built only a short distance from Camp X-Ray—a dusty area of temporary shacks surrounded by double fences of razor wire that had been used to hold some of the Haitian refugees a decade earlier. Camp Delta, also filled with barrackslike structures designated Camps 1–4 and surrounded by razor-wire fencing, can house more than four hundred prisoners.

While domestic and international voices have been calling for the shutdown of Guantánamo for years, during my three visits to the prison during 2006, I saw that the Bush administration was paying no heed. In fact, two new state-of-the-art permanent concrete and steel prison structures were going up right across the road from Camp Delta. When I visited in March, Camp 5 had just been completed and Camp 6 was under construction. By the time of my visit in December, both prisons were in full operation. While Adel had not been moved there, one of my office's other clients had. The habeas attorneys who visited clients in the new prisons reported that the men are kept in isolation much of the time and that conditions are much harsher than in Camp Delta.

The tougher conditions in the new sections of the prison came as no surprise to the habeas lawyers given the continued statements by Bush's team, including the commander of the forces at the prison at Guantánamo known as JTF, or Joint Task Force, Guantánamo, Admiral Harry Harris, who told the *New York Times,* "They're all terrorists; they're all enemy combatants. . . . I don't think there is such a thing as a medium security terrorist."[3]

Seton Hall Professor Mark Denbeaux's analysis of the Department of Defense material released in the Associated Press lawsuit revealed that the overwhelming majority of the men were not in fact combatants picked up on battlefields.[4] Many, like Adel, were arrested in their homes. Some were even literally sold for bounties when the administration offered $5,000 for Al Qaeda fighters in Afghanistan and Pakistan in 2001 and 2002. Some of the bounty payments ended up going to people supporting rival warlords and other unscrupulous characters. Despite Admiral Harris's statement, a fair number of the prisoners, including Adel, had long and distinguished careers, including histories of working for legitimate charities that served thousands of starving and uprooted people. Denbeaux's research has been supported by reports from prisoners who have been released, such as Shafiq Rasul, Asif Iqbal, Moazzam Begg, and others.[5] Similar comprehensive studies have been produced by Human Rights Watch and Amnesty International.[6]

In July 2007, a government-commissioned study by the Combating Terrorism Center at the army's military academy at West Point criticized some of Denbeaux's findings, but even their research concluded that only 53 percent of the detainees "definitively supported or waged hostile activities."

Only 35 percent, according to the study, were identified as fighters for Al Qaeda, the Taliban, or affiliated groups.[7]

The competing claims about the prisoners have never been tested in a court of law, military or civilian, or by any independent visitors, as a result of the policies of the Bush administration. No one can visit the prison without a military clearance. Hence no pickets, no protests, no escapes, no attacks, no visits, no reporters, and no independent observers. And the administration's view at the beginning, as it is today, is that Guantánamo Bay, Cuba, is outside the jurisdiction of the U.S. courts. So there has been no review by any federal judges. For five years now, the administration has acted as though U.S. law and the Constitution do not reach Guantánamo and has done everything in its power to obstruct Adel and the other prisoners from having a day in court or contact with the outside world. This even after two Supreme Court decisions told the administration that the courts did have jurisdiction there.

The administration has not simply been holding the men in Guantánamo as regular prisoners in cells but rather as intelligence assets, men who could tell them about Al Qaeda, its structure, and its methods of operation. From the beginning, as was done with Adel, the prisoners were squeezed for all their interrogators could get. There is no question that some of the men held in Guantánamo had information about the opposition forces in Afghanistan that would be useful to the military. Some had information about Al Qaeda and Bin Laden. Some men with valuable information, including one of my clients, talked freely, while others did not. Still others, including Adel, were innocent and knew nothing.

Regular interrogations continue with nearly all of the prisoners today. Three and a half years after Adel was seized, he asked me, "If I ever knew anything, what could I add today that would have any value?"

Adel's question was echoed by several of my other clients. Four or five years is surely long enough to get any reliable information the men ever possessed. The first time the Supreme Court looked at Guantánamo during Hamdi, Rasul, and Padilla's cases in June 2004, it concluded not only that it made no sense to hold prisoners for years just to interrogate them but also that it violates our Constitution to imprison men for prolonged periods if the only purpose is interrogation.[8]

But timing is not the only issue here. As the first reports about our government's treatment of the prisoners in Guantánamo began to leak out in 2002 and 2003, it became clear that the government had a great deal more to be worried about if the situation were brought to light in a court of law. Interrogation techniques that violated international norms and that many consider torture were being used, and they were approved and justified at the top.[9]

According to a Department of Defense report released in April 2005 called "Investigation into FBI Allegations of Abuse at Guantánamo Bay Detention Facility," on December 2, 2002, Secretary of Defense Rumsfeld approved a list of sixteen interrogation techniques.[10] These practices were detailed in a lawsuit the American Civil Liberties Union filed against Rumsfeld and included chaining prisoners' hands and feet to the floor in a "stress position," twenty-hour interrogations, stripping detainees of all their clothes during interrogations, inducing stress through detainee phobias, isolation for up to thirty days, sensory deprivation, use of falsified documents, and pretending interrogators were from countries known to use outright torture or that prisoners were about to be flown to those countries.[11]

None of these methods are new. What was new was that they were being sanctioned by the U.S. secretary of defense rather than a dictator.

Fortunately, Rumsfeld's list was too extreme for the professional interrogators in the FBI and some of the secretary's colleagues within the Department of Defense, and he succumbed to the pressure, rescinding his original directive. He was not done with the issue, however, and soon approved a new list that eliminated some of the techniques but still included thirty-day isolation, dietary, sensory, and environmental manipulation, sleep adjustment, and the method of pretending interrogators were from countries that overtly use torture.[12]

Rumsfeld's lists ratified most of the interrogation methods used in Guantánamo throughout 2002. The first interrogations took place in Camp X-Ray, where the prisoners were subjected to them daily by agents from the armed forces, the FBI, the CIA, and other civilian agencies. These were not gentle interrogations. The sleep deprivation, standing for long periods, and constant bullying that Adel had experienced in Baghram were only the tip of the iceberg.

Numerous interviews with men still imprisoned in Guantánamo, and with some who have been released, have described weeks of little sleep, being forced to dress in women's underwear, sexual advances by menstruating women, urination on the Koran, and simulated drowning by putting burlap bags over a prisoner's head and pouring water over the bag. Men were told that they were being sent home, blindfolded, earmuffed, muzzled, chained, and put on airplanes that flew in circles for hours only to land back at Guantánamo. Interrogators told the detainees that they were lawyers sent to help them. Some men were subjected to prolonged sensory deprivation—seeing no one, some for days, others for months on end. Others were then bombarded with blaring sounds, leading to sensory overload.[13]

Complaints about these techniques did not come only from the detainees and their habeas lawyers. FBI agents who were sent to Guantánamo to participate in the interrogations reported back to headquarters that things were out of control, that the methods being used were over the top, unnecessary, and might be illegal. The stream of FBI complaints flowed so strongly that the Department of Defense was finally impelled to respond.

While its "Investigation into FBI Allegations of Abuse at Guantánamo Bay Detention Facility" whitewashes many of the incidents cited by FBI agents, finding them consistent with the Rumsfeld directives or noting that offending personnel had left the military, the report does confirm that most of the incidents that offended the FBI's professional interrogators had taken place. Some of the agents' letters, e-mails, and reports that led to the military's investigation are available thanks to a Freedom of Information Act lawsuit filed by the ACLU.[14] The fact that under our system a group like the ACLU was able to force the government to disclose this information is about the only thing that distinguishes the goings-on in Guantánamo from the types of regimes Americans generally abhor.

Although large portions of the FBI complaints were heavily censored when the Department of Defense released them to the ACLU, enough remains to get a chilling picture of the interrogation sessions. One report stated that female personnel were repeatedly used in interrogations to cross the strict Islamic rules against male-female contact. The female interrogators would approach the prisoners in a sexual way, perfume was rubbed on one detainee, an interrogator rubbed her body against a prisoner's back while whispering in his ear and running her fingers through his hair, and a third showed a prisoner a blood-covered hand (actually ink), then wiped her hand on the prisoner's arm and told him it was menstrual blood—a contact that would be degrading in any culture and is anathema in Islam.[15] The report does not say whether the women volunteered to approach the men in this way or were asked or directed to use their sex to get to the prisoners.

Although the report details sexual interrogations by women, most of the interrogators at Guantánamo are men, who use their strength rather than sex to bully and frighten their subjects. The report also confirmed a long litany of the less overtly physical techniques, such as painfully loud music, extreme heat or extreme cold, short shackling—chaining a prisoner's hands and legs to the floor so he has to stay in a stooped position for hours at a time, and use of dogs.

In 2006, the habeas team at the Center for Constitutional Rights published a comprehensive report detailing the treatment of the prisoners in Guantánamo.[16] Lakhdar Boumediene, whose habeas corpus case became the focus of much of the legal fighting in 2006 and 2007, described several occasions in early 2002 when guards returned him to his cell following interrogation, grabbed him under his armpits, lifted him up, and threw him to his cage floor repeatedly while his wrists were shackled to his waist and his feet to an anchor in the floor. Sami Al-Laithi, a prodemocracy English teacher from Egypt who was determined to be "no longer an enemy combatant" on May 10, 2005, and was later released, is now confined to a wheelchair as a result of beatings he sustained by the U.S. military. In an affidavit filed in the district court in Washington, DC, in 2006, Al-Laithi stated, "Once they stomped my back, an MP threw me on the floor, and they lifted me up and slammed me back down. A doctor said I have two broken vertebrae and I risk being paralyzed if the spinal cord is injured more." A juvenile prisoner listed only as "O.K." was held for a month in isolation in a room that was kept at a chilled temperature, much like a refrigerator. Abdallah Najez Sayyah Hassal Al Noaimi was one of many men who reported being short-shackled. Another prisoner, Mohammed Al-Qahtani, reported fifty days of sleep deprivation.

Al-Qahtani, who is alleged to be a confidant of Bin Laden and the "twentieth hijacker" who tried, but failed, to get into the United States in August 2001, was seen as such an important source of information and so impervious to standard techniques of interrogation that a special plan was devised for him.[17] His interrogators not only subjected him to sleep deprivation but also interrogation that lasted for twenty hours each day, poured water over his head at least seventeen times, strip-searched him in front of women, forced him to wear a bra and also a thong on his head, led him around on a leash tied to his chains, called his mother and sister whores, and restricted his ability to pray.

When Illinois senator Richard Durbin learned in June 2005 about the degradation of Al-Qahtani, he could not contain himself: "If I read this to you and did not tell you that it was an FBI agent describing what Americans had done to prisoners in their control, you would most certainly believe this must have been done by Nazis, Soviets in their gulags, or some mad regime—Pol Pot or others—that had no concern for human beings."[18]

Vice President Cheney also spoke out about Al-Qahtani's treatment, but his reaction could not have been more different from Durbin's. "The important thing here to understand," he said, "is that the people that are at Guantánamo are bad people."[19]

One of the premises of the "torture memos" justifying these harsh techniques was the belief that the tougher the interrogation, the better the information that could be obtained to help fight the war on terror. However, the FBI complaints questioned not only the morality and legality of these methods but also their efficacy, saying the tough techniques didn't work and were likely to produce false information.

"In my weekly meetings with the Department of Justice," wrote Thomas Harrington, an FBI counterterrorism expert who led a team of investigators at Guantánamo, "we often discussed techniques and how they were not effective or producing intelligence that was reliable." Harrington's assessment was echoed by another agent who wrote in an e-mail dated May 4, 2004: "Our Behavioral Assessment Unit disagreed with the use of specific techniques in the case of [redacted] as they opined that the techniques would not be successful and they could produce unreliable results."[20]

The concern about the reliability of the information obtained in Guantánamo went beyond the FBI. Retired Colonel Jack Jacobs, a Vietnam Medal of Honor recipient and faculty member at West Point and the National War College, told *Newsweek* in November 2005, "At the end of the day, it's very easy to distinguish between the right thing and the wrong thing to do. If you do the wrong thing, you're not going to get any positive payoff from it and it's going to be at some great cost. We get much more information if we treat people properly."[21] Jacobs added that an interrogator needs to be aggressive, but "if you treat people inhumanely, they're just going to tell you what they think you want to hear" to get the mistreatment to stop.

My staff and I learned all about the lies people tell under torture from one of our other clients in Guantánamo, Abdur Rahim Al Ginco. When we were assigned to represent him in the spring of 2006, Al Ginco had been in prison longer than anyone else in Guantánamo, but in a cruel twist of fate, his first year and a half had been in a Taliban prison. Al Ginco, a Syrian Kurd visiting in Afghanistan in 2000, was conscripted by the Taliban and sent to a military training camp. He did not adjust well and after only eighteen days was denounced as an Israeli and American spy and thrown in prison. For a year and a half he was tortured, beaten, abused, and humiliated. He was beaten on the soles of his feet until they were so swollen and blackened that he could not walk. He was subjected to electrotorture, hung from the ceiling by his arms, and nearly drowned. Under the torture, Al Ginco made at least two tapes for the Taliban, confessing that he was a spy (he was not), confessing that he was a homosexual (he is not), and saying that he was now ready to atone for his past by becoming a jihadist and suicide bomber (he was not). Unfortunately, when the tapes were found, Attorney General Ashcroft got into the act and announced their discovery personally. We will never know whether the Americans had any knowledge of the circumstances under which the tapes were made, but Al Ginco, who had been staying in the prison in Kandahar as a guest of the Americans after our army had liberated it in December 2001, was thrown back in as a prisoner and soon taken to Guantánamo. Our efforts to convince the government that the tapes were a product of torture finally bore some fruit in the fall of 2007, when the government looked at the evidence we had given them, looked again at its own records, and decided to take another look at Al Ginco's case.

. ▪ ▪

Fortunately for Adel, my six other clients, and the rest of the prisoners in Guantánamo, when Base Commander Geoffrey Miller left the base in 2003 for Abu Ghraib, calmer heads prevailed and the intensive interrogation techniques pervasively used in the first year and a half were stopped.[22] But the prison still remained a horrific place, where the men were cut off from the outside world, denied the treatment required for prisoners of war under the Geneva Conventions, denied any way to prove their innocence, and forced to live indefinitely as prisoners of a war in a place run with ever-changing rules. From what I have witnessed, the result has been hopelessness and despair. Some of the prisoners, like Adel and several of my other clients, are remarkable human beings with an inner strength and grace that enables them to carry on with humor and dignity. Others, however, are not as resilient. Psychosis is a serious problem in Guantánamo. So is suicide.

Late spring 2006 was a particularly difficult time for the prisoners. When I saw Adel at the end of May, he was in reasonable spirits and his sense of self and humor were intact. Two of my other clients, on the other hand, were not doing well, and shortly after I left the base, three other prisoners, Manei Shaman turki al Habadi, Yasser Khalial al Zahrani, and Ali Abdullah Ahmed, committed suicide.[23] Over the weekend of June 10, they succeeded in taking their lives, probably by stuffing their mouths with wads of cloth that Colonel Mike Baumgarner, the commander of the guards at the prison, reported finding in each man's mouth. Habadi had been protesting his imprisonment as a hunger striker since June of 2005. Zahrani had been imprisoned since he was eighteen and, like Habadi, had been on a hunger strike for more than one year. He was only twenty-two years old when he took his life. In the statement he gave on the suicides, Admiral Harris, who had just taken over command of JTF-Guantánamo on April 1 from General Jay Hood, said that Ahmed had not been on a continuous hunger strike but he had gone on strike several times in the past year.

Just how vast the divide is between the military's and prisoners' views of who they are and what is happening in the prison can be seen in Admiral Harris's press statement about the deaths on June 10. According to the admiral, these were not suicides: They "were not an act of desperation, but an act of asymmetrical warfare committed against us." The deaths he said showed that the detainees "have no regard for life."[24]

"Asymmetrical warfare" is a phrase used by military planners at least since the early 1990s to describe tactics of a smaller, perhaps guerrilla, force against a much stronger power.[25] The smaller power knows it is no match for the larger's army, so it uses hit-and-run or disruptive tactics, like IEDs against American Humvees or tanks in Iraq. In calling "suicide" an act of warfare, Admiral Harris was saying that the control the JTF had over the prisoners in Guantánamo was so great that the only way they had of striking back at the Americans was to take their own lives. He could not acknowledge that the total control may have driven some of the men to total despair about their conditions.

While overt torture was stopped in Guantánamo several years ago, men who are not immediately compliant with the arbitrary and ever-changing rules, or are too psychotic to understand what is wanted of them, still experience forceful beatings, disrespectful treatment, and prolonged isolation and sensory deprivation. And for some of the hunger strikers, said by the Department of Defense to have peaked at 130 prisoners in 2005, the prolonged force-feeding they are subjected to amounts to torture of a different kind.[26]

.   .   .

In the face of international reports, reports from released detainees, and complaints by FBI agents, the administration has continued to assert that all is well in Guantánamo and that all the prisoners are fighters. Commenting on an International Committee for the Red Cross report on conditions in Guantánamo in November 2004, General Richard B. Myers, chairman of the Joint Chiefs of Staff, said, "We certainly don't think it's torture." He continued, "Let's not forget the kind of people we have down there. These are the people that don't know any moral values."[27] Two years later, President Bush continued to assert that all the prisoners were "picked up off the battlefield in Afghanistan."[28]

No matter how damning the reports about Guantánamo and continual the stream of reports about innocent men like Adel who were seized far from any battlefield, the Bush administration has continued to spout its line that there are no innocent men at Guantánamo and has gone to extreme lengths to keep from being challenged by an airing of the truth in court where sworn testimony could be taken in a public forum. In doing so, the administration has asserted powers that threaten the fabric of our government.

15 | The Cavalry Is Coming

The constitution will endure as a vital charter of human liberty as along as there are those with the courage to defend it, the vision to interpret it, and the fidelity to live by it.

—Justice William J. Brennan Jr.[1]

LATE IN THE SUMMER OF 2005, WHEN I got word from the district court in Washington that it was going to assign federal defenders to represent some of the prisoners in Guantánamo and that my office was on the list, I put myself and my team through a crash course on the history of the habeas corpus litigation. The three and a half years since CCR had filed the first habeas petitions had been packed with legal action, and we needed to understand what had come before if we were to have any chance of pushing forward for our clients.

As I delved into the history of the litigation, I studied the case of Yaser Hamdi that had reached the Supreme Court in 2004 and was chilled to see the reality of my warning to Brandon that he might be taken out of the justice system to a military brig. Hamdi, a U.S. citizen of Saudi descent, had been picked up on the battlefields in Afghanistan and taken to Camp X-Ray in Guantánamo.[2] When the DOD was finally convinced that Hamdi was an American citizen, they did not release him or bring him back to face criminal charges for conspiring to wage war against the United States. Instead, the DOD transferred Hamdi to the brig at the naval station in Norfolk, Virginia, where he was held in legal limbo without either military or civilian charges.

While Hamdi was still in Guantánamo, the lawyers at CCR filed what is called a "next friend" habeas petition for him, a petition filed at the request of a family member or friend on behalf of a prisoner who is being held incommunicado. After Hamdi was moved to the brig in Virginia, CCR's habeas petition moved through the courts on a track parallel to the petitions for the men who were still imprisoned in Guantánamo. The administration told the court it had to dismiss Hamdi's petition for many of the same reasons it said the Guantánamo petitions needed to be thrown out—he was not a prisoner of war so had no rights and the Geneva Conventions were not applicable. They also added the argument that no petition could go forward unless the "next friend" met and got permission from the prisoner, an impossibility given the full restrictions on visitation.[3]

When CCR filed its massive "John Doe" petition in 2005 to try to get all the detainees who had never met a lawyer into court, the administration said CCR had no basis for speaking on behalf of men they had never met. This was a classic Catch-22 argument because, as they had with Hamdi, the administration would not let the lawyers contact any prisoners who had not sought help.

The first legal battles for Rasul, the Kuwaitis, and Hamdi raged for more than two years. Every day, during which the administration's arguments that the federal courts had no power or jurisdiction to act were being contested, was a victory for the administration because the prisoners remained incarcerated and the interrogations went on. Meanwhile, the administration continued to bring in more prisoners, eventually running nearly eight hundred men through the prison between 2002 and 2007.[4]

CCR lost the first two rounds of the legal battle in the District of Columbia district court and then in the DC court of appeals, the intermediate appellate court in Washington that has been stacked with supporters of President Bush. Both courts bowed to the president's arguments that the U.S. courts had no jurisdiction in Guantánamo.

The lawyers at CCR, Tom Wilner for the Kuwaitis, and their pro bono colleagues were not daunted by the defeats and asked the Supreme Court to take the case. The administration vigorously objected but, on November 10, 2003, the Court agreed to hear Rasul's and Hamdi's cases. The Court also granted review of the habeas petition that had been filed by José Padilla, the U.S. citizen who had been arrested at the Chicago airport and taken out of the federal court system to be held indefinitely in military custody.

The problem was that as soon as the Supreme Court granted the petitions for writs of certiorari and agreed to hear the cases, the administration switched tactics. As part of its campaign to throw every conceivable obstacle in the way of judicial review of its actions in Guantánamo, the president and his staff apparently decided that putting a benign face to the world might help defuse any negative court action. Less than a month after the Supreme Court accepted the cases, the administration granted the first ever visit by an attorney to a prisoner. They allowed Stephen Kenny, an Australian human rights lawyer who had joined CCR in the representation of the Australian David Hicks, to visit Guantánamo.[5] This turned out to be the first in a series of public relations moves strategically timed around various court actions over the prisoners and something I was personally to experience several years later.

While the administration orchestrated its PR campaign, its briefs and arguments in the Supreme Court did not stop at the question of federal court jurisdiction in Guantánamo but went on to make sweeping statements about presidential power to detain enemy combatants indefinitely without any charges or trial in any court, civil or military. Solicitor General Ted Olson told the Supreme Court in the administration's brief, "Exercising jurisdiction over habeas actions filed on behalf of the Guantánamo detainees would directly interfere with the Executive's conduct of the military campaign against al Qaeda and its supporters."[6]

In the district court, Attorney General Ashcroft had asserted that there should be no habeas corpus jurisdiction to question the petitioner's detention because that involves "determinations left to the President's sole discretion."[7] As former deputy secretary of defense John Hamre told the Judicial Conference of the Ninth Circuit Court of Appeals, the federal appeals court that hears 38 percent of all federal appeals, at its annual meeting in July 2005, the Bush administration's assertions of presidential power are unprecedented and dangerous.

The prisoners' cases were set for argument in the Court on April 20, 2004. Just weeks before its brief was due, the administration made another move that could have been calculated only to affect the cases. On March 9, after two years of steadfastly maintaining that the British citizens Rasul and Iqbal were among "the worst of the worst," the DOD simply announced that the men were going to be released.[8] There was no revelation about new evidence or a statement that the military had discovered, after all, that neither man was a terrorist or supporter of Al Qaeda. The decision seemed to be driven purely by legal politics.

The Supreme Court, however, did not bite and duck the cases but went forward with the argument as scheduled. The primary lawyer for the prisoners was retired Federal Judge John Gibbons, a Nixon appointee who was never known as a liberal. The fact that a lawyer of Gibbons's stature and conservative background argued for the prisoners underscored the importance of the cases and how far out of the mainstream the administration's arguments were.

But the moral force in the cases was Fred Korematsu, who joined the Guantánamo prisoners' cause by filing an amicus, or friend of the court, brief with the Supreme Court. Korematsu was one of the 112,000 Japanese Americans who had been "interned" under an earlier presidential directive that the nation eventually repudiated. On February 14, 1942, General Dewitt, the commander of the Western Defense Command, had recommended the removal of "Japanese and other subversives" from large parts of the West Coast. Five days later, President Roosevelt issued Executive Order 9066, authorizing the secretary of war to establish military areas on the West Coast. Then on March 2, General Dewitt set the removals in motion.[9]

Korematsu, whose family lived in Oakland, California, where he worked in a shipyard, refused to comply with the directive to report to the local "processing center." He was charged with violating the order, convicted, and sent to the Topaz internment camp in Utah. But he did not give up and two years later took his case to the Supreme Court. In a ruling issued in 1944, which William O. Douglas later called the worst mistake he ever made as a Justice, the Court upheld the internments.

The brief Korematsu filed in support of Rasul and Iqbal decried their indefinite detention. Pointing to his own internment, Korematsu reminded the Court that "history teaches that, in time of war, we have often sacrificed fundamental freedoms unnecessarily." He urged the Court to avoid "repeating the mistakes of the past."[10]

Writing for a six–three majority of the Court in Rasul's case, Justice John Paul Stevens's opinion handed the Bush administration a stinging defeat. He wrote that the Guantánamo detainees could challenge the legality of their

detention in federal court under 28 USC 2241, the statute that has effectu-
ated the writ of habeas corpus since 1789.

The Court's strong language about the historic importance of habeas
corpus as a check on the power of kings and presidents underscored its
rejection of the administration's efforts to avoid judicial scrutiny by placing
the detainees in Guantánamo.[11] The Court flatly rejected the administration's arguments that the writ did not reach to the prison based on the fact
that the treaty between the United States and Cuba had given the United
States virtual sovereignty on the base for a century. The Supreme Court's
ruling in June should have sent many of the prisoners home, but, as I was
soon to find out, the administration refused to accept the core of what the
Supreme Court decided and, instead, seized upon the fact that the Court
had ruled only based on the statute that enacted habeas corpus and not on
any of the underlying constitutional rights.

While six justices joined in the opinion of the Court for Rasul, there was
no clear majority in Hamdi's case, which fractured the Court four ways.
Justice O'Connor wrote an opinion that three of her colleagues joined that
tried to balance the competing needs of the executive during a time of war
against the rights of American citizens to due process of law. While refusing to order Hamdi's release or trial, Justice O'Connor did write that the
executive's power was clearly limited even in a time of war and that Hamdi
was due some process to determine whether the government could keep
him in prison any longer. She did not spell out the type of process that was
due but said it was clearly not necessary to insist on a full criminal trial.
As for detaining men "for the purpose of interrogation," Justice O'Connor
said it "is not authorized."[12]

Justices David Souter and Ruth Bader Ginsburg disagreed that the government could hold Hamdi without charge but joined Justice O'Connor's
discussion about the limits on the process he should have. Justice Clarence
Thomas, on the other hand, followed much of the administration's line and
said that the Court should not intervene in Hamdi's detention and that Justice O'Connor had gone too far in saying he was entitled to any process.

The final opinion was the most unusual. It brought together the two justices who normally sit on the ideological poles of the Court: Justice Stevens,
the oldest justice, a Republican appointed by President Ford who has held
the mantle as the most progressive justice since Justice Thurgood Marshall's

retirement in 1991, and Justice Antonin Scalia, the acerbic Reagan appointee who repeatedly rails against the opinions of even his conservative Republican colleagues. These strange bedfellows united in stating that the government must either put up or shut up—indict Hamdi on criminal charges or let him go. They saw no middle ground under our Constitution for holding a civilian American citizen in military custody without a formal criminal charge.[13]

But in the end, the debate over the type of hearings required for men charged by the military in the war on terror did not affect Hamdi. In yet another of its moves to avoid an adverse court ruling, the administration announced on September 27 that it had reached an agreement with Saudi Arabia to send Hamdi there. The deal called for this U.S. citizen to be permanently banished from the United States, to renounce his citizenship, and to stay in Saudi Arabia for at least five years. He was also required to agree not to sue the government over his arrest and imprisonment. On October 10, Hamdi was flown to Saudi Arabia.[14] Even though he had won a right to a hearing from the Supreme Court, his case was officially over.

Padilla, on the other hand, did not fare as well as Rasul or Hamdi. Padilla, who had filed his habeas petition in New York and won an order of release, was told by the Supreme Court that he should have filed his case where he was imprisoned, and his case was sent back to Virginia for him to start all over. He succeeded there, and by the end of February 2005, Judge Henry Floyd too ordered the administration to charge Padilla with a crime or release him.[15]

The administration appealed again, this time winning in the Fourth Circuit Court of Appeals (the court with jurisdiction over appeals from Virginia federal courts), which held that the administration could detain Padilla indefinitely. Padilla then asked the Supreme Court to review his case again, but in November 2005, the administration changed direction and indicted him in federal court in Miami for conspiring to murder and maim overseas—charges entirely unrelated to September 11 or the supposed radioactive bomb plot on which he was originally held.[16]

This change in direction was too much for even the conservative judges of the Fourth Circuit who had just upheld the president's assertion that he could indefinitely detain people. On December 21, that court blocked Padilla's transfer from military custody to a civilian jail. In his opinion for the court, Judge J. Michael Luttig questioned the administration's "credibility," commenting that their actions left the "impression" that they believed that "principle" could "yield to expediency."[17] Judge Luttig's order stopping the transfer was, however, short-lived. In the spring, the Supreme Court held that the administration's transfer of Padilla from military to civilian custody mooted his challenge to his military detention and required dismissal of his habeas case.[18] The battle over his future shifted to the federal criminal court in Miami, where Padilla fought unsuccessfully to have the charges dismissed because of the torture he had endured at the administration's hands over the past four years. After a bitterly contested trial, Padilla was convicted in August 2007.[19] His appeals are pending and may well end up back at the Supreme Court.

Word of the Supreme Court decisions in Rasul, Iqbal, and Hamdi's cases filtered back to Guantánamo. As hard as the JTF-Guantánamo tries to keep the men isolated from world events, there is a prison grapevine in Guantánamo, much as there is in all prisons. When I talked with Adel in 2006, he told me that he was vaguely aware of these habeas cases as they worked their way up to the Supreme Court, but it wasn't until six months later that he learned that the decision in Rasul's case might have some meaning for him.

Two weeks after the Court spoke in June 2004, the JTF posted a preliminary notice in the prison that the "United States courts have jurisdiction to consider petitions brought by enemy combatants held at this facility that challenge the legality of their detention. You will be notified in the near future what procedures are available should you seek to challenge your detention."[20]

It took the administration five months to reach that "near future" and, at the same time that it was arguing to the courts in Washington that the prisoners had no rights, the JTF told the men they could file habeas corpus petitions like Rasul's and gave them the address of the court in Washington, DC.[21] This was the key for Adel who, without influential family or friends or a government that could pressure the United States, needed to start the fight for his release from Guantánamo on his own. He did so in the spring of 2005, taking the government at its word and filing his handwritten petition with the court:

I request your honorable court to look into my request with consideration and that is that I object to my detention at the Guantánamo Bay, Cuba detention camp as an enemy combatant.

Therefore I wish to file a petition for a Writ of Habeas Corpus.

With my appreciation and my respect to you and my trust you will do me justice.

■   ■   ■

It had taken the DOD five months after Rasul's case was decided to get the prisoners the address of the court in Washington but only a couple of weeks to set up the Combatant Status Review Tribunals (CSRT). While the language of the *Rasul* and *Hamdi* decisions allowed the administration to argue, as the litigation went forward, that they were very narrow in scope, the Supreme Court had clearly required the administration to adopt some procedure to legitimize the imprisonment of the five to six hundred men it was holding in Guantánamo in July 2004.

Deputy Secretary of Defense Paul Wolfowitz took the first step in setting up a procedure on July 7, when he issued a memorandum that provided a definition of "enemy combatant." After nearly three years of seizing and imprisoning men, this was the first definition the DOD had published: "The term 'enemy combatant' shall mean an individual who was part of or supporting Taliban or al Qaeda forces, or associated forces that are engaged in hostilities against the United States or its coalition partners. This includes any person who has committed a belligerent act or has directly supported hostilities in aid of enemy armed forces."[22]

The Administrative Review Board process had actually been established two months earlier, while the *Rasul, Hamdi*, and *Padilla* cases were still pending. Perhaps that was another of the moves timed to influence the judicial process. Regardless, the memorandum establishing the ARBs is replete with justifications for the military's actions but makes clear that the prisoners never had any hearing process at which they could challenge the government's assertions.[23]

Just what a CSRT hearing should entail was set out in a memorandum issued on July 29, 2004, although decisions had already been issued on a handful of prisoners.[24] Hearings for the majority of the men, including Adel and my other clients, started four days after the second memorandum. As

I later learned, Adel's CSRT was not held until November 4, 2004. By early winter, the Department of Defense had held tribunals on the 558 detainees who were in the prison then and found nearly all to be enemy combatants.[25] Even the few who were found not to be were still held in custody, and some remained in Guantánamo for years before being freed.

The *Hamdi* decision changed life in the prison for a few of the prisoners in an even more dramatic way than the CSRT process. In July, as the CSRTs were just getting under way, JTF filed formal charges against ten men, alleging actual acts of terrorism and violations of the laws of war.[26] Following Justice O'Connor's vague directives in Hamdi's case, the Department of Defense set up what it called military commissions to try these prisoners. The procedures created for these commissions gave the ten charged men a little more access to the evidence the military had against them than the CSRT procedures allowed and permitted them to have lawyers, but they stopped far short of the types of procedures required for prisoners of war.

One of the ten men charged was Salim Ahmed Hamdan, a Yemeni accused of being a personal driver for Osama Bin Laden. Hamdan, who had earlier been designated for trial by a military commission by order of President Bush, was formally charged on July 9, 2004, two weeks after the decision in Hamdi's case. The specific charges against him were attacking civilians and civilian targets, murder by an "unprivileged belligerent," and terrorism.[27]

Arguing that commission rules were unfair because they did not let him see enough of the evidence to mount a defense or in any meaningful way confront his accusers, Hamdan tried to stop the commission proceedings in the federal courts through habeas corpus. His efforts set up a litigation track that, like Hamdi's before him, ran all the way to the Supreme Court alongside the cases of the majority of the prisoners who, like Adel were not charged with crimes but were held as "enemy combatants." Unfortunately, this separate track ended up delaying the litigation process for everyone.

■   ■   ■

While the JTF was gearing up the CSRTs and trying to get military commissions started for the ten men it had already charged, pro bono lawyers from some of the nation's largest, best-connected, and well-heeled law firms, like Wilmer Cutler Pickering and Clifford Chance in Washington, DC, joined the pro bono corps of attorneys and filed a series of habeas petitions on behalf of scores of detainees.

The rash of new cases begun in July 2004, after the *Rasul* decision, were assigned randomly to all of the judges on the DC district court, a division that had the Justice Department worried. The lawyers at Justice handling the litigation for the administration, Terry Henry and his crew, did not want to have to litigate prisoner petitions in fifteen different courtrooms, so, by July 23, Henry started filing motions to consolidate the cases.[28] Fearing designation to an unsympathetic judge, and knowing that there would be at least some judges open to their claims, the petitioners' lawyers opposed the motions. In a highly unusual move, the judges of the court met in executive session to discuss the issue and on September 15 they passed a resolution transferring the cases to Judge Joyce Hens Green.[29] Green seemed like a reasonable choice, a judge appointed by Democratic President Carter but with experience as a member of the Foreign Intelligence Surveillance Court and who carried a reduced caseload as a senior judge.[30]

Full of hope that the *Rasul* decision had provided a green light for habeas corpus challenges to their imprisonment in Guantánamo, the petitioners demanded that the administration provide "returns" with the evidence supposedly proving they were terrorists, Al Qaeda, or Taliban fighters. But nothing was produced and, on October 4, acting as if the administration had won Rasul's case, Henry filed motions to dismiss the cases.[31] He argued that all the Supreme Court had decided in *Rasul* was that the federal courts had jurisdiction in Guantánamo and went on to repeat all the other arguments the administration had been making since the cases had begun in 2002: that the prisoners had no rights under the U.S. Constitution or laws, the Geneva Conventions, or any other international law.

While the petitioners' motions for returns and the administration's motions to dismiss were being litigated, CCR continued its efforts to get petitions on file for all of the prisoners, but they needed the names of these men to be able to move beyond the John Doe stage. In mid-December, the CCR team sent a letter to the new deputy secretary of defense, Gordon England, asking for names and identifying information on all the prisoners so they could contact them and their families.[32] England had taken over for Wolfowitz as second in command in the Department of Defense with experience as secretary of the navy, but his appointment had been controversial since he had no real military experience. He had spent his career working for two of the biggest defense contractors, as president of Lockheed and executive vice president at General Dynamics.[33]

England passed CCR's letter to the Department of Justice, which denied the request for the names on January 14, 2005, in a letter signed by Principal Deputy Associate Attorney General Brian Boyle.[34] Undaunted, CCR moved forward anyway and filed the massive "John Doe" petition in February. The administration immediately moved to dismiss.

One naval officer, Lieutenant Commander Mathew Diaz, was sufficiently incensed at the administration's position that, in February 2005, he put a list of all the prisoners' names in an unsigned Valentine's Day card and mailed it to CCR attorney Barbara Olshansky. As he told Tim Golden of the *New York Times*, "We were just throwing up these obstacles in the way of implementing the *Rasul* decision."[35] Olshansky, a brilliant 1985 Stanford Law graduate who was named Public Interest Lawyer of the Year by the Stanford Public Interest Law Foundation for her work on the Guantánamo cases in 2005, had been working on the habeas cases since their inception in 2002 and had seen nothing like this from anyone in the government.[36] Quickly moving to stop anyone else from helping the habeas counsel in this way, the navy convened a court-martial against Diaz. Even though all the prisoners' names were officially released by the Department of Defense a year later, the court-martial was continued and, in May of 2007, Diaz was convicted of communicating information that could be injurious to the United States.[37]

When Henry filed his motions to dismiss all the pending petitions in early October 2004, all of the judges in the DC court followed the consolidation agreement they had reached a few weeks earlier and let Judge Green handle the motions—except one. Richard Leon, a 2002 Bush appointee who had served as counsel to Republicans in the House on the Iran-contra scandal under President Reagan and in one of the investigations into the Clintons' business activities surrounding Whitewater, kept the cases he had been assigned and then beat Judge Green to a decision on the administration's motions to dismiss.[38] On January 21, 2005, Judge Leon accepted virtually all of the administration's arguments and, in a case called *Khalid v. Bush*, dismissed seven cases pending in his court.[39] Judge Green's decision nine days later upholding the prisoners' claims that they had enforceable rights under the Constitution in what was called *In re Guantánamo Detainee Cases* came as a bitter anticlimax.[40]

Neither Judge Leon nor Judge Green wrote about the plight of any individual prisoner. As with the Supreme Court's decisions in *Rasul* and *Hamdi*, the focus was clinically legal, and none of the prisoners received anything meaningful from Judge Green's decision. Within a week, Henry filed a motion to stay the effect of her decision so he could appeal. The motion was granted the day it was filed, and the prison gates stayed shut for all the prisoners, including Adel.[41]

Meanwhile, Hamdan's efforts to get the federal courts to stop his commission trial were moving forward. He won in the district court with Judge James Robertson agreeing that he was entitled to the rights the Geneva Conventions give all prisoners of war and that the military commission procedures were unfair in several respects—particularly because the government was allowed to kick Hamdan out of the hearing for certain evidence.[42] That victory turned out, however, to be short-lived. The DC Court of Appeals heard Hamdan's case in the summer of 2005, and with soon to be Supreme Court Chief Justice John Roberts participating in the decision, the court reversed Judge Robertson's decision, finding there were no problems with the commission procedures and that Hamdan could not make any arguments based on the Geneva Conventions.[43]

．　．　．

The efforts my staff and I were making to catch up on the litigation history got a tremendous boost even before our formal assignment orders arrived. In September 2005, CCR held an all-day training session for the federal defenders and some new pro bono attorneys at the New York City offices of one of the pro bono firms, Clifford Chance. I took Steve Sady, Amy Baggio, Chris Dahl, and William Teesdale with me.

Life's wonderful twists and turns had my Czech friend Michal in New York at the same time, so the night before the training, a few of my colleagues and I ate dinner with him and a Romanian Jewish expatriate friend of his at an open-air fish restaurant in Queens. Sitting on the patio in plastic chairs with the sparkling Manhattan skyline on one side and the elevated subway trains roaring by on the other, we defenders talked about our work and learned about the experiences of these two Jewish children of Holocaust survivors and political prisoners of the Communists. The talk of history, repression, fear, and persecution of people of all religions and politics was a perfect prelude for the training we were soon to have.

When the CCR meeting began the next morning, Gita Gitanjali, one of the lead lawyers on their beleaguered staff, looked out over the new recruits, including lawyers from nearly thirty federal defender offices, breathed a sigh of relief, and greeted us with, "It feels like the cavalry has finally arrived."

Having read about the twists, turns, and complexities of the litigation, I had some understanding of her sentiments. But while the defenders' arrival may have felt like a godsend that fall, it turned out that our guns were quickly muzzled.

16 | The DTA and the Second Rebuke

If we are to keep our democracy, there must be one command-ment: Thou halt not ration justice.

—Judge Learned Hand[1]

WHEN I FIRST SAW ADEL'S HANDWRITTEN habeas petition in the fall of 2005, it reminded me of another handwritten petition that had been filed forty years earlier. On June 3, 1961, Clarence Earl Gideon, a small-time crook, was charged with a petty theft for stealing $65 and some beer and wine from a pool hall in Panama City, Florida.[2] Mr. Gideon had pled guilty many times before, but this time he told the judge he was innocent and requested a trial.

When Gideon appeared on the day of trial without a lawyer, Florida Judge Robert McCrary Jr. asked him if he was ready.

Gideon told him, "No sir. . . . I have no counsel."

When the judge asked why not, Gideon replied, "Your Honor, . . . I request this court to appoint counsel to represent me."

The judge responded, "Sorry Mr. Gideon, I can't appoint a lawyer to represent you."

Gideon did not back down. "The United States Supreme Court says I am entitled to counsel."[3]

There was no public defender in Florida at that time and the court had no money to pay a lawyer so, representing himself, Gideon was convicted and sentenced to five years in prison. But he did not give up. Sitting in his prison cell in January 1962, he wrote a petition to the United States Supreme Court asking how he could be put in prison without a lawyer to represent him when the Constitution, specifically the Sixth Amendment, said he was entitled to one.

The Supreme Court took his case and asked Abe Fortas, one of Washington's most powerful lawyers, friend of then Vice President Lyndon Johnson, and soon to be appointed to the Court, to argue on Mr. Gideon's behalf. Justice Fortas wrote a compelling brief on the importance of the right to counsel in balancing the scales of justice and convinced the Court that Gideon was correct. The unanimous decision of the Supreme Court revolutionized the criminal justice system in America, requiring the federal and state governments to fulfill the promise of the Founding Fathers in the Sixth Amendment that no one could be sent to prison without having government-appointed representation if he or she could not afford a lawyer.[4]

Four decades later, I was the public defender representing a black Sudanese Arab held as a terrorist who had appealed to the American courts for justice. There certainly had been progress in our justice system in the intervening years but, as I started to experience the administration's obstructionism first-hand, I was reminded of how fragile our liberties really are.

. . .

By the time the assignment orders and petitions for Adel and two other clients arrived in my office, I had learned enough about the history of the habeas litigation to start thinking about how to move forward. But before I could do anything meaningful, including filing anything with the court, I had to contend with security issues and the Protective Order that had been negotiated during the summer and fall of 2004 following the decision in Rasul's case.

The Protective Order, which had prevented me from telling Adel about the classified return on my second visit to Guantánamo, intruded on our relationship in several other ways as well and ran counter to everything I had experienced in my career about the confidentiality between an attorney and his client. It caused me to question whether I could establish a meaningful relationship with any of my clients in Guantánamo. I soon learned the history of negotiation behind the Protective Order, which helped explain how CCR and its allies ended up having to accept it.

On June 29, 2004, in the immediate wake of the *Rasul* decision, District Judge Colleen Kollar-Kotelly, who had originally ruled for the administration in July 2002 and dismissed the petitions filed by Rasul, Iqbal, et al., recognized the import of the Supreme Court's statements and held a telephone conference with the CCR, other habeas lawyers, and their Department of Justice counterparts to discuss the question of habeas counsel's access to their clients.[5] At this point there were approximately thirteen separate habeas cases filed involving seventy detainees and a score of lawyers.

Opening the administration's next obstructionist front, Terry Henry pointed out that while the Supreme Court had ruled in *Rasul* that the prisoners had a right to their day in court, it had not said anything about lawyers. He told Judge Kollar-Kotelly that the prisoners had no right to counsel and the government would not permit visits to Guantánamo.

Dismayed by Henry's positions, CCR Legal Director Jeffrey Folgel wrote to the secretary of defense in an effort to gain access to Guantánamo without court intervention. Rumsfeld did not reply, so, on July 14, Folgel wrote again, this time to Deputy Secretary of Defense Gordon England.[6] This letter did elicit a response, from Alberto Mora, the navy's general counsel. In typical government fashion, it advised CCR that it was "exploring" the access issue.[7]

On July 30, the administration backed off its absolute position and stated that it would allow visits to the prison, but only on the condition that its agents listen in and tape the attorney-client meetings. Such an intrusion would have cut the heart out of the attorney-client relationship, which is based on the confidentiality of communications—a privilege that is enforced by ethics rules in every state. The idea behind this is that a client needs to be able to tell his lawyer everything about his case, the good and the bad, without fear that the lawyer will help the government prosecute him or, in a civil matter, sell his secrets to a business adversary. Not ready to jettison hundreds of years of practice, the habeas lawyers rejected Henry's proposal, beginning a four-month process of negotiation over the protocols for attorney visits to the base.

The negotiations culminated in November 2004, when the District of Columbia court issued the first of the Protective Orders.[8] While not as intrusive as the administration's initial proposals for taping all conversations, the Protective Orders severely restricted attorney access to the base and attorney-client communications.

When my staff and I got going on the cases a year later, as much as we resented it, we had no choice but to accept the Protective Orders and file Memoranda of Understanding. The Protective Order prevented me from writing directly to Adel or receiving mail directly from him. Instead, all correspondence went through a Privilege Team from the Department of Justice. When I visited Adel, I could not take my notes out of the prison; instead, I had to give them to my military escorts. If I wanted to get the notes for use in my office, I had to let the Privilege Team read them, a process that can take anywhere from one to four weeks. Anything they thought should be classified was censored and locked in the secure facility outside of Washington. And everything Adel told me, including such things as the name of his wife and his brother-in-law's phone number, which he gave me on the first visit, was presumptively classified.

The Privilege Team was a hindrance and a puzzle. A hindrance because the fact that the notes of my conversations with Adel and the other clients were censored sometimes limited what I wrote down. A puzzle, because on some visits all of my notes, and all of Pat's or William's notes, were cleared, but on others, some pages were retained in the secure facility. When I went on site to look at the classified notes, it was impossible to tell why. More puzzling was the fact that after some visits, the notes from one person in the office were cleared in full, but a page or two from the other person covering the same issues was held back. Different censors with different perspectives? Just another example of the arbitrariness of the situation in Guantánamo.

As bad as it is to have what my clients tell me open to the government, the fact that I could not discuss the classified portions of the returns was even worse. Fortunately for Adel, what I wanted to discuss from the classified return would only have been icing on the cake of our investigation, but that was not the case with one of our other clients. Because there was so much in the unclassified portion of that client's case that we knew the Department of Defense got wrong about where he was, whom he was fighting with, and when, we were confident that there were similar mistakes in the classified portion. But we couldn't talk to him about that material or investigate what we read. Because the entire litigation had been held up over the fundamental question of whether there is a right to appear in court at all, I was not able to challenge the orders and the administration's position that what Adel and my other clients told me about their own life experiences was presumptively classified.

The government's access to and control of the flow of information between habeas counsel and their clients created real problems of trust with some of the prisoners. Some see their lawyers but tell them nothing; others refuse to see the lawyers at all. I was fortunate with Adel and we built a positive relationship. But even that was fouled for several months by an interpretation error.

The abusive and arbitrary treatment of the prisoners in Guantánamo breeds a certain level of distrust of all Americans, and that distrust is only heightened for some of the men whose strict Islamic beliefs cause them to reject participation in our secular legal system. In fact, some of the fundamentalist believers have tried to discourage their fellow prisoners from participating in any lawsuits. Overlaying those obstacles to trust is the fact that some of the prisoners report interrogators in Guantánamo posing as prisoners' counsel, trying to gain their trust in a new way, only to break it in the end.[9] I asked Adel about this type of interrogation. He confirmed these methods were real and also that the interrogators have told the prisoners they will never get out if they cooperate with lawyers. Prisoners have also reported being told that the lawyers coming to "help" them are Jews who just want to see them rot—religious stereotyping akin to what I saw in the affidavit in Brandon's case about Muslims.

As one of the "Jew lawyers" the interrogators warned the prisoners about and who has poured his heart and soul into their fight for more than two years, I find myself alternately shaking my head at the irony of the situation and angry at my government for allowing the interrogators to say this. I consider myself fortunate that trust has been a significant issue with only one of the seven clients my office is representing.

As I first immersed myself in the limits imposed by the protective orders and the rules governing the CSRT proceedings, my mind went back to a book I had read in college, Kafka's *The Trial*. Joseph K. awoke one morning to find himself arrested for a crime that is never revealed based on evidence that he is never shown:

K. must remember that the proceedings were not public; they could certainly, if the court considered it necessary become public, but the Law did not prescribe that they must be made public. Naturally, therefore, the legal records of the case, and above all the actual charge-sheets, were inaccessible to the accused and his counsel, consequently one did not know in general, or at least did not know with any precision, what charges to meet in the first plea.

Translated to Guantánamo, *The Trial* would go like this:

We say you are guilty of being an enemy combatant but won't tell you why or what evidence we have. We won't give you a lawyer in our CSRT proceeding, won't let your habeas corpus lawyer help you there, and won't let him tell you anything he learns from any classified source. Now defend yourself.

.   .   .

My first personal experience with the administration's strategies and changes of direction was on the very first issue I had to address: obtaining security clearances so I could write to and visit Adel and my other clients in Guantánamo. Having been told it could take up to sixty days to get through the FBI background investigation that would have agents out interviewing neighbors, family, friends, and even ex-spouses before a security clearance could be granted, I attempted to reason with the government. In November, I pointed out to Terry Henry and Andrew Warden that as federal and assistant federal defenders, my staff, unlike all of the other lawyers who had been involved so far, worked for the government. We were required to file annual financial disclosures. To obtain my job, I had been subjected to what is called a "full field" FBI investigation, an inquiry into my life even more thorough than the security investigation. In order to see the clients on our regular caseload in Oregon, my staff and I had already been screened by numerous state and federal jails. We even have access cards, issued by the United States marshal, that open the doors to the federal courthouse. I reminded Henry of the incredible delay that my clients had suffered, not only since being captured but also since they had filed their petitions with the court. Henry's response was: procedure is procedure; nothing could be done to expedite the process. So on November 18, I filed a motion asking the court to order the government to expedite the security clearance process.

At the end of January, I received notice from Washington that a hearing had been scheduled for Tuesday, February 7, 2006, before Magistrate Judge Alan Kay, the judge to whom the district judges had referred all issues regarding access to Guantánamo. As I was learning, there were continual problems with access, involving security clearances, the timing of visits, and the materials attorneys could bring in to their clients. In the federal system, the judges are appointed for life by the president and confirmed by the Senate. They are then authorized to appoint what are called magistrate judges to eight-year terms. Judge Kay, white haired and in his late sixties, had served as both a public defender and an assistant United States attorney earlier in his career.[10] The even-tempered and soft-spoken Judge Kay is often asked by his colleagues to mediate tough cases, which is the role he took on for the Guantánamo access issues.

Used to practicing in a system where judges, like Judge Jones, take control of litigation, I was pleased to get notice of the hearing, though it didn't seem like anything out of the ordinary. Assistant Defender Chris Dahl, who had taken the lead on writing the access motions, and I cleared our calendars for the following week and got our plane tickets. Then, the Friday before the hearing, around 4:30 DC time, I got a call from the judge's law clerk telling me that the Justice Department had just informed them that my office would receive five of the sixteen security clearances we had applied for the following week, the week of the hearing.

The judge's clerk added, with more than a note of irony in her voice, "This is how things seem to happen in these cases. As soon as something is scheduled, the government moves a little."

Five of sixteen clearances was certainly better than nothing, but it meant we would not be able to divide up the client work as I had planned, so I asked the court to keep the hearing on the judge's calendar.

February 7 in Washington was a crisp and clear respite from the rainy Oregon winter as Chris and I made our way to the Prettyman Courthouse, a large multiwinged structure where we got lost trying to find Judge Kay's chambers. When we finally turned the right corner, the judge and his law clerk greeted us warmly and I had my first and only glimpse of a human adversary in the entire fight for Adel—Terry Henry was in attendance. Also present for the meeting were Jennifer Campbell and Kent Bond, the Department of Justice staff who coordinate all security matters between the DOJ and the federal courts nationwide.

We spent an awkward two hours sitting around a conference table in the judge's chambers. Henry's response to almost everything was either "no" or "I really don't think so." It was difficult to tell if he truly believed in the positions he was taking or whether he was just following the directives of his client, the Department of Defense. While Judge Kay occasionally suggested that Henry consider a different tack, it quickly became clear that the judge was there to facilitate conversation and mediate, not order the government to do anything.

The most productive part of the meeting was the opportunity to see Campbell and Bond. It turned out that Bond had been in Oregon several years before and had helped my colleague Steve Sady through a security clearance process and with classified documents in an espionage case. Bond had come away highly impressed with my office. This earlier experience and the personal contact we made that afternoon with him and Campbell have helped us through the often labyrinthine security processes required under the Protective Order for filing all documents in the Guantánamo cases.

As it turned out, one other thing did come out of the hearing: Bond checked on the status of our security clearance applications while we were there and by the time we left, seven more had been approved. The last four came through a few weeks later.

. . .

While we had been waiting for our security clearances so we could visit our clients, we confronted the same problems that CCR and the pro bono counsel had grappled with: whether and how to file detailed amended habeas petitions for clients we had not met and about whom we knew nothing, and whether we should ask the judges to enter orders that would prevent the administration from taking the clients out of Guantánamo and sending them home or to other countries. We knew from other lawyers that some prisoners were afraid that if they were sent home they would be tortured or killed. We also had heard rumors that the administration was using so-called rendition to send some prisoners to third countries where even more intense interrogations were commonplace. Our original thought was to wait until we could meet the clients before filing so we could make the petitions and motions specific to their cases as we do with all other clients, but political forces that transcended the Guantánamo situation forced us to act immediately.

By the fall of 2005, Senator John McCain's concerns about the importance of humane treatment of prisoners of war had resonated with the American people and many of his colleagues in Congress. Perhaps out of a belief that torture was morally wrong, or perhaps out of self-interest and a desire to protect Americans captured overseas, Congress was seriously considering a "McCain Amendment" prohibiting torture as a rider to the 2005–2006 military appropriations bill.[11]

For most of 2005, the Bush administration resisted McCain's efforts and continued its opposition to any legislative limit on its behavior in interrogation rooms in Guantánamo and around the world. Then, in mid-December, the administration switched tactics and announced that it would support a torture ban. But its support came with a price that would tie up the Guantánamo litigation and keep Adel out of court for yet another year.

Working with Senator Lindsay Graham of South Carolina, the administration achieved a strategic compromise attached to the military appropriations bill that was passed by Congress and signed by the President on December 30, 2005. Section 1003 of what was called the Detainee Treatment Act (DTA) of 2005 included the McCain antitorture provision. It was clear and direct: "No individual in the custody or under the physical control of the United States Government, regardless of nationality or physical location, shall be subject to cruel, inhuman, or degrading treatment or punishment." And the prohibition extended worldwide: Nothing "shall be construed to impose any geographical limitation on the applicability of the prohibition against cruel, inhuman, or degrading treatment or punishment under this section."[12]

Given my concern about torture in Guantánamo, I was pleased to see the ban passed. But Section 1005 of the DTA rendered the ban all but irrelevant for the prisoners in Guantánamo. Pushed by Senators Graham and Jon Kyl of Arizona, Section 1005 stripped the federal courts of jurisdiction to hear any claim brought by any person detained in Guantánamo. The one little piece of jurisdiction that the DTA left for the courts was a very limited review in the DC Court of Appeals. All Congress said that appellate court could look into was whether the military had followed the procedures it set up for its CSRT process. It could not look at any new evidence. It had to presume the military's actions were correct. And while the law said the circuit court might be able to consider whether the military's procedures were so unfair that they violated the Constitution, it could do so only if the Constitution applied in Guantánamo. And another section of the law said the Constitution was inapplicable there. Kafka could not have imagined a more absurd set of provisons.

The prohibition against torture in Section 1003 was rendered even more irrelevant by the signing statement President Bush issued when he signed the DTA into law. Signing statements, utilized by many presidents to state how they intend to enforce the law, have been pushed to new heights by the Bush administration.[13] The statement issued for the DTA directed that it be construed so that it would in no manner limit the president's author- ity as commander in chief to direct foreign intelligence operations.[14]

Less than a week after the president signed the DTA, the administration relied on it to try to get all the Guantánamo cases dismissed. The first case in line on the way to the Supreme Court at that point was Hamdan's chal- lenge to the circuit court's decision that he could be tried by a military com- mission in Guantánamo, on which the Supreme Court had set argument for April 2006. The Justice Department lawyers asked the Court to dismiss Hamdan's case.[15] The next cases in line were the appeals from the jurisdic- tional decisions Judges Green and Leon had handed down in January 2005 that were now consolidated in the DC circuit court under the names of two of the petitioners, Khalid Al Odah and Lakhdar Boumediene. These two pris- oners, who had been designated as enemy combatants, had been fighting their detention since 2002 through their lawyers Tom Wilner and Neil Koslowe of Shearman & Sterling and Stephen Oleskey and his team at Wilmer Cutler Pickering. Their appeals governed the fate of all of the enemy combatant prisoners. The government lawyers asked the DC circuit court to dismiss these cases. And, on January 4, 2006, Terry Henry filed formal notices with each of the judges in the district courts of the administration's intent to move to dismiss all the pending enemy combatant cases, includ- ing Adel's.[16] The administration's new argument for dismissal was that the DTA eliminated the jurisdiction of all federal courts, including the Supreme Court, over the habeas corpus cases and other lawsuits filed by any prison- ers in Guantánamo.

While all of us in the office had tremendous respect for the East Coast lawyers who were going to be briefing the issues in the appellate courts, I am always reluctant to leave a client's fate in another lawyer's hands. My staff and I had been researching and debating the constitutionality of the DTA even before it passed, and we had come up with several constitional challenges that some of the East Coasters were not keen on pursuing. Steve Sady and I started speaking up at the regular habeas counsel conference calls where these issues were discussed, and after a month or so, we suggested that we would be willing to write an amicus brief that pushed our positions. The "brain trust," as the inner circle of habeas lawyers was known, agreed. After I did several rounds of e-mails to get all of the defender offices on board, on March 10 Sady and I filed an amicus, or "friend of the court," brief with the circuit court on behalf of all of the federal defender clients.[17]

We took a slightly different tack than that in the briefs filed by Al Odah's and Boumediene's lawyers. We argued that the DTA violated the provision of the Constitution that prohibits suspension of the writ of habeas corpus and the constitutional guarantee of due process of law, as well as the Constitution's prohibition against laws that single out a disfavored minority. When we started on the brief, we had not yet been able to see any of our clients, so it felt good to be getting into the fray.

The arguments in the Supreme Court on Hamdan's case were heard in late March, three weeks after my first visit to Guantánamo, and, as it turned out, the Supreme Court action pushed the action in the circuit court off to the side. Hamdan's lawyers, Lieutenant Commander Charlie Swift, who had been detailed by the Navy to represent him in the commission proceedings and had been giving the military fits because he was taking his job quite seriously, and Neil Katyal, a professor at Georgetown Law Center, focused their attack on the statute, telling the Supreme Court that the habeas corpus Suspension Clause was violated by the section of the DTA that purported to strip the courts of jurisdiction over habeas cases.[18] Swift and Katyal also told the Supreme Court that it did not have to decide the big constitutional question because Congress did not intend the DTA to apply to cases that had already been filed, but only to cases that might be filed for other prisoners in the future. The Bush administration countered that the law was just fine, applied to all cases past, present, and future, including Hamdan's case in the Supreme Court, and that the DTA review procedure was an adequate substitute for habeas corpus so there were no constitutional problems.[19]

As in Rasul's case when Korematsu filed one of many friend of the court briefs, scores of amicus briefs were filed for Hamdan. Many more supported

Hamdan than the administration. Legal scholars, British historians, retired generals, and the private bar all told the Court how important habeas corpus is to our constitutional framework and in keeping executive power in check. Senators Graham and Kyl then filed a brief in support of the administration, telling the Court how important the law was to the war on terror.[20]

Taking the same tack it used when it released Rasul and Iqbal just before the arguments in the Supreme Court during their case in 2004, the administration announced a significant change in policy just six days before the arguments were scheduled in Hamdan's case—it would no longer use the fruits of torture. This decision went to the heart of one of the more visible objections to the "trials" the administration was trying to have against Hamdan and the nine other prisoners in Guantánamo it had actually charged. The transparency of the ploy was highlighted by the fact that the Defense Department announced the rule before it became final. Even the *Wall Street Journal*, traditionally friendly to the Bush administration, saw the connection. It reported that "the new rule, expected to be issued this week, comes before the Supreme Court arguments next Tuesday over the legality of the special courts, known as military commissions."[21]

The statement about the change in policy over the fruits of torture wasn't the administration's only public relations move before the arguments in Hamdan's case. Earlier in March, Guantánamo Joint Task Force commander Jay Hood invited reporters to a previously secret part of the base, a huge warehouse crammed with dark green boxes and garbage bags that he said contained more than 120,000 documents that had been taken from the prisoners.[22] The point he was trying to make, that the prisoners had intelligence value the military needed to exploit through its interrogations, may have been helpful in some way, but that was lost on me when the admiral acknowledged that the material had been sitting unread for four years. The JTF was just then getting to its review. Given the administration's repeated assertions that they continue to interrogate the prisoners for their intelligence value, it is difficult to comprehend why they would not have bothered to look through the seized material sooner.

While the administration's conveniently timed announcements of changes in direction were most visible in the Supreme Court cases, as my experience with the clearance issue had shown, the changes were not reserved for that court. The situation with the Chinese Uighurs in Guantánamo was one of the most glaring examples. These men, who had been pushing their habeas cases along with the rest of the Guantánamo prisoners, finally made it out of the district court and to the DC Court of Appeals in 2006. Hundreds of hours were spent writing legal briefs on the complex issues and in judicial preparation. Everyone involved with the habeas litigation saw these as strong cases for the petitioners because they involved some men even the DOD had recognized as innocent noncombatants. Perhaps this is why, just days before the arguments were going to be made in the Court of Appeals in the spring of 2006, the Department of Justice lawyers called the court to say that they had released five of the men to Albania. The call to the court was followed by an Emergency Motion to Dismiss the Case as Moot, a motion the court granted with alacrity even though only five of the eighteen Uighur prisoners had been freed.[23]

We waited with some trepidation through the spring for the Court to rule on Hamdan's case. By then, Justice Roberts had moved from the circuit to the Supreme Court, and while he could not participate in the case because he had been part of the circuit decision that was being appealed, we were worried that his presence might affect the outcome. We knew that if Hamdan lost, it could spell disaster for all our clients, turning the notice the JTF had given the prisoners of their right to seek habeas corpus relief into a very hollow promise. Because my authority to spend federal funds on the Guantánamo cases was based on the assignment orders from the court in Washington, I also knew that a ruling in favor of the administration could end our representation. Unlike CCR and the pro bono and retained lawyers, who had no restrictions tied to their funding and would be able to continue to fight in Congress and in the CSRT and ARB processes, without the court's authorization to represent my clients in the habeas cases, I would have to stop all my office's work.

When I visited Adel in Guantánamo for the second time at the end of May, I had to tell him all this, that his case, like all the other prisoners', was in jeopardy as long as it was tied up in the jurisdictional battle over the DTA being fought out in Hamdan's case. I tried to explain through our interpreter that things would look a little brighter if the facts before the Supreme Court involved an innocent person like him rather than a person alleged to have been Bin Laden's driver, but that there was nothing I could do about it. Hamdan's case was ahead of Adel's in line.

. . .

Even though a ruling for the administration in Hamdan's case could end my representation of Adel and all of the office's Guantánamo clients, I decided that we could not sit idly by throughout the spring and await the *Hamdan* ruling. As soon as Pat's and my notes from our first visits to Guantánamo were cleared through the Privilege Team, we started trying to contact Al Tayeb and Salwa in Khartoum, Adel's brother Hashem in Port Sudan, and Abu Hadifa, Adel's supervisor at WAMY, in Pakistan. The rest of my staff, Chris, Bryan, Amy, and Ruben, had also come back from their first visits with Chaman and Gul armed with names and numbers of family and friends in Aghanistan, and we started the hunt for them as well.

In April, we also started work for three new clients. Just before leaving for Guantánamo for the first visit to Adel in March, I had received a call from CCR asking if we could take on three more clients whose cases had originally been assigned to the federal defender office in Los Angeles. That office had been unable to get into their cases, and CCR, which had been impressed with the work we had been doing, hoped we could help out. Our initial progress on behalf of Adel, Chaman, Shabaan, and Gul had whetted my appetite and I quickly agreed. The new assignment orders for Al Ginco, Yasin Basardh, a Yemeni who had actually been with Bin Laden for a while, and Amin Ullah, an Afghan who had fought with the Northern Alliance against the Taliban, came through later that month. I divided the cases among the members of the team, Al Ginco to Steve Sady, Pat Ehlers, and myself, Amin Ullah to Ruben Iniguez and Bryan Lessley, and Basardh to Sady and myself.

Since December 30, 2005, the administration has opposed the entry of any new Protective Orders, the agreed upon restrictions on access, so I was worried that we might never get to see the new clients. Fortunately, we found that orders had been entered in the fall so we were able to get going on the cases, entered Memoranda of Understanding agreeing to abide by the Protective Orders, amended the pro se petitions (requests from prisoners asking to defend themselves in court), and started investigation on the Internet. I met Mr. Basardh at the end of May when I saw Adel for the second time.

On June 29, the wait for the Supreme Court's ruling on Hamdan's case ended with the Court's second rebuke of the Bush administration.[24] Not swayed by the the fact that Hamdan was alleged to have been Bin Laden's driver, Justice Stevens, writing for the court, rejected the administration's argument that the DTA had stripped it of jurisdiction. The DTA, he said, did not apply to Hamdan's case because it had been pending when the law was passed. He went on to hold that Article III of the Geneva Conventions (the part that defines humane treatment for prisoners of war) applied to Hamdan and that the commission procedures violated the conventions and the "laws of war."

The administration's first reaction to the decision was positive, a memorandum from Deputy Secretary of Defense Gordon England informing all military personnel that Common Article III of the Geneva Conventions was to be applied to all the prisoners in Guantánamo, and elsewhere.[25]

We were thrilled with the Hamdan decision and England's memorandum and I gave the green light to go ahead with plans to take our investigations overseas. But the decision had a gaping hole in it: The Court had thrown out the DTA and the commision procedures not on Constitutional grounds but based only on the language of the DTA. This left the door open for the administration and its friends in Congress to come back and rewrite the law again, something they promptly set out to do.

17 | Homeland Security

What Hamilton is saying is that the Constitution is a Constitution of limitations. It is a Constitution where nobody becomes too powerful. It's a constitution where we have a democracy, but it's a certain kind of democracy that protects human liberty, and a degree of equality, and a rule of law, and separation of powers, and federalism. Nobody gets all the power in the United States of America. And those are limitations.

—Justice Stephen Breyer

THE DECISION TO RESPOND TO THE ATTACKS of September 11 as a military rather than criminal justice matter, the incursions in Afghanistan and Iraq, and the torture memos were only part of the administration's war on terror. In the wake of September 11, the Bush administration geared up for the war it intended to fight at home as well as abroad. The policies it implemented had a profound effect on Brandon and his family and have set in motion forces about which all Americans should be concerned.

Within weeks of the attacks, the administration started submitting proposals to Congress to expand executive power and began implementing others through executive orders. The president created the Office of Homeland Security by executive order in October 2001.[1] A year later, on November 25, 2002, the office was upgraded to cabinet status as the Department of Homeland Security in the Homeland Security Act of 2002.[2] The new department brought together a score of federal agencies including the Immigration and Naturalization Service, Customs, the Coast Guard, and the Federal Emergency Management Agency. Its purpose is to coordinate protection of the nation in a variety of ways including the efforts to combat domestic terrorism.

By mid-September 2001, the administration's friends in Congress had introduced the bill that was to become the Patriot Act, the Uniting and Strengthening America by Providing Appropriate Tools Required to Intercept and Obstruct Terrorism Act of 2001 (U.S.A.P.A.T.R.I.O.T.). That legislation, which greatly expanded the executive's power to conduct domestic surveillance, was signed into law on October 26, 2001, and several sections were to play a prominent role in the violation of Brandon's privacy three years later.[3] Section 213 authorized, for the first time in our nation's history, "sneak-and-peek" searches. From the founding of the republic, police executing searches authorized under the Fourth Amendment have been required to let the subject of the search know that it has taken place. Under the new sneak-and-peek authority, the searches could take place in secret. As they did with Brandon, government agents are now authorized to break into someone's home, take photographs, copy computer drives, or take DNA swabs, and simply lock up and leave. While they are required to give notice of the search at some point, the time for disclosure can be repeatedly extended.

Historically, grand jury matters are kept secret to protect the integrity of the investigations, the subjects, in case they are not indicted, and the witnesses. Prosecutors and police are not allowed to share information from grand jury proceedings with anyone. The secrecy of the grand jury as it relates to intelligence matters was even written into the law in 1978. Responding to revelations about abuse of wiretaps and domestic spying by the Nixon administration in the late 1960s and early 1970s, a partisan effort carefully crafted a new law, the Foreign Intelligence Surveillance Act (FISA).[4] The law was intended to balance the need to obtain intelligence information believed necessary to protect the nation from foreign powers yet ensure that the government would not again engage in politically motivated domestic spying. The FISA specifically precluded information sharing between intelligence and law enforcement agencies.

Section 203 of the Patriot Act changed all that and broke down the wall between law enforcement and intelligence, and permitted information to be shared. The government used Section 203 in Brandon's case.

In 1978, the FISA had also established a special court in Washington to authorize wiretaps for the government to eavesdrop on foreign intelligence agents and allowed the court to issue warrants using a lower legal standard than applies in all other cases. Section 218 of the Patriot Act then expanded the court's authority under the FISA and allowed the government to obtain FISA warrants not only when the subject of the tap is exclusively foreign intelligence but also when foreign intelligence is only one part of the reason behind the search. The FBI went to the FISA court to obtain the warrants permitting them to tap Brandon's home and office.

A third section of the Patriot Act was also used against Brandon. Section 505 greatly expanded the use of what are called National Security Letters. These are administrative subpoenas under which government agents are allowed to gather private records about a person from his or her bank, accountant, credit card companies, Internet service providers, and the like. Under the act, National Security Letters are kept secret and a person ordered to furnish records is prohibited from telling anyone about them. The Patriot Act allowed not just the attorney general but also the heads of all FBI field offices to issue the letters. And they may be issued without any proof of probable cause, the usual legal standard for search warrants that was relaxed by the FISA, or any judicial oversight. Brandon's life had been exposed by the use of National Security Letters.

While the Patriot Act passed the Senate with only one dissenting vote (from Wisconsin's Senator Russ Feingold) and passed with overwhelming support in the House, it stirred tremendous opposition throughout the country. During the winter of 2002, John Podesta, formerly President Clinton's chief of staff, said of the early opponents of the Act, "We should not forget what gave rise to the original opposition—many aspects of the bill increase the opportunity for law enforcement and the intelligence community to return to an era where they monitored and sometimes harassed individuals who were merely exercising their First Amendment rights. Nothing that occurred on September 11 mandates that we return to such an era."[5]

Warnings such as Podesta's have been met with cries of outrage from the administration ever since. "In the war on terror we cannot afford to be without this law for a single moment," the president reinforced late in 2005, and he added that we need not worry about abuse.[6] Coming to the president's defense in 2006, former Attorney General Ashcroft said, "The president has been more respectful of civil liberties and civil rights than any previous wartime president in the history of the United States."[7]

Not everyone believed the president's and attorney general's assurances that federal agents would stay strictly within the law. By 2005, concerns about the Patriot Act had led to anti–Patriot Act resolutions in 379 communities in 43 states, including six statewide resolutions.[8] A nationwide coalition to limit the act was formed, bringing together groups from all parts of the political spectrum, ranging from former conservative Republican congressman Bob Barr of Georgia and the American Conservative Union to the ACLU. The anti–Patriot Act groups were not strong enough to repeal the act, but they may have prevented the administration from passing even more intrusive measures.

As far-reaching as were some of the powers granted to the executive in the Patriot Act, at least they were granted openly and by Congress. At the same time, however, the president had initiated a secret program of domestic surveillance of telephone calls and e-mails outside the Patriot Act and the FISA without even the more relaxed judicial oversight those laws had allowed. The government listened in on calls and read e-mails of tens of thousands of people until the existence of this secret program was revealed by the *New York Times* in December 2005.[9] When the existence of this covert, warrantless surveillance was revealed, the president and his attorney general insisted that it was necessary to protect the country from future attacks. The justification that we need these powers to protect you is very difficult to refute.

Those who were skeptical of the administration's promises that the American people could trust the expanded powers given to government agents under the Patriot Act turned out to be right. In March 2007, the inspector general of the Department of Justice, Glenn Fine, revealed that the department had been underreporting its use of National Security Letters for years, and that far more than anyone had imagined, nearly 150,000, had been issued.[10] Fine also revealed that the government had been using the letters for improper purposes, such as gathering personal data on Americans. People from all over the political spectrum were outraged. Conservative California Republican Congressman Darrell Issa said, "From the Attorney General on down, you should be ashamed of yourself. . . . We stretched to try to give you the tools necessary to make America safe, and it is very, very clear that you've abused that trust."[11]

In part stemming from my family history of murder—in state-sponsored pogroms and repression under institutionalized anti-Semitism—I have been particularly concerned about the policies of the Bush administration that insinuate themselves into and change the fabric of our open and tolerant society. One of the most pernicious of such policies—and one that undoubtedly affected Brandon and his family—was the TIPS program, or Terrorism Information and Prevention System. Under this system, all citizens were encouraged to look for and pass on suspicious information to government agents. Sensitive to the impact that informing can have on a free society, Congress balked at this proposal, but the idea continued to circulate within the administration.[12] At a Public Preparedness Symposium in July 2004, Homeland Security Secretary Tom Ridge said, "Efforts each of you make to be vigilant, such as reporting suspicious items or activities to authorities, do make a difference. Every citizen, using their common sense and their eyes and ears, can support our national effort to stop the terrorists."[13]

From the beginning, Americans have taken pride in the fact that the First Amendment protects us from government intrusion into our political and religious thoughts and associations. During the height of the cold war, the Soviet Union's reliance on the KGB and the East German reliance on the Cheka to infiltrate all political groups was rightly condemned. The way a nation of informers, as the fascist and totalitarian states of the twentieth century were called, contrasts with a free society has always been part of our national self-definition. When a society is riddled with informers, trust between neighbors breaks down.[14] While the TIPS program never got off the ground in any formal way, the administration's urgings led to a spate of calls to federal, state, and local law enforcement about a myriad of benign acts and pointed fingers at innocent people—most of whom were of Middle Eastern descent, Muslim, or people of color. TIPS gave a boost to the Muslim profiling that infected Brandon's case.

Another of the administration programs that was easy to sell was the Office of Homeland Security's effort to beef up airport security. At first, the new security was handled by private contractors. Lines were abysmally long as contractors searched passengers before they entered airports or as they headed to departure concourses and again as they tried to board planes at the gates. All tests of the screening process showed, however, that knives and other weapons were easy to get through.[15] The Homeland Security Department then set up the Transportation Security Administration (TSA) to handle the work, and slowly the TSA replaced the contractors with government employees. The TSA is our first real national police force, an idea that conservatives had bitterly fought for decades. Air travelers were soon greeted at airports throughout the country by uniformed federal police frisking eighty-year-old grandmothers. Whether there has been any true increase in security from these measures is open to debate.

There is no question, however, that the TSA presence and searches at all of our airports has had at least one effect. Many of the tens of millions of people who fly each year have become used to the commonplace spread-eagle searches and rummaging through personal papers and toiletry kits by federal police, a treatment that was formerly reserved for those caught in criminal acts and regulated by the courts. While we can lose our freedoms overnight to foreign invaders, we can also lose them slowly through a day-to-day acceptance of a series of incremental steps that will alter our lives forever.

One of the more curious aspects of the administration's domestic war on terror was the color-coded security alert system. Since the spring of 2002, Americans have been greeted each day with a kaleidoscope of colors: red for a serious threat, orange for one somewhat less serious, and so on downward. But what did this mean? What were the local police supposed to do? What was each of us supposed to do in our daily life? Did red mean Portland was facing a real terrorist threat?

The color system clearly succeeded in increasing anxiety and confusion. I saw this at home through the reaction of my son, Michael, who was eleven at the time and could not figure out what to do with the new color code for terrorist alerts. As I drove him to school during 2002 and 2003 when there were many "red" days, we often saw police cruisers guarding both ends of the bridges that spanned the Willamette River. Michael wanted to know why they were there. Was there a real danger? If so, why were we driving over the bridge? I had no satisfactory answers, and eventually their presence became a subject of his jokes.

Even more telling was Michael's reaction to the sudden interest in the city reservoirs in Mt. Tabor Park that abuts our house. The Homeland Security Department had called upon municipalities around the nation to ensure the integrity of their infrastructure, and Portland had responded by hiring private security guards to patrol the reservoirs. There are three reservoirs in the park, spread out in different locations. The one-man teams, rotating in eight-hour shifts, would walk around one reservoir for a while, then drive to the second in their Geo Metros and Honda Civics, patrol there, then move on to the third and back again. The full cycle took about an hour.

We walk in the park regularly, sometimes spurred by the need to exercise our Scottish terrier, sometimes just to enjoy the day. The path around the lower reservoir, the one behind our house, is a little more than a quarter mile from corner to corner. A few evenings after the watch began, Kathleen, Michael, and I went out for a walk. The guard's car was parked at the far corner of the reservoir that sits behind our house and, as we came near, he got out of the car and started his foot patrol. The guard that night was typical; he must have been between sixty and sixty-five and extremely overweight. Michael looked him up and down, eyes stopping on the belly, then looked back across the reservoir toward our house. He then looked at me and asked, "Dad, how is that guy going to stop anyone from doing anything on the other side of the reservoir?" I felt a profound sadness as I looked at him without any reassuring answer.

Two years later, when I met Brandon's children while he was still in jail, I recalled that walk and my concern about the messages the security alert system, airport searches, police cruisers, and reservoir guards were conveying to Michael. Were they undermining the sense of security that is so important in child development? Were they teaching him cynicism about the steps our government was taking to protect us? But my worry about the effect of all this on Michael was nothing compared to the pain Brandon's children felt when their father was thrown in jail and held up to the world as a Muslim terrorist.

18 | Proffer and Immunity

*The fight is won or lost far away from witnesses—behind the
lines, in the gym, and out there on the road, long before I dance
under those lights.*

—Muhammad Ali

BRANDON DESPERATELY WANTED OUT. As we huddled in the county jail cell
and Judge Jones's chambers, Brandon kept coming back to the big question, "When can I get out of here?" He was worried about his family and
his law practice—and himself. He knew he had nothing to do with the
bombings, but as he told me later about his days in the jail, "It was creepy
in there, not knowing when someone might decide to get patriotic."

The get-out-of-jail card being dangled in front of Brandon by Gorder and
his colleagues required him to testify in the grand jury. But Chris and I
continually had to remind Brandon that this was not a get-out-free card. It
came with a price: possible indictment for capital murder or for perjury.
No one in the United States attorney's office, Justice Department, or FBI
could move past the 100 percent fingerprint identification.

Monday morning, May 10, Chris and I met with Gorder, Atkinson, and
Holsinger in a conference room of the United States attorney's office, located on the fifth and sixth floors of the courthouse. The U.S. attorney's
presence in that building gave them a slight advantage over the lawyers in
my office in dealing with the judges because they bumped into each other
in the hallways, forging informal relationships. When the Hatfield courthouse was in development in the late 1990s, I had the option of asking for

office space but turned it down. I felt that whatever advantage we might gain by being in the building was outweighed by the message our presence there would convey to our clients, their families, and witnesses. It is hard enough sometimes to convince clients that we really are independent without them seeing us under the same roof as the government employees who are prosecuting them.

Being in the courthouse would also have meant that anyone coming to our office would have to pass through the U.S. marshal security station at the front door, submit to a search, and present identification. That scenario has been a problem at times when we need to get undocumented family members and witnesses into court in our illegal reentry cases. Some won't come out of fear of arrest, while others have run into problems with knives or drugs when they have forgotten to empty their pockets or backpacks. I did not want to risk that type of problem on routine office visits.

Chris and I had held a team meeting before our appointment with Gorder to go over what we hoped to get—information on the sneak-and-peek searches; return of the property the FBI had seized, or at least the computers that Mona needed to keep Brandon's law practice going; information on what the Spanish were saying about the fingerprint. We wanted to discuss the leaks, a gag order, and the law office files. We also wanted to review parameters on the grand jury testimony Gorder wanted from Brandon, whether he would offer immunity, and whether he would take the possibility of a capital prosecution off the table.

When we got started in the United States attorney's office, I laid out the areas we wanted to cover. We all agreed we should start with something on which we might reach agreement, but there was only one—the leaks to the media and a gag order. Gorder was as upset as we were about the leaks and he knew they could become a problem for the government if they ever wanted to indict Brandon.

After those points were cleared, we were back to running up against a brick wall. Gorder would not reveal any information about Spain, or even give us a phone number to contact someone on our own. He also refused to give us a list of what had been seized from Brandon's home or office and would not return the computers or even copies of the hard drives.

Other than agreement on the gag order for the leaks, the only positive outcome of the meeting was that Gorder did not completely rule out immunity for Brandon in return for his testimony.

"No decision has been made," he said.

"Decision by whom?" I asked.

"Steve, we are not calling the shots on something like that," Gorder replied. "Any decision on immunity is going to be made in Washington."

Chris and I were not surprised. The magnitude of the case on the international stage and leaks emanating from Washington had suggested to us that the authority of the United States attorney in Oregon was going to be limited, something that did not please us. The assistant United States attorneys in Oregon are almost all career, professional prosecutors. While I don't always agree with their decisions, I know that they are made based on the assistant's analysis of the facts, rather than being driven by political calculations. With the decisions in Brandon's case coming from Washington, I was worried that politics was going to skew the way the case was handled. Given the press conferences by Attorney General Ashcroft over the Portland Six, Hawash, and Imam Kariye, the possibility loomed that the Bush administration might try to use Brandon's situation for political fodder.

We didn't get much farther when we asked Gorder whether Brandon was really a witness in the grand jury or just in a holding pattern to be indicted.

"Charles, you want Brandon's testimony?" I asked. "Take the possibility of a capital prosecution off the table."

"Steve, you know I can't do that."

"He's already told you that he knows nothing. That first day in court he told you and the judge he had nothing to do with the bombing, it's not his print, and if somehow it is, he has no idea how it got there. There's nothing more he can say. Give him immunity."

"Tell us what he will say."

"You know we can't say anything more than we already have."

Here we were only five days into the case and "that first day" felt like eons ago. When you are in a big case, time bends, expands, and contracts, and you lose sight of much of the rest of the world. Brandon's case was so intense that time ceased to exist.

We had tried and failed an informal approach to learn more about the evidence the FBI had seized. Now we had to turn to the court, and somehow on Tuesday the eleventh, Chris and I filed five motions.[1] The first two asked Judge Jones to order Gorder to give us what he had refused to provide: disclosure of the search warrant affidavits and the returns, the legal documents the FBI was required to provide to the court and to the subject of a search after it was completed, and return of all property that had been seized from Brandon's home and law office. We felt this was the least we needed in order to advise Brandon whether to testify at all, or testify only if Gorder gave him immunity. We couldn't give Brandon any meaningful advice unless we knew more specifically what the prosecutors had in their hands.

The next two motions sought to protect Brandon, his family, and his clients from any more damage to their reputations by asking Judge Jones to freeze all of the material that had been taken from his office and to stop the FBI and the U.S. attorney's office from conducting investigations of these materials until the judge had ruled on our claim of privilege. I also asked the judge to stop Gorder and the FBI from disseminating information to any other agencies from the law office seizures.

The final motion took us on the offensive and asked for a formal investigation into the media leaks and violation of grand jury secrecy. We knew from Judge Jones's tone during the Monday conference in chambers that he was angered by the government leaks, and we felt that putting Gorder on the defensive with a formal motion would help in further negotiations on the testimony issue and might also start setting up possible defenses if the prosecutors took Brandon out of the witness basket and charged him with capital murder.

Looking back, I have no idea how we got all this done in such a short span—talking to Brandon, talking to his family, researching the law, learning the art and science of fingerprinting, working with the investigative team, negotiating with Gorder, appearing in Judge Jones's chambers. Each was an intense and complex task that stretched the incredibly talented and dedicated team that was working for Brandon. Fortunately, the elasticity of time was at its zenith.

▪   ▪   ▪

The morning of Wednesday the twelfth, I met with Brandon in the marshal's lockup to update him on our work and filings of the night before and to go over the meeting Chris and I planned to have with Gorder later in the day.

Chris stayed behind in the office to work on a comprehensive memorandum in support of our motions. Because lawyers were coming in from the state bar to help with Brandon's own law practice, he and I would have no time for a private conversation once the marshal took him upstairs. There was one decision we needed to make. On Tuesday, Gorder had broached the possibility of Brandon taking a polygraph, something Brandon, Chris, and I had talked about briefly over the weekend. We had been lukewarm to the idea since a polygraph by an FBI examiner would give them a free shot at questioning Brandon. After all, a polygraph is simply a specialized type of interrogation. When we met Wednesday morning, Brandon and I decided to take it off the table unless Gorder offered us something in return.

However, we didn't want to just say no to Gorder. So we talked about giving him a letter or affidavit stating Brandon's position, something that could jump-start the negotiation process. The idea was to send Gorder a formal statement from Brandon denying any knowledge of the bombings and agreeing to help if he had information of significance he was not aware of having. It would be a miniproffer, a statement of good faith, something that gave them a little more than the initial denial Brandon had made on his first appearance in court the previous Thursday.

We also talked again about the difference between the formal immunity we could insist on in the grand jury and the more limited immunity that would be given if Brandon talked in an informal proffer session.[2] Both possibilities had advantages and disadvantages. The grand jury gave protection against use of Brandon's words and anything that the prosecutors might develop from them. While Gorder would also be prohibited from using Brandon's words in a proffer session, he would be able to use any leads he got from Brandon to investigate and could then use any material he subsequently uncovered. The difference in protection from grand jury to proffer was potentially huge if Brandon said anything that fit with the evidence the FBI had seized and to which we had not yet had access.

Even though, Gorder could not force grand jury testimony without giving the broader immunity, there was a downside to the grand jury because Brandon would face it alone. Grand jury witnesses, even if they are suspects, are not allowed to have their lawyers in the room. In a proffer session, Chris and I would be right next to Brandon; we could stop the questioning instantly if we did not like the direction it was going, or interpret questions or answers if we felt that something had been missed.

The reality was that we could probably arrange a proffer sooner, and Gorder had made it clear that some testimony was a prerequisite to getting Brandon out of jail.

We agreed to keep both options on the table. The last thing we wanted was to draw any lines in the sand and push the prosecutors into a position where they felt they had to seek an indictment. The possibility of the death penalty loomed large over Brandon and over us.

. . .

Following my morning meeting with Brandon, Chris and I met with Gorder and his team late that afternoon in the conference room that is part of the suite where the United States attorney has her personal office. Gorder's position was even clearer than it had been two days before that he had "no authority to do anything." He had not even asked Washington about immunity. Dave Atkinson did more of the talking this time around and used a phrase we would hear repeatedly over the next week: "We want unvarnished answers."

Atkinson told us that they were going to oppose all our motions for access to the evidence they had seized because they did not want Brandon to have the opportunity to think about the materials and prepare explanations.

"But Dave, you are talking about material you seized from Brandon. It's his, but some of it may be old, he might not remember offhand unless he can see what's there."

"That's our point," Atkinson said. "We want it unvarnished. We don't want you going over explanations with him. I'm sure you understand we can't agree to release him unless we're satisfied that he's not involved."

We were getting nowhere fast. I then explained that we saw four possibilities and were concerned that what they were suggesting was setting Brandon up for a perjury charge.

"If Brandon is involved, he is not going to talk and there is no point to any of these conversations. He's not. That's why we are here. The second possibility is that he knows something and knows he knows. If that was what we are dealing with, we would be negotiating in an entirely different way. If the fingerprint is his, and he has any knowledge, he doesn't know it. He's an unwitting witness to something he's completely unaware of. That's the most likely scenario and Brandon wants to help in any way he can, but we can't advise him to talk to you unless he's protected. The fourth possibility is that the print is not his and he has nothing at all to offer."

Atkinson's response was to go back to a polygraph—they really wanted it. I threw back the idea of an affidavit, the jump-start Brandon, Chris, and I had been discussing to get things going. "Dave, give us the parameters of what you want to test and we can give you an affidavit."

Something in what I had been saying must have resonated because Gorder took over then and put the idea of a proffer session with immunity on the table. He went much farther than before, using a phrase that sprang from our childhood television experiences and that we were all familiar with from our regular caseload, "queen for a day," meaning come in and talk about anything, no limits, and we won't use it against you in our case if there ever is a trial. The prosecutors could still investigate based on what Brandon might say and use his statements to impeach him if he ever took a different position. While Gorder put the "queen for a day" idea on the table and wanted us to think seriously about it, he also made it clear that he was not authorized to make a formal offer. That night, we sent the prosecutors the jump-start letter we had gone over with Brandon, denying any involvement or knowledge or possibility that Brandon's "fingerprints can be on any items connected with the bombing."

The next day, Thursday the thirteenth, my whole team got together at the round table in my office at noon. Jim, William, and Janan reported on the progress they had been making on their investigations. Jim had pretty much locked down the money issues, Janan had a good start on Brandon's family history, and William was immersed in the loops, whorls, and arches of fingerprinting. Chris, Amy, and I reported our progress on a comprehensive motion for release that not only argued from the facts of Brandon's life that he posed no risk of flight or any danger if he was released before he was called to the grand jury but also challenged the way the government was using the material witness statute to detain people.

After we were all up-to-date, we reviewed the next stages of the investigation and agreed that we needed to see if we could find reference to Brandon in any of the reports about the Moroccans who had been charged in Spain. Had any of them mentioned Brandon, or anything American, in the statements they had made to the Spanish investigators? We agreed that Jim would spend more time combing the Internet and William would try to find someone in Spain to talk to and a lawyer or investigator to help us there.

We needed a lawyer in Spain for another reason. If Gorder was serious about offering some type of immunity, whether in the grand jury or a proffer, we needed to know whether a U.S. grant of immunity would give Brandon any protection in Spain. Many crimes can be prosecuted in multiple jurisdictions, and the constitutional protection against double jeopardy covers a defendant only against multiple prosecutions by the same sovereign.[3] This meant that both the Americans and the Spanish could charge Brandon with murder and he could be forced to stand trial in both countries even if acquitted in one. The bombings in Madrid had already led to charges there against the Moroccans, and there was no bar against the Spanish charging an American. We had not been able to obtain any information from Spain, and Gorder either could not or would not tell us if he knew whether the Spanish were now convinced by the FBI's fingerprint work. We needed to know what was happening abroad to know if statements given under immunity in America could still be used in Spain.

The meeting ended at the decision we had been up against since the case began. If we did not keep the dialogue going for some form of testimony, the risk that Brandon would be indicted increased because there was no way the U.S. attorney and FBI would free Brandon as long as they had the fingerprint. But we still did not have enough information to give him any meaningful advice.

Chris and I trooped back over to Gorder's office. Both sides kept circling around the same points. Atkinson restated the prosecutors' desire for the "unvarnished truth." Chris and I then upped the ante on our need for information before we could advise Brandon whether he should testify, reminding the prosecutors that we did not believe we would be providing effective assistance of counsel if we gave Brandon advice about testifying without knowing what he was up against. We told them that if Brandon talked and they went ahead and indicted him, any conviction they got could be challenged based on his lawyers' ineffectiveness.

"Dave, please understand our predicament," Chris said. "It's in everyone's interest to make some progress here. There must be something you can tell us. You must be in contact with Spain. Do they have anything more on Brandon?"

As in the previous meeting, Gorder spoke up at that point and said that the Spanish had had no interest in Mayfield before the fingerprint identification. "It was a cold hit," he said. Apparently the Spanish had no information on Brandon, but Atkinson then chimed in that there are "several things that create inferences beyond the affidavit." But no matter how hard we pushed, none of the prosecutors would say anything more.

At four that afternoon, Amy, Jim, Chris, and I rendezvoused briefly with Brandon in the marshal's lockup after he had finished working with the bar counsel in Judge Jones's chambers. While agreeing to hold off on any decisions a while longer, we were all disappointed in what felt like the lack of progress. On the surface, our jump-start letter had not accomplished anything.

Chris and I spent most of the following day working on the release motion and checking in on our other clients. I asked Amy to spend the afternoon in the jail with Brandon reviewing the voluminous motions we had filed earlier that week and going over some of the facts with Brandon in the hope that a new face and different approach might produce some additional information. Late in the day, Gorder called with bad news about Spain and immunity. He had discussed the issue with his superiors in the DOJ and they did not believe they could tie the Spanish hands with any agreement they might make and would not agree with us to withhold the results of any proffer or grand jury testimony from their counterparts in Madrid.

Friday afternoon's mail run from the courthouse brought us more bad news from the United States attorney's office. Gorder had filed a Notice of Disclosure earlier in the day under the federal rules governing grand jury proceedings, advising the court that information gathered for the grand jury matter involving Brandon "has been and will be disclosed" outside the grand jury process. The list was chilling in the extreme; the CIA, National Security Council, Department of Defense, Department of Homeland Security, Department of Justice, FBI, Department of the Treasury, and National Security Agency had all been given copies of the information.[4] Under the Patriot Act's breaching of the wall between criminal investigations and intelligence gathering, dissemination of the information obtained from Brandon and his family in the searches of his home and office was now perfectly legal. The breadth of the list meant that hundreds, if not thousands, of our nation's spy agencies' field offices were in possession of pieces of Brandon, Mona, and their children's personal lives.

Late Sunday morning, Chris and I met in the public lobby of the jail, filled out the visitor cards, checked in at the desk, and headed up. When we signed in, it was to visit Brandon under his true name, everyone having given up the Randy Taylor pretense a couple of days earlier. When Brandon was brought into the contact visit room, we could see a marked difference in his mood. When I had said good-bye to him on Thursday evening in Judge Jones's chambers, he had just finished working on his files, thinking and acting like a lawyer in the quiet confines of the courthouse, even though he was dressed in his jailhouse blues. He had seemed tired but okay. Sunday morning he was not; he looked drawn and thinner, and the lines under his eyes indicated he had not been sleeping. He told us that the ten days in jail "seemed like an eternity," and that with nothing to do over the past two days the reality of his situation had sunk in. The separation from his family and the specter of the death penalty had plunged him into a deep trough of despondency.

Brandon's location on the fourth floor of the jail, where the sheriff had put him for his own protection, was not helping his frame of mind. The administrative segregation section of the county jail is where the sheriff houses inmates who cause disciplinary problems either because they are violent or mentally ill. It is a loud and sometimes scary place that Brandon wanted to get out of, and it was difficult for him to shift from talking about his feelings to an objective discussion of his legal options. When Chris told Brandon about the Notice of Disclosure, Brandon's despondency was heightened by the anger he felt at the violation of his privacy.

We had to go over the possibilities: testify if Gorder made an offer for some form of immunity or agreement on release, testify even if there was no offer, testify in the grand jury, testify by proffer, don't testify even if there was an offer, don't testify if there was none, insist on getting more information first, and other multiple possible outcomes we put into a decision tree that ended up with fifty-eight branches. While we were trying our best to make objective decisions, we recognized the reality that we had little control over what would happen.

"So," Brandon said, "I could give a proffer and they could still refuse to release me?"

I had to tell Brandon that was a possibility—Gorder might not believe him. Or maybe he would, but the FBI or decision makers in Washington might not.

On top of that, we had no control over other facts that might be out there. In criminal cases, the prosecutors and police are always trying to get information through informants. When there is more than one person involved in a crime, they often bargain with one defendant, agreeing to give him a lesser charge or to argue for a lesser sentence in return for testimony against his crime partners. The unfortunate reality is that information obtained by deals is not always reliable. As former associate attorney general under President Reagan and judge on the Ninth Circuit Court of Appeals, Stephen Trott, has written, "By definition, informants are cut from untrustworthy cloth." They must be carefully watched "to prevent them from falsely accusing the innocent, from manufacturing evidence against those under suspicion of crime."[5]

As Brandon succinctly put it, "The Moroccans could lie against me." We had no idea if any of them had confessed and said anything about Brandon. By the time I left the meeting hours later, my head felt like it was going to explode, but we had made some decisions. In court on Monday the seventeenth, we were going to focus on the fingerprint, getting returns on the search warrants, and pushing on the release motion. Outside of court, we were going to keep up our efforts in Spain.

19 | Catch-22

Okay, let me see if I've got this straight. In order to be grounded, I've got to be crazy, and I must be crazy to be flying, but if I ask to be grounded, that means I'm not crazy anymore and have to keep flying.

—Yossarian, in Joseph Heller's *Catch-22*

TWO O'CLOCK MONDAY AFTERNOON, MAY 17, Chris and I walked into Judge Jones's wood-paneled courtroom a minute ahead of the contingent from the United States attorney's office. The deputy marshal brought Brandon in from the side door, where they have a little holding cell for court proceedings. When the judge took the bench, we were ready to jump right into our motions, but he had a different agenda in mind. Judge Jones asked if we had seen Gorder's response to our motion for release, a pleading that he had just received from the government.[1]

"No, Your Honor," Chris replied.

After reminding us all of "the utmost importance" of getting documents to each other, the judge moved ahead without waiting for the copy he had just asked his clerk to make for us. His face became more severe than usual as he spoke, clearly thinking he was dropping a bombshell on Brandon and his team. Referring to Gorder's pleading, Judge Jones said, "One of the issues that this document raises is the affidavit of indigency . . . for appointment of counsel . . . The Government . . . points out that a warrant on the safe deposit box turned up 10,000 dollars cash in 100-dollar bills, which I doubt you were aware of."

It was instantly apparent that the safe-deposit money threatened to derail our efforts to get Brandon out of jail. The box filled with money and passports "has a lot of relevancy in respect to his ability to flee," the judge said. Judge Jones was also angry because he had not known about the money when he assigned my office to represent Brandon. While $10,000 would not have covered even a fraction of the cost of the representation the case required, if Brandon had hidden the money from his lawyers and the court, Judge Jones said it would be most relevant "to his credibility."

Having aired his concerns about the money, and before Chris and I could get into our arguments for releasing Brandon, the judge shifted gears and cut to the heart of the problem that had prevented any significant progress during the past week.

"As I look at it, both sides are in a catch-22 position. Legally, the defense doesn't want to commit to giving a proffer or deposition or grand jury testimony until they know what the Government's got against them.

"The Government doesn't want to tell the . . . material witness what they have, in addition to what you know, so that answers can't be tailored to any questions that they normally have to ask a witness."

This was the practical Judge Jones I had come to respect, and his next words were music to my ears, proposing to break the Catch-22 circle precisely as we had hoped. "One thing," the judge said, "that I have been thinking about, just to put to rest one way or the other, there's no secret about the fingerprint—in Spain. The issue is how valid it is."

Judge Jones then went on to suggest we all consider a series of steps, testimony about the print from the FBI examiners and production of the print for review by a defense expert.

Seeing an opening, Chris pressed ahead, telling the judge that Spanish newspapers were reporting what was in the arrest warrant affidavit and that the Spanish forensic police were continuing to question the fingerprint. He reminded the judge that everything he had seen so far in Brandon's law office files was exculpatory. We wanted, Chris concluded, access not only to the fingerprint but also to the other material the FBI had seized.

Dave Atkinson responded for the United States attorney's office, telling Judge Jones that his office had put together a list of fifteen to twenty items they would return to Brandon, but he recycled his arguments about wanting the "unvarnished truth." As for disclosure of the fingerprint, Gorder stepped back in, telling the judge that there was no legal precedent for a court to order the government to provide a witness anything in a grand jury proceeding. While he could "provide a copy of the FBI's fingerprint report," he said he did not "have the authority to provide . . . a copy of the actual fingerprint from Spain."

"Why not?" Judge Jones barked back.

Gorder held his ground. "There . . . is some sensitivity to issues with the Spanish government." Then he went back to the Justice Department's concern that they "don't want to establish a precedent."

The judge wasn't moved and explained to the prosecutors why he was going to order production of the print. Losing patience with everyone at that point, he snapped at Brandon, who had leaned over to ask me a question, to "cease talking." It's bad enough for a lawyer when the judge talks to you that way, I am glad I have never experienced Judge Jones's ire as a defendant. When the judge finished, Gorder, still holding his ground, asked if they could delay getting the print "until tomorrow to discuss the issue with the folks back in Washington, DC."

The judge leaned forward on the bench, eyes boring into Gorder, his entire body rigid. "I'm not dependent upon your approval or Washington, DC. This is a court order."

The power of the federal judiciary was on display in all its majesty at that moment.

Established as a separate and equal branch of the government in Article III of the Constitution, federal judges enjoy life tenure precisely for moments like this—when one of the other branches needs to be reminded that there are limits to its power and that the judiciary must stand as the guardian of individual liberty. During the Guantánamo litigation with Adel, I was continually disappointed that the judges in the District of Columbia failed to stand up to the executive branch in the same way as did Judge Jones with Brandon and Judge Brown with Steitiye.

We were thrilled about the order; Brandon was adamant that an independent examination would exonerate him. But there was one part of the judge's order I had to oppose.

"As a condition of being able to have it examined," Judge Jones said, we would have to "supply the Court with a report from the examiner, irrespective of what the examiner comes up with."

Regardless of Brandon's assurances, if we accepted these terms and somehow the examiner confirmed the FBI's identification, we could literally be putting a nail in Brandon's coffin because the United States attorney would be able to use our evidence in prosecuting Brandon for capital murder. Judge Jones heard me out but said, "It's pretty obvious that if you proceeded not to give me anything, I would make—I would be—"

I had to concede it would be obvious that the results were bad for Brandon if we did not come running with an exculpatory report, but I told the judge that if we proceeded in the normal course with an expert, even though he might know, the results would be protected by the attorney-client privilege. We needed a guarantee that the results could not be used against Brandon. Ever practical, Judge Jones agreed he "could go that far."

We then won another piece as the judge ordered Gorder to give us the affidavits that had been filed in support of the search warrants that Judge Jones had issued for Brandon's house and car. It wasn't a complete victory because the judge allowed Gorder to black out certain parts of the affidavits. When we saw them the next day, though, only one paragraph had been blacked out in each. Based on our years of experience analyzing search warrant affidavits, the place of the blacked out paragraphs added fuel to our suspicions that these warrants had been preceded by sneak-and-peek and wiretap warrants from the Foreign Intelligence Surveillance Court and under the Patriot Act. I asked Gorder about that, but he would make no comment, further confirming my suspicions.

When we finally got back to arguing for Brandon's release, it was clear we had won all we were going to win that day. The judge heard us out politely, but from his side of the bench looking at the fingerprint and the safe-deposit box, it was eminently reasonable to have Brandon wait in jail a couple more days while we got the independent fingerprint test.

My investigator, William, spent the rest of Monday afternoon and evening on the phone sounding out possible experts. Under the gag order, he could not tell anyone precisely why we needed a top expert immediately, but it was obvious to everyone he called what the issue at hand was. By Tuesday morning, William had compiled a short list. Allan Bayle was our first choice, a retired Scotland Yard man who had broken the case of the Pan Am 747 jetliner that was blown out of the skies over Lockerbie, Scotland, linking latent prints picked up at the scene of the downed plane to Libyan terrorists.[2] We liked Bayle because he had an independent streak, having taken on Scotland Yard a couple of years after his success in the Lockerbie case and helping to expose a frame-up of one of his colleagues.

Our second choice was Professor John Thornton, who questioned "ridge-ology," one of the points of disagreement between the Spanish and the FBI. Our third choice was Kenneth Moses, a retired San Francisco police officer and independent criminalist who had done a fair amount of work for defense attorneys in recent years. He came to us highly recommended by the Innocence Project, a group created by defense attorney Barry Scheck that investigates the cases of people on death row and has produced DNA and fingerprint evidence that has led to more than 125 exonerations.

At 10:25 Tuesday morning, Pam Holsinger called to say that the FBI had a digital copy of the print at their laboratory in Quantico, and were working on the mechanics of sending it via e-mail to the FBI office in Portland. At 11:00 A.M., the prosecution team and I convened in Judge Jones's chambers for an off-the-record discussion of the mechanics of our examination. Holsinger reported that the FBI was working on the transmission issues. Judge Jones turned to me and asked, "Who do you want to use, Steve?" In normal proceedings, I would have told the judge that it was none of his business, but this was anything but normal and the judge had gone out on a limb to order the print produced, so I gave him our list of experts.

Holsinger went down to her office for a few minutes to consult with the FBI and, given Bayle's work against Scotland Yard, I was not surprised when she reported that the FBI "had problems with Bayle." The judge vetoed the professor, saying he had too little practical experience. Holsinger said Moses was acceptable but suggested another former police officer, Allan McRoberts, who, like Moses, was working independently. William had vetted and included McRoberts in our list of possible experts, but the word we had received suggested that he might be a little less independent than Moses. We all agreed that Moses would be the man.

At 1:15, Chris and I met with Brandon in the marshal's lockup in the courthouse to update him on the situation and give Brandon one last chance to call off the examination. I reminded him that, regardless of the agreement that the government could not use the results if they confirmed the FBI analysis, the reality was likely to be indictment if the identification was confirmed. Brandon said he understood and remained adamant that he was not worried. Chris and I headed up to court.

Everything both sides had been doing during this grand jury proceeding was confidential, a gag order was in place, and all our pleadings had been filed under seal. Nonetheless, Judge Jones added a real cloak-and-dagger element to the fingerprint examination when he took the bench.

"First of all," he directed, ". . . this whole exercise must be kept absolutely confidential. . . . Make sure not even any other judge is aware of what we are doing or any clerk."

I had never before experienced a judge so overtly keen on keeping something confidential from his fellow judges.

Gorder, who had gotten an earful from the higher-ups in the Justice Department and the FBI about the production order the night before, asked the judge "to reconsider its order just slightly." The DOJ and the FBI could not accept the precedent of a grand jury witness in a terrorism case getting access to evidence, he told the judge, so he proposed having Moses designated as a "court expert." From their perspective, this would lessen the impact on the Justice Department of what the judge had ordered, since it would not involve disclosure directly to the witness. As I was gearing up to object that designating Moses as a court expert would put Brandon at risk since a court expert's report would be equally available to the prosecutors, Gorder offered a concession. The government felt so strongly about the precedent issue, he said, that he was "willing to give up the right to call [the expert] as a witness down the road if it is a positive match." With this assurance, it made little difference what we called Moses and so I agreed.

There were two more pieces we wanted for the examination: the right to talk freely to Moses about his findings and to make sure that he was insulated from any FBI pressure by preventing anyone in the FBI or Justice Department from contacting him. The first part was easy: Gorder and Judge Jones agreed we could discuss everything with Moses. However, Gorder did not want Moses insulated from the FBI. After wrangling back and forth, in the end we all agreed that Moses could call the primary FBI fingerprint examiner, Terry Green, if he needed information on the FBI examination, but that no one from the FBI would be permitted to initiate contact with him.

Anticipating that we would get a copy of the fingerprint on a disk, William was ready to fly to San Francisco that afternoon. As soon as court ended, William headed for Portland International to fly to San Francisco where he would rendezvous with Moses, who had agreed to work all night if necessary to complete his analysis of the fingerprint and call us at 8:30 the next morning.

. . .

A little before 8:30 on the nineteenth, Chris and William stepped sharply into my office. William, who had not gotten back to Portland until late the night before, reported that the fingerprint transfer to Moses had gone off without a hitch. When Moses phoned moments later, we were all more excited than nervous, looking forward to the vindication Brandon assured us we would get.

Moses began by telling us that the latent "was a pretty good print." There were no difficulties in making a comparison. The "substrate," the material the latent was taken from, was a "plastic bag." Okay, Ken, I thought, cut to the chase, is it Brandon's print or not. Then he hit us, hard.

"There are sixteen points that match; I have marked them on the prints and can e-mail the comparison to you."

Sixteen points. The FBI had only noted fifteen points that matched. Had we really just heard that our expert had not only agreed with the FBI's analysis but had added to their work? Moses's e-mail arrived within seconds, and Chris, William, and I huddled around the computer screen, heads brushing against each other as we conducted our own instant analysis, looking for any weaknesses in Moses's work. Chris immediately focused on several ridges on the top left of the latent that, to his lay eyes, appeared to be different from the ridges in the same area on Brandon's prints. Yes, Moses agreed, they were different, "this is an anomaly," but he ascribed the difference to "distortion by motion of the finger," or possibly "underlay of another print."

I had focused on a mark on the latent in the lower right part of the print that I thought showed a ridge that shifted from the horizontal to the vertical. Again Moses attributed the difference to the way the latent was laid down. William then noted a circular ridge area also on the top left of the latent that we did not see on Brandon's print. Moses agreed it appeared on the latent but said it had nothing to do with the fingerprint and was, rather, the result of distortion in the surface of the bag from which the print was lifted.

In our review of literature on fingerprinting, the "one dissimilarity doctrine" says that even if there are points of comparison, you don't have a match if there are any significant differences. There are many articles about this doctrine regarding its validity, its relevance, and what constitutes an important dissimilarity. William put it directly to Ken, who said he did not subscribe to the doctrine.[3]

We were concerned and confused. In only a couple of minutes, each of us had seen a different dissimilarity. Ken's answer to each was based on an assumption about the surface material, a moving finger, or an overlay. While they were plausible assumptions, they were, nonetheless, assumptions. Chris, who was going to handle examination of Moses when we got to court, spent some more time with him on the phone, questioning the assumptions, establishing that he was not certain of his identification, and that his degree of confidence would be affected by access to the original of the latent.

At 10:00, a dejected team left for the courthouse and the marshal's lockup where we would have to give Brandon the bad news. Even though we tried to tell Brandon that Ken's opinion was not final, there was no way to downplay the fact that Ken's opinion squashed any possibility of a quick resolution and release. I don't think Brandon was able to accept the reality of the news and the fact that a capital prosecution was now likely.[4]

. . .

Gorder, Holsinger, and Atkinson were already sitting at counsel table when Chris and I walked into the courtroom. There was no time for anything more than a quick hello as we made our way past the bar to our seats, where Brandon was already waiting. William and the rest of my team came in and sat in the public seats as Chris and I sat on either side of Brandon.

Judge Jones's secretary and courtroom deputy clerk, Cindy, had Moses on the speakerphone by the time the judge took the bench.[5] Dispensing with any preliminaries, Judge Jones got to the heart of the matter: "In a nutshell, can you tell me what your ultimate conclusion is as to whether this fingerprint can be identified as that of Mr. Mayfield?"

Moses's disembodied voice boomed like the voice of doom from the speakers in the courtroom. "Yes. I compared the latent prints to the known prints that were submitted on Brandon Mayfield, and I concluded that the latent print is the left index finger of Mr. Mayfield."

Poker-faced at the time, but as he told me years later, as surprised as we had been, Judge Jones turned the witness over to Chris, who asked a few questions, bringing out the possibility that it would be important for a fingerprint examiner to have access to the original print so he could assess whether the "anomalies" we had seen were really the result of shifting substrate or print overlay, or whether they existed because the two prints were made by two different people. When Chris turned the questioning over to Holsinger, she asked only one question, whether the digital print Moses had worked from was sufficient to use for making a comparison. Moses's terse, "Yes, it was," was all she needed to hear.

We were unsure what direction things would take now that the FBI identification had been confirmed. One thing is certain: None of Brandon's team were prepared for what happened next. Judge Jones turned to Gorder, who rose slowly to address the court.

"Yes, Your Honor, just briefly. I advised the Court that we had received some information from Spain this morning that casts some doubt on the identification." Gorder went on to say that the information was classified so he could not tell us anything more. Judge Jones, who had a security clearance, told them to follow him into his chambers.

I have lived through any number of strange moments in court since I tried my first case more than thirty-five years ago, but none as surreal as this. I had just gone through the agony of telling my client that our expert confirmed that his fingerprint was on a bag full of detonators at a terror bombing site. My client, colleagues, and I had just finished presenting defense-generated testimony to the court that could ensure we would be dealing with a capital prosecution. And after allowing the testimony to be taken, the prosecutor's reaction was to tell the court that the fingerprint might not be my client's after all. When the prosecution team went back into chambers to give Judge Jones the classified details, I truly felt as though I had slipped down Alice's rabbit hole.

An interminable twenty minutes later, Judge Jones, Gorder, and his team emerged from chambers and the mystery only intensified. The new information, the judge said, "is not of such a caliber that would justify immediate release of the material witness." What were we hearing? I wondered. Did the new information confirm it was Brandon's print or not? Judge Jones forged ahead, further dashing our hopes, and announced that the grand jury would be brought in on Friday but then asked all the lawyers, investigators, and FBI agents to confer about a possible proffer agreement in his conference room. I had to tell the judge I was not sure any of that made sense if the government was going to stay firm in its position that it was

Brandon's print. If so, there was no way, given Moses's analysis, I could advise him to testify without full immunity. Regardless, the judge had set a firm deadline for the grand jury and for the government to decide on the type, if any, of immunity it would offer.

All the lawyers filed into the judge's conference room. None of us were comfortable with what had just transpired, and there was none of the banter and professional friendliness that usually marked our meetings. Chris finally broke the ice, trying to get Gorder to tell us informally what was going on. He looked uncomfortable with his position, but consummate professional that he is, would not talk. Worse yet, he reported that the FBI felt that the potential exculpatory information "might wash out." He also made it clear that the government would not be offering Brandon immunity if he testified in the grand jury.

Our focus turned to the terms of an informal proffer agreement under which the prosecutors would be strictly limited to areas of questioning around three or four matters arising from the searches that they and the FBI were concerned about, and they would also agree that if Brandon appeared to be truthful, they would recommend his release.

It was a full hour before Chris and I made it down to the marshal's lockup to talk to Brandon, who was as confused as I had ever seen him. The roller coaster of Moses's testimony, Gorder's mysterious revelation, and Judge Jones's statements had taken a serious toll. Judge Jones had also put us in a terrible bind, as we finally had to decide whether Brandon would assert his Fifth Amendment privilege. I did not see any choice at that point but to advise Brandon to refuse to provide any information unless we received more information on Thursday.

20 | The Road to Kabul

It is no surprise that danger and suffering surround us. What astonishes is the singing.

—Jack Gilbert, "Horses at Midnight Without a Moon"

PREPARATIONS FOR A TRIP TO AFGHANISTAN had started the second week in March, as soon as we had all returned from our first visits to Guantánamo. I called an office meeting and we gathered in the large conference room to relay our firsthand accounts of what we had found in the prison. Full of Adel, Gul, and Chaman's stories, we wanted to share them with everyone in the office, but we could not under the Protective Order. Everything we had learned was considered classified information and could be shared only within the core group of sixteen who had received security clearances, unless and until the notes of the visits with our clients were declassified. Instead, we put on a little slide show with photos of Guantánamo, talked about Cuba, the beach near our funky hotel, and the CBQ, and described our visits with the clients in very general terms. Then I had to ask all but the team members with security clearances to leave so we could get down to business. Following the instructions from the Department of Justice security officers who had given us our classified briefings, we shut the drapes and started the serious business of figuring out how we could try to investigate our clients' claims in the hostile environments of Afghanistan, Pakistan, Saudi Arabia, and Sudan.

While I had come back from my first visit believing in Adel, I also knew that I had gotten only his side of the story and had not seen any of the classified information. My mood was also tempered by my skepticism, something that has guided me throughout my career. Of course not all of my clients are guilty, but many are, and some have difficulty confiding in me, particularly in the first meetings. I tell all my clients, as I did Brandon when he got upset two years before, that I don't judge them and will fight just as hard for them whether they've "done it" or if they are innocent. I ask them to be honest with me, then do what I can to test what they have told me. It takes more than belief to help a client.

As challenging as it was to prove a negative for Brandon, that he had not been involved in the Madrid bombings, it would be that much more difficult to test Adel's story. Brandon was local, and he was in the jail across the street, not in Guantánamo; we could see or call him whenever we wanted. His family and coworkers were ten minutes away, not in the war zones in Afghanistan or Sudan; he had been in Oregon for a decade, and, while he had converted to Islam, there were no cultural or language barriers to overcome with him or with any potential witnesses. Also, the gag order we had negotiated with Gorder and Judge Jones had allowed us to investigate, even using information that was deemed secret in the grand jury.

Of all the pieces Adel had given us in Guantánamo that we could use to start testing his assertions of innocence, the most important were a phone number in Khartoum that Adel said used to belong to his brother-in-law, Adil Al Tayeb, and the names of the hospital director, Dr. Najib, and Adel's supervisor at WAMY in Pakistan, Abu Hadifa. Pat and I had both memorized Adel's brother-in-law's name and phone number, but under the Protective Order we could not put them to use. Even writing them down on a piece of paper that would be locked in my desk would be a violation of the order. Until our notes passed through classification review and were released from the secure facility, we were not allowed to use the information that was in our heads.

My team started figuring out not only how to test Adel's account and prove his innocence but also what we could do for our two Afghan clients, Chaman and Gul. During their visit to the base, Chris, Bryan, Amy, and Ruben had also received family contact information.

As we started planning our work for Adel, Gul, and Chaman at that first postvisit meeting in March, Adel's situation looked the most straightforward. We needed to find a way to confirm that he was an innocent charity worker and hospital administrator. Gul's situation also appeared relatively straightforward. After being caught in a firefight during which Gul, then three, lost an eye, his family had fled the Soviet invasion of Afghanistan for Pakistan. He had grown up as a refugee outside of Peshawar, working in the family bakery, and had returned to Afghanistan only after the fall of the Taliban. A few weeks after his return, he had gone for medical treatment and was staying with a friend of a friend when the American military raided the house looking for someone else and seized him.

Chaman's case was more complex because he had been a fighter against the Soviets and later in the Afghan civil wars. Our government alleged that Chaman had gone over to the dark side sometime in the late 1990s or early 2000s and had become a supporter of the Taliban. Chaman denied the charge, saying that he had remained loyal to President Karzai, had been working for him, and was the victim of a double cross. To do anything for him, we were going to have to find some way to reach into the netherworld of Afghan politics.

The situation with Gul and Chaman was complicated by the fact that Gul's nickname was "Chaman," and it was possible that our military had confused the two men.

. . .

While we couldn't try to call Adel's brother-in-law, Al Tayeb, until our notes were cleared, we could start trying to contact Adel's employers, WAMY and LDI, since we had an independent source for that information in the material William had downloaded from the Internet. I asked Toni Pisani, the investigator in my branch office in Eugene who was working on the Guantánamo cases, to try to find the hospital where Adel had worked and any doctors who had worked there. We needed proof that Adel was a legitimate charity worker.

Toni's first step paid off. Mining the Internet, she found references to a hospital in Chamkani, Afghanistan, that seemed, from the location, to be the one where Adel had worked. But then she ran into a brick wall. Over the next month and a half, Toni logged close to one hundred calls and e-mails to the United Nations offices in New York and Geneva, offices of the World Health Organization, Doctors Without Borders, and Mercy Corps.

No one could, or would, give her the name of a hospital WAMY ran in Chamkani province or the name of anyone from the UN or WHO who had worked with a hospital there. Most people did not even return her calls. Were they afraid of being seen as helping a terrorist? Or were records so poorly maintained that the information we needed was not available? All we knew was that we were getting nowhere.

William was running into a similar problem with WAMY. He started by looking for offices in the United States and found there had been one in Virginia, but it had closed in 2004 or 2005. Then, on the Internet, William found two phone numbers for WAMY in Saudi Arabia, one in Jedda and one in Mecca. The first time he tried to call, William and I met in my office with our interpreter, Dr. Sbait, at 7 P.M., 6 A.M. Saudi time, on Thursday night. While the office system allows for direct dial overseas, the call would not go through. The overseas operator, a woman in Dallas with a nice Texas accent, had no more luck. Eventually she got through to an operator in Mecca. I smiled as the two operators tried to converse in English, the American with a thick drawl and the Saudi with a crisp, easy-to-understand British accent. When they had trouble understanding each other, Dr. Sbait interrupted in Arabic. The drawl tightened up as the Texan told him to be quiet, she would handle it in English. Finally the Saudi operator told Dr. Sbait, in Arabic, that it was a holiday weekend and we might have better luck on Saturday.

Saturday came around and William did get through to WAMY in Mecca, but he got nowhere again. The person he spoke with would not put him through to the WAMY director and would confirm nothing, not even the name of the hospital in Afghanistan. Shifting continents and starting over, William tried London to see if there was a WAMY office there. Finally he got something. The London office confirmed that WAMY had run a hospital in Afghanistan near Pakistan, that it was in Chamkani, and agreed to send us some literature. We waited less and less patiently as the weeks went by, but it never arrived.

We clearly needed to go in a different direction, so I asked William to see if he could find a lawyer or investigator in Peshawar who would be interested in working for us. After searching the Internet, he finally found several people in Pakistan who held themselves out as English-speaking lawyers, including the third Adil in this case, Adil Butt, a Pakistani lawyer based in Peshawar.

. . .

A week after our return from Guantánamo in March, the deadline set in the Protective Order for classification review of our notes, Pat called Jennifer Campbell, our main contact in the court security office and one of the people I had met in Washington the month before in Judge Kay's chambers. We were both worried by her news that the notes had not even made it from Guantánamo to the secure facility. Having heard horror stories from other habeas lawyers of notes never showing up, Pat asked Jennifer to try to track them down. A tense week later, Jennifer e-mailed Pat that the notes had arrived and she would press the classification review team to move quickly.

On March 29 at 1:10 in the afternoon, the notes finally arrived in my office via fax. Pat and I jokingly congratulated ourselves on our memory of the number sequencing. We had both written Al Tayeb's number down the same way, but we had very different phonetic versions of Al Tayeb's name. While this didn't trip us up with Al Tayeb, we later learned that the multiple spellings and misspellings of Arabic names by the government had caused some problems.

Pat took a set of the notes back to his office and I left William a voice mail asking him to arrange with Dr. Sbait a call to what we hoped was Al Tayeb's number in Sudan. As I was walking down the hall to speak with one of the assistants, I passed Pat's office, where, phone in one hand, he signaled me in with the other. Always the go-getter, Pat had not waited for Sbait but had picked up the phone and just dialed the number. He hit the speaker button, and after a half dozen more rings a groggy voice answered. Pat had not thought of the time difference—1:30 P.M. our time was 12:30 A.M. in Khartoum.

Pat spat out briskly, "Hello, Adil Al Tayeb. Do you speak any English?"

The answer was hard to understand, but there was a "yes" somewhere in it. A soft voice spoke in broken English with a thick Sudanese accent, but it was English. Pat explained that he was a lawyer representing Adel Hamad.

Language was no barrier to the emotion that poured back through the line.

"Helping Adel?"

"Yes," Pat said. The conversation broke down, but Pat managed to convey that we would call with an interpreter at 11 P.M. Al Tayeb's time, on Friday the thirty-first.

I whispered to Pat, "Ask him to have Adel's wife there."

The first call to Al Tayeb with Dr. Sbait lasted an hour. It took several tries to get through, then the connection, as sometimes happened on our calls to Sudan, would fade in and out. Al Tayeb did not have Salwa on the phone, but we understood she was there in the background listening to his end of the conversation. The taboo against speaking with men outside the family was too strong for Salwa to get on the phone during that first call.

Al Tayeb wanted as much detail as we could give about Adel. How was his health? Did he look okay? How were his spirits? When we had satisfied his appetite for information about his brother-in-law, we turned to trying to explain who we were and what we hoped to accomplish for Adel. This was no easy task. The arcane habeas corpus process that was bogged down in procedure and the CSRT process are difficult enough to explain to an American lawyer, let alone a Sudanese where there is no analog in the law. I am not sure how much Al Tayeb understood, but it probably was not important. What mattered most was that he understood very clearly there was a team working for his brother-in-law and there were Americans who cared and who promised to stay in touch with him.

As for providing us with information about Adel, Al Tayeb helped a little in that first call but did not know much about Adel's life and work in Pakistan and Afghanistan, the areas that were most essential to us. We put the phone on mute and caucused for a minute among ourselves about talking to Salwa, and with Dr. Sbait's guidance that most Sudanese are not as strict as Muslims in some other Middle Eastern countries, decided to push forward.

"We understand that it may be difficult for Salwa to speak with us, but we need to talk to her and the older daughters. We need to hear about their life in Pakistan, what Adel was doing, his job, his politics. Please talk to Salwa and explain how important this is. While we are looking, we don't have anyone else right now who can tell us about Adel's life."

Al Tayeb said he would talk to her and that "it should be possible." We agreed to call again the next Friday at the same time.

A week later, Dr. Sbait arrived shortly before noon and William dialed Al Tayeb's number. The call went through on the second try and a male voice answered. It was Al Tayeb. We could hear female voices in the background.

"*Salaam Alechem,*" Dr. Sbait began.

Al Tayeb answered, "*Alechem Salaam*," the traditional Arabic greeting, the equivalent of "Peace be with you," a phrase we would repeat hundreds of times over the next two years, hoping it would come true. We had a few more sentences of greeting, then Al Tayeb told us Salwa, the two oldest daughters, and one of Adel's sisters were there with him. Then he asked, "When will Adel have his trial? How long will it be?"

It hurt to hear such a rational question. Even in Sudan with its Islamist dictatorship, the assumption was that a man who was put in prison would eventually be charged with something and have a trial. But not in Guantánamo. In more detail than we had the week before, Pat painstakingly explained, or tried to explain, habeas corpus, the stay of all proceedings, and the CSRT and ARB processes.

"How is Adel's family getting on?" I asked.

"The financial condition is not good since Adel went back to Sudan. His wife and children live in one room with my family. But *Inshallah*, we all survive," Al Tayeb answered.

"*Inshallah*" was another phrase I would hear hundreds of times in the coming years. Meaning "God willing," it is sometimes a fatalistic view of the world that stops people from trying, but for many others, including Al Tayeb and Adel, it's a phrase said with a reverence and acceptance of the results of their efforts.

I then asked Al Tayeb if he could put Salwa on the phone. He said yes, she would speak with us, and we heard a female voice on the line.

"*Salaam Alechem*."

Worried about her husband and hesitant to talk to male strangers, Salwa's voice was weak and cautious at first. There was often a long gap between our questions and her answers. But, slowly, as the conversation progressed, Salwa's voice grew stronger and, over a full two hours, Salwa confirmed what Adel had told us and what he had told the CSRT about his life and work in Pakistan and Afghanistan.

"Adel left in July and I did not hear from him. What had happened? I called Sakhina in Sudan."

"Who is Sakhina?" William asked.

"The wife of the downstairs neighbor, Ammeur Mammar, from Algeria. But there was no answer. I waited to hear, but nothing. Then I went with my uncle to the Sudan government. They had no information. I never heard back from them."

"How did you learn what had happened to Adel?"

"Around four months after he left, some students who had been in Pakistan came to the house. They had been in Peshawar and knew he had been arrested, but they could not tell me anything more than that. I tried again with the WAMY office, but they would tell me nothing."

Salwa then told us about the letter Adel had sent her from Baghram. She still had a copy and said she would send it to us.

After several hours on the phone with Salwa, we talked briefly with Adel's oldest daughter, Zaynab, who added to our understanding of the ordinariness of their life in Pakistan. She told us that she never saw or heard anything or anyone around their house that seemed suspicious in any way. A university student in Khartoum, Zaynab spoke some English and had access to the Internet, something we were hopeful could be used to establish regular e-mail communication with the family. It did not work out with Zaynab, but Al Tayeb was able to establish an Internet account, which helped immeasurably over the next year.

A few weeks later we were reading a faxed copy of the letter Adel had sent home from the prison in Baghram that Dr. Sbait had translated for us.

> My Dear wife Salwa Uthman, my Daughters, my Mother Awatif, my brothers, My Sisters, and all my folks and in-laws,
>
> Peace be with you, the Mercy of God, and His Blessings.
>
> If you would like to know how I am doing, thank God, I am very well. I would like to inform you that I am still imprisoned in Afghanistan for seven months and a half, not to [not legible] thanks to your prayers. I know that you are in need of expenses. You can receive a sum of money from brother Sliman. Don't deprive yourself but don't overspend either; be in between.
>
> My greetings and peace to all of you, and hope to see you soon, God willing.

Since that first contact, either William, Pat, or I have spoken with Al Tayeb several times a month. Some of the calls have just been to check in with them to say hello, see how the family is doing, and let them know we are still trying to get Adel home. Other calls describe our visits with Adel, let the family know he is still in good spirits. Others focus on the legal aspects, what we have been doing in the case, what motions we have filed, what happened in the Supreme Court. From late June on, after we had made our first contacts with witnesses overseas, the calls took on a much more serious purpose as we checked what we were learning against what they knew.

.   .   .

As soon as Pat and I received our notes from the reviewers in Washington, I asked William to see if he could track down Abu Hadifa, the supervisor Adel had called just before going back to Peshawar in July 2002. From the London offices of WAMY, he was eventually able to get through to someone in the headquarters in Saudi Arabia who then referred us to a lawyer in New York, Omar Mohammedi. But he would not help. WAMY, which had been sued for alleged connections to terrorist activities, did not want to do anything that could be seen as helpful to a former employee who was in Guantánamo.

It was at this point that the Pakistani lawyer, Adil Butt, got involved in the case. Butt assured us that he was willing to be retained to look for Abu Hadifa and to track down Adel's landlord in Peshawar. He came through quickly, contacting the WAMY office in Islamabad and finding a number we could use to call Abu Hadifa.

On May 9, William and Pat got a call through to Islamabad. With Dr. Sbait's help they got our first confirmation, independent of the family, of Adel's work in Afghanistan. Abu Hadifa was guarded, telling them at first, "I will be happy to look for information on Adel Hamad, but I need to speak with the headquarters in Saudi Arabia."

A good investigator knows that even when a witness says, "I won't talk to you," if you keep him on the line, eventually you will get some information. William and Pat did just that, and twenty minutes later, Abu Hadifa had confirmed that WAMY had run a hospital in Chamkani, Afghanistan, from the early 1990s until 2004; Adel had worked for WAMY from 2000 to 2002 and served as the director of the hospital in Chamkani in 2000 and 2001. Abu Hadifa also confirmed that he had been instrumental in selling the possessions in Adel's home in Peshawar after his seizure and sending the money to Salwa along with Adel's last wages. The conversation ended with Abu Hadifa promising to get permission from his headquarters to get us employment records through Adil Butt.

While Butt had started strong with the contact information for Abu Hadifa, William's contact with him soon took a very different turn. A couple of times a week they e-mailed back and forth. Butt would promise to get on the case "tomorrow"; he was at a wedding; he had tried a call but no one was there; he did not return e-mails. It was a terribly frustrating time. We were concerned that Butt had been frightened off the case until, finally, at the end of May, Butt came through again with an e-mail explaining that he had spoken with Abu Hadifa on May 24. Hadifa was still waiting for permission from headquarters in Saudi Arabia to provide any records.

A week later, Butt e-mailed again. He had made contact with Engineer Ishmail, the landlord of Adel's house on Bilal Lane in Peshawar, and Ishmail recalled Adel and Ammeur fondly, they were good tenants, there was nothing political about them, they always paid the rent on time.

. . .

When we first got involved with the Guantánamo cases, we had quickly hooked up with Dr. Sbait at Portland State to help our Arabic-speaking clients but had not found anyone in Portland with experience as a Pashto interpreter, the primary language of our Afghan clients. I asked Rod Saiki, one of the team's investigators in Portland, to line up a Pashto speaker. Rod, of Japanese descent, became more and more intense about the Guantánamo cases as they dragged on. Like Korematsu in his amicus brief, Rod was personally aware through his family's history of how easy it is for a person to be a "good citizen" one day and a number in a concentration camp the next.

Rod followed a series of leads for a Pashto interpreter from Portland to Eugene to a graduade student at the University of Oregon, Zabihullah "Zabi" Noori. Zabi had graduated from the Balkh University in Mazar-e-Sharif, Afghanistan, with a degree from the English Department in 1997, then worked for eight years teaching English and as a travel agent in exile in Peshawar, then, after Karzai took power, went back to Afghanistan as a humanitarian organizer and aid worker. In 2005, Zabi won a Fulbright scholarship to study at the University of Oregon.

At first, Zabi helped introduce our team to Afghan culture and tribal politics, then when the notes of our first visits in Guantánamo with Chaman and Gul were cleared, he interpreted the team's calls to their families in Afghanistan. Throughout the spring and early summer, Zabi was in the office several times a week on one mission or another. Feeling the pain of his countrymen who were locked up in Guantánamo, Zabi was easily swept up in our cases. From his time spent around the office, he had also heard the basic facts of Adel's case and asked if it would be all right if he contacted his friends in some humanitarian organizations back in Afghanistan to see if they could track down information about the hospital in Chamkani.

We enthusiastically took Zabi up on his offer and he spread the word among his friends back home. It took only a week to get our first results, official confirmation from the Karzai government through Dr. Hakim Nasiry, a deputy with the Department of Education in Gardez, the capital city of Paktia province where Chamkani is located, that the Chamkani hospital had an excellent reputation while it was run by WAMY. But more important, Dr. Nasiry confirmed the name of the former medical director of the hospital, Dr. Najib.

We asked Zabi to have his friends try to locate the doctor. Although "Najib" was the nickname of Dr. Najibullah Zalmai, locating him turned out to be an easy task since he was a prominent physician in Kabul. On June 20, William and I reached Dr. Najib by phone. Zabi stood by to translate, but Dr. Najib's English was strong enough for much of the conversation to take place without his help. Fortunately for us, Dr. Najib spoke without any hesitation or fear.

"Tell us about the hospital, please," William asked.

"This was full hospital, sixty beds. Set up to see surgical patients. The hospital also had obstetrics and gynecological facilities."

"How long did you work there?"

"I was general surgeon from March 1994 to January 2004 and became director."

"Did the hospital have any contact with any outside organization?" William asked.

"Of course. United Nations. Assistance from the United Nations. There was monthly visits from UNHCR [the UN Refugee Agency]. The World Food Program sent food, wheat, sugar, oil."

"Did you know a man named Adel Hassan Hamad at the hospital?"

"Yes. The hospital administrator was Abu Doujana. From 2000 to maybe 2002."

We were pretty sure that Abu Doujana and Adel were the same person. Dr. Najib did not have the English word "nickname," but that was what we believed he was saying, though we were not sure. Hoping for the best, we pressed ahead.

Dr. Najib confirmed what Adel had told us about living in the hospital for most of the month with the rest of the staff and traveling back to Peshawar to be with his family for about a week each month.

"What do you remember about Adel?"

He recalled that Adel had three or four daughters and that "he was a very nice man. Always in a good mood, joking."

"What about politics?" I asked.

"Abu Doujana never talked anything political or have any contacts in Chamkani. That was not the type of person he was; no one ever thought anything bad about him."

"Was there anything political at all about the hospital?"

"No. Just a hospital."

Then Dr. Najib went on. "An excellent hospital. Since WAMY stop the funding, the new sponsor is not so good. Much smaller hospital now. This not good for Paktia provinces because the hospital was the best medical [source] in the area."

"What do you remember most about Adel?"

"Ping-Pong," Dr. Najib said.

"Ping-Pong?"

"Yes. We work and then there is not much to do at the hospital. So we play much Ping-Pong. I could never beat him. Abu Doujana a good winner."

Dr. Najib told us that he had brochures from the hospital and staff photos. He wished Abu Doujana well and said he would send what he had. It took only a few days for the FedEx package to arrive from Kabul with brochures, government and UN reports, and a staff photo. Dr. Najib had not marked the photo, and Pat, William, and I spent far too much time speculating about which of the thirty or so men in white coats was Dr. Najib, and while we all thought we recognized Adel, we could not be positive.

Over the next weeks, we traded e-mails back and forth with Dr. Najib, who continued to send us more photo attachments from Kabul. We also received photos from Salwa, including one of Adel and his nieces that was taken the day before he left Khartoum for Peshawar for the last time in July 2002, and a photo of Salwa and the girls that they had taken at a photography shop at our request. We scanned the photos from Salwa into our computer system and e-mailed them to Dr. Najib. He e-mailed back, confirming that the man in the picture with the girls was Abu Doujana, or Adel Hamad. We then had Dr. Najib mark up another copy of the staff photo, circling himself and Adel and writing in their names. The doctor told us that he would be pleased to give us a sworn statement if we came to Kabul and was confident he could help us locate several other doctors who had been at Chamkani during the same period.

21 | Defenders in the War Zones

Under the stipulation of the Red Terror, mistaken ruthlessness
would be forgiven, mistaken mercy might not.

—William Vollmann, *Europe Central*

AFTER OUR PHONE SUCCESSES IN MAY and June, I moved preparations for
trips to Afghanistan and Pakistan into high gear. Zabi and his friends had
been as tireless in their efforts for our clients as my staff investigators, and
we had leads to follow on the ground not only for Adel but also for Nazar
Gul and Chaman. By mid-June, it was clear that we were going to have to
send two teams to Afghanistan, one for Chaman that would include investigation into Afghan tribalism and politics and a separate trip for Adel and Gul.
Separating the investigation for Chaman and Gul would also make it easier
to look into the confusion over Gul's nickname of "Chaman." I made the call
that Chris Schatz and Bruce Daily would go to Afghanistan first for Chaman.

As part of the preparations, Chris and Bruce subscribed to a service provided by ANSO, the Afghan NGO Safety Office, which provided daily updates
on the military and safety situation in Afghanistan for all nongovernmen-
tal organizations working there, including stories of the Taliban resurgence
and accounts of the steadily increasing attacks and suicide bombings.[1]
While telling the teams to move ahead with the trip, I asked to see regular
reports from ANSO, and the generally rosy picture of Afghanistan under
Karzai portrayed by our government quickly darkened. There was one
particularly disturbing report:

June 28, Subject: ANSO South—incident report—Suicide VBEID [Vehicle-borne improvised explosive device] Attack—Zabul Province . . . Kandahar—Kabul main route

Information: Initial reports stated that a suicide VBEID attack took place in the close proximity of a CF convoy in the area. . . .

A week later, I read:

5 July 2006 03:53.42, Dear All, This morning at around 0700 hrs, 2 explosions were heard in Kabul city. . . . An RCEID detonated next to a government bus, injuring 4 government workers at District 11, Labi Kar areas. . . .

I had made it very clear to both teams that I would pull the plug on the trip if the situation deteriorated or, perhaps, limit their work to Kabul. As much as I wanted to get the evidence of innocence for our clients, I was also responsible for my staff. While the reports were grim, our contacts in Kabul assured us there were many Western civilians working safely there. We needed to investigate on the ground for our clients, so I gave the green light for the first trip.

Chris and Bruce arrived in Kabul on July 10, 2006. "Arrived safely. Long flight, customs was interesting. The hotel is ok. More later." This was the first of the daily e-mails Bruce sent the office from the Park Residence. One of the few places Westerners stayed in Kabul, the hotel was surrounded by barbed wire, a daily reminder of the realities of life there. Though it may have been one of the "nicer" hotels and in a "safe" district, the rooms were small, the electricity unreliable with Kabul's frequent brownouts, and the view nonexistent.

Chris and Bruce moved nonstop, interviewing family members, tribal leaders, fighters, and government officials. They got confirmation of how Chaman had fought the Soviets and the Taliban and how the Taliban had massacred members of Chaman's village in the mid-1990s and forced relatives to carry ten bodies back to a mass grave.

During a meeting with several government officials in the presidential palace, Chris and Bruce were told that the Afghans and United States had reached an agreement for repatriation of nearly all the Afghans in Guantánamo, which was supposed to take place in February 2007. When we tried to get confirmation from the State Department, we ran into a brick wall. Our government would not confirm or deny anything. The reality turned out to be that only a handful of Afghans have been sent home since the summer of 2006.

The security situation in Kabul briefly caught up with Bruce and Chris on their visit to the presidential palace. On their way in, the palace security detail had a dog sniff their car for explosives, leaving them out in the baking sun for four harrowing hours. As Bruce described it with the humor of hindsight, "Besides, if you go in and the dog detects explosive residue, you have to sit in a big SUV with a guy in a T-shirt packing a Glock while another guy runs off with your passports to photocopy them. And the copy machine must be a long way from the checkpoint, because it took an awfully long time for him to get back."

Bruce and Chris realized during those four hours how vulnerable they were to the police apparatus. When Bruce checked into his hotel in New Delhi on the way home, he felt that vulnerability all over again. When he left Kabul, Bruce had carefully packed all the interview videos in bubble wrap and placed them in his suitcase. But when he opened his case in the hotel in New Delhi, the bubble wrap was empty, the tapes were gone! Bruce was furious, and worried that his trip was about to unravel. Had someone taken the tapes thinking they were exotic pornography? Or, as he suspected, had the Afghan or U.S. intelligence services been following their work and taken them at the Kabul airport? There had been no way to keep the trip a secret; the Afghan and U.S. governments both knew we were investigating for Chaman and had had plenty of time with Chris and Bruce's passports to track their departure. We will never know. What we did know was that the redundancy we had built into the trip had paid off in the end. Even though the original tapes were gone, Bruce had FedExed copies to the office before he had left Kabul and they all arrived safely.

.   .   .

Chris and Bruce landed safely at the Portland airport early in the afternoon on Friday, July 28. Tired as they were, they came to the office to hand over the camera, computer, and DVD equipment to the next team. William, Ruben, and Martin Caballero, the investigator who had been doing most of the work on Gul's case, were flying out on Sunday to investigate for Adel and Nazar Gul. The full complement of the second team included our University of Oregon Fulbright fellow, Zabi, who was so taken by the work we were doing on the cases for his fellow Afghans and for Adel that he volunteered to help investigate without pay—all we covered was his airfare.

The second team's route took them through London to New Delhi. Exhausted from the full day–plus of traveling, and reeling from the extreme heat that greeted them on the ground and "total insanity" of the noise, they tried to explain to an overly curious Indian customs inspector why they were traveling to Afghanistan. Taking the lead, Ruben matter-of-factly said that they were American lawyers, heading to Afghanistan on business. The customs man was not satisfied, asking, "What kind of business?" When Ruben told him that it had to do with the men in prison in Guantánamo, the inspector's attitude of bored hostility shifted 180 degrees. He now thought he understood why two of the men, Martin and Ruben, were traveling with official red U.S. government passports, an option we have as federal employees when going overseas on business. Ending the inspection of the men he now saw as terrorism fighters of some sort, he whisked them through, wishing them well with, "Give my regards to Mullah Omar and say hi to Osama for me."

The assumption that our team was CIA, or at least army intelligence, was repeated at the airport in Kabul. Bruce and Chris had traveled on regular blue passports so that the witnesses in Chaman's case would have less reason to suspect they were part of the U.S. government, stayed in a regular hotel, and waited for hours in the lines at the airport. The second team was met by the staff from Global Security, a British-based firm specializing in a variety of "services" for governments and businessmen in Afghanistan we had hired to help with the investigation. They were taken immediately out the side entrance of the airport to an open-air VIP section where they lounged for a half hour while everything was handled for them, then whisked in an armored Land Cruiser to the Country House, the compound in the heart of Kabul run by Global that was to be their home for the next week. Piling out of the Land Cruiser, my team was greeted by Radies Rademeyer, manager of the Country House and former lieutenant colonel in the South African Special Forces before the fall of the apartheid government.

Following Bruce's lead, William sent daily e-mails on their progress. I was back east, out of computer contact, for much of the second trip but asked Sandra Showard, my patient and dedicated legal assistant, to read the e-mails to me whenever I called to check in. As William described the team's arrival in Kabul, they were taken from the airport "to the 'Country House,' a purposely built villa in an armed compound in two armor plated Ford Excursions, driven by British former SBS [Special Boat Service] staff. One got the impression they would have been able to handle the situation if something unpleasant arose. Apparently they have had some IED's on the road between the airport and Kabul."

On the very first day of interviews, William's insistence that an investigator can always get more in person than on the phone paid off. The first round of interviews went very well, with Dr. Najib providing wonderful detail about Adel and the hospital in Chamkani in a sworn video statement.[2] He also told William about another doctor from the hospital who spoke English, Dr. Roghman. Although Dr. Najib thought he was living in Pakistan, Zabi was able to track him down in Jalalabad, on the road from Kabul to Pakistan, and a few days later they spent several hours filming and sweating in his broom-closet-sized office. The doctor really liked Adel and was upset when he learned about his situation. Dr. Roghman explained that all staff had lived together at the hospital and got to know each other "like family." He remembered Adel well as "an honest and loving man."

Weeks later, when I watched the video of the interview with Dr. Roghman, I was struck by his emotion as he recalled Adel. Roghman told William how he was disappointed when his second daughter was born. "Afghan and Muslim men prefer a son," he said. When he had shared his disappointment with Adel at the hospital in Chamkani, Adel would have none of it.

"You should not be disappointed," Adel told Roghman. "She is a gift of the merciful Allah. No person alone can create such a being."

It is that openness and reverence for life that we heard repeated time and again about Adel.

Dr. Roghman was the third of the doctors from Chamkani who gave William a sworn statement. The second, Dr. Sailani, like Dr. Najib, was in Kabul and like Najib and Roghman, was very troubled that Adel was in prison.

"I think he was a very good man," he told William. "I never heard anything political from his mouth."

Adel's prowess at Ping-Pong had also impressed Dr. Sailani. "Abu Doujana was very smart in Ping-Pong." Gesturing with his hand on the video, he went on, "I play hard but he defeat. He defeat. He own me in Ping-Pong."

Dr. Sailani also gave us the best piece of information about the anti-Taliban nature of the hospital in Chamkani. Previously working in a hospital in Kabul, Sailani told how when the Taliban came to power, they would "inspect" the hospital, and on one of their early visits, they ordered him to cut his hair. Sensing that this was just a foreshadowing of the interference in his practice and life, Dr. Sailani went into exile in Peshawar, Pakistan, for several years. In the late 1990s, he heard about the hospital in Chamkani and that it was not under the sway of the Taliban, and took a job there.

"Myself, I escape from the political to work there," Dr. Sailani explained. As for Adel, "with the rule of the Taliban, he did not agree."

The team was struck by the devastation everywhere in Kabul. More than twenty-five years of war had left the city pockmarked, with buildings in various states of collapse, and burnt-out tanks scattered around the countryside. But they also saw the beauty of the stark landscape and ever-present, colorful kites.

Eight A.M., Friday, August 11, 2006. The armored Toyota Land Cruiser was loaded with suitcases, cameras, computers, and other electronic gear, ready to leave the Country House. William, Martin, and Ruben finished their good-byes to Radies Rademeyer, thanking him for Global's efforts in escorting them safely to interviews with Adel's employer and physician colleagues, the people who made up the trail of Nazar Gul's return to Afghanistan, and for the help their "fixer," Shakur, had provided in opening doors in the Afghan Ministries of Education and Labor and Social Affairs. Shakur, armed as always with a handgun and an AK-47, was going to drive the team out of Kabul, through Jalalabad, and up and over the Khyber Pass to Peshawar.

The Khyber Pass. I had first heard of the historic 28-mile-long opening in the high mountains of the Hindu Kush that connects Afghanistan with Pakistan as a child reading about Alexander the Great's march to India in 326 B.C. The pass had been the scene of countless battles over the centuries as Afghans, Mongols, Tatars, Russians, and others sought conquest and riches in India and Pakistan. Now I was sitting in my office in Portland reading an e-mail from my team that was searching not for empires to conquer but for justice.

William's e-mail had spared us the dangerous details of the trip. Gathered in my office a few weeks later, he told the full story about how they had just escaped another violent encounter. An hour out of Kabul as the "highway," which was just crisscrossing ruts in the desert, narrowed, the traffic slowed, then stopped. Their driver started swearing in English, Pashto, and Dari. William had been around armed guards, Stinger missile buyers, soldiers, and assorted "spooks" for a week but had not seen anyone react like this, looking around constantly on all sides, gun at the ready. William told how Shakur shouted, "There's a convoy up ahead. Americans and Canadians. We need to get out of here."

While the road from Kabul to Jalalabad and then on to the Khyber Pass was safe enough to risk the drive in an armored car with an armed guard, nowhere in Afghanistan was really safe. As Shakur had told my team, "Anywhere near an American army convoy is a likely target, especially if the convoy was stopped. That's how the Taliban often strike."

With my team in his care, Shakur was desperately searching for a place to turn off the highway when a dust cloud started growing nearby in the desert. The American convoy had turned off the road. An hour later, William recalled, Shakur was still looking around, occasionally checking his gun, and the contagion of his fear had my team on the alert.

Safe in Pakistan two days later, the team read in the newspapers that a truck had been blown up by an IED at the very spot on the road where they had been stopped less than twenty-four hours earlier.

When the team made it over the Khyber Pass into Pakistan and on into Peshawar, they connected with Adil Butt. Having received little work from him in months, they were concerned that their time in Pakistan might be wasted, but they were pleasantly surprised to find Butt fully engaged in our mission.

By the time they left Pakistan, William, Ruben, and Martin had conducted nearly twenty interviews in both countries. In addition to the three doctors, William had videotaped interviews with the Afghan deputy minister of labor and social affairs, Dr. Wasil Murmond; Hakim Nasiry from the Afghan Department of Education; the WAMY director in Afghanistan, Engineer Naquibudin; Abu Hadifa from the WAMY office in Islamabad; and Adel's landlord, Engineer Ishmail. Not on tape was the chief of the Pakistani police in Peshawar, who searched the available records for anything regarding Adel's arrest. Finding no references, he told William that

Adel must have been taken by the ISI (Inter-Services Intelligence), Pakistan's top security agency. In addition to the interviews, William had scores of brochures and official documents on WAMY and photos of Adel's home in Peshawar.

. . .

The investigation for Nazar Gul was equally successful.[3] The team spent a wonderful day with his extended family and village elders at their home on the outskirts of Kabul and taped confirmation of the family's flight from the Soviets and exile in Pakistan. With Zabi and his friends scouring the Gardez area and bringing people to Kabul, the trail Martin and Ruben were able to trace from Pakistan to Guantánamo was unbroken. They found and interviewed two of the three friends who had returned with Gul from Pakistan in the spring of 2003 full of excitement about the possibilities for their country under its new regime, the man who hired Gul and his friends soon after their return to Afghanistan to help guard a fuel depot outside of Gardez, the taxi driver who drove Gul to Gardez to get medical treatment and then to the house of a man named Akhtiar where he was seized, and the pharmacist who had treated Gul for an infection in his swollen mouth.

Gul had told his captors why he was at Akhtiar's house, but they ignored him. A year and a half later he gave the same account at his CSRT in Guantánamo and asked the tribunal to bring in Akhtiar, who had also been seized, as a witness. The CSRTs never brought in witnesses from outside the prison and rarely called witnesses who were also prisoners, but they actually did bring in a witness in Gul's case, allowing Akhtiar to testify. He confirmed Gul's account, but as with the men who captured Gul, the tribunal ignored what they had heard and declared Gul an enemy combatant.

. . .

In early September, a third team from my office, Steve Sady and Pat Ehlers, set out overseas, this time to Dubai in the United Arab Emirates for one of the clients added in the spring, a Taliban torture victim. This team was as successful as the first two in obtaining sworn statements confirming Al Ginco's account. Months later, our investigators tracked down two of the other men who had been liberated by the Americans at Kandahar but then imprisoned along with Al Ginco, and they provided statements confirming Al Ginco's innocence.

Because Al Ginco suffers from post-traumatic stress disorder as a result of his prolonged imprisonment and the torture he suffered at the hands of the Taliban and then again by his "liberators," the U.S. military, he has been having an exceedingly difficult time in Guantánamo and we have tried to see him as much as possible.[4] As soon as Steve and Pat returned from Dubai, Steve headed to Guantánamo. Because of the expense of travel there and the press of other cases, I asked Steve also to visit with Adel and give him a far more detailed account of the great material William had brought back from Afghanistan and Pakistan than we had been able to put in a letter.

Adel had weathered the summer well, was in great spirits, and was thrilled as Steve filled him in on the details of William's investigation. Steve was also able to get some details for us about some of Adel's travels in the short time he had worked in importing between his stints with LDI and WAMY. Everything checked out as a legitimate business. When Steve, who had not previously met Adel, got back to Portland, he shared his heightened understanding of the passion we felt for our fight for his freedom. He had been tremendously impressed with Adel's spirit and humanity.

Armed with confirmation of Adel's, Gul's, Al Ginco's, and Chaman's innocence, we were ready to take the offensive in the habeas litigation.

22 | Spanish Truths/ American Lies

A lie exposed is a fantasy revealed.

—Benjamin Kunkel

ON THURSDAY MORNING, MAY 20, I CALLED Gorder to see if I could get anything more out of him about the "new information" from Spain. While he hinted that there was yet more information, all he would say outright was that the classification issues had not been resolved. Our repeated calls to the lawyer we had hired in Madrid didn't get us anywhere either.

Deeply frustrated, Chris and I went to see Brandon in the lockup late that morning. The confusion I had seen in him on Wednesday after Moses's testimony identifying latent print #17 as his had been replaced by anger. Brandon had looked over the search warrant affidavit again and was steaming about the "profiling" he felt permeated it, the paragraphs about his religion, his representation of Battle, and Battle's views about Jews.

"They have nothing to do with anything," Brandon said.

He was right, except for their context. As the prosecutors went over the evidence, they kept seeing things that related to terrorism and Spain. Although each separate piece looked innocent to us, the fact that the prosecutors and FBI saw something new each time they turned a corner kept them looking. From their perspective, what they were finding meant far more than empty Internet trails leading to fantasy football games or books on the Dalai Lama. While I understood their point of view, the way the information was used also underscored the dangers raised by focusing on religion or race in trying to decide if someone was involved in criminal acts.

The difference between profiling and context was irrelevant to Judge Jones's decision to call in the grand jury for the following day, and it forced us to refocus on whether Brandon should give the prosecutors any information. Chris cut to the bottom line by asking Brandon, "How badly do you want to get out of jail and how much risk are you willing to take?" Brandon's response was short and firm: "I want out." Recognizing the impact the decision could have on his family, Brandon wanted to discuss the final decision with his wife, and the marshal was kind enough to agree to a special visit between them.

I was very uncomfortable with his decision to speak to the prosecution. Although I understood Brandon's desire to get out of jail, over the years I had seen too many clients hurt themselves by focusing on a short-term goal that ended up having disastrous consequences. I was still stewing about Brandon's decision at 1:30 when Gorder called.

"Can you come over to my office? I have news."

The Spanish had just announced, Gorder said, that they had "identified the latent print as belonging to an Algerian. The FBI lab is looking at it as fast as they can." Chris and I could not wait to get down to the marshal's lockup to tell our client. Brandon, who was still waiting for his visit with Mona, was surprised to see us step back into the visitor's side of the caged area. I will never forget how the consternation on his face melted into relief as we gave him the news.

We were all thrilled that the Spanish government voted into office only three days after the Madrid bombings, and which had promptly pulled out of the "coalition of the willing" in Iraq, had not been buffaloed by the FBI. The Spanish forensic police had continued their own investigation and now had taken on the American agency that proclaimed itself the most proficient forensic laboratory in the world. But the announcement raised a host of new issues.

Brandon's release was now possible; Gorder could no longer oppose sending him home. But when Chris and I went back to Gorder's office after speaking with Brandon, he told us that until the FBI had finished its work, he was not ready to dismiss the material witness proceeding or let Brandon go home without conditions. While we were adamant that there should be no conditions, Chris and I knew that Brandon would agree to almost anything to get out of jail.

After a half hour of wrangling that got us nowhere, Judge Jones's judicial assistant called to say the judge wanted us all in his chambers. We had barely started replaying the discussion we had been having in the U.S. attorney's office when the judge made it clear that Brandon was going home and that there would, indeed, be some conditions.

The lawyers all trooped from his chambers into the courtroom, the marshal brought Brandon in, and, at 2:40, Judge Jones took the bench for the formal hearing. Gorder stated that the FBI continued to believe it was "Mayfield's print on the blue bag."[1] But "in light of this information," he moved for Brandon's release. Judge Jones jumped right in, ordering release but setting strict conditions—Brandon had to remain at home unless he was at work, his mosque, or his children's schools; the $10,000 that had been seized, as well as all the Mayfields' passports, would remain with the court; and the court's pretrial services office would be making random calls to Brandon's home.

No one on Brandon's team liked the fact that his release was conditional, least of all Brandon, but Judge Jones made it clear that as far as he was concerned the grand jury proceeding was not over and he still expected testimony from Brandon. If Brandon wanted to go home, he had no choice but to accept these terms. And he did.

The last piece of the release decision involved the media. The Spanish position on the print and Brandon's release were going to be huge stories, and I wanted to make some statement to the press about Brandon's release that would lead people to think of him as an innocent and wronged man. When we were in chambers with Judge Jones before the court hearing, we had pressed the point, urging the judge to lift the gag order and let us talk. After several minutes of pushing back and forth, he had agreed that we could say something, but he would not lift the gag order. Sitting around the judge's desk we had all hammered out a statement focusing on what a "fine young lawyer" Brandon is and how "terrible" his "ordeal" has been. Judge Jones's secretary had typed the statement for us before we headed into court. Like the release conditions, it was not what we wanted, but it was much better than nothing at all.

. . .

Thursday night, Brandon was home and could sleep in his own bed for the first time in two weeks. Mona described her feelings the next day: "The kids are so very happy. Brandon is quiet like he usually is. That's just him. I'm in shock. I need time to be with my husband."[2]

Even though Brandon was out of jail, no one in the Mayfield home or on his team could relax over the weekend; reports out of Washington made it clear that the case was far from over. As Gorder had said in court, the FBI had not backed off its identification. The Spanish National Forensic Police probably had told the FBI in detail what was running in their media on Thursday: that their "meticulous work" had "determined completely" that they had identified two latent prints, including #17, as belonging to Algerian Ouhnane Daoud.[3]

The FBI was not ready to back down. The late edition of the *New York Times* reported on Saturday that the FBI had not ruled Mayfield "out as a suspect."[4] I was worried that we would return to court on Monday to hear that the FBI believed, as they had in April, that they had again convinced the Spanish they were right and it was Brandon's print.

The usual Oregon spring rains had taken a break Monday morning, and Kathleen and I drove to work under a glorious sun that brought out the color from the spring flowers, but my mood was not light. Although I trusted Gorder, I did not have any confidence that the FBI would be able to admit it had made a mistake or that the local prosecutors would be able to control Washington.

Brandon's team gathered in my office around 8:30 to review the possibilities for the day—would Gorder move to dismiss or would the FBI stand firm?—and the options we would have depending on the direction they took. At 9:30, Brandon arrived with Mona for our first meeting outside a jail setting. Out of the jail blues, he radiated a confidence I had not seen before. We had barely finished our hellos when Holsinger called to say that the United States attorney was going to be filing a motion to dismiss the grand jury proceeding but it was not yet ready.

Smiles, high fives, and hugs all around. But we were soon back to the serious business of trying to put Brandon and Mona's life back together. While the United States attorney and FBI wanted the matter to be over, we had motions pending to get back all of Brandon's property, stop its further dissemination, pursue an official investigation of the leaks and abuse of the material witness statute, and find out if Brandon's home had been invaded by sneak-and-peek searches under the FISA or Patriot Act. Brandon did not want to slink away quietly. He felt wronged and wanted to tell the world.

In our discussions with the United States attorney's office that morning, Gorder advised that the FBI agent in charge in Portland, Robert Jordan, would be apologizing to Brandon. In a statement issued later that day, Jordan formally "apologized to Mr. Mayfield and his family for the hardships that this matter has caused."[5] The written apology and Jordan's offer to meet personally with Brandon were unprecedented. The local expression of goodwill was, however, trumped by the position taken by the FBI in Washington.

Late in the morning, Judge Jones initiated a conference call to Gorder and me. Gorder officially confirmed his desire to dismiss the proceeding and dissolve the grand jury. We wanted orders entered on our motions and we wanted to hold a press conference, assuming that the gag order would be lifted. At that point, Gorder's opposition to our motions was muted.

By early afternoon we had won everything we could in the grand jury matter. Judge Jones entered orders dismissing the material witness proceeding, terminating any supervision of Brandon by the Pre-Trial Services Office, dissolving the gag order, and unsealing all of the pleadings and transcripts of the court hearings. The judge granted all our motions to protect Brandon, ordering the FBI to preserve the fingerprint evidence, something Brandon needed if he was ever going to sue the government for damages, and ordering the government to return all the property it had seized from Brandon and to destroy any copies it retained. The order of destruction was a huge victory for us. Since the fruits of the searches had been disseminated to U.S. intelligence agencies around the world, we wanted an order requiring every copy destroyed so that Brandon's name would not keep cropping up in terrorism intelligence reports for years to come. The FBI was not happy about this and the order would prove to be short-lived.

At 2:30 P.M., I convened a press conference in my office's training room. Chairs were pushed back to the sides to make room for a podium and equipment. The large room was packed with cameras, microphones, and print reporters, and that evening and the next morning our words were carried around the world.

Brandon said, "The experience has been a nightmare for all of us from the very beginning. . . . I believe that the government's handling of this case has been prejudicial and discriminatory in the extreme."

After describing the pain and fear he suffered while in jail, Brandon noted that "some good has come out of this ordeal" and talked about the support he and his family had enjoyed.

He closed by looking to the future, saying of, and to, his fellow American Muslims, "Although we know that the days of our being targeted simply because of our faith are certainly not over, our collective hope is that the hate-mongers of this land will take pause and reflect on today's events."[6]

I focused my words on the fear spreading through our country. "This matter should be seen as a cautionary tale about how civil liberties need to be defended most in times of national stress . . . of how the fear of terror can lead even well-meaning individuals to take precipitous action that can have a devastating impact on an innocent individual, eroding civil liberties, and traumatizing a community."

After a half hour of questions, one of the reporters asked Brandon somewhat hostilely about his representation of Mr. Battle, as if that still mattered somehow. Brandon looked at me, we both broke into large smiles, and our arms reached out to wrap around the other's shoulders. We stood there beaming at the cameras. Lawyer and client standing together. The world did not always keep us separate. I thought, if Chris and I are not already in a government database, we are sure headed there now.

I concluded our press conference by complimenting Brandon "for the grace and calm with which he handled this ordeal." Whatever rough spots we had encountered were minor bumps in a very tough road. Brandon's ability to maintain his dignity and keep his focus had been remarkable.

·   ·   ·

The Brandon Mayfield grand jury matter could have ended there for my office. Brandon was free, his property had been ordered returned, and the FBI had apologized. If he wanted to pursue matters and sue the government, he would need to hire civil attorneys in private practice.

While relations among the prosecution, FBI, and Brandon's team were civil in Portland, they were not in Washington, and the position the FBI took there kept the fires of the case burning. Even before the dismissal order was entered, the FBI in Washington started a cover-up of misinformation and deceit and, as I understand it, pushed the U.S. attorney to try to undo Judge Jones's last orders.

Monday afternoon, while we were having our press conference, the FBI in Washington issued a "Statement on Brandon Mayfield Case." Rather than admit their mistake as their agent in charge in Portland had done, the explanation from Washington was starkly misleading: "The FBI identification was based on an image of substandard quality."[7] As far as we knew from Moses and our own review, there was nothing "substandard" about the latent print. Indeed, a report sponsored by the FBI months later confirmed that the latent print was of good quality and was also used by the Spanish against Daoud.

The cover-up was even more brazenly set out in the Motion to Dismiss Material Witness Proceeding filed with the court on May 24.[8] Although filed by United States Attorney Karin Immergut's office, she had received the language in the motion from the FBI in Washington and relied on their supposed knowledge of the facts. The motion to dismiss explained that, after learning the Spanish had identified latent print #17 as belonging to Dauod, the FBI had sent a two-person team back to Spain. The purpose of the mission was described in the motion as "to obtain images with the highest possible resolution to help resolve the concerns." The motion went on to say that "the two examiners were granted full access to the fingerprints of the other individual and the item on which the latent had been left." Upon their return, four examiners "began work to sort out the issue." They agreed "that the latent print had multiple separations—that is, it was divided by many lines of demarcation possibly caused by creases in the underlying material, multiple touches by one or more fingers, or both." The motion concluded that "utilizing the additional information acquired this weekend in Spain," the FBI lab had determined that the latent was "of no value for identification purposes."

The motion made no sense. While the FBI examiners may have gone to Spain intending to take high-resolution images of the latent print, they could not have done so. The latent print had been destroyed months before by the Spanish effort to get DNA samples off the bag. There were, therefore, no new photos of the print for the examiners to have looked at. Even more disturbing was the statement that latent print #17 had "no value for identification purposes." The Spanish certainly disagreed; they were using the print to identify Daoud.

Apparently concerned about the impact of Brandon's case on their image and funding from Congress, senior-level FBI officials took the cover-up directly to Capitol Hill. During the week of May 24, they made the rounds of congressional offices, explaining that the mistake was an honest one, involving no profiling based on religion, and that Congress did not have to worry about the science of fingerprinting because the misidentification had been based on a copy of a poor print.

I learned about the Capitol Hill action from Sarah Kershaw, a reporter for the *New York Times*. For a week after the press conference, I was deluged with calls from the media. Everyone wanted some inside scoop, and I told them all the same thing—I did not believe the FBI had been honest with the court about the fingerprint. Time after time, I went over the dismissal motion in detail, pointing out the cover-up, and read the reporters the statements in paragraph 8 in the affidavit in support of the search warrant that said the Spanish findings on the fingerprint were "inconsistent" with the FBI's. I urged them all to push the FBI, the DOJ, and the United States attorney in Portland to disclose precisely what the Spanish had told the FBI in April.

Of all the reporters, Kershaw was the one who understood best, or was willing to act on, the significance of the misstatements in the motion to dismiss and the possibility that the FBI had outright lied to the court about the April meeting in Spain. It took two hours of going over the facts with her in my office on May 25 before she was willing to take on the issue. The following day, the *Times* ran a front-page story by Kershaw and Eric Lichtblau headlined, "Spain Had Doubts Before U.S. Held Lawyer in Blast."

I repeatedly tried to get the Associated Press, television and radio, and our local reporters from the *Oregonian* to push the issue but without success. Tomas Tizon of the *Los Angeles Times* mentioned my concerns, but very few people were willing to believe, or tell, a story about gross incompetence by the FBI or the FBI lying to a court.[9] The stories the *Oregonian* ran were typical. On May 26, they wrote about the science of fingerprinting that led with the reassuring paragraph that the FBI was investigating how the error was made. There was no reference to any possibility of misstatements in the affidavit or the motion to dismiss. The *Oregonian* then ran a comprehensive story on the Mayfield matter on May 30 that did mention the April meeting and my suspicions but stopped short of questioning the FBI directly and put my suspicions aside by saying the Spanish had used a second print found on the bag, not latent print #17, to identify Daoud.[10] That was simply not true; the Spanish used two prints, latent print #17 and an additional one.

∎ ∎ ∎

The lies we believed the FBI was telling on Capitol Hill and the rumblings we heard from the U.S. attorney about seeking modification of Judge Jones's order to return everything to Brandon understandably upset him. As soon as we had received Moses's report, we had contacted the fingerprint examiner who had been our first choice, the former Scotland Yard man, Allan Bayle. We now pushed forward with Bayle, who agreed to analyze the FBI work and do an independent comparison. I asked William to e-mail Bayle copies of latent print #17, a set of Brandon's prints, the FBI report, the affidavit in support of the arrest warrant, the motion to dismiss, and the comparisons we had received by e-mail from Moses. Bayle reported back to us within a day. Contrary to the FBI's statement in the motion to dismiss, latent #17 was of significant value and "contained a sufficient degree of uniqueness to individualize."[11] At what Bayle called "level one" of analysis, the core pattern of the fingerprint, the pattern in latent print #17 "was not the same" as Brandon's. As any examiner should have learned in basic fingerprint analysis 101, the latent could not belong to Brandon because "the core area in the latent was an open delta in an arch pattern" and in the prints known to be Brandon's it "was a closed delta in an arch pattern." Bayle's report went on to point out numerous inconsistencies in the ridge patterns.

Bayle's report added fuel to the fire of speculation that Brandon had been the victim of religious profiling and something other than an honest mistake. When the government moved to reconsider the order to return all of the property it had seized, we knew that Bayle's report would be a critical piece of evidence, because the legal standard we would have to meet required us to show that the government had acted in bad faith when it searched Brandon's home and law office. Any profiling would be one key, and evidence that the fingerprint identification was something other than an honest mistake would be another important part of that proof. So late on Friday, May 28, I filed Bayle's report with the court and started packing up to go home for what I hoped would be my first restful weekend in a month.

A few minutes after five, the phone rang, and I heard the angry voice of United States Attorney Karin Immergut. A product of Brooklyn like me, Immergut and I generally got along well, but that afternoon she was incensed that I had filed Bayle's report with the court. I responded as diplomatically as I could that I believed both the affidavit and the motion to dismiss had presented the court with an inaccurate account of what had happened in Spain and that those facts were most relevant if she was going to seek modification of the return and destroy order. We shared our different perspectives for a few minutes, professionally but coldly, and I told Karin that I would not withdraw the report. She then said she wanted to try to get Judge Jones to put it under seal. I agreed to stay in the office for a few minutes while she tried to reach the judge at home.

Ten minutes later, the three of us were on a conference call, Karin and me in our offices, and Judge Jones at home. Karin started explaining why she was upset, but the judge quickly cut her off: "We're all trying to do the right thing here, there is no advantage or disadvantage to anyone." He told Karin she could make any response she wanted, but "don't make it personal." He went on to remind me that with everything unsealed and things still being filed, the United States attorney or FBI could disclose the results of the search warrants, which included some items that might be embarrassing to Brandon, such as the number of hits on his computers for travel in Spain and his possession of the Patriot missile material.

Brandon, Chris, and I had had numerous discussions about the possibility of embarrassment if some of the seized items were released, but it still did not feel right to have that put on the table by the judge. I reminded him and Immergut that there were questions about the legality of the entire proceeding and that Brandon was thinking about filing a civil suit. This was the one point in the phone call when I felt the judge getting angry at me, and he barked back that Brandon was free to do whatever he wanted and that he might end up as a witness in any civil suit.

As for the order to destroy all copies, the judge told Immergut that the government could keep anything it believed it needed to defend against a civil suit and he would be open to formally amending his order if she asked him. As we anticipated, a week later, Gorder filed the motion.

The FBI, knowing that with Bayle's report in the public domain it would be more difficult to continue with their cover up, must have pressured the United States attorney's office all weekend because I received a call from

Gorder first thing Monday morning asking if he could talk to Moses and urging me not to provide copies of the prints to anyone else. I had no problem with him calling Moses, but in light of my call with Judge Jones and Immergut on Friday, I was not going to agree to limit what we could do with the prints. I did, however, agree to hold off on any disclosures until Gorder could get the judge, who was out of town, on the telephone for another conference.

Tuesday morning, Dave Atkinson patched together a call with the judge at the hotel in Coeur D'Alene, Idaho, where he was attending a conference. The FBI, Atkinson argued, wanted to convene an international team to review the fingerprint issue before the prints and comparisons were out in the public domain. Time and again in my life I had heard the "big lie" from government officials and seen how one-sided access to information limited everyone else's ability to get at the truth—the Watergate scandal that brought down President Nixon, the Iran-contra scandal in which the United States sold arms to the Iranians to fund the contras to fight the Sandinistas in Nicaragua, and a host of lesser issues. Now I was in possession of facts in a case in which the FBI had tremendous incentive to keep them hidden, because both the integrity of their investigation as free of religious profiling and the science of fingerprinting were being questioned.

I agreed that an international review would be commendable, but I went on to say I did not see any basis for limiting dissemination of Bayle's report. Judge Jones heard Atkinson out for a few minutes, then cut the call short, reiterating what he had said on Friday, that I could make Bayle's report public and the United States attorney and FBI could respond in any way they chose. By the weekend, Bayle's report and the prints were online for anyone who wanted to look at them. This was one investigation that would not take place behind closed doors.

Meanwhile, Kershaw and her colleagues at the *Times* had not rested after their story appeared on the twenty-sixth. They got their Spanish bureau on the case, and Dale Fuchs obtained an interview with Pedro Luis Melida Lledo, the head of the fingerprint unit of the Spanish forensic police.[12] Melida Lledo explained that on April 13, the Spanish had sent the FBI a formal letter expressing their views about latent print #17 and Brandon. The letter did not specifically say that the Spanish had questions about the

FBI work, but it did state that the results of their comparison of latent print #17 with Brandon's prints was "conclusively negative." Melida Lledo went on to tell Fuchs that the FBI account of the meeting that took place in Spain in April, as reported in the affidavit used to arrest Brandon, was inaccurate. The meeting did not end with the Spanish telling the FBI that they agreed it was Mayfield's print; all they said at the end was that they would take another look.

While I trusted the *Times* reports, I knew we were taking a risk pushing the bad faith issue without having spoken directly to the Spanish and asked William to keep up our efforts to get something firsthand out of them. Finally, on June 8, using the contact information provided by Kershaw, William got through to the source. Melida Lledo was pleasant and remarkably open. He confirmed every aspect of the *Times* account of the meeting that took place between the FBI and Spanish authorities on April 21–22—the Spanish had never agreed with the FBI's conclusion that the print was Brandon's. We were confident now having heard from Melida Lledo directly, because if we were going to keep pushing, at some point the FBI would push back hard.

The same day that we got direct confirmation from Spain about the disagreement with the FBI and only three days after the *Times*'s comprehensive article, the cover-up reached the highest level of the administration.

Tuesday afternoon, June 8, the Senate Judiciary Committee convened to discuss the Bush administration's antiterrorism efforts with Attorney General John Ashcroft.[13]

In the midst of the hearing, Wisconsin Senator Russell Feingold turned to Brandon's case. "General, Brandon Mayfield is an innocent American citizen who was falsely implicated and detained for the [March] 11 terrorist bombing in Spain."

Foreshadowing my fight for Adel and my other clients in Guantánamo, the senator went on, "But for the fact that he had access to counsel and judicial review, Mr. Mayfield might still be in jail today. If held as an enemy combatant, Mr. Mayfield would be in a military jail without the right to an attorney and his truthful statements of innocence would simply be taken as failures of his interrogators."

Senator Feingold then turned to the profiling issues in the case, expressing great concern about the statements in the arrest warrant affidavit that Brandon had attended a mosque. "Mr. Mayfield appears to have been singled out for heightened scrutiny based on a number of legitimate tests, but also because of his religious beliefs."

Attorney General Ashcroft offered the senator assurances that there was no religious profiling. Then, under oath, he turned to the fingerprint. He stuck to the line we had been told the FBI had been giving Congress behind closed doors for the past two weeks. "The fingerprint had been a photograph from a partial print, and obviously when the real print became available and additional analysis was engaged in, it was determined . . ."

In the lectures I have given on Brandon's case since his release, I have come back to this sworn testimony many times. With all respect to the attorney general, I still cannot square it with the truth. Latent print #17 that the FBI worked with was always a photograph; they never had access to the "real print," because it was destroyed by the Spanish efforts to obtain DNA samples; the latent analyzed by the FBI in May was the same as the latent they analyzed two months earlier. Neither the attorney general nor anyone in the FBI has ever been called to account for their statements.

23 | Mayfield: The Aftermath

Which office do I go to to get my reputation back?
—former Reagan labor secretary Ray Donovan
after a jury acquitted him of fraud charges[1]

BRANDON'S CASE CAUGHT THE PUBLIC EYE in a different way from any other in the national debates over the war on terror and the costs of expansion of the Patriot Act. The forensic fingerprint issues were important. But the deeper significance of the case lay in its exposure of the devastating harm that individual citizens suffer through overzealous prosecution of the war on terror. Two government reports, one by a team of international experts convened by the FBI to examine the fingerprint fiasco and the other by the inspector general of the Department of Justice, and materials produced in the civil suit Brandon filed against the attorney general and the FBI revealed a great deal about the FBI's bungling of the fingerprint, the blind eye they turned to evidence that did not add up, the extent of the intrusions on Brandon's and his family's privacy and the role of the Patriot Act in those intrusions, and the role religion played in his arrest. While parts of the government reports stop short of the truth, they were generally critical of the investigation. Because the government eventually settled most of Brandon's civil suit for $2 million, none of the FBI agents are likely to ever be questioned under oath, but the suit did produce a number of documents that provided significant insight into the workings of the government in the war on terror. The picture that has emerged confirmed many of the worst fears I harbored during my representation of Brandon.

The first report was issued in November 2004 by a team of international experts convened by the FBI to examine the fingerprint issues in Brandon's case. Authored by Robert B. Stacey, head of the FBI laboratory's Quality Assurance and Training Unit, the report was objective as far as it went and placed the blame for the FBI's mistake entirely on human error and the identification procedures used by the FBI.[2] The panel had worked rapidly to complete the report in order to calm the forensic community, which was rattled throughout the summer and fall by public discussions of fingerprinting and Brandon's situation.[3] Something had to be done to shore up the FBI's image as a pillar of police science.

The second report emerged from the many discussions on Capitol Hill that explored the delicate balance between security and freedom that followed the June 8 exchange between Senator Feingold and Attorney General Ashcroft. I became involved in the debate through a call from Kristen Wells, staffer for Representative John Conyers of Michigan, the ranking Democrat on the House Judiciary Committee. Wells explained that Rep. Conyers was considering a request to the inspector general in the Department of Justice for a full inquiry into Brandon's case and wanted my input. I told her I believed the administration was involved in a cover-up about the mistaken identification of Brandon, including outright lies that reached the highest levels.

On June 16, Representatives Conyers and Robert C. Scott of Virginia and Senator Feingold wrote a joint letter to Inspector General Glenn Fine asking for a formal investigation into the "multitude of errors" that led to Brandon's arrest and detention.[4] Most government agencies have an inspector general whose job is to conduct investigations into questionable actions of the agency. By law, they can act on their own or at the request of, and with a requirement that they report to, Congress. The Conyers/Scott/Feingold letter called for a wide-ranging investigation into the fingerprint issues, whether the material witness statute was misused, any role Mayfield's religion played in his arrest, and whether he had been the target of sneak-and-peek searches.[5]

My initial reaction to the idea of an investigation conducted within the Department of Justice was not very enthusiastic. It seemed like asking the fox to guard the henhouse. But one of my assistants, Francesca Freccero, was a former assistant in the DOJ and knew Glenn Fine. She assured me that he was a man of integrity and would do a professional job.

The civil suit that Brandon filed on October 4, 2004, produced still more information.[6] In the weeks after his release, Brandon's thoughts about a civil suit against the government became more and more concrete, and on July 11 Brandon's team met with Gerry Spence, a nationally prominent attorney based in Jackson Hole, Wyoming, who had been taking on the government in civil and criminal cases all over the country for decades; prominent Portland civil rights attorney Eldon Rosenthal, who had successfully sued a neo-Nazi group a decade earlier, winning a multimillion-dollar verdict that put them out of business; and Michelle Longo, a fine attorney who practiced on the Oregon coast and had cocounseled a murder case with Spence in the 1980s. The meeting took place in my office's conference room.

Chris and I went over the case, pointing out the places where we believed the government had crossed the line—the inclusion of the religious information in the warrant affidavit, failure to tell Judge Jones about the "negative" statement in the April 13 letter, the media leaks, use of the material witness statute to hold a person when there was no probable cause to arrest him, and Brandon's incarceration with charged and convicted criminals. We pointed out the areas where we believed it was important to get more information—who in the FBI knew what about Brandon at what stage in the investigation; the weaknesses in the case such as the Patriot missile material; some of the information that was found on Brandon's computer. We went back and forth for hours, sweat rolling down our backs with the air conditioning off on the weekend, Rosenthal doing most of the probing on the facts and Spence charming us with his gloss on the big picture.

Spence was interested in the case but was not yet ready to make a commitment. We agreed that Chris and I would push ahead negotiating with Gorder and Immergut about getting Brandon's property back. On August 24, Spence, Rosenthal, and Longo committed to taking on the civil case and the property matter, and our formal work was over. The civil suit was filed on behalf of Brandon, Mona, and each of the children, and alleged violations of their civil rights based on the profiling, leaks, sneak-and-peek searches, and misuse of the material witness statute. The suit sought money damages and an injunction against further use of portions of the Patriot Act. Because Judge Jones was a potential witness, the case was assigned to Judge Ann Aiken, whose chambers are in Eugene, two hours south of Portland. Like

Judge Jones, Judge Aiken held the government's feet to the fire, requiring them to produce a number of important documents. In September 2007, she issued a strong opinion on the part of the suit that challenged the constitutionality of the Patriot Act.[7]

The story that follows, pieced together from these sources, confirmed some our worst fears about the intrusions into Brandon's, Mona's, and their children's lives, and how the FBI misled the federal courts.[8]

．　．　．

The FBI's involvement in the investigation of the Madrid bombings got off to a slow start because the initial copy of latent print #17 sent out by Interpol on March 13 was not of the best quality. But the very next day, not two months later as Attorney General Ashcroft had told the Senate, Interpol followed up with higher-resolution images that were perfectly usable for forensic purposes. All of the FBI's work was based on those higher-resolution images. The FBI's report concluded, "The quality of the images that were used to make the erroneous identification was not a factor."[9] The FBI's and Attorney General's statements to Congress in May and June were simply not true.

After receiving an electronic copy of latent print #17 on March 14, supervisory fingerprint examiner Terry Green coded seven points from the latent and ran them through several FBI databases including the forty-seven-million-item IAFIS (Integrated Automated Fingerprint Identification System) database and a special terrorism database called the Special Latent Cognizant File (SLCF) that contains known prints of people identified or suspected of being involved in terrorism activities.[10]

Green has said that the first computer run of the Madrid latent print #17 was against the three thousand or so prints in the SLCF, but there were no possible matches identified.[11] Whether Brandon's prints were in that database is not publicly known. It was from the second run in the general IAFIS database, which includes all prints the FBI has been able to gather from criminal investigations, that Brandon's print appeared, based on a juvenile arrest that had been dismissed. Green then made a third computer run against the civil database that includes military prints and the like. Even though Brandon's military prints should have appeared on that list, the computer did not identify any possible matches.[12]

After the computer generated the list of twenty possibles, Green began to manually compare each to the latent. After deciding he had found a match, he went back to the original coding he had done for the IAFIS search and found that the points he had encoded did not match. Rather than question his identification of Brandon, however, Green went back and changed five of his seven original points in type or location.[13] There is no indication he told his supervisor of these changes. When the Spanish identified Daoud and his prints were compared against Green's work, it turned out that four of the five points he changed matched Daoud.[14]

John T. Massey was then called in to "verify" Green's work.[15] In March 2004, Massey, who had spent his career at the FBI before retiring, was working with the bureau on a contract basis. It is difficult to understand the FBI calling Massey in on a case of this magnitude because, as reported by *Seattle Times* investigative reporter David Heath in a postmortem he wrote on the fingerprint issue in the case, "Court records show that Massey was reprimanded three times early in his career for mistakes, including two false fingerprint identifications."[16] Massey proceeded to make a fourth mistake here, verifying Green's identification. They were quickly joined by Michael Weiners, one of three Unit chiefs in the Latent Print unit, who also "verified" the identification.[17]

The international panel that looked at this procedure was highly critical, faulting the FBI for failing to provide a scientifically acceptable check on its examiners' work. As the report put it, "Once the mind-set occurred with the initial examiner, the subsequent examinations were tainted." The panel called this "confirmation bias," explaining that disagreement with the first examiner "was not an expected response." The examination was also tainted by the fact that this was a "high profile case," a case in which everyone involved was eager to find the culprits.[18]

The international panel concluded that this mind-set infected far more than the FBI's initial work. The FBI examiners carried this mind-set to Spain on their first trip there in April, taking a "defensive posture" that made it difficult for them to hear what the Spanish were telling them.[19]

While the international panel was blunt about "confirmation bias," it did not reveal that months after Brandon's release, when the FBI was trying to unravel the mess it had created, Weiners said that he had seen "distinct features" in the upper left-hand part of the print and that this "gave him heartburn" from the get-go. That information came out only in the inspector general's report more than a year later.[20] Weiners may have had heartburn, but he never put the brakes on the investigation, even after the Spanish told the FBI on April 13, 2004, that their comparison was "NEGATIVE." The irony of Weiners's "heartburn" statement was not lost on Chris, William, and me when we saw this part of the inspector general's report. The upper left-hand part of the print was one of the areas we had focused on that day in May when we had huddled around the computer in my office listening to Moses.

Green has stated in an affidavit filed in Brandon's civil suit that he did not know anything about the people and the database from which their known prints had been pulled before he made his identification.[21] The international panel's report is silent on the question of what information the FBI examiners knew about Brandon when the identification was first made, whether they ran his name through their databases or even through a search engine such as Google. When Judge Aiken issued her opinion in September 2007 on the portion of Brandon's civil suit that involved the Patriot Act (a part of the suit that had been allowed to continue after the money settlement), she said that the list of twenty "possibles" generated by the IAFIS computer included some sort of identifying number. As the judge put it, "This information allowed the FBI to perform background checks on each of the twenty candidates."[22] Because no live testimony has been taken in the suit, the judge's opinion stops there.

Suspicions continue to swirl around this issue because any foreknowledge of the possible subjects would have tainted the comparison, and it is possible that Brandon's prints were in the terrorism database because of his representation of the convicted terrorist Mr. Battle and the fact that he was a Muslim himself. What is known from an internal document that was released a year and a half after Brandon's arrest and Fine's report is that the Portland office of the FBI had opened a file on Brandon related to the Madrid bombings before March 20 and had made the link among Brandon, the Bilal mosque, and the Portland Seven the day the FBI told Spain they had found one of the bombers.[23] The inspector general reported that twenty-four hour surveillance was begun on Brandon on March 19.[24] Whether anything had happened or was known before that day remains a mystery.

It is clear that once the FBI began its investigation of Brandon, his religion did play a role. From the outset, Brandon believed he had been the victim of religious profiling, and his claim drew many adherents.

When Judge Aiken held a hearing on July 15, 2006, in the civil suit, Gerry Spence was at his grandiloquent best in arguing that Brandon's religion had played a major role in his arrest: "I am sure that had it been Billy Graham, or one of Billy Graham's children, the FBI might have said that we'd better check it out. No airline tickets. How did he get over there to Spain? Must have been that magic carpet. The Muslim magic carpet."[25]

Inspector General Fine asked a lot of people in the Justice Department, FBI, and United States attorney's office whether Brandon's religion influenced the investigation, and many said it had not been a factor. However, a number of the people questioned showed more insight, and Fine reported that "several witnesses acknowledged . . . that Mayfield's religion was a factor in the investigation."[26] One assistant in Immergut's office called Brandon's religion a "mildly corroborating factor."[27] Immergut herself stated that "the fact that he was a Muslim couldn't be ignored."[28] The inspector general agreed with Immergut's assessment that the arrest warrant affidavit should have more clearly explained why the government believed that Brandon's religion and attendance at a mosque was important—because it was the mosque the Portland Seven had attended.[29] Given the statements from the people in the United States attorney's office, it is reasonable to believe that the FBI agents found comfort in the fact that Brandon was a Muslim and were less inclined than they otherwise might have been to seriously question what they were doing. However, the bottom line, as Fine saw it, was that the investigation would have gone forward regardless of Brandon's religion.[30]

It was several days after they had made the identification of Brandon that the FBI provided the information to the Spanish. The next day, the Spanish sent the FBI the photographs of the blue bag that they had requested earlier in the week. More photos of the bag arrived on March 23, but, neither Green, Weiners, nor Massey ever reviewed them as part of their fingerprint comparison.[31] Agents who did examine the photos after Brandon's release state that the location of latent print #17 on the bag undermines the identifications, but by then it was too late to spare Brandon and his family the pain they had endured.[32]

By the end of the third week in March, the Spanish National Police had developed significant leads to a group of Moroccans. In fact, by March 20, they had already made at least five arrests, so they were baffled when they received word from the FBI about Brandon's identification. As Melida Lledo later told us, Brandon's supposed involvement just did not make sense. An Oregonian who did not even speak Spanish was a most unlikely confederate for the Moroccans. Unable, or unwilling, to see the inconsistency between the Spanish investigation and their work, the FBI ordered a full-court press on Brandon.

When the twenty-four hour surveillance of Brandon was begun on March 19, agents were stationed outside his home and office to follow him around.[33] But the FBI was not satisfied with visual surveillance and shortly turned to the Foreign Intelligence Surveillance Act for authorization to engage in electronic surveillance.[34] The prosecutors went to the lead-lined room in the Justice Department's main building in Washington where the Foreign Intelligence Surveillance Court (FISC) sits and requested warrants to engage in surveillance of Brandon. Since its establishment in 1978, this court has authorized more than twenty thousand warrants.[35] There is a public record of it turning down a government request only once, a decision that was then reversed by the special Foreign Intelligence Appeals Court.[36]

If the government considers even the streamlined and secret FISC process too cumbersome, it can start surveillance on an emergency basis with a warrant issued by the attorney general, which is exactly what happened in Brandon's case.[37] The FBI was so hyped up by its identification of Brandon's fingerprint and the background information it had generated on him that it sought and obtained permission from Attorney General Ashcroft to proceed without waiting for a FISC warrant. From the beginning, everything about Brandon's case was handled at the highest level and under tight security to avoid leaks. As it turned out, Washington maintained the security only until Brandon's arrest, when it began leaking information about him.

After starting surveillance on Brandon on his own say-so, the attorney general went to the FISC for a judicial warrant.[38] While that warrant has not been made public, government documents that have been made available make clear that it closely paralleled the regular judicial warrant later used to arrest Brandon, reciting the fingerprint match and detailing what was known of Brandon's religion, religious practice, and representation of Mr. Battle. The FISC authorized electronic surveillance at both Brandon's home and law office, as well as sneak-and-peek searches.

When, in mid-April, the Mayfields started suspecting that their home had been invaded, they were not being paranoid. The inspector general's report confirms what Brandon and Mona suspected: The FBI had intruded into their home for sneak-and-peek searches at least twice.[39] The report also makes clear that the Mayfields had no idea of the extent of the secret invasions. The agents who intruded in the Mayfield home inspected and photographed many documents; they brought in computer experts and made mirror images of the hard drives in the computers; they rummaged through and took the Mayfields' trash. They took DNA swabs.[40] In the opinion she wrote in 2007, Judge Aiken said that the material may also have included "summaries of confidential conversations between husband and wife, parents and children, and other private activities of a family's life within their home."[41]

It is this complete stripping of privacy of American citizens by their government that now occurs in the name of protecting ourselves from terrorists. This type of intrusion, when botched, as it was in Brandon's case, engenders terror in its victims, who are aware that their homes have been invaded but have no idea by whom or why. When we don't know but are left to wonder whether we have been victimized in this way, the fear may be even more insidious than the fear of a known terrorist group.

The FBI admitted to Inspector General Fine that all of its surveillance on Brandon turned up nothing concrete linking him to the bombings.[42] But they kept at it.

The United States attorney received regular reports from the FBI about the investigation. Throughout March and the first part of April, Immergut and Gorder had no reason to question the FBI, but Fine's report makes clear that, while Washington was calling the shots, the United States attorneys in Portland were not just rubber stamps. When, in mid-April, the Department of Justice Counterterrorism Section told the United States attorney in Portland something about the Spanish letter of April 13, Immergut and Gorder were not pleased and urged the FBI to send a delegation to Spain.[43] It is not clear whether they actually had a copy of the letter at that time. They did, however, have it in hand later on.

On April 15, Immergut received a report of an e-mail from a supervisory FBI agent that advised, "I spoke with the lab this morning and they are absolutely confident that they have a match on the print—No doubt about it!!!—They will testify in any court you swear them into."[44]

Hard charging, but not zealots, Immergut and Gorder were still sufficiently concerned about the Spanish position that they continued to press for a meeting between Spanish and FBI forensic agents that resulted in the trip to Spain on April 21 and 22. It was only after receiving the FBI account of these meetings, which included their assessment that the Spanish agreed with the FBI's fingerprint identification, that Immergut, Gorder, and the Portland FBI stepped up preparation of federal court arrest and search warrants.[45]

While the FBI in Washington was still convinced of Brandon's involvement, the people in Portland were not so sure. As they subsequently admitted, the physical and electronic surveillance had turned up nothing concrete.[46] Gorder and Portland's FBI chief Robert Jordan began making plans simply to approach Brandon and ask him some questions, and it is likely that Brandon's life would have turned out quite differently if, on May 4, the *Los Angeles Times* reporter in Paris had not called authorities in Madrid with questions about the fingerprints.

Fine described on the reporter asking "about this American" whose fingerprint was linked to the bombings.[47] Somewhere, there had been a leak. Top people in the FBI and the Justice Department felt that they had to move against Brandon and arrest him, and after a heated debate about whether there was enough evidence for an arrest, the decision was made.[48] Gorder went to Judge Jones and, relying on the information provided by the FBI, sought the arrest warrant.

During Brandon's civil suit, however, the FBI was forced to cough up a document about Brandon's arrest that puts the FBI decision in a very different light. On May 5, 2004, the day before Brandon's arrest, an e-mail was sent by Beth Ann Steele in the Portland FBI office to the Los Angeles FBI office. After recounting the fact that news was leaking out of Spain about the FBI's interest in Brandon, Steele wrote her colleague, "The problem is there is not enough other evidence to arrest [Brandon] on a criminal charge. There is a plan to arrest him as a material witness if and when he gets outed by the media."[49]

This e-mail, coupled with the statement out of Washington that had been reported in the media right after Brandon's arrest that the FBI never expected to get any information from him, provides powerful evidence that use of the material witness statute to secure Brandon's arrest was illegal. Rather than being used to hold Brandon for the sole purpose of obtaining his testimony, which is the reason the statute exists, the FBI apparently planned to use the material witness warrant to keep Brandon in a holding pattern while they tried to develop enough information to file criminal charges.

Brandon is far from the only person whose arrest in the years after September 11 was an abuse of the material witness statute. In 2005, Human Rights Watch and the American Civil Liberties Union published a joint report called "Witness to Abuse" in which they documented seventy similar cases, sixty-nine involving Muslim men, sixty-four of them of Middle Eastern or South Asian descent.[50] One of the men described in the report, Abdullah al-Kidd, a U.S.–born American citizen, sued Attorney General Ashcroft, alleging that he was improperly arrested in Idaho and held in jail and then under severe restrictions for thirteen months under the material witness statute while the government investigated him. He was ultimately freed without ever being charged or called to testify. In allowing a civil suit al-Kidd filed to go forward in September 2006, Idaho Federal Judge Edward Lodge said, "It would be improper for the government to use the material witness statute for . . . the detention of persons suspected of criminal activity for which probable cause has not yet been established."[51]

Of course the threat from terrorists is real, but the unfortunate reality is that the threat from an overzealous response to terrorism is real as well. When we recalibrate the balance that has served this country for more than two hundred years, innocent people suffer at the hands of our government.

. . .

I was gratified when the international fingerprint panel's report was released in November to see confirmation of the opinion about the fingerprint error Bayle had given me. The mistaken identification of latent #17 as Brandon's was about as basic as a mistake could be. The report concluded that "the identification is filled with dissimilarities that were easily observed when a detailed analysis of the latent print was conducted."[52] The panel also provided a number of critical suggestions so that similar mistakes could be avoided in the future, including a requirement that print examiners obtain information about a print surface before making a comparison, ensure blind verification, and include charts of both similarities and discrepancies.[53]

But one section of the international panel's work really bothered me, the description of the April 13 memo from the Spanish to the FBI. The FBI cover-up about the Spanish position continued in the report, which stated only that the Spanish "arrived at an inconclusive finding."[54] I knew that this was simply not true.

Back in June, my confidence in the *New York Times* report had been temporarily shaken by word that the FBI had taken a third trip to Spain on June 9 and 10. This time the FBI team had been accompanied by Assistant United States Attorney Pam Holsinger. As relayed to me by Immergut, Melida Lledo had denied the quotes attributed to him in the *Times* article on June 5 and confirmed the FBI version of events. Immergut had a copy of the letter then, but she would not give it to me. When I pressed Gorder about the letter the next day, he said the FBI believed that the more important piece was what the Spanish had told the FBI at their first meetings on April 21 and 22.

Even though William had obtained confirmation of the *Times* report the week before, I needed to hear from Melida Lledo myself, and on the fifteenth I asked William to try to get him on the phone again. There was no mistaking what Melida Lledo told me—the Spanish had written to the FBI on April 13 saying their review of the prints was "negative." Perhaps equally important, he told me that the Spanish had never agreed with the FBI. The information available to Judge Aiken led her to the same conclusion in the opinion she issued in September 2007: "Spanish authorities who met with the FBI agents [on April 21] 'refused to validate' the FBI's conclusion."[55]

The FBI was eventually forced to make the April 13 memo public during the civil suit, and there is no ambiguity in it. The one-page document was captioned "Official Letter" and was printed on the letterhead of the Police Headquarters Forensics Sciences Division.[56] It said in simple English: "The result was NEGATIVE." Capitals were used in the original letter, underscoring the conclusiveness of the Spanish comparison of latent #17 with Brandon's prints. The characterization that the FBI agents had put in the affidavits used to arrest Brandon and get warrants to search his home and office grossly misled the court—the Spanish conclusion was far more definite than "inconsistent."

How the United States attorney's office handled the April 13 letter still bothers me, and I know that Immergut and Gorder continue to deal with the devastation wrought by Brandon's arrest. As Immergut put it, Brandon's case was "a particularly low point in my career. The case was very hard on the individual assistants." Immergut, Gorder, and their colleagues became prosecutors because they wanted to help society. I believe they were acting in good faith when Brandon was arrested, and they were exonerated in a review conducted by the Justice Department's Office of Professional Responsibility. There is no question they were misled by the FBI and relied on what they were told.

Brandon's civil suit also seemed to reflect this view because it named as defendants Attorney General John Ashcroft, the Department of Justice; the FBI; FBI Agents Green, Massey, and Werder, who conducted the fingerprint examination, and Agent Weiner, who signed the affidavits in support of the warrants to arrest Brandon and search his home, office, and cars. It did not name Immergut and her staff. There are legal immunity issues for this, but the reality is that the shots in the case had been called in Washington and that was where any civil liability was going to lie.

But when it came to the April 13 letter, it seems Immergut and her staff succumbed to the same type of big case pressures that infected the FBI's identification mistake in the first place, particularly when they gave Judge Jones the Motion to Dismiss the grand jury proceeding at the end of May. They were also operating in a system in which the leadership in Washington wanted to score political points by prosecuting people in the war on terror. The attorney general would bring local United States attorneys to Washington for press conferences, as Ashcroft had with Immergut's predecessor in the Portland Six case. Because the prosecutors have far greater powers under the Patriot Act and are pushed by the administration, the potential for people like Brandon to suffer is far greater than it used to be.

■   ■   ■

Even before the fingerprint and inspector general's reports or the disclosures in the civil suit, Brandon's case had a direct impact on the local political scene, particularly in debates over the Joint Terrorism Task Forces. JTTFs had been set up in a number of cities, including Portland, in the late 1990s. Portland's participation had remained under the radar until it came up for renewal in November 2000, and the debate on whether to continue raged for more than four years.[57] Whenever the subject came up, city council sessions were jammed by those opposed to the city's participation in the JTTF. The councilors heard time and again about the fears harbored by many Portlanders of overzealous law enforcement and racial profiling. They heard from Japanese Americans who reminded the council of their internment in 1942, from civil rights, antinuclear, and antiwar protesters who testified about police and FBI interference in legitimate political activity and protests in the 1960s and 1970s.

In public testimony and behind the scenes, the Portland police chief, Immergut, Jordan, and other local federal officials were equally strong in their advice to the council that Portland needed to play its role in the fight against international terrorism. The law enforcement community played down the past abuses and sought to assure the council that everything had been corrected. Those voices won out, and the council voted in 2003 and 2004 to continue the city's participation.

It looked as though the opposition to the city's participation was fading when Brandon's case broke. Andrea Meyer, Oregon ACLU attorney, detailed for the city council documentation of countless cases of interference with legitimate political activity around the country, and she asked if I would lend my voice as a counterweight to Immergut and Jordan's strong statements about the importance of the JTTF with the city council.[58] I agreed and weighed in, meeting with one of the lead members of the city council.

The surveillance on political activists Andrea described was nothing new. The *Portland Tribune* reported on September 13, 2002, that Winfield Falk, who worked as a terrorism expert for the Portland police for many years, took home thirty-six boxes of files when he left the force.[59] The files, discovered in his garage years after he died, covered at least three decades of spying on Portlanders from the 1960s to the 1980s. Files had been kept on at least 3,000 people in 576 organizations that included the People's Food Store co-op, the Northwest Oregon Voter Registration Project, the Women's Rights Coalition, and even the Bicycle Repair Collective, described as "a city program offering a $24 course on how to fix flat tires and adjust brakes." The activities monitored included "writing letters, signing petitions, joining organizations and attending lectures or school board meetings."

Portlanders demanded to know why their police had been spying on them. Where was the oversight? Was the spying kept secret from the mayors during those years? And how did officer Falk come to have all those files in his garage? There were no good answers.

On April 28, 2005, Portland became the first, and only, city in the nation to pull its local police out of a JTTF. As national ACLU legal director Ann Beeson said about the decision, "We all want the police to protect us from real criminals and terrorists. But resources and funds established to fight terrorism should not be misused to target innocent Americans who have done nothing more than speak out or practice their faith. Investigations should be based on actual evidence of wrongdoing."[60] While preventive measures require a different approach, the problem is that the FBI, JTTF, and local police investigations too often fail to distinguish between the different types of work.

Portland's experience with police officers carrying surveillance beyond the bounds of the law into legitimate political activity was not a historic anomaly. In the spring of 2007, Inspector General Fine issued another report critical of the FBI, focusing on abuse of National Security Letters, a number of which had been issued in Brandon's case.[61] This 267-page audit concluded that the reports the FBI was required to submit to Congress had seriously underreported its use of NSLs. Fine also found too many instances of NSLs being used for improper reasons, to secure personal information about people when the bureau had no legal basis for doing so. The report concluded, "We believe the improper or illegal uses we found involve serious misuses of security letter authorities."

. . .

The battle for Brandon's freedom begun by my federal defender team on the first Thursday in May 2004 ended three years later. In late 2006, the government agreed to settle most of his civil suit. The apology Portland's FBI director Robert Jordan had given Brandon when he was released from jail was not enough to undo the harm he and his family had suffered. In the settlement, the government agreed to pay the Mayfields $2 million. It also resolved the motions Chris and I had filed about searches and surveillance, requiring destruction of all the material obtained during the eavesdropping and sneak-and-peek searches of Brandon's home, although not the derivative material that was disseminated to all of the spy agencies. The last piece of the settlement allowed Brandon to continue the part of his suit that sought an injunction against sections of the Patriot Act that permit searches meeting the standard required in all other searches—probable cause that criminal activity is afoot.[62]

While Brandon, like most Americans, wants our police and intelligence agencies to have sufficient authority to protect us from terrorists, he knows too well how important it is to ensure that law enforcement agencies stay within the confines of the law. Being able to challenge the Patriot Act, to do whatever he could to see that other Americans did not suffer as he had, was a critical part of the settlement for Brandon.

For a while, Brandon's case helped fuel the debate over the Patriot Act but without concrete evidence that its expanded powers had been used. One such discussion occurred in April 2005 in the Senate Judiciary Committee. Senator Dianne Feinstein of California asked Attorney General Alberto Gonzales whether the Patriot Act had played a role in Brandon's case. His initial response was that it had not, but then he corrected himself, providing the first, albeit limited, acknowledgment that the act had indeed played a role in the invasion of Brandon's privacy.[63]

A year later, Inspector General Fine's report provided the concrete and detailed evidence that the Patriot Act had been used against Brandon. The inspector general concluded that the Patriot Act had come into play, particularly in its relaxation of the wall between criminal investigation and national security that allowed all of the information the FBI gathered to be shared around the world.[64] He also acknowledged that under the Patriot Act, the FBI was allowed twice the time under the FISA authorized sneak-and-peek searches before it was required to give notice that it had conducted any searches. Fine reported that the Patriot Act also played a role in the intrusion into the Mayfields' lives through the use of National Security Letters issued by Portland's FBI chief Jordan that were used to obtain telephone and financial records without any court authorization.[65] How many NSLs Jordan issued and who received them was, however, kept classified in the inspector general's report.

Brandon's attack on the Patriot Act prevailed in September 2007, when Judge Aiken handed the government a stinging defeat, declaring two key provisions unconstitutional. The first was that which allows search or surveillance warrants to be issued by the FISC without a showing of probable cause of criminal activity not only when this is the "primary" purpose but also when it is a "significant purpose." That section also allows such warrants to be used in criminal investigations. The second part Judge Aiken struck down significantly limits the role of the judiciary in reviewing warrants, requiring the judges on the FISC to accept the government's representations that a person is an agent of a foreign power unless it is clearly erroneous. The judge found that the drafters of our Constitution had struck the "appropriate balance between intelligence gathering and criminal law enforcement" in the Fourth Amendment. "For over two hundred years," she said, "this Nation has adhered to the rule of law—with unparalleled success. A shift to a Nation based on extra-constitutional authority is prohibited, as well as ill-advised."[66]

I can't help but think that my Guantánamo clients' cases would have gone far differently if they had been heard by Judge Aiken, or Brown, or Jones.

24 | The MCA and the Third Procedural Stall

The spirit of liberty is the spirit which is not too sure that it is right.

—Judge Learned Hand[1]

READY TO TAKE THE OFFENSIVE IN THE habeas litigation armed with the evidence of innocence William brought back from Afghanistan and Pakistan, we were more convinced than ever that Adel's imprisonment was indeed unconscionable and that we would be able to convince the court to order his freedom. As the summer of 2006 turned into fall, however, it became clear that the administration was not going to accept the Supreme Court's second directive from Hamdan's case any more than it had accepted the first from Rasul's. I wondered, as I had so many times before, what they were afraid of.

Because the Supreme Court had specifically said in Hamdan's case that it was rejecting the administration's arguments about the DTA based only on interpretation of the statute and that it was not deciding if their effort to eliminate habeas corpus review violated the Constitution, the administration and Congress were free to rewrite the statute. And they immediately set out to change the rules again and seek another law to strip the federal courts of jurisdiction and keep the prisoners out of court.

While the administration wanted to rewrite the law, they were also facing increasing opposition at home and abroad to their policies in Guantánamo. So once again, they changed the facts. On September 6, President Bush announced that fourteen "high value" detainees had been brought to Guantánamo from undisclosed CIA-run sites around the world.[2] It was impossible to mistake the political in the president's statement since it was coupled with a call for passage of the Military Commissions Act so that these terrorists, who included one of the alleged masterminds of the September 11 attacks, Khalid Sheikh Mohammed, could be tried.

With the administration pressing hard for a new habeas-stripping law, my staff and I found ourselves confronting the same problem in September 2006 as when we first got into the cases. We were in a race to get something filed before Congress passed a law that could throw us out of court entirely. We worked feverishly to wrestle the evidence we had gathered on Adel, Gul, Al Ginco, and Chaman into bite-sized and coherent pleadings called motions for summary judgment. In order to get those motions heard, however, we first had to convince the judges to lift the orders that stayed the cases while the battles over jurisdiction raged on in other cases.

We had made a limited effort to get Judge Bates to lift the stay in Adel's case in August, using a little of our overseas evidence as a lever to ask the judge to order the DOD to give us more information about Adel, if any existed. Objecting on their behalf, Terry Henry argued that the Supreme Court's decision in Hamdan's case was limited and that the DTA jurisdiction stripping provision still applied to Adel and all the other prisoners who had never been charged with a war crime. Judge Bates ducked this constitutional issue, refusing to lift the stay, saying we had not presented any "concrete" evidence of "irreparable harm."[3]

Undaunted, we continued working on our main motions and, on September 21, we filed the first motions by any of the prisoners that presented new facts based on field investigation. From the beginning, our approach to the Guantánamo cases had paralleled what we do in all of our cases— we read the government's material, listened to the clients, and investigated. Based on the information we had seen on many of the other prisoners, it was clear that similar work could have been done for them.

Only six days after we filed, the Senate passed its version of the Military Commissions Act (MCA) of 2006 by a vote of 65 to 34. The next day the act passed the house 250 to 170, with only 7 Republicans voting against the bill. The law was a mixed bag.[4] On the positive side, it included procedures for military trials of men the administration actually charged with war crimes, like the ten against whom charges had been filed in 2004. That part was a tremendous advance over the procedures the Supreme Court had rejected in Hamdan's case, the new rules more or less conforming to the procedures generally required for prisoners of war under the Military Code of Justice.

The most controversial part of the MCA, and the section that has kept Adel from having his day in court, was the provision to strip the federal courts of habeas corpus jurisdiction. This time the stripping language was far more sweeping than in the DTA of 2005, including those detained as enemy combatants not just in Guantánamo but anywhere in the world. It was also written in such a way as to make clear that Congress intended not only to prevent any future habeas actions but also to throw out all the pending cases.[5]

After a fierce and partisan debate, the Senate barely passed the habeas stripping section by a vote of fifty-one to forty-eight with only four Republicans voting to preserve habeas corpus—Oregon's Gordon Smith, Judiciary Committee chairman Arlen Specter, Rhode Island's Lincoln Chafee, and New Hampshire's John Sununu.[6] The debate in the Senate mirrored the arguments that had been made repeatedly during the past four years in all the habeas cases. Senator Smith spoke about the "damage" to "our moral integrity" by stripping foreigners of rights, questioning how giving them a day in court could possibly cost American lives. Senator Leahy asked "why would we allow the terrorists to win" by giving up the democratic principles for which we were fighting voluntarily. Speaking for the bill, Senator Lindsay Graham, one of the primary sponsors of both the MCA and DTA, said that stripping habeas was necessary because habeas corpus fights in the civilian courts would impede our war effort. The overriding theme of the sponsor's rhetoric was the continued and mistaken assertion that all the men in Guantánamo were fighters.[7]

But no one said it more directly than the president in a speech on September 6, 2006, that, as he did so often, preyed on fear:

> It's important for Americans and others across the world to understand the kind of people held in Guantánamo. These aren't common criminals or bystanders accidentally swept up on the battlefield—we have in place a rigorous process to ensure those held at Guantánamo Bay belong at Guantánamo. Those held at Guantánamo include suspected bomb makers, terrorist trainers, recruiters and facilitators, and

potential suicide bombers. They are in custody so they cannot murder our people. One detainee held at Guantánamo told a questioner
questioning him—he said this: "I'll never forget your face. I will kill
you, your brothers, your mother, and sisters."[8]

Some of the prisoners at Guantánamo fit the president's description;
many others, including Adel and most of my other clients, do not. And the
processes the president described, the CSRT and ARB, are anything but
rigorous in weeding out the guilty from the innocent.

While not as dangerous to our constitutional structure as the provision-
stripping habeas jurisdiction from the courts, perhaps the most cynical part
of the act was the part that significantly narrowed the scope of the War Crimes
Act of 1996, the law that made it illegal for U.S. government agents to treat
prisoners harshly.[9] Apparently recognizing that its actions, in Guantánamo
and elsewhere, had crossed the line, the administration insisted that the MCA
make the changes retroactive to 1997, essentially granting immunity from
prosecution for many of the interrogation techniques used in the war on terror.

The MCA was too much for some human rights lawyers in Germany. In
November, they filed suits in German courts seeking to have the German
government prosecute Secretary Rumsfeld, Attorney General Gonzales, and
torture memo authors Yoo and Bybee, among others for war crimes.[10] While
the suits may never lead to convictions or judgments for damages, they
demonstrated the depth of the anti-American feelings that the imprisonment and interrogation policies of the Bush administration have generated
even among our allies.

■   ■   ■

Passage of the MCA only deepened the procedural morass that stopped my
team and me from making any progress in court for Adel and our other
clients. Terry Henry's response to my motion to lift the stay in Adel's case
and grant his release was to tell district Judge Bates that the MCA took away
his jurisdiction to hear the motions and to urge him not to rule on that jurisdictional question until the DC circuit court ruled on the same issues in
Al Odah's and Boumediene's cases.

The circuit court, where those cases had been pending when the MCA
was passed, ordered new briefing on the jurisdictional issues raised by the

MCA, which meant more months of delay. As during the previous winter, I did not want to trust Adel's fate to the other habeas lawyers and offered to write another amicus brief. The habeas litigation "brain trust" again jumped at the chance to have my staff and me file an amicus brief with the circuit that explained our innocence investigation, how important it was to have a full habeas corpus process that allowed the courts to look at new facts, and how unfair it would be if the court could review only the "evidence" the military had presented at the CSRT hearings. Two weeks after the MCA was signed into law, Steve Sady and I filed our second amicus brief with the circuit.[11]

The whole process was incredibly frustrating. My staff and I strongly believed that Adel and four of our other clients were innocent, but we were still blocked in the courts by the fights over jurisdiction. We had been looking for some other way to help our clients when, in late September, during the congressional debates over the MCA, the lawyers at CCR invited my staff and me to join a major press conference they had organized in New York City to humanize the prisoners. Their hope was that by publicizing the fact that there were innocent men in Guantánamo, some senators might buck the administration and save habeas corpus. CCR, which had been in the forefront of efforts to combat the administration's continued drumbeat that the prisoners were the "worst of the worst," distributed a report called "Faces of Guantánamo" at the press conference. It told the stories of a score of innocent detainees and featured a picture of Adel with his daughters on the cover. "Faces" also told Gul's story.[12]

Energized by the press conference, which we had joined via satellite from Portland, my team managed to get stories about Adel and our other clients into the *New York Times, Washington Post, Boston Globe, Miami Herald,* and *San Francisco Chronicle,* and in scores of smaller markets as AP wire stories.[13] After the articles ran, I was contacted by several Senate Judiciary staffers, and for a while we thought I might be invited to testify in Washington, but nothing ever came of the contacts. Even after the Democrats took control of both houses in November 2006, no one ever scheduled a hearing on habeas corpus and Guantánamo where our evidence of innocence could be presented.

In October, we took the publicity campaign to a new level and a new medium. William and Pat had been contacted by two Portlanders, David Naimon, a naturopathic physician, and Laura Moulton, an educator, who had read about Adel and wanted to do something for him. The five of us had a preliminary meeting, where Naimon and Moulton explained that they were hooked up with Ben Parzybok, a Web developer, and suggested the creation of a Web site to publicize Adel's situation and the lack of process for any of the prisoners in Guantánamo. I gave Pat and William a tentative go-ahead if the trio checked out as neither police agents nor violent activists. When they came back clean, meetings began in earnest, and Project Hamad was born—a Web site that features news about Adel and tries to rally people to press for fair hearings for all the prisoners.[14]

Their work with the Project Hamad team got Pat and William, who are twenty years younger than I am, thinking about the Internet, and they came to me in December with a suggestion that we put out a video about Adel on YouTube.

That night, knowing nothing about YouTube, I toured the site in earnest, reading the comments viewers posted and tracking YouTube pieces that appeared on other Web sites. I quickly realized that it is a form of publicity that reaches a different audience from the newspapers I was more familiar with. When, several weeks later, the guys showed me a preliminary draft of the video they proposed to post, I was sold.

At the same time that Adel's team was moving forward with Project Hamad and YouTube, we had to divert our energies to fighting another of the administration's stonewall tactics. This time it was a skirmish over release of the sworn video exhibits we had filed with the court. Under the Protective Order, all court filings were presumptively classified until the Department of Justice Privilege Team completed its review. While the review was ongoing, we could not release the exhibits to the press or post them on the CCR habeas lawyer's Web site where all counsel shared their work. From February to October, filing under the Protective Order had not been a problem, all of the court papers we had filed had been cleared within a week.

Given the volume of documents we filed in September for Adel and the other clients, additional time for the administration to complete the review seemed reasonable, but not the two and a half months it eventually took for our exhibits to be cleared. As October turned into November, the thought crossed my mind that the review was being deliberately delayed to avoid more embarrassment before the elections of the first public disclosure of court documents proving that some of the prisoners were innocent. The delay was particularly galling because I could not see how any of the exhibits could be considered classified, particularly since we had been free to publish them until they were filed in the court.

On November 1, we had had enough, and Pat fired off an e-mail to Andrew Warden: "I have to tell you that we are getting frustrated. . . . This is especially the case with the Exhibit 1 DVD [a twenty-five-minute summary of the investigation] . . . that . . . provides no different information than what has already been cleared in the written exhibits." Pat went on to ask whether we would need to litigate the classification issue.

Warden responded that "review of the DVD's present unique classification issues given their format," and told Pat that he would oppose any motion to expedite the process.

"What format issue?" Pat shot back. "DVD is a standard video format."

Warden had no answer to that, so in mid-November I filed a motion asking the court to order the classification review and, just as Judge Kay had told me when we were fighting for security clearances the previous February, the administration blinked when it was faced with a court hearing. On November 29, Warden telephoned Pat to say that he expected the documents to be cleared "very soon." Perhaps revealing a little of how he felt about the legal positions he was sometimes required to take, Warden told Pat he expected the exhibits would be cleared "before the Department of Justice had to respond to our motion as he did not want to write the brief on it." Somehow the "problem with the format" evaporated and the exhibits were cleared the very next day.

With morale in the office plummeting over the new jurisdictional roadblocks thrown up by the MCA and the stall over our exhibits, my team got a much-needed boost from an unexpected source. The American Jewish Committee decided to bestow its annual Learned Hand Award, for people who work for democratic values, on the Portland lawyers working on the Guantánamo cases. On November 9, the Guantánamo lawyers in my office and six other Portland lawyers in private practice were honored at a luncheon at Portland's Governor Hotel. Paul Fortino, the most senior of the recipients, spoke for us all in accepting the award: "Look how wonderful this is. Here I am a Roman Catholic, Italian American being given an award by a Jewish Organization for representing Muslims. Thank you." As much as I appreciated the acknowledgment and Paul's words, they had a hollow ring. My clients' freedom was the only award I wanted.

Stymied in court and unable to count on Congress to restore habeas corpus, in mid-October of 2006, my team and I decided to take our fight for Adel's freedom to the military itself. Nine months earlier, my assistants and I, along with all habeas counsel, had received notices from the DOD's Office for the Administrative Review of the Detention of Enemy Combatants (OARDEC) that we could make submissions for our clients in the ARB process. When the notices arrived, we had not even met any of our clients and had nothing to say, but after our overseas investigations, we certainly did. Even though our experiences with the Department of Justice and JTF gave us little hope that anything we said would have a positive effect, our approach was to push every lever, so we sent a copy of the summary judgment motions and exhibits we had filed for Adel, Gul, and Al Ginco to OARDEC. But we did not just ask for release under the ARB; we asked to have our clients declared innocent.

I sent a separate copy of Adel's material directly to Deputy Secretary of Defense Gordon England with a cover letter appealing to his "conscience." In the world of the ARB and CSRT, England was the DCO, or designated civilian official, who had the final say over all the prisoners' status. My Internet research on England suggested that he was cut from different cloth than his boss, Secretary Rumsfeld. Word was that England had been dressed down for a memorandum he had sent to all military personnel in July after the Supreme Court's decision in *Hamdan* directing that all prisoners were to be treated in accord with Common Article III of the Geneva Conventions.[15] As we were to learn months later, our submissions started a chain of events within the Pentagon that eventually moved the entire government—even if only an inch.

Late on Friday, November 3, I received an e-mail acknowledgment from OARDEC stating that my submissions had been received. At 8:11 A.M. Monday morning, I fired off a response, explaining how "disturbed" I was about Adel's situation and asking whether Adel had even had a second ARB in 2006. While an Administrative Review Board is supposed to be held annually for each prisoner, Adel had told us that he had had only one review. At 8:49, I received an "out of office auto reply" that I surmise was meant for Major Peter's* secure e-mail rather than the public e-mail OARDEC used for its rare communications with habeas counsel. As I was to learn later, many people in the Pentagon have two e-mail addresses that differ by one or two numbers, one that is secure and for internal use and another that is for use with the public. The auto reply I received included Major Peter's personal cell number.

Even though communications from habeas counsel were generally supposed to go through the Department of Justice, it seemed reasonable to communicate directly with OARDEC, because the subject was not in reference to our lawsuit but rather the ARB process on which OARDEC had invited direct communication. Having Major Peter's cell number was too good an opportunity to ignore, so I called, getting a voice mail recording, and left the major a message. Later that day, he replied by e-mail saying that he was the proper "point of contact," but in line with all other responses we had received since we entered the cases, he went on to say, "Unfortunately, I am not able to provide you an answer to most of your questions."

When new staff join the office, I give them an introductory orientation that includes my philosophy for defense work. We just can't take no for an answer. You make your point and if the judge rules against you, you politely and respectfully shift a little and make the argument again, maybe in your next breath, maybe in a new pleading a few days later, or maybe, if you believe you are right, repeatedly in pleadings over the years. We owe that to the clients. I then go on to tell them about the time Steve Sady was arguing a point with Judge Redden. The judge ruled against him, but Steve pressed on; the judge ruled again, and Steve pressed on; after the fourth time, the judge barked in exasperation, "Mr. Sady, don't you know the meaning of the word no?" Unbowed, Steve respectfully told the judge that he believed he was right and the reasons why. After a pause, pregnant with anxiety for Steve and his client, the judge changed his ruling.

Following my own advice, I ignored the major's e-mail and called his personal cell number again. When I introduced myself, he was clearly taken aback. "How did you get this number?"

"You gave it to me," I replied matter-of-factly.

While he did not challenge me again, the major reiterated what he had said in the e-mail, that he could not tell me anything. But when we hung

---

* My correspondent's name and rank have been changed for security reasons.

up fifteen minutes later, he had told me quite a bit about the ARB process in general and that there were two lawyers working on Adel's case. Major Peter had not yet seen any of the material himself, so I pressed the case for Adel's innocence and urged him to review the DVD summary exhibit as quickly as he could. Later that morning, I sent an e-mail thanking him for the conversation and, much to my surprise, received an immediate reply assuring me that he would give the matter "immediate attention." Later in the week, my assistants followed up with e-mails about our clients Gul and Al Ginco, and, while we did not have new evidence for him, a plea for another of our clients who appeared to be completely innocent.

Fully engaged with my other cases and on other Guantánamo fronts over the winter, I did not call Major Peter again until the end of February 2007. Now his tone was entirely different, and I felt I had finally gotten through to a human being. The major explained that my team's submissions in November 2006 were the first of their kind OARDEC had seen. While OARDEC had received numerous ARB submissions from habeas counsel, no one else had gone out and investigated his client's case, gathered evidence of innocence, and submitted it to the military.

"Frankly, we did not have any procedure in place to handle any material like this," the major admitted. He apologized for the fact that no final decisions had been made about Adel but went on to explain that it had been necessary to write an entire SOP (procedure) on how to handle new evidence that went to the heart of the CSRT decision and that "it had to be approved all over the place." The final procedure was not in place, but the Major explained that a report on Adel had already been sent to the head of OARDEC, Frank Sweigart. Sweigart, a 1974 Annapolis graduate and career naval flyer, had retired from the navy in 2004 just before he took over as the head of OARDEC.[16] From Sweigart, the recommendation would go to Deputy Secretary England.

Before he hung up, Major Peter invited me to stay in touch and, throughout the spring, I did. On March 23, I called to see if there had been any progress on his recommendation. We talked for quite a while about the major's plans and about me (the major had seen some articles about my representation of Brandon), about the SOP, and about new CSRTs. I was disappointed to learn about a delay in finalizing the SOP but even more discouraged to hear that there was not going to be any movement on new CSRTs because the decision had been made to give CSRTs to the fourteen "high value detainees" who had been brought to Guantánamo in September.

Since Peter had been so open, I called again a few days later to tell him I was planning a trip to Sudan and did not want to waste government money if Adel's release was imminent. Peter dropped any pretense about not telling me he had made a positive recommendation in Adel's case and assured me he would press for a new hearing. By May, Peter had left OARDEC but gave me numbers for other staff who were still there. While they were civil when I called, none of them had reviewed Adel's material and would give me no information. It did not seem like we were any farther ahead than we had been in November.

25 | The Dark Winter

We cannot learn real patience and tolerance from a guru or a friend. They can be practiced only when we come in contact with someone who creates unpleasant experiences. According to Shantideva, enemies are really good for us as we can learn a lot from them and build our inner strength.

—attributed to the Dalai Lama

Khartoum, Sudan

November 2006
Mr. George Bush
The President of the United States of America

Dear. Mr. President

Peace be with you, the mercy of God, and His blessings.

I am the wife of the Sudanesse Detainee Adel Hassan Hamad. I am writing to you from the Sudan. My Husband has been detained in the military prison in Cuba for more than four years.

Mr. President, My husband is a good and innocent man. He did not do anything to harm the United States of America. He worked for charities that tried to help the poor and sick people of Pakistan and Afghanistan.

My husband has been away from me because he has been detained. He left me four daughters. Our human condition is at its worst, and it is the most difficult due to thee absence of my husband, Adel, the only person who used to provide for our family. He left us living miserable life, all of us in one single room, summer and winter, and a courtyard surrounded with a fend of molded bricks. We live in the worst possible condition and we are struggling in earning our living, because we have little income to use for our living expenses.

Mr. President, I am a wife and I am a mother, and I suffer a great deal from the absence of my husband. My daughters suffer exactly the same from missing their father. I have to carry the responsibility because it is far more than what human beings can endure. Now we know that you have impassioned affection and noble feelings towards the family, that makes you live the compassion of fatherhood, and of being a son, a compassion that excites the heart of every human being.

Mr. President, how tough life has been while my husband, Adel, is still detained and far away from me and from his daughters. It is true that we are alive, but without him, our life has no taste, no color, and nor smell to it. What can you say to very young children who have no water and no trees, no means of living, and the person who can clothe them has been placed in a dark pit. Be merciful sir, and peace be with you. How great is our need for the warmth, compassion, love and support of him.

Mr. President, with all due respect, please look into my husband's detention and the facts and you will see that he is a good man who should be free. We are waiting for you to free him any minute, for our sake, and for the sake of his daughters. My youngest daughter, who is five years old, frequently asks me when her father will come home, but I cannot answer her. She forgot even what her father looks like, because she has been deprived of seeing him for such a long time. Mr. President, please help me answer that question for her. Thank you.

Salwa Othman Ahmad Othman
The wife of the detainee Adel Hassan Hamad,
in the military prison in Cuba.

In Khartoum, Guantánamo, and Portland, the winter of 2006–2007 seemed to go on forever. It was not easy in our calls to Sudan to tell Salwa and Al

Tayeb about the MCA. They could not understand what was going on in America, why the new evidence we had brought back from Afghanistan and Pakistan did not free Adel, and why the president and the Congress were so afraid of letting him have a day in court. In one of the calls in early October, Pat suggested that Salwa write a letter to President Bush and tell him how she felt. Dr. Sbait looked at him like he had slipped a gear, writing to the president of the greatest country in the world was beyond the ken of a traditional Muslim woman, he told us. Over the next several weeks, William brought up the subject each time he called Khartoum, suggesting several approaches to help Salwa get going and finally getting agreement that she would try to write a letter. When it arrived via e-mail in mid-November, what she had written bore little relation to what William had suggested, but it was sheer poetry, exposing her anguish in a way that no one could have expected. I mailed the letter to the president in December with a cover letter on office stationery. No one from the White House ever replied.

In mid-December, I made my third trip to Guantánamo. The CBQ and the ferry and bus rides over to the prison were no different from before, but things were changed once we arrived. Camp 6, the second of the new modern maximum-security prisons, was open and some of the attorneys who were visiting their clients there reported that the conditions were awful. The men were locked down twenty-two hours a day, isolated in windowless cells; "rec" time was in a fifteen-by-four-yard concrete enclosure that was subdivided into five separate cages so that prisoners who were there at the same time could not even hit a soccer ball back and forth; the guards were particularly surly; and the visiting room walls so thin that everything could be heard.[1]

When William and I checked in at Camp Echo, the mood was different as well. The funky metal table next to the small guard booth where we were frisked and our papers searched was the same, but when I touched the table after putting my papers down on it, the young guard barked at me, "Don't touch the table."

Not sure what I had done, or what the issue was, and not wanting to slow down the process of getting in to see Adel, I just stepped back. Review of our papers was more thorough than ever, and even though we had approval from the powers that be to bring in photos, our DVD summary exhibit, and the DVD player, the guard would not let them through until we got the head of the JTF legal unit to come over and clear it.

Forty-five minutes later, one-third of the allotted morning visiting time, William and I finally stepped into unit 1 in Echo. As soon as I walked in the door and Adel opened his mouth, I could tell that he was having a more difficult time than in September.

"It is so good to see you." Even without Felice's interpretation, the "so" sounded heavy.

Adel's reaction to the food we brought reflected the same mood. In addition to Janan's baklava, we had brought some store-bought baked goods. Adel looked at the box and said, "They are not from my country." There was no demand in his voice or criticism of the bearers of the gifts. It was a simple statement of fact, reflecting how much he missed Sudan and Salwa and the girls. Adel was also embarrassed because he had nothing to give us in return. As William and I were to learn a few months later, in Sudan it is considered impolite to bring a gift when you go to someone's house. In the prison, we were bringing gifts to Adel's house, even if it was not a house of his own choosing.

While somewhat less buoyant than before, my introduction of William as the infamous "interrogator" from our first letter brought a broad smile to Adel's face as William unloaded family photographs and the summary DVD exhibit of our investigation that we had gotten permission from the JTF to bring in and show Adel.

His reaction to the first photograph, of Salwa and the girls, was not at all what we expected. "Where is the little girl?"

There was almost panic in Adel's voice. William and I looked closely at the photo but saw nothing wrong. Adel pointed at the right side and I realized that when we had blown up the photograph to bring to the prison, Rahmah, Adel's youngest daughter, was cut out. Only her elbow remained in the frame. Adel, who had already lost one daughter while he was in prison, was afraid he had lost a second.

I quickly explained what had happened as William fumbled for another photo with Rahmah, her expressive eyes shining out at her dad.

When William started the DVD, Adel's face lit up again. For the first seven or eight minutes, he was having a ball watching the video of William's investigation. Slowly, however, the reality of what was happening set in.

This was not a home movie of a nice trip; he was in his fourth year in prison, watching a video of his home, family, and colleagues that we were using to try to get him out of the pit, or as he put it "this grave," in which his life was wasting away. The video brought him closer to his family but also reinforced the gulf that kept them apart.

When we started talking about his situation, Adel told us that he was back in the dorms in Camp Delta after the brief time he spent locked down after the disturbance in May. He was still being seen by interrogators every few weeks and was told on nearly every visit that he should be going home soon, though one of his interrogators had told him that with the political situation between the United States and Sudan over Darfur,[2] it might take a long time actually to get him out of the prison. He had told the interrogators he was depressed, "This is not a hotel here," he told us. "Every day the situation worsens. Every day there is a new rule."

The boredom was extreme. "There is nothing to develop your mind."

Adel went on, "Even the desert would be better than here." I was quite concerned about his mood and asked Adel if there was anything in particular we could do.

He did not answer right away but looked at the pictures on the table in front of him. Finally, pointing to one of the photographs of his family, he said, "What pushed me to say this was when I saw the picture of the little girl here." He told us again, the sadness taking over his voice, "The last time I saw her, her mother was feeding her." After a pause, he went on, "When you trust in the merciful Allah it will work, that does not mean you always see the peaceful end. I sometimes feel I am losing my life here."

I reached out and held Adel's arm, telling him we would keep pushing in every way to get him home. It wasn't much, but it was all I could do. Adel looked up and said, "I know. I even hear of the efforts your institution is making from the other prisoners."

We slowly shifted back to talking about the case, clarifying some facts and discussing our plans for continuing to push on all fronts. By the time we said good-bye at the end of the day, the full strength was back in Adel's voice and he was smiling easily again. The resilience I had seen on the first two visits had triumphed over despair.

Leaving the prison that night in the bus, the sky reflected the mood of the day, red tendrils in gray clouds. Our JTF escort told me he was lonely on the island—of the 300 people in his platoon, more than 290 were men.

But he was still glad he was there rather than at a base back home. "I feel like I did something, being here," he said. "I feel bad for the people in Iraq but at least I am contributing." Once again the complexity of the situation with Iraq and Guantánamo for the entire country struck me. There are many different ways we Americans express our patriotism and compassion, and it is important to honor them all.

.   .   .

Within a few days of my return from Guantánamo in December, the disconnect between my experiences and the administration's continued drumbeat was underscored yet again by an article in the *New York Times* reporting a major shift in policy at the prison under the new command. In June 2005, JTF commander Brigadier General Jay Hood had been reported in a press release put out on the American Forces Information Service as saying that an incentive system he had instituted allowing more privileges for prisoners in the different camps based on their behavior had been highly successful. He was said to be planning to extend the privilege system even to the not yet completed Camp 6.

"Everyone here knows about Camp 4," he said about the camp where Adel spent most of his time, "and everyone wants to be here."[3]

But Hood's successor as JTF commander, Admiral Harris, took a very different view. As reported in the *Times*, Harris believed "they're all terrorists; they're all enemy combatants. . . . There is no such thing as a medium-security terrorist."[4]

Having just visited Adel, and listened to my colleague Steve Sady's account of the problems our client Al Ginco was having, Harris's comments were just too much to take. I sent him a letter with some of our evidence of innocence, urging him to take another look at who was actually in the prison. I never received a reply.

On January 5, 2007, we were finally ready to take our response to the administration's distortions to the Internet and YouTube. My team's video, *Guantánamo Unclassified*, opened with William standing on the beach in Guantánamo with the sound of waves rolling ashore in the background before moving on to excerpts from the sworn video statements gathered in Afghanistan and Pakistan. The video quickly rose to the number one spot on the YouTube News and Politics Site.[5] Sabin Willett, one of the more active of the pro bono counsel and fellow graduate of Harvard Law School, applauded our effort on the CCR habeas lawyers' Web site: "With the courts closed to us, this may be the single most powerful piece of advocacy yet in these cases. All should view and pass along."

The synergy of the Internet was apparent on January 11 when the world news media noted the fifth anniversary of the opening of the prison in Guantánamo. Our YouTube piece was discussed around the world, and a photo of a protester in Miami, dressed in prison garb and wearing Adel's inmate number around her neck, appeared in papers as far away as New Zealand.[6] Everyone on Adel's team was buoyed to see that we were making an impact of some sort, but it wasn't the one thing that really mattered— Adel's freedom.

Apparently concerned about the storm of protests and negative publicity surrounding the fifth Guantánamo anniversary, the administration went on the offensive through deputy assistant secretary of defense for detainee affairs, Cully Stimson. After calling Guantánamo the "most transparent and open facility around the world," Stimson dismissively called the protests "something drummed up by Amnesty International."[7] He then went on the attack, calling out the large firms that were representing the detainees, labeling their representation of the detainees "shocking," and warning them that as news of their work spread, the executives of their corporate clients were going to make them "choose between representing terrorists or representing reputable firms." The *Wall Street Journal* immediately joined in, praising Stimson's attack.[8]

Fortunately for the prisoners and their attorneys, the attack died right there. Congress, the American Bar Association, the *New York Times*, and a host of other media outlets condemned Stimson, pointing out that representing the poor, downtrodden, and despised was the highest calling of the legal profession in America.[9] This time the administration's goal of achieving action through fear backfired, and by the end of the month the administration had backed away from Stimson's statements, and the position of the habeas lawyers, pro bono, retained, and federal defender, was more secure than ever.

Even though the broadside attack on counsel failed, my staff and I could not rest easy. On January 23, 2007, the military turned a more focused weapon on my office. A letter from Terry Henry to William advised him that the footage of the shore at Guantánamo that opened the YouTube video violated the Protective Order, which prohibited unauthorized photography at the prison. As a sanction, everyone from the office, not just William, was banned from the base.[10]

To say the banishment letter cast a pall on the office would be an understatement. If we could not visit our clients, we would not be able to continue our representation. Our upset quickly turned to anger as William, Pat, Steve Sady, and I pored over the Protective Order again. It prohibited photography on the prison side of the base but not the leeward side where we stayed and where William had done his filming. Equally important, William reminded us that he had obtained permission from the JTF escorts to use his cameras on the leeward side. We prepared a tight response, explaining the facts and our understanding of the Protective Order. Since Pat had a visit scheduled at the prison for the end of February, we needed a quick resolution.

Surprisingly, we got it in an e-mail from Henry within a week, advising that we could go forward with the visits we had planned. We can't know why Henry resolved the matter so quickly; maybe he agreed with our response, or maybe he just did not want another fight. Regardless, I was relieved that the matter was behind us and we had not had to burn more energy fighting another side issue.

As January came to a close without a decision from the DC circuit court on the MCA jurisdictional question, I decided to go back to Judge Bates in the district court and file another motion asking him to lift the stay in Adel's case and get to the merits. While I strongly disagreed with the judge's earlier decisions that the dripping away of Adel's life in the prison was not enough "concrete, impending and irreparable harm" to get him a hearing, my strategy in the renewed motion was to accept the judge's premise, cite his findings back to him, and say that our sworn evidence of innocence provided the "concrete" proof he said had been missing. The judge acted within one day and ordered Henry to respond within twenty days. When Henry filed his response with Judge Bates on February 15, all he talked about was the MCA; we learned nothing new about Adel's case and he was no closer to getting a decision that could free him.

The roller coaster of despair and optimism never moved faster than in the second half of February. Rumors had been flying once again that some prisoners were going to be sent home. Then, the day after Henry filed his response in Adel's case, Henry and Warden sent e-mails to a handful of lawyers around the country telling them one of their clients was going home. One e-mail came to Amy and Ruben, our primary lawyers for Nazar Gul, the man who had fled the Soviets with his parents and had been arrested a few short weeks after his return to Afghanistan. Coming while all the habeas lawyers were anticipating a ruling from the circuit on the jurisdictional issue, this may have been another of the administration's cynical moves to try to influence the judicial process. But this time the negative reaction in the office was tempered by the fact that one of the men released was ours.

As with nearly everything about our work with Guantánamo, Gul's return to his family was bittersweet. We were happy for him but had no way to know if our work had made any difference, and our other clients, including Adel, were still in the prison.

The week after Gul went home, the circuit staggered all of the prisoners and habeas counsel when it handed down its decision in *Boumediene*, holding the MCA constitutional and that the Constitution did not apply at all in Guantánamo.[11] Even more devastating, the circuit believed that all of the habeas corpus cases needed to be dismissed. The limited review created in the circuit by the DTA was all that was required.

From the pit of the *Boumediene* setback, the roller coaster headed upward again on the very afternoon Boumediene's case was decided, when e-mails arrived from OARDEC advising that Adel, his downstairs neighbor Ammeur, and Amin Ullah, the Afghan client for whom we had not been able to investigate yet at his home in the wild north of Afghanistan, had "been approved to leave Guantánamo." In the Kafkaesque world of Guantánamo, the e-mail went on that this did not "equate to a determination that your client is not an enemy combatant." Since the ARB permitted determinations that a person had been an enemy combatant but no longer posed a threat, this phrase was at least consistent with their rules. But the next phrase made no sense, "nor is it a determination that he does not pose a threat to the United States or its allies." As absurd as it seemed, our military was approving the departure of prisoners it had held in Guantánamo who still might pose a threat to our country. Of course, we did not believe that was the case with any of our clients, but apparently the Department of Defense did not care.

The real-world import of the notice for Adel was in one of the other clauses in the notice, a clause that was in all the notices, and said his approval to leave "was subject to the making of appropriate diplomatic arrangements for his departure." We were concerned that the rift between the United States and Sudan over the fighting and deaths in Darfur and the sanctions that had been imposed against Sudan by the United Nations would impede any diplomatic efforts to repatriate Adel.

.   .   .

Adel learned about the "approval" for his departure from Pat, who visited him in the prison during the last week of February. Upon his return, Pat told William and me that Adel was ecstatic about the news but he was also able to hear Pat's explanations about the reality of the strained diplomatic situation between the United States and Sudan. Since we were still pushing the DOD to exonerate Adel through a new CSRT, Pat also prepared Adel on how to respond if a new CSRT was held: He should participate fully, insist that any new CSRT consider the evidence we had submitted, and ask to have William called as a witness.

Stung by the decision in Boumediene's case and certain of nothing with OARDEC, we pressed ahead in March with our efforts to publicize Adel's plight and, shortly after Pat got back from Guantánamo, we put out a second YouTube video, *Guantánamo: Waiting for Justice*.[12] Pat and William thought we could generate an even broader audience on the Web if they enlisted a famous actor in Adel's cause, and through a series of who-do-you-know? phone calls, Pat ended up speaking with Academy Award–winning documentary director Frieda Mock. Her neighbor was Martin Sheen, a progressive political activist as well as an award-winning actor who had starred for years as the president on the television show *West Wing*. Sheen agreed and put together a powerful introduction, reminding the viewers that "no one should be locked up based solely on the word of a president, any president."

Sheen ended by referring to Salwa's letter to the president, which was featured in the second half of the video, read by a local student, and asked his audience to join in asking the president when Adel would go home.

.   .   .

While the *Boumediene* decision was a major setback, his lawyers immediately pressed onward, preparing certiorari petitions that sought a third round of litigation in the Supreme Court. We all hoped the Court would take the case and cut through the procedural morass, address the constitutional questions about jurisdiction it had ducked in *Rasul* and *Hamdan*, place clear limits on executive power to do away with habeas corpus, and pave the way for Adel's release.

Then, during the week of March 20, while the certiorari petition in *Boumediene* was still pending, the new secretary of defense, Robert Gates, joined Secretary of State Rice in calling for the closure of Guantánamo.[13] While their break from the president and vice president was welcome, the timing was suspect, paralleling as it did similar carefully calculated moves by the administration over the years to influence the judicial process.

The next week the administration struck again, announcing that it had reached an agreement with Australian prisoner David Hicks, one of the ten men it had actually charged in a military commission process.[14] Under the agreement, Hicks admitted that he had provided material support for terrorism, a charge similar to the one the Portland Seven had been convicted of for their efforts to get to Afghanistan. But in return for his admission of guilt, Hicks was not going to serve the same time in prison as the Portlanders. Rather, this man, who had been called repeatedly one of the "worst of the worst," was going home, where he would have to spend only nine more months in prison. Meanwhile, Adel, who had been approved to leave Guantánamo, was still there, as were our other clients who had never been, and likely never would be, charged with anything. The perversity of the situation was difficult to accept.

On April 2, 2007, a week after the Hicks deal was announced, the darkness of winter carried over into spring when the Supreme Court surprised most of the habeas counsel and voted four–three–two to deny the petitions for certiorari in the *Boumediene* and *Al Odah* cases.[15] The new Bush justices, Roberts and Alito, joined with the conservative justices Scalia and Thomas in voting to deny the petitions outright. The only two Democratic appointees of the past forty years, Justices Breyer and Ginsburg, joined with Justice Souter to vote to hear the case. Justices Stevens and Kennedy joined in an unusual opinion, saying that they were not prepared to grant certiorari— yet. They first wanted to see whether the DTA process was an effective substitute for habeas corpus.

The Supreme Court's refusal to hear the cases had potentially devastating consequences. Not only were we relegated to the limited review under the DTA, but a number of district court judges felt that they had no choice under the circuit court's ruling and started dismissing the habeas cases. With no case pending, the Protective Orders were no longer in effect and all visits to the base and communication with the clients were in jeopardy. I was worried Judge Bates might follow some of his colleagues and dismiss Adel's case and, as dismissals trickled in over the next few months, my apprehension never dissipated, but the outcome I feared did not materialize.

The next round of litigation was about to begin on a new playing field in the circuit court while Adel, still approved to leave, continued to languish in the prison.

. . .

April 2 was also the first night of Passover, the Jewish holiday that celebrates the liberation of the Jews from their captivity in Egypt thousands of years ago. Kathleen, Michael, and I, as we have ever since my father died and my mother stopped traveling to Portland in the late 1990s, celebrated the Passover seder at my friend Peter Korn's house. Coincidentally, the Haggadah, the books that tell the Passover story, that Peter and I both inherited from our parents, are the 1940–1941 version of the Jewish Reconstructionist Foundation—a version that has a decidedly political introduction. In light of the Supreme Court's refusal to act and Adel's continued imprisonment at the hands of my government, the words in the Haggadah that introduce the seder had special meaning for me that night:

> The age-old struggle between those who cherish freedom and those who would deny it to their fellow-men has become more embittered than ever. In that struggle the Jews are deeply involved. They have a great stake in the ultimate victory of the cause of freedom. . . . We live in a new world; we are confronted with new conditions. But the problem is still the same: how, in the face of setbacks and despite the demagogic appeals of false prophets, to keep alive in men the love of freedom, and their faith in it.

26 | Tea with the Ministers in Sudan

Winter is on my head but eternal spring is in my heart.

—Victor Hugo

WHILE THE LITIGATION AND RELEASE ROLLER coaster was taking us to dark places throughout the winter, William and I started preparations for a trip to Sudan. For months William had been urging Adel's brother-in-law to get us a lawyer to work with in Khartoum. Al Tayeb tried hard throughout the fall and early winter, visited with several lawyers, and gave us a number of possible contacts. But no one was willing to step up for a prisoner in Guantánamo who might not be in favor with the Sudanese government. Even though self-described as an Islamic republic, the Sudanese government had no love for Muslim extremists who could upset the precarious political balance there. Then, our YouTube piece changed the landscape for Al Tayeb.

The World Wide Web carried *Guantánamo Unclassified* to Sudan, where it was not only watched but also led to stories in several newspapers about Adel and his innocence. Adel became front-page news in Khartoum. Late in January 2007, the publicity paid off when Al Tayeb made contact with Hassan Saeed El Mogummer, the director of Civic Aid International Organization, an NGO based in Khartoum that devoted its efforts to human rights work and had recently taken up the cause of the Sudanese imprisoned in Guantánamo. The information we made available online about

Adel's innocence was just what Civic Aid needed to bolster its work. Now they could point to facts rather than simply attack the U.S. policies.

El Mogummer agreed to help in any way he could, and William started calling him regularly on Fridays when he spoke to Al Tayeb and Salwa in Khartoum. El Mogummer reported that the Sudanese foreign minister would facilitate the processing of visas for our visit, a process that often took months, and that we would be able to have high-level meetings with members of the government. The bad news was that the foreign minister had told El Mogummer that there were no negotiations ongoing with the United States about bringing the Sudanese prisoners home.

When we first started preparations for our trip early in the winter, William and I considered joining forces with Clive Stafford Smith, whose thirty some clients in Guantánamo included Sami Al Haj, a Sudanese cameraman for the Al Jazeera television network who had been seized in December 2001 by the Pakistanis as he attempted to cross the border into Afghanistan.[1] Because of his affiliation with Al Jazeera, Sami had become something of a celebrity detainee and a powerful political symbol, especially in Sudan. Smith also contacted El Mogummer and set up a trip for the end of March, but his timing did not work for us—I had other responsibilities in the office and needed to clear some bureaucratic hurdles with the Administrative Office of Courts in Washington before we could go.

El Mogummer came through for Smith in every way he had promised: meetings with all the prisoners' families, Civic Aid staff and their allies, the media, and top government officials. In his meetings with the government officials, Clive kept pressing them to take the initiative with the United States to get their citizens home, including a formal letter to Secretary of State Rice urging their repatriation. No letter was produced despite many promises, but Smith's trip generated a lot of energy in Sudan that proved invaluable when William and I got there three weeks later.

. ▪ ▪ ▪

Because the Supreme Court had refused to hear the jurisdictional question that was blocking the habeas corpus cases, review was thrown into the circuit court under the DTA. As limited as that process was likely to be, I had to pursue it for Adel and, in order to try to demonstrate the urgency of the situation, I wanted to file before leaving for Sudan. I spent the first two weeks in April working feverishly on Adel's DTA petition, while my assistants put together petitions for three of our other clients. Our approach was multileveled. First, we urged the court to follow the narrow scope of review in the DTA statute and just review the CSRT record in Adel's case, which is devoid of any evidence that could be used to declare him an enemy combatant and, under any standard, Adel should be declared innocent and ordered released. Second, we urged the court to follow the DTA statute and look at the CSRT process, which is a sham and violates the Constitution. Third, in order to provide meaningful review and be a constitutionally adequate substitute for habeas corpus, we said the DTA requires the court to move rapidly and consider our evidence of Adel's innocence.[2]

The first DTA petitioners, who had filed before the Supreme Court's denial of certiorari in Boumediene's and Al Odah's cases, had gotten bogged down in procedural wrangling with the Department of Justice, represented in the circuit court by Robert Loeb rather than Henry and Warden. With argument on procedure for these petitioners, Haji Bismullah and Huzaifa Parhat, set for May 15, it was apparent that there would be no hearings on the merits anytime soon.[3] Trying to avoid that morass, we accompanied our eighty-five-page petition with a motion for expedited consideration, arguing that the Court could rule on Adel's case without having to address the procedural matters. I called Loeb the day before I left for Sudan to try to reason with him about Adel but ran into the usual stone wall; he would tell me nothing about Adel's situation and would do nothing.

.   .   .

I tried pushing two more levers for Adel in April before I left for Sudan. My sister's husband, Ed, was worried by the prospects of a Jewish guy from Brooklyn traveling to the Islamic Republic of Sudan and called on a childhood friend, Larry Frankel, who was working closely with former President Carter at the Carter Center in Atlanta. Ed had seen the same travel warning about Sudan I had read on the State Department Web site:

> This Travel Warning for Sudan reminds U.S. citizens of the continued threat of terrorism and notes restrictions on travel by American citizens outside Khartoum . . . and to remind travelers that the U.S. government has received indications of terrorist threats aimed

at American and Western interests in Sudan. Terrorist actions may
include . . . kidnappings.

Frankel assured Ed that the Carter Center did business in Sudan. More
important, Frankel was sufficiently intrigued by our work in Adel's case
that he suggested I call. During the first two weeks in April I spoke with
him and Karin Ryan, the staff person who worked most closely with President Carter on humanitarian issues of this nature, and provided them all
of our material on Adel. Ryan told me that the center had taken up the cause
of Ahmed Errachidi, a Moroccan businessman who was sold for a bounty
in Pakistan in late 2001 after being injured in an automobile accident. The
center's role was to help convince the under secretary of state for democracy and global affairs and his Bureau of Democracy Human Rights and
Labor that it was safe for Mr. Errachidi to go home. Although Ryan was
interested in our case, she wanted to see what happened with Errachidi and
our trip to Sudan before deciding whether they would help Adel.[4]

The second new lever William and I pushed was with the Sudanese
ambassador in Washington. I had met with the Sudanese consul there in
May of 2006 but had gotten nowhere. In April, as part of his efforts to make
sure our Sudanese visas arrived on time, William managed to get through
to Ambassador Ukec and took the opportunity to bend his ear about Adel's
case. With our government refusing to give us any meaningful information, we were skeptical that the Sudanese would be any more forthcom-
ing. When Ambassador Ukec took a second call from William a week later,
it generated a little more hope that he would turn out to be a helpful
resource.

By mid-April, I had teed up the DTA petition, William and I had laid
whatever groundwork we could in Sudan, and the team had touched base
with everyone we could think of here at home. The stage was set for our
departure for Sudan.

•   •   •

On April 19, William and I took a late-afternoon flight to London. At
Heathrow we hooked up with Tom Durgin, the third member of our group,
a lawyer from Chicago who was representing one of the seven Sudanese
who had not been approved to leave. Tom, a former assistant United

States attorney with a blunt big-city manner, was a good addition to our little team.

The British Airways flight from London to Khartoum was full, until it stopped in Amman, Jordan, where we were unsettled by the exodus of all but fifteen passengers. I would have been a little more concerned that they knew something about Sudan that I did not had my seatmate not been a Sudanese ex-patriot who had spent the last thirty years living and teaching in Boston and was returning for a nephew's wedding. He assured me that we would find Khartoum quite safe. In the end we did, and it was a good thing because the sanctions that have been imposed on Sudan over the killings and human rights violations in its Darfur region prohibit any financial transactions by Americans—including credit card purchases—and William and I were carrying more than $10,000 in cash between us.

The sanctions don't seem to have hurt Khartoum much—it is bustling and booming. The Chinese, who are the biggest group of foreign investors, are ignoring them. From my hotel window, I faced one of the many construction cranes putting up new high-rises that were marked with Chinese lettering, and on the street in front of the hotel was a billboard featuring three beatific Chinese construction workers promoting a power company with the decidedly Maoist slogan "Power through Harmony."

After a few hours' sleep, we went down to the hotel lobby Saturday morning to wait for El Mogummer and took in our first clear-eyed views of the people in Khartoum. About three-quarters were in Western dress, the rest in white Arab robes and turbans or kufis. El Mogummer walked in a few minutes later. A lawyer devoting his career to humanitarian causes, he is in his midthirties, and although he was dressed in Western clothes, we soon learned that he is a religious man who stopped whenever he could to pray five times a day. With El Mogummer were his Civic Aid colleague, Hatim, also a lawyer, and the man who would serve as our interpreter for the week, Dr. Mohammed Osman Maki.

We drove to the Civic Aid offices through the city center with its wide boulevards left over from the British colonial period and modern buildings that went up only six or eight stories, giving the city a feel like Washington, DC. But the ubiquitous sweeps and piles of sand on the side of the roads blown in from the deserts, broken curbs, piles of rubble where construction had been started and abandoned, or finished but not cleaned up, bottles, cans, garbage everywhere, and plastic shopping bags blown onto every branch and fence post reminded us we were in a very distant place. The cars and trucks were almost all small Japanese and Korean models and were fighting for space on the roads with motorcycles, mopeds, and tuk tuks, three-wheeled motorized rickshaws.

The Civic Aid offices are in a nice walled compound of typical Sudanese architecture, with the organization's emphasis on Guantánamo visible as soon as we stepped into the courtyard, where two eight-foot cube cages the organization used in protests stood. Banners calling for the shutdown of Guantánamo were hung on the walls inside and out. The Civic Aid staff, around ten men and women, all greeted us warmly, and we had some time to chat before we headed for Adel's home.

When we got to Adel's house, the first face-to-face contact with Adel's wife and children was awkward. Understandably, they did not really want to see us; they wanted to see their father and husband. One of the first things Salwa said was, "Why isn't my husband home if he is innocent?" Nor was it not easy for William and me to see the poverty of their home. Inside the walled compound, Salwa and the girls live in one mud-walled room with their beds placed outside under a wood thatch shelter.

Al Tayeb's greeting was not restrained; he was filled with emotion at meeting his brother-in-law's advocates. He and his wife, Insaf, were thrilled to meet us and wanted to know how Adel was doing. Maryam, Adel's twelve-year-old, and Rahmah, the five-year-old, were wearing dark blouses and pants. Maryam wore a constant wide-mouthed smile, though it seemed she was smiling from nervousness rather than joy. Rahmah, beautiful, with round and sad dark brown eyes, was shy and clung to her mother or aunt for the first hour we were there. She eventually got up the courage to wander over to me, where she stuck for the rest of the day and on our other visits, perhaps sensing my presence as some connection to her father. We did little more that first day than say hello, offer reassurances that Adel was okay and his dignity and humor intact, and explain what we could about our efforts to win his freedom.

Jet-lagged and emotionally drained when we got back to the hotel, Tom, William, and I decided to walk about a mile to, and across, the bridge that spans the White Nile near its confluence with the Blue Nile. This is a powerful spot in Africa, the place where the branch of the Nile that comes out of Lake Victoria, the largest lake in Africa, shared by Tanzania, Uganda, and Kenya, merges with the Blue branch that roars into Sudan from the mountains of Ethiopia. We were reminded that we were in a police state when we were temporarily seized by secret police as we crossed the bridge, which was guarded by soldiers with fixed machine guns. When William and I identified ourselves as the American lawyers working for the Sudanese prisoners in Guantánamo, the head man looked us up and down then said in a knowing tone, "You are the American lawyers." He knew all about us and our visit and work for his countrymen. Suddenly, we were friends and there were smiles and handshakes all around.

Sunday we began our meetings with government officials, other human rights organizations, the media, and the families of the other eight Sudanese detainees. It was a long and productive day, starting with the chair of the National Commission on International Human Rights, who is also the brother of the first vice president (the compromise that ended Sudan's twenty-year civil war called for one vice president from each faction).[5] We then moved on to the Justice Ministry for a positive meeting with the deputy minister, and then the first of our daily press conferences, this one attended by more than fifty reporters. It was much more civilized than a press conference at home—no shouting or cutting people off—and women were well represented, roughly 40 percent of the reporters.

Our most important meeting of the day, and perhaps the entire trip, took place that afternoon at the Foreign Ministry. We were able to walk right into the building, there were no guards with guns and no search of any type. When we got off the elevator on the sixth floor, we walked into the spacious outer office of the state minister, Elsamani Elsawila Elsamani, with its dark green leather furniture and polished wood tables. With him were Ambassador Elsanosi, the person holding down the American desk in the Foreign Ministry; Minister Plenipotentiary Sharfi; and Dr. Ahmed Belal Osman, President Bashir's Kissinger-type adviser on foreign affairs. All were in Western garb save Dr. Osman, who was much lighter skinned and dressed in white robe and turban.

After brief introductions, I gave my pitch for Adel's innocence. There were some questions, but none from the president's man. Tom Durgin then talked a little about his client. When he stopped, the state minister asked, "What do you want us to do?" Tom, William, and I urged a variety of actions, then I suggested a formal written request from the Foreign Ministry to Secretary of State Rice for the return of the Sudanese. The Foreign Ministry men talked among themselves in Arabic for a few minutes. President

Bashir's man still said nothing, but then he nodded at the state minister and I understood that his presence probably said it all. Bashir had approved the meeting, and now he had his adviser approve a formal letter. We were feeling quite good when we arrived at the *Al Wattan* newspaper's offices for our next press conference.

Sunday ended with a lecture at Al Sharaf hall at the University of Khartoum that was broadcast live on Al Jazeera. Millions of Sudanese and other Arabic speakers in neighboring countries heard about Adel's plight. Al Sudani television, the state network, also ran stories on Adel that night and over the next three nights. During many of our meetings with government officials, they invited Al Sudani television cameras in for photo ops, and after the meetings, camera crews were waiting to interview us. These were mainly softball interviews in which we said we were fighting for the innocent Adel and how pleased we were to be greeted so warmly by the justice minister or the deputy in the National Assembly. What was important was that Adel's profile rose every day and we were hopeful that all the publicity would help him when he got home both with the government and with jobs, that he would be seen as a returning hero/victim, not a returning jihadist.

The following morning, as we were leaving a meeting with the deputy chairman of the National Assembly, Mr. Garang, El Mogummer got word that Minister Plenipotentiary Sharfi wanted a follow-up meeting with us at the Foreign Ministry to discuss the letter to Secretary Rice. Cutting short a third press conference, with the *Al Sahafa* newspaper, we made it to the ministry by noon, where we were ushered into a conference room. Sharfi's staff had the room set up with soda and water bottles in front of five microphones on one side for us, "the habeas lawyers' delegation," and three set up across the horseshoe-shaped table for the minister, Ambassador Omar from the consular department, and Ms. Selma, the legal adviser for the Human Rights Commission. After exchanging pleasantries, we all sat down on our respective sides and the minister started the meeting with a "statement" about the draft letter.

Rolling with the diplomatic formality, I made a "statement" about our appreciation of their willingness to work with us. The minister then walked around the table and gave Tom, William, and me copies of a handwritten draft. Overall we were thrilled—a letter in progress and they wanted our input. The only negative, as William and I saw it, was that the letter asked for the return of all the Sudanese detainees. Tom, whose client had not been approved to leave Guantánamo, wanted to keep it that way, while William and I wanted the letter to focus on Adel. The three of us caucused and debated a one-letter versus two-letter approach, eventually agreeing that one letter was more likely actually to get finished. I then suggested that the minister add a paragraph specifically mentioning Adel and gave him the language I wanted. The Sudanese "delegation" seemed quite open to the suggestion. We left with the understanding that the minister would get the draft typed and circulated that afternoon.

The time in the Foreign Ministry was fascinating, but the day's drama arrived during a meeting with Justice Minister Al Mardi, a meeting that had been ordered by President Bashir himself. Al Mardi is a southerner, and El Mogummer told us that although Al Mardi has the title, the northern deputy we had seen the day before has the real power.

Minister Al Mardi seemed like a kindly old gentleman with his curly gray hair, plastic-rimmed glassed, and chocolate brown leisure suit, sitting on an overstuffed mustard yellow leather sofa with white silk flowers on his tables. We all chatted pleasantly about our investigation and justice systems in general, then the conversation turned to the process the Sudanese Justice Ministry would go through when the prisoners returned home. Minister Al Mardi assured us it would be "fair." Perhaps sensing our concern for Adel and any process that might unfold in Sudan, Al Mardi gave us his personal pledge that we, William and I, were invited to participate in any investigation or hearing into Adel's situation once he returned. This commitment would become important later in the summer.

Then the conversation turned to what we were trying to accomplish, and I brought up the letter. "What letter?" the minister asked, suddenly looking anything but kindly. He had not been filled in by his deputy on the letter the Foreign Ministry was preparing for Secretary Rice, and he was furious. Out came his cell phone and a torrent of Arabic laced with the English word "fax" several times. Dr. Osman, who was sitting next to me, whispered that the minister had demanded to see the letter and ordered that it go nowhere until he had signed off on it. There goes the letter, I thought, tied up in a turf battle. So much of human nature is universal. I don't think any of us hid our disappointment.

We left Minister Al Mardi kicking ourselves for having seen him. In the midst of the bitterness between the United States and Sudan over Darfur, someone needed to take the first step in negotiation. Up to then it looked like we had managed to jump-start the process in the Foreign Ministry with President Bashir's backing. Fortunately, our worry that the justice minister had scuttled our efforts was short-lived. Around five o'clock, El Mogummer received a call from the minister plenipotentiary that his office had faxed a draft of the letter to Al Mardi, who had already signed off. The minister had been included and, apparently, that was what counted.

William and I had been pressing El Mogummer for several quiet and uninterrupted hours with Adel's family so we could conduct video interviews, and we did not understand why several of the Civic Aid staffers packed into the Toyota 4Runner for the ride when we left the Justice Ministry. We bumped over the unpaved streets that wound around the poor Haj Yusef neighborhood where Adel's family lived and pulled up to the compound entrance.

As soon as the door opened, we realized that El Mogummer had something entirely different planned. The area in front of the kitchen, sleeping area, and Al Tayeb's room was covered and backed with large squares of cloth in reds, yellows, and blues, some with patterns, some solid. Under and in front of the cloths were folding tables and plastic chairs.

After about a half hour, a bus swayed to a stop outside the outer door and a mess of teenagers piled out. They were there to work on the new rooms for Adel's wife and daughters and were led in by the directors of Ana Sudan, the NGO that was sponsoring the work. A few minutes later, the crowd doubled in size as a local politician, the equivalent of a city councilman in the States, arrived surrounded by an entourage and a television crew. It seemed everyone wanted a piece of the action with the American lawyers; we obliged, shook hands, posed, and watched construction begin.

Adel's older brother Hashem, who had taken the twelve-hour bus ride over from Port Sudan where he was a teacher, needed to return home, so we somehow managed to find enough quiet to film his interview and get more details of Adel's life as a child and after his return from college in Egypt. While the afternoon was not what we had planned, it was eminently worthwhile.

Over the next two days, we shuttled around Khartoum, shirts plastered to our backs in temperatures that climbed over 120 degrees, working on the next draft of the letter with Minister Sharfi; testifying before the Sudanese National Assembly Committee for Human Rights; meeting with the director of the Khartoum International Center for Human Rights, the leaders of the Women's Center for Human Rights, and the chair of the International Law Faculty at the University of Khartoum; filming interviews for a documentary on Adel; and appearing on a one-hour talk show on Al Sudani television, making the commentator uncomfortable several times with reminders that there are terrorists in Guantánamo and the overt torture he kept asking about stopped several years ago. It was not easy walking the line between politeness and honesty.

One of the most disturbing aspects of the trip was learning firsthand how badly the U.S. policies in Guantánamo have hurt my country's reputation around the world and damaged the cause of liberty. We heard time and again in our meetings, with no malice, "We understand what your country is doing in Iraq. You are imperialists and there is oil there."

But then the person would go on with genuine concern, "But we cannot understand Guantánamo. You are supposed to be the beacon of liberty in the world. If you do not uphold the rule of law, how can we here?"

Ashamed of the Guantánamo policies, the answer I gave repeatedly, individually, in press conferences, and to millions of viewers on television, was that the policies of the Bush administration and Guantánamo do not represent all of America. I patiently explained time and again that many people in America abhor what our government is doing in Guantánamo. I would defend my country, explaining how my presence in Sudan demonstrated the continuing vitality of the rule of law in America, how my government was paying me to fight it, and leaving me alone while I did. While some people were skeptical, most were amazed by my account, and I believe that our work in Sudan helped the U.S. image, at least a little.

But the concerns the Sudanese expressed reinforced for me the fact that when the United States forgets that people around the world look to us for leadership and ignores morality and the rule of law, we free others to do the same. Since most countries lack the checks, balances, and freedoms we have, the consequences are far more devastating to human life and freedom elsewhere than they are at home.

As wonderful as El Mogummer and Civic Aid were, I could not understand why they were devoting so much effort to the prisoners in Guantánamo when there seemed to be so much work to do on human rights issues in Sudan. This all became clear on Thursday when we were driving back to the Civic

Aid offices from the Foreign Ministry where William and I had pushed El Mogummer to seek another face-to-face meeting with one of the ministers when the phone calls about the letter seemed to be just so much stonewalling. El Mogummer said to his colleague, Hatim, "I wonder if we will be arrested after they leave."

Before the sentence was even finished, William and I were looking at each other with alarm. As bad as things seemed at home, this was a reality we never had to face. America is not a police state and Sudan is. El Mogummer tried to reassure us that he had been joking, but without much success. Slowly the reason behind Civic Aid's work on Guantánamo came out. The organization had devoted a lot of effort in 2006 to the plight of political prisoners in Darfur, work that had gotten them in such trouble with the government that they could not get their annual registration renewed. They chose Guantánamo as their next project because it was safer, an attack primarily on the United States rather than the Sudanese government, in the hope that their administration would let them continue in operation. As reflected by the governmental doors that were opened to us during our visit, trying to free the Sudanese prisoners in Guantánamo was a mission the government not only accepted but also decided to exploit for its own ends, as it put a benign face forward to the world in contrast with the American jailers at Guantánamo and their own image in the West as "butchers"[6] in Darfur. As of the publication of this book, El Mogummer and Civic Aid are doing fine.

Since we had not completed our interviews in our last visit to Adel's house, we returned Thursday evening. I continue to play over the bittersweet images of the five hours William and I spent at Adel's house interviewing the family members. We started filming outside, but as dusk fell and we needed more light, we moved inside the house where the only light came from bare forty-watt bulbs, one hanging loose from the ceiling in Al Tayeb and his wife's room and one in Salwa and the girls' room. Al Tayeb ran out to a Sudanese equivalent of a convenience store and got an extra bulb for a lamp he rigged up in his room. William sat on one of the twin beds, our interviewee on the other; the background was the same wall where Adel had his picture taken the day before he left for Pakistan in July 2002. The phone, a 1960s model that Al Tayeb used for the regular calls with William, sat on a dresser behind me.

Our first interviewee, Nusaiba, is Adel's niece and a medical student with a perfect grasp of English. Her father is also employed by WAMY but in a higher position than Adel had been. Nusaiba talked animatedly about Adel as the kind, funny uncle, the one who always brought something when he visited. She then translated for us for the rest of the interviews.

Adel's daughter Tasneen, seventeen when we interviewed her, remembered the Hira Institute, the Algerian neighbors, and school in Pakistan. We all choked up when she said in a voice dropping to a whisper, "I need my dad."

Insaf, Adel's younger sister, went to school in Pakistan for several years and she told us how Adel treated the orphans "like his own children." "He doesn't look to himself; he always thinks of others."

Our last nationwide television show was on Friday night on the Blue Nile station and the most animated of all meetings with the media. Our host, El Rasheed Khidar, who had been the head of the U.S. desk in the Foreign Ministry for many years and had also lived in America, pushed William and me with charges of racism in the United States relative to the Arabs in Guantánamo. Several million Sudanese heard me hit back, pointing out that racism is endemic throughout the world and that Adel is in prison because of the racism of the Sudanese's fellow Muslims in Pakistan who turned him in. As I said to William afterward, I should probably not go to Pakistan for a while.

After taking Saturday off for sightseeing at ancient Egyptian and Sudanese ruins in the north, we started Sunday by pushing El Mogummer hard for action on the letter. We were set to leave the following morning, and I could see that he was very uncomfortable with our American refusal to take no for an answer, but he reluctantly put in a call to the Foreign Ministry. Finally, in midmorning, someone from the ministry returned El Mogummer's call with the news that the foreign minster was in Libya and could not see us. There was no word about the letter. We were all upset, and William and I wondered if El Mogummer had been right in thinking we had pushed too far. Regardless, we felt we had nothing to lose and urged El Mogummer to try for a meeting with the state minister.

El Mogummer got nowhere, but around 2 P.M. a call came from the Foreign Ministry that Dr. Sulieman Mohammed, the ministry's executive director, would see us if we could get right over. He was all smiles when we walked into his office and we chatted about his time in the States, but after a few minutes, he got down to business.

"The foreign minister has been called to Libya. I am so sorry he cannot meet you."

Before he could say anything more, William interrupted, "What about the letter? Will we be getting it today?"

"I am so sorry, that is not possible. The foreign minister must sign it himself."

William got hot. "We have been promised that we would have a letter since Sunday. Can't the state minister sign it? That was what we were originally told would happen."

I could see El Mogummer trying to meld himself into the fabric of the couch. William's tone was not one a Sudanese would, or could, use with a government official.

I decided to step in, and referring back to some of the small talk we had started with, I asked, "Where did you live when you were stationed in New York?"

"Roosevelt Island."

Dr. Mohammed and I went off on a discussion about New York City, putting the unpleasantness behind us. When I steered the conversation back to the letter, he assured us that Foreign Minister Akol would sign it as soon as he got back from Libya. If we could delay our flight forty-eight hours, he would make sure we received a copy while we were still in Khartoum. As much as we wanted to have the letter before we left, after all the other promises that we would have the letter, it didn't make sense to trust that this time the letter would come through.

William and I left early the next morning as scheduled, sad as we flew home that Adel continued to languish in the prison.

27 | The Final Rounds for Adel

In these matters, the only certainty is that nothing is certain.

—Pliny the Elder

Date:30/04/2007

H.E. Condoleezza Rice
Secretary of State
U.S.A. Washington DC

Excellency:

I trust you are aware that nine Sudanese nationals were appre-
hended, some held in detention for long periods lasting five years, at
the U.S. Guantanamo Base prison in Cuba without charges or trials.

It is evident that, under International Law standards, Human
Rights norms and International Humanitarian Law, the detention
period the Sudanese nationals have spent in confinement is longer
than necessary and unwarranted. . . .

It is worth mentioning that, detainees Hamad (ISN #940) and
Bin Amir (ISN 716) have not been released despite a declaration
made, specifically in respect of Hamad, by the US Defense Department on February 22nd, 2007. . . .

No doubt, the detention of these Sudanese nationals has contributed negatively to the state of relations between the two countries and earned the US government, contrary to the good reputation and respect it had enjoyed years before in our peoples perception, an overt expression of displeasure and reproach from the public. ....

While the government of Sudan is urging the immediate release and eventual repatriation of its citizens, it ensures that due process and prosecution will be accorded to the trial of its nationals should proceedings be brought against any before the court of Law. In addition, it will provide the necessary guarantees and legal remedies for a free and fair trial to benefit the defendants, inter alia, public proceedings, right to counseling, evidence disclosure, . . . etc.

Finally, I have noted that Mr. Hamad's attorneys have been consistent in litigating the case and have provided proof of his innocence to US courts. It is therefore imperative that the US government grant a waiver declaring him a "non-enemy combatant." Such a measure, in my view, would constitute a positive step to speed up efforts leading to his return home concurrently with the visit of his attorneys to Sudan this week.

Sincerely Yours,

Dr. Lam Akol Ajawin
Minister of Foreign Affairs
Khartoum, Sudan

While it seemed to be such a long shot the day we left, the foreign minister did as he had promised and sent the letter the very same day, starting what we hoped would be the last round in our fight for Adel's freedom. I immediately called Loeb at the Department of Justice and sent him and Henry copies of the foreign minster's letter and asked them to send the letter to their people in the State Department. I explained the extent of my contact with the top Sudanese government officials and went on to say, "I believe these meetings gave me significant insights into the Sudanese government that could be most useful to the State Department in efforts to repatriate Mr. Hamad and the other Sudanese detainees."

My offer was not, however, limited to Mr. Hamad. I am a patriotic American and told them, "I believe the insights I gained could also be of more general use to the government and would be happy to provide the information to the appropriate personnel."

The first week in May also appeared to bring our efforts to have OARDEC hold a new CSRT a step closer. On May 7, the Department of Defense filed "OARDEC Instruction 5421.1," a brand new "Procedure for Review of 'New Evidence' Relatiing to Enemy Combatant (EC) Status" as an exhibit in the circuit court litigation about procedures for DTA hearings.[1] This was the document Major Peter had started working on after OARDEC received my office's evidence of innocence on Adel, Gul, and Al Ginco the previous fall. And, as the major had told me over the winter, the definition of "new evidence" was written specifically to track and include the types of material we had sent—"information that contends the detainee is not an enemy combatant and that contains photographs, affidavits, videotaped witness statements, or other supporting exhibits . . . as would documentation of investigative results." In an effort to make sure new evidence review did not get bogged down, the instruction included a time limit of ninety days within which OARDEC was to decide whether new evidence required a new CSRT.

I put in another informal call to Major Peter, complimented him on the procedures, and asked about Adel. He assured me Adel's case was first in line for consideration for a new CSRT.

But from that point on, all my efforts to communicate officially with OARDEC about a new CSRT and with the State Department ran into a stone wall. For two and a half months, the only answer I received from the State Department about Adel's repatriation was silence. As I told Loeb and Henry in one e-mail, "As I am sure you can imagine, it is quite frustrating to have had the opportunity to meet with high Sudanese officials and to be told that my government has no interest in meeting with me."

While my government would not speak with me, the Sudanese continued to get in touch. State Minister Elsamani e-mailed, Ambassador Ukec took William's and my calls, and they both told us that my government would not enter any dialogue with them either. On the broader diplomatic front, relations between the United States and Sudan took a turn for the worse. The Bush administration announced that it was going to increase sanctions on Sudan;[2] the Sudanese denied a visa to Senator Bill Nelson and other members of a U.S. delegation that was headed to visit the Darfur region.[3] It looked like the release of Adel and the other Sudanese in Guantánamo was enmeshed in negotiations over Darfur.

I was surprised then to receive an e-mail from Terry Henry on July 11 asking if I would be "available for a phone call with someone from the State Department" later that afternoon. I responded with alacrity, "Whenever." The call was as Kafkaesque as anything I had yet experienced. A man who asked me not to reveal the fact of his call identified himself as from the State Department's "Legal Department." There are scores of legal departments at State but that was as specific as he would get. He then proceeded to tell me, "You should have no expectations of future communications. This call does not set any precedent."

"What is going on with Adel?" I asked. "What would you like to accomplish during the call?"

"We will provide you no information," he said.

"Okay. So what specifically would you like to hear? What are your areas of concern?"

"I'm sorry. I can't answer that."

"Okay. Would it help Adel if I told you why I came back from Sudan believing it would be safe for him to go home?"

"You've told Terry that you would be happy to debrief us on your trip. That would be a good place to start."

So I did. For forty-five minutes I provided a detailed account of my time in Sudan, what was said during the meetings with government officials, the media coverage, and Adel's high profile as an innocent man, why I believed President Bashir supported our work there, Civic Aid's role, and the family support Adel enjoyed. When I mentioned the justice minister's commitment that I could participate in any proceedings in Sudan, the caller seemed concerned that the Sudanese were planning something nefarious. I explained that the minister's promise stemmed from my explanation to him that the U.S. government has insisted that some of the home countries investigate and try some of the detainees who had already been sent back.

What irony. After torturing Adel in Baghram and holding him for five years in a prison without any fair process, my government would not release him because the Sudanese might treat him unfairly. While I wanted to believe the person from State when he said, "We don't send people back where they will be tortured," I was furious at the monstrosity of the situation. There are good people in our government working on the Guantánamo situation, trying to uphold our core American values even in the midst of the nightmare that the administration has created. I am sure, like Gorder and Immergut in Brandon's case, some of them are aware of the context in which they are working. I could only hope that the State Department person was one, that he was doing his "due diligence" before Adel would finally go home.

A few days later I e-mailed Karin Ryan at the Carter Center about the call and that I had mentioned the center's interest in Adel. She too was hopeful that this meant the State Department was actively working on Adel's repatriation and agreed to speak to her contacts at the State Department again. "I would also mention that President Carter has been personally approached and that he has asked me to brief him on the situation—that tends to get their attention," she e-mailed back.

While former President Carter's concern might still get the attention of career foreign services officers, I was worried that it was unlikely to motivate anyone higher up in the administration given the former president's views about Bush. In an interview with the *Arkansas Democrat-Gazette* on May 19, Carter had called Bush's international relations "the worst in history."[4]

When there was no word from OARDEC by the beginning of July, I called Major Peter again to see if he could find out what was happening. He told me there were now several requests for new CSRTs in addition to those my office had submitted but assured me that Adel's should still be first in line. He agreed that more than enough time had passed for a decision to be made and he would check on the status of Adel's file, which was still with the head of OARDEC, Frank Sweigart. But then he stopped taking my calls, and when another month had passed with no news, I wrote to Sweigart and Deputy Secretary England, reminding them of the ninety-day time limit and urging them to act. Once again there was no reply.

.   .   .

After the Democratic takeover in both the House and Senate in the elections of 2006, the habeas counsel legislative groups had been in constant contact with senators Dodd, Leahy, and Specter about restoring habeas rights for the prisoners in Guantánamo. While a number of bills were introduced, the habeas issue kept getting pushed to the sidelines. First, there was the president's announcement, timed just before the January 11 fifth anniversary of the delivery of the first prisoners to Guantánamo, that he was going to be pushing a "surge" in troops in Iraq which, of course, focused Congress on the war and a series of ill-fated moves to pass a resolution to bring the troops home. Then a scandal broke over the attorney general's firing of eight United States attorneys. Restoring habeas for the prisoners in Guantánamo just could not get any traction.

Even though there was little movement in Congress, the media was paying close attention to the habeas restoration issue. On May 3, a *New York Times* editorial supported a new move by California's Senator Dianne Feinstein that would order closure of the prison.[5] The *Times* opined that many of the men in Guantánamo might not be terrorists at all and urged traditional judicial review of their cases rather than "dubious military commission proceedings, which produce implausible wide-ranging confessions or plea deals that exchange early release for pledges of public silence."

The first real action on any of the bills occurred on May 24, when Senate Judiciary Committee Chair Patrick Leahy took up the issue at an executive business meeting of the committee. In his opening statement he urged his colleagues to "reconsider this historic error" and "restore our legal traditions and re-establish this fundamental check on the ability of the government to lock someone away without meaningful judicial review of its actions."[6] He drew a parallel between the "stain on America's reputation in the world" from Guantánamo and the "internment of Japanese Americans during World War II." Ranking Republican Arlen Specter was just as concerned, but when the committee voted on June 7, he was the only Republican to join the Democrats in the disappointing eleven-to-eight vote.[7]

The animosity toward, and fear of, Muslims accused of terrorism was just too hot a political issue for our elected officials. In late June, word leaked out of Washington that the administration was seriously considering shutting down Guantánamo, and the Associated Press reported "consensus is building for a proposal" that would have moved the prisoners to other DOD facilities, including the military prison in Fort Leavenworth, Kansas. Within an hour, the administration issued a denial and National Security Council spokesman Gordon Johndroe was reported as saying the idea "was no longer on the schedule for tomorrow."[8]

Congress's reaction to the notion of moving the prisoners was even stronger. No one wanted "terrorists" in his backyard. On July 19, the Senate, which had not brought the bill for habeas restoration to the floor for a vote, overwhelmingly passed a resolution sponsored by Republican Minority Leader Mitch McConnell, ninety-four to three, saying that the men imprisoned in Guantánamo could not be brought into the United States.[9]

.　.　.

Shortly after getting back from Sudan, we learned that the strategy we had devised to get our DTA petitions moving on a fast track had not fared any better than our efforts with the State Department or OARDEC. Instead of expediting consideration of Adel's petition, the circuit court ordered any action deferred until it decided the procedural matters that were scheduled for oral argument in Bismullah's and Parhat's cases on May 15.

We watched Bismullah's and Parthat's litigation warily. At stake were important questions about whether the government would have to give any evidence to the habeas lawyers, the evidence the circuit court could look at, and whether the court could consider any new evidence from the prisoners. The administration was also arguing that the circuit court should throw out the Protective Order that had served everyone well for the past two years and enter a new order that would significantly limit all habeas counsels' access to their clients and what we could talk about.[10]

Loeb told the circuit court that habeas attorney-client contacts and mail transmittals were rife with abuse and had caused "intractable problems and threats to security at Guantánamo." Arguing for all the habeas and DTA lawyers, Sabin Willett, Jeffrey Lang, and Susan Baker Manning vigorously objected, pointing out that no district court had taken action against any of the lawyers in five years of litigation. The administration's extreme position was too much even for Guantánamo Base Commander Admiral Harris, who was quoted in the *Miami Herald* on May 4, "I have no issue with habeas visits. The detainees ought to have an opportunity to visit with lawyers to discuss their cases."[11] The DOJ lawyers quickly withdrew their request for a limited number of visits but continued to press for the other limitations.

The administration did not back away from its position that the DTA provided for limited review by the court. In an effort to show that court it did not have to worry about the fairness of the CSRTs, the administration submitted a declaration from Rear Admiral James M. McGarrah, who had been the director of OARDEC from July 2004, when the first CSRTs were held, until March of 2006.[12] McGarrah's declaration described the CSRTs as full and fair hearings and the obligations of the "recorder," the person described in the CSRT rules as responsible for gathering all evidence in the possession of the government about the prisoner, as broad. He also described how the recorders searched far and wide for both incriminating evidence and evidence of innocence and presented it all to the tribunals.

McGarrah's declaration bore no relationship to the procedure Adel and my other clients had described. All the habeas counsel believed that McGarrah had painted a grossly distorted picture of the CSRT process, but we knew belief and clients' statements would not get us very far with the court. We needed an insider to break ranks.

On June 15, we got the break we needed. After the McGarrah declaration was filed, the lawyers at Pillsbury Winthrop, the firm representing a number of prisoners including Fawzi Al Odah whose case was joined with Boumediene's, were trying to figure out how to respond. One of the employees in the firm spoke up. Her brother was a lieutenant colonel in the army reserves. He had been involved in the CSRT process, and she thought he might be willing to talk to them. So the Pillsbury lawyers made contact with Lieutenant Colonel Stephen Abraham and, on June 15, he signed a declaration that put the CSRT process in an entirely different light.[13]

Lieutenant Colonel Abraham, an intelligence officer, worked in OARDEC from September 2004 to March 2005, serving on one and reviewing numerous CSRT proceedings. Abraham described most of the recorders as junior officers with "little training or experience" working with "intelligence material." Contrary to what McGarrah had described, Abraham said the recorders "exercised little control" over the process of gathering information for the CSRTs, which was actually done by lower-level "case writers." The information they had to rely on, contrary to what McGarrah had said, was limited. Even though Abraham had intelligence training and was "suitably cleared," when he tried to get information, he was provided only "limited access." When he asked for permission to review further information, the request was denied. Abraham went on that he had "communicated" his concerns to McGarrah.

Abraham's descriptions of the shortcomings with the CSRT process did not stop with the information gathering. The hearing process itself, he said, was tainted by pressure from the command. "It was well known by the officers in OARDEC that any time a CSRT panel determined that a detainee was not properly classified as an enemy combatant, the panel members would have to explain their findings to the OARDEC deputy director. There would be intensive scrutiny of the findings by Rear Admiral McGarrah who would, in turn, have to explain the finding to his superiors, including the Under Secretary of the Navy." In Brandon's case, the task force that reviewed the FBI's process of fingerprint analysis concluded it was tainted by "confirmation bias" and the pressures of a big case. What Abraham described paralleled the failings with the fingerprint but were even worse: There was command pressure to reach a particular result before any hearing had even begun.

In a last-ditch effort after the Supreme Court's refusal in April to hear Boumediene's and Al Odah's cases, their lawyers had gone back to the Court and asked it to reconsider. The motion was still pending when Abraham signed his declaration and the lawyers filed it with the Court. On June 29, 2007, the last day of the term, the Court issued a most unusual order that once again set the habeas litigation on yet another path. The Supreme Court granted the petitions for rehearing the lawyers for Boumediene and Al Odah had filed.[14] Court-watchers noted that a turnaround like this was virtually unprecedented.[15] Because it takes five votes to grant a petition for rehearing, the move suggested that both Justices Stevens and Kennedy were ready to rule. Perhaps the Abraham affidavit had affected one of the justices, or, perhaps the delay in the circuit court's handling of the DTA petitions had shown the Supreme Court that the DTA might not be an adequate substitute for habeas corpus.

This time, it looked like the Supreme Court would have to rule on the fundamental constitutional questions about habeas corpus and executive power and decide whether the president could, as he continued to argue, unilaterally seize and imprison people without full judicial review in habeas corpus. As with the *Rasul*, *Hamdi*, and *Hamdan* cases, the Court was flooded with briefs urging it to rein in the administration.[16] Oral arguments were held in December 2007.

While the Supreme Court's change of direction was great news, it came with a price. With the Supreme Court getting back into the action, we were concerned the DTA process would stall all over again. While many prisoners needed the full scope of habeas review to have any chance at winning their freedom, the shortcomings in Adel's CSRT were so great we hoped we could prevail even under the limited scrutiny the DTA left for the courts.

We were pleasantly surprised then when, on July 20, the circuit handed down its procedural ruling in Bismullah's case, rejecting the adminstration's limited view of what it could look at and ordered the administration to provide the DTA petitioners with all the information that had been considered in the CSRTs.[17] At the same time the court did accept the administration's request for a new more restrictive Protective Order that included significant limits on attorney-client communication.

Freed by the *Bismullah* decision to press the court to move on Adel's case, I spent the weekend putting together new pleadings that urged the circuit court to rule on the merits of Adel's challenge to the sufficiency of the evidence against him without further delay. As I expected, the administration opposed any special procedure or timing for Adel, and a full month crawled by without any ruling from the court on our request that it move quickly.

When the court finally ruled at the end of August, our efforts to put Adel's case on a fast track were vindicated. The court granted our motion to expedite, though the "expedited" schedule did not require the administration to give us all the information it had looked at on Adel until October 15 and set the deadline for the last briefing on the case for December 31.

Confronted with the reality that it might finally have to produce some evidence about its prisoners and face a hearing in court, even the very limited hearing under the DTA, the administration brought out its big guns at the beginning of September—the directors of the CIA, NSA, FBI, and Deputy Secretary of Defense England.[18] Filed as exhibits to its request for the circuit to reconsider its order of July 20 that it produce all information it had reviewed in the CSRTs, the declarations said that "production of the sensitive classified material" could cause "exceptionally grave damage to national security." Underscoring the extent of its concerns, the administration filed CIA Director Michael Hayden and NSA Director Keith Alexander's declarations under seal, requesting that only the judges, not even their clerks, have access to them. The pleadings also said that the government did not have the staff to compile the records in the time the circuit was directing. At the time, these seemed like statements that were impossible to prove and impossible to refute. The government then filed motions to stay the orders of production in all the pending DTA cases, Adel now appearing as the lead petitioner in the consolidated motion the administration filed in sixty-four cases.

At the beginning of October, the circuit court denied the administration's request for rehearing but in an opinion that all but begged the Department of Defense to make all the DTA cases go away by giving every prisoner a new CSRT and in a way that did not resolve the delay issue by leaving open the possibility that the full court would grant rehearing.[19] Trying to salvage the progress we felt we had made, I filed an opposition to the administration's request for delay in Adel's case that had repercussions for all of the prisoners.

Earlier in the summer, in our search for something that would get Adel home, William and I had called Lieutenant Colonel Abraham. He was not familiar with Adel's case and did not add much beyond his affidavit, but he did agree to review the unclassified version of Adel's CSRT to see if he could offer us any ideas. When I asked him why, as an officer still active in the reserves, he had spoken up, Abraham told me, "McGarrah's declaration stepped over the line." He could not sit by in the face of a submission to the court that he believed contained statements that were "materially false." He had spoken up while he worked at OARDEC but no one had listened to him, and he believed what McGarrah told the court in his declaration "impugned the integrity of all the officers who were there." He did not believe it was right to let that happen.

The most helpful thought Lieutenant Colonel Abraham gave us after he had had a chance to review Adel's CSRT involved the classification process. He told us that the name of the major who had dissented in Adel's CSRT should not have been classified and suggested we check with the Privilege Team that had blacked out his name on the version of the CSRT the administration had filed as the return in Adel's habeas case. William, Pat, and I had been dying to speak with our dissenter ever since we first read his powerful words in hopes that he could tell us something more about Adel, or the unfairness of the CSRT process, anything that might help us win Adel's freedom.

William quickly followed Abraham's suggestion and started working with the Privilege Team to get the major's name. Within a week he prevailed and the Privilege Team sent us another copy of the dissenting major's opinion with his name visible. We were advised it was still "protected," which meant we could not disclose it, but since it was not classified, we were allowed to locate him and see if he would speak with us.

After negotiation with the major and his legal adviser in the army general counsel's office in Washington, William and I were finally able to meet with him in mid-August, and by September he had approved a declaration recounting his statements that William had prepared.[20] I included his statements when I told the circuit I opposed any further delay in Adel's case. Although the major, who had sat on forty-nine CSRTs, was limited in what he could say about any individual case, he said that "there was no separate exculpatory evidence presented in Mr. Hamad's case." In fact, "there was no exculpatory evidence presented separately, as required in the CSRT rules, in any CSRT" he sat on. He knows exculpatory information existed because at times they would stumble on it "by accident." As for the overall process, the dissenting major confirmed Lieutenant Colonel Abraham's statements about command influence, telling us that in all six panels he sat on where they found a prisoner not to be an enemy combatant, a new CSRT was ordered. Other habeas counsel immediately picked up the declaration and included it in their arguments about the importance of judicial review of the detention decisions.

October 15, the day set by the circuit for the government to provide us all the information it had on Adel, came and went with no ruling from the court and no information from the government. Looking for something more to add to our arguments that Adel's DTA case should move forward, William contacted Lieutenant Colonel Abraham again at the end of October. This time they talked about the affidavits the government had filed saying that requiring production of information on the prisoners would undermine national security. Once again Abraham had the courage to speak up, telling us that the reality of the situation in Guantánamo bore very little relation to what the intelligence directors had said. There had been hardly any significant intelligence about any of the prisoners. Moreover, Guantánamo was not even set up to handle and secure the types of intelligence the directors had described. Suddenly we had evidence from the inside that could rebut the exaggerated claims.

▪ ▪ ▪

Although it looked like we were making some progress in court over the summer, we were still hoping to get Adel home without a court order, so I asked William to check in with the Sudanese embassy in Washington to see if they would tell us whether there had been any progress in negotiation, or, indeed, if there had been any negotiations at all. Once again, the openness of the Sudanese was a painful contrast to the cone of silence in which my government continued to wrap itself. Ambassador Ukec was in Sudan during the first week in August, but Deputy Ambassador Elguneid took William's call. What he had to say opened yet another window into the "unconscionable" detention of Adel and put William on a plane to DC to see the documents he had described.

We learned that the United States military had actually cleared Adel for return home on November 10, 2005. We were later able to find a heavily censored copy of the clearance decision on the Department of Defense Web site, confirming that the decision on Adel was made immediately after the ARB reviewed his case.[21] On February 21, 2006, the State Department sent a delegation from its Office of War Crimes Issues to the Sudanese embassy, where they delivered a one-and-a-half-page document in which our government sought assurances from the Sudanese about the treatment its citizens would receive if they were repatriated. The United States also gave the Sudanese a synopsis of the information they had on Adel which, while it had none of the independent corroboration my team produced in our investigation, stated that he was indeed an innocent aid worker and hospital administrator.[22]

On June 9, 2006, a second meeting took place between the Sudanese and the United States, this time in the State Department. The Sudanese delivered an official reply to the State Department's request for assurances of fair treatment for the prisoners upon their return home. The deputy ambassador came away from the meeting believing the U.S. delegation was satisfied with the Sudanese assurances. At least ten times over the next year, the Sudanese told William, they requested a follow-up meeting and tried to find out from the new ambassador-at-large for war crimes issues, Clint Williamson, whether the United States needed something more from them. At least ten times since June 2006, the Sudanese ran into the same stone wall that I encounter when I try to get information from my government.

The breakthrough we had begun to fear would never happen finally arrived at the end of August. State Minister Elsamani Elwasila came to Washington to meet with Deputy Secretary of State John Negroponte for negotiations on Darfur. The status of the Sudanese prisoners in Guantánamo was also on the agenda. As the ambassador described the meeting to William and me by phone during the first week in September, he understood that a deal had been made and that Adel would be going home soon. He told us that he had been assured he could visit the Sudanese in Guantánamo but that Adel would likely be home by then.

A week later, I visited Adel in Guantánamo for what I hoped would be the last time. It was the most difficult meeting we had had. He was angry that he was still there, particularly because he had seen more men leave over the summer who had not been approved for transfer, and men he knew had been fighters. As he put it, "I have been through so many tests and I have been patient, up till now, but it is getting difficult." I explained what was happening in court and on the diplomatic front and tried to give Adel some hope, but I could see it was getting more and more difficult for him to trust American justice.

When nothing had happened by the end of September, William and I called the ambassador again. For the first time, this polished diplomat sounded frustrated. The State Department had stonewalled his request to visit Guantánamo. He had no news about Adel's repatriation.

28 | The Fight for Freedom
Is Never Won

Eternal vigilance is the price of liberty.
                                    —John Philpot Curran[1]

As HAS HAPPENED PERIODICALLY THROUGHOUT history, the tension between security and freedom is once again starkly visible. Bombs explode and people die. We feel real fear. When will the next attack take place? Who will do it? Is the fellow down the street who attends a mosque just a lawyer, or is he really a terrorist? Let's lock up the hospital administrator because he might be a terrorist.

Then we wonder, What should we do about bombs and the fear? Are the terrorists criminals who should be dealt with through prosecution and imprisonment? Or are they soldiers in a war that should be fought with no rules? Are new tools needed for our government to keep us safe? Do we need to give up freedom in order to maintain our security? What are the costs if we give our local police, the FBI, the attorney general, secretary of defense, and president more power? Will they abuse it?

Brandon and Adel's stories help focus the debate over these questions. Their fates, the citizen and the alien, are linked; they are a cautionary tale for all of us. The arguments for greater power to fight international terrorism necessarily spill over to the home front. When we start changing and ignoring the rules, we don't stop with just one group. When we lift the restraints on police and executive power, abuse is inevitable.

The arguments the Bush administration has made to justify the expanded powers it has sought and wielded—we need these powers to protect you from further terrorist attacks—are very difficult to refute. We all want to be protected, and protection of its citizens is the first priority of government. Terrorist bombs, collapsing buildings, and dead bodies are immediately visible and produce strong emotional responses. Our freedoms, on the other hand, are less tangible and exist for the most part in the realm of ideas. Most people say they want freedom in the abstract, but when given an immediate choice between more terrorism and less intrusion by government into our lives, many opt for safety.

There are several problems with this choice. One is that the safety offered is often illusory. The searches of baby strollers at airports does little or nothing for safety in the air and nothing at all for the safety of trains, trucks, shipping, and chemical and power plants.

A second problem is that the administration's policies have done nothing to address whatever grievances are shared by those people who attack, or want to attack, this nation. There may be nothing we can do to win over some of these people, and there may be nothing they want that we are willing or able to give, but there is much that we could do if we at least tried to understand and respond to what motivates them with something other than a gun.

Related to the second problem is the reality that some of the administration's policies have not only done nothing to address the concerns of those who would attack us but actually have helped them by presenting only an ugly side of America to the world. In the end, this turns more people against the United States and prevents us from exercising moral leadership in the world. These costs go far beyond the pool of potential terrorists and by doing so gives them far more fertile ground in which to breed. When we give up the moral high ground, we also free governments everywhere to do far worse.

A third problem is that while many of the people who implement the administration's policies are men and women of goodwill, some are corrupted by the power they wield and abuse it. This is far more likely when the nation's leaders engage in a campaign that demonizes our enemies. The abuses at Abu Ghraib and Guantánamo are but two of the most visible examples, as are the theft and petty indignities inflicted by TSA personnel. For some who wield the power of the government, the problem is not manifested overtly in theft or abuse but involves a moral ambiguity about their actions, the searches or break-ins or surveillance of fellow citizens. They feel uncomfortable about what they are doing, but it is sanctioned by the government. The ambiguity may be less than that felt by the Nazis, the Soviet KGB, or the the former East German Stasi, but there are significant lessens to be learned from the difficulty they, and their countrymen, have had in coming to terms with their actions.

A fourth problem is that the government's demonization and intentional creation of a climate of fear unleash the baser instincts not only in government officials but throughout the nation. People of Middle Eastern origin who have suffered the knock on the door by FBI agents have also felt the sting of their neighbors calling the FBI to report "unusual behavior" and fellow passengers refusing to board airplanes if the Middle Easterners are permitted to fly. If not checked, the unleashing of these base instincts feeds the demagoguery that can lead to the election of leaders who will push even farther.

A fifth problem involves incrementalism. The erosion of our freedoms can occur step by step. We say that this is a small price to pay for security. But the small steps add up to something far greater, and some steps may even be so small that we are not aware of them. As one of my mentors in Oregon, Senior Judge Owen Panner, wrote in an opinion about the erosion of judicial power in sentencing, "Like frogs in a simmering pot, we adjust to the new temperature, and complain among ourselves that it seems a tad warm, but then accept the new order of things, to repeat that process anew after the next encroachment."[2]

Although this is a book about the abuses of executive power, the corrupting effects of fear, and the importance of vigilance when confronted with a government's grasp for more power, it is also a story about the strength of America and its institutions. While both Brandon's and Adel's lives were turned upside down based on a mistake and devastated by the government's assertions of additional power and creation of new rules, in the end our system offered both of them help. The courts assigned me to represent both men, the citizen and the alien, and the government paid me to fight for them and put no restrictions on what I could do. As I told the Sudanese who were hostile to America, "I am American too. There is no other country in the world that would pay one of its citizens to fight against it in this way."

We are a great country whose people value human life and liberty, and there are few other places in the world where a nation's citizens can engage in the type of questioning, protest, and attacks on a government via its own legal system through which the world has learned the details about Guantánamo.

After a horrific beginning, the traditional criminal justice system worked in Brandon's case with Judge Jones issuing orders that the United States attorney and FBI were required to follow. While the nineteen days were an eternity for him and his family, it was lightning speed for the system. Then Congress ordered the inspector general in the Department of Justice to investigate the case and provide a report that is open to public scrutiny, albeit with classified portions removed. The civil justice system was open to Brandon, and he was able to achieve both personal recompense and vindication of his beliefs that parts of the Patriot Act that had been used to invade his privacy were unconstitutional.

Adel's case is more ambiguous. The administration's strategy in the habeas litigation, in the DTA litigation, and within the DOD has been remarkably successful. They delayed and prevented hearings in every way possible. As of the winter of 2008, after six years of litigation, not one court hearing has been held, not one detainee has had a day in court.

During those six years, the administration has been rebuked twice by the Supreme Court. While it has won a number of rounds of litigation in the lower courts, it has also lost several major decisions in the District of Columbia Court of Appeals. But it has not backed down from the position President Bush staked out in 2001, that he has the authority as commander in chief to order men seized, imprisoned, and subjected to extreme interrogation techniques and that the federal judiciary has no authority to question his actions through the writ of habeas corpus. And the Congress, whether led by Republicans or Democrats, has not reined the administration in.

Since the first prisoners were brought to Guantánamo in 2002, nearly 800 have been held in the island prison. More than half have been sent home, with fewer than 350 remaining on the island. All of the returned prisoners were, however, sent home by executive grace. In a clearly cynical pattern, the countries most closely allied with the United States—Great Britain, Australia, Germany, and Saudi Arabia—got their men home first. Some of the returned prisoners have been innocent, some have not. Some, like my Afghan client Nazar Gul, are home with their families, and we know that all our work on his behalf was not in vain because my staff's investigation was cited by the military as a factor in his release.[3] Other released prisoners, like my office's Afghan client Amin Ullah, were sent home with the express agreement between the United States and their home governments that they would be imprisoned at home.[4] Within the military system, only one prisoner has had a new CSRT ordered under the instructions that were published in May 2007, my client, the Taliban torture victim Al Ginco.[5]

As for Adel, while I have been paid by the government to represent him, I have not been able to have him set free. The administration continues to use the vast resources at its disposal to fight his release. We need to ask: Why does the administration continue to lie about the men it has imprisoned in Guantánamo? Why does it fight so desperately to keep men in prison it knows are innocent? What is it so afraid will come to light if any of the prisoners have a day in court? What does its continued use of fear to manipulate policy tell us?

I have felt time and again in my battles over the past four years that my fellow defenders and habeas counsel are the true believers in American values and that many members of the administration actually fear them. We lawyers believe in and trust our legal system. In fighting for our clients, we are fighting for the values that have set America apart. Some of the members of the administration act as though they fear "the rabble," as the kings of the seventeenth century and the Founding Fathers of this nation who wanted a far stronger executive branch than the constitutional convention produced called the citizens of this great land.

Every time we are stressed as a society, the executive branch flexes its muscles for more power and seeks to shift the balance struck in the constitutional convention. Every time Congress and the Supreme Court step aside, the executive gains more power, though we have been fortunate that when the crises pass, Congress and the Court usually reassert themselves. The grab for power during the past seven years has been more far reaching than ever before. Correcting the balance is going to require that we all speak up, reassert our rights, live our American values, and demand that our congresspeople reassert themselves and cease the intrusions on the power of the independent judiciary. While our governmental structure and system of checks and balances is stronger than those in other countries, America is not immune to the types of forces and abuses that have devastated other advanced societies through fascism and dictatorship.

What happens is up to us. America today is like the old Cherokee chief who was telling his grandson about life:

"A fight is going on inside me," the chief said to the boy. "It is a terrible fight and it is between two wolves. One is evil—he is anger, envy, sorrow, regret, greed, arrogance, self-pity, guilt, resentment, inferiority, lies, false pride, superiority, self-doubt, and ego. The other is good—he is joy, peace, love, hope, serenity, humility, kindness, benevolence, empathy, generosity, truth, compassion, and faith. This same fight is going on inside you—and inside every other person, too."

The grandson thought about it for a minute and then asked his grandfather, "Which wolf will win?"

The old chief replied simply, "The one you feed."

Postscript

There are no hereditary kings in America and no powers not created by the Constitution.

> —Judge Anna Diggs Taylor, ruling that warrantless wiretaps conducted by the NSA are unconstitutional.[1]

THE FRUSTRATION WE FELT THROUGHOUT FALL 2007 over the lack of progress on Adel's repatriation was relieved somewhat on October 31 when the Court of Appeals granted our request and reinstated the briefing schedule for hearing the merits of his case. Anticipating that the Department of Defense would now comply with the court's order and file a new version of the classified record from Adel's CSRT in 2004, I made arrangements to travel to the secure facility outside Washington on November 12. But the administration was still unwilling to allow a public hearing on any matters related to Guantánamo and on November 8 filed yet another motion asking the court to stay proceedings in Adel's case. Their reason for delay this time was the decision to grant Adel's request for a new CSRT.

While I was pleased that the Department of Defense had finally agreed to our earlier request for a fresh CSRT, I immediately told the court that I did not trust it would be held any time soon or that it would be fair. I pointed out that it was likely more than a coincidence that the decision to order a new CSRT had been made the very same day the court ordered a public hearing on Adel's case—a charge the administration later denied. It took the court only one day to grant the administration's motion and strike the briefing schedule, although it did order the Department of Defense to file frequent reports on the status of the CSRT. Fed up with the interminable delays and wanting to push the issue as hard as possible, I decided to go to Washington anyway to read the newly filed classified material and file my brief on the merits.

As originally planned, I headed to DC on Monday the twelfth. It did not take me long to review the material, and by the end of the day I had filed, with help from Lisa Powell, my security-cleared legal assistant, a full classified brief on the merits arguing Adel's innocence and an unclassified motion that asked the full DC circuit court to reconsider its decision to strike the schedule for hearing Adel's case on the merits.

With the motion, I also filed a new declaration from Lieutenant Colonel Abraham that had come in over the weekend, refuting the statements that the directors of the CIA, NSA, FBI, and Department of Defense had filed in September about the scope of the CSRT process. Based on his first-hand knowledge of the CSRTs, Lieutenant Colonel Abraham explained, in full detail, the misrepresentations contained in the declarations of the directors.[2]

Returning to the office on Wednesday afternoon after a pressure-packed trip to Washington, I called Bob Loeb, the Justice Department attorney who was still handling Adel's DTA case. Given the administration's frequent maneuvers throughout the litigation, I was cynically bemused when he told me that the "impediment that has been delaying Adel's release has been lifted." I also knew that if Adel was sent home before the new CSRT was held, it would never take place and the Department of Defense would not have to deal with the repercussions of the terrible mistake it had made through that first process.

No matter how I pressed, Loeb would not tell me anything more, so I asked William to see if he could get any information from the Sudanese. When he got through a couple of days later, the word was not good—the U.S. had demanded a new agreement from them with even more restrictions. The Sudanese were not willing to go along. The momentum that had been building for Adel's release once again seemed to have collapsed.

The court, however, held up its end and kept the pressure on the Department of Defense with an order on November 20 directing the administration to respond to our motion to keep things moving. The very same day, my congressman, Earl Blumenauer, wrote a stinging letter to Deputy Secretary of Defense England, urging prompt action on Adel's case.

Even though I hoped Adel would be home, in mid-October I had started making arrangements for another trip to Guantánamo. With Adel still languishing in prison, I left Portland on November 28 and was waiting for the flight from Fort Lauderdale to Guantánamo when William, who was also making the trip, pushed his computer over toward me and said, "Look at this." He had received an e-mail from Sudanese Ambassador Ukec stating, "I have just been informed . . . that the two will be transferred to Sudan Dec. 10, 2007." Inclusion of a firm date gave this news a much stronger sense of an impending reality than Loeb's earlier comment about an "impediment."

It was fortunate that we had something reliable to tell Adel when we saw him the next day because he was more depressed than I had ever seen him. Not only was his imprisonment weighing more heavily with each passing day, but since my previous visit in September, he had also been brooding about the possible conditions on his return to Sudan. It took a full hour before William and I were able to straighten out a misunderstanding left over from my September visit about exactly what he was likely to face at home. We then spent the rest of the day planning our strategy for the court cases and CSRT in the event Adel was released soon. While Adel was happy to learn he would likely be released in the near future, he remained skeptical and did not like the fact that he would leave under an enemy combatant designation. His voice was firm as he explained that he wanted us to continue pursuing efforts to clear his name: "I want justice."

Upon our return to Portland, we received another confirmation that Adel would be freed on December 10—this time from State Minister Elsamani Elwasila himself. As William told me, "My cell phone rang while I was driving in this morning. I couldn't make out the name at first, then realized the person was saying 'Elsamani Elwasila!'" I could not get through to even a low-level bureaucrat in our State Department but the Sudanese minister was so moved by our efforts that he called personally to tell us that Adel would be home in a week.

The next day, the Supreme Court heard arguments on the *Boumediene* and *Al Odah* challenges to the habeas-stripping provisions of the MCA and DTA. Solicitor General Paul Clement for the administration, and Seth Waxman (solicitor general under President Clinton) for the prisoners, presented the Court for the third time with the competing claims about the importance of habeas corpus in our constitutional scheme and the scope of the president's power. The outcome, which remains unknown as of publication of this book, may well determine Adel's ability to obtain justice in a U.S. court. And, unless the Court ducks the issue, the decision will be an historic statement about the extent of the president's authority and whether habeas corpus retains its centuries-old role as a fundamental check on executive power.

The following week dragged by. The tenth came and went with no news, as did the eleventh. Then, on the twelfth, William and I got great news from Al Tayeb: representatives from the Foreign Ministry had visited Adel's home that morning. It had been a friendly visit, and they had told Al Tayeb and Salwa that Adel "will be home with you tomorrow."

■   ■   ■

At 1 A.M. on December 13, a U.S. military transport touched down in Khartoum and Adel Hassan Hamad stepped out onto Sudanese soil. Thirty hours before, he had been taken from his cell in Guantánamo, blindfolded, earmuffed, and muzzled by the United States military for the last time and chained to a seat in the plane. Upon arrival in his country, the Sudanese intelligence authorities who took custody of Adel brought him inside the terminal and gave him a beautiful new jallabiyah and kufi. After a short debriefing, he was taken to a hospital for a checkup and then driven home. At 5 A.M. he was reunited with his family after five years, four months, and twenty-five days of imprisonment.

At 10:30 that night William and I called to make sure Adel was indeed home and free. Having had our hopes raised and dashed so many times over the past two years, no one on Adel's team could fully believe he was safe at home until we actually heard his voice on the phone from Khartoum. His niece Nusaiba, the English-speaking medical student who had been so helpful during our visit in April, answered the phone. We could hear music in the background. The homecoming celebration was still going strong. Adel got on the line and we heard his voice as a free man for the first time. "I thank God Almighty and express my thanks to you and your staff. Finally, I can see the light after the darkness."

Acknowledgments

This book started pouring out of me on the flight back to the mainland from Guantánamo at the end of May 2006. At first I thought I would write a magazine article on the situation in Guantánamo, but my experience with Brandon and the larger context of my life kept intruding. Lunch with fellow criminal defense attorney and noted author Phil Margolin resulted in an introduction to his agent, and while that did not work out, it led me to Barbara Kyle, Canadian author, writing teacher, and coach. She had the patience to work with a man who had not written anything other than a legal brief or college paper in forty years. And she was moved by the story I wanted to tell. After eight months of helping me learn to write without constant resort to legalisms and shape the book, Barbara took the unusual step of introducing me to her agent, Al Zuckerman, founder of Writers House. Al took a chance on me, as did Judith Gurewich, publisher at Other Press. Once launched at Other Press, my editor, Corinna Barsan, spent countless hours helping refine the story and work the prose. Corinna's assistance has been invaluable and reminded me of the first editors in my life, my parents, Anne and Jack, both wordsmiths in their professional lives who brought the love of learning and the English language into my life.

As I have looked back over the work my staff has performed on Brandon's case and on the Guantánamo cases, I have marveled at their creativity and passion. When we took on our Guantánamo clients, it was with the understanding that there would be no reductions in anyone's regular caseload. They have displayed the utmost professionalism in this extraordinary situation, as has Professor Dirgham Sbait, our tireless translator, who helped us understand Islam and Sudanese culture.

Thanks are also due to the work of the national habeas litigation team for their unceasing efforts over the past six years and sage words of advice as we started work for our clients, and to Robbie Hamilton, who took time away from his new daughter to help with the notes.

My most heartfelt thanks go to my wife, Kathleen, and son, Michael. For the past year and a half they have put up with me as my writing hours before dawn and late into the night stretched into our weekends. Kathleen has been my strongest supporter, first reader, and toughest critic, continually steering me back on course, while Michael has leavened the project with his ever-present humor.

Of course, this book would not have been possible without the grace and strength of Brandon and Adel.

Notes

Unless otherwise referenced, all of the facts about Brandon and his family and Adel and his family were gathered personally by the author during his representation of Brandon and Adel or by the author's staff at the Federal Defender Office. Dialogue between the author and Brandon and Adel and their families, the author and other witnesses or participants in the cases, and between Brandon and Adel and their captors is based on the notes and recollections of the author and the recollections of Brandon and Adel. Use of the notes and the author's observations is with the permission of Brandon and Adel.

The court pleadings and transcripts in Brandon's grand jury matter were originally filed under seal. All were unsealed after the matter was dismissed and are now open to the public. *In re Federal Grand Jury 03-01*, United States District Court for the District of Oregon Misc. No. 04–9071. Dialogue from court proceedings is taken directly from the transcripts.

Most of the pleadings in Adel's habeas corpus case in the United States District Court for the District of Columbia and his petition under the Detainee Treatment Act in the United States Court of Appeals for the District of Columbia are unsealed and unclassified. *Hamad v. Bush et al.*, No. 05-1009 (United States District Court for the District of Columbia); *Hamad v. Gates*, No. 07-1098 (United States Court of Appeals for the District of Columbia). This includes the transcript of Adel's CSRT proceeding and videotapes of witness interviews submitted as exhibits to the courts.

Prologue

1. Edward R Murrow, CBS newsman taking on Senator Joseph McCarthy and his communist witch hunts on his television show *See It Now*, March 9, 1954.
2. A number of books and articles have been written about Cox and the "Saturday night massacre." One that tells the story is Ken Gormley, *Archibald Cox: Conscience of a Nation* (New York: Perseus Books, 1997).

Chapter 2

1. Neibuhr was a Protestant theologian who wrote about the dangers of American idealism and excess at the height of the Cold War and the McCarthy era. *The Irony of American History*, Scribner Contemporary Classics (New York: Scribner, 1952).
2. Brandon's recollection of his response to the FBI agents was confirmed in the report by the Justice Department inspector general. *A Review of the FBI's Handling of the Brandon Mayfield Case*, Office of the Inspector General, March 2006, 67. The report is hereafter identified as Fine, for Glenn Fine, the inspector general who was responsible for preparing the report.
3. Brandon's recollection of the "media" comment was confirmed ibid., 68.
4. Carlton Smith, "Holy Warrior," *Willamette Week*, July 21, 2004.
5. 18 U.S.C. 3144.
6. The headline on the Web site for one of Portland's largest television stations that ran under the byline "KGW, NBC, CNN and AP Staff" was typical.
7. Les Zaitz, Noelle Crombie, Joseph Rose, and Mark Larabee, "Fingerprint Links Oregon with Spain," *Oregonian*, May 8, 2004, A1.
8. Fine, 69.
9. Ibid.
10. Zaitz, et al., Fingerprint Links Oregon," A8.
11. Transcript May 6, 2004, 7.
12. "Justice Department Covers Partially Nude Statues," *USA Today*, January 29, 2002.
13. *United States v. Awadallah*, 349 F.3d 42 (2nd Cir. 2003).
14. Zaitz, et al., Fingerprint Links Oregon," A8.
15. The transcripts of the oral argument held on April 28, 2004, in *Hamdi v. Rumsfeld*, No. 03–6696, *Rumsfeld v. Padilla*, No. 03-1027, and on April 20 in *Rasul et al. v. Bush et al.*, No. 03–334 are publicly available on the Supreme Court Web site, www.supremecourtus.gov_arguments/argument_transcripts.
16. Transcript of *Padilla* argument, 24–26.
17. Quoted in Ron Susskind, *The One Percent Doctrine* (New York: Simon and Schuster, 2006), 18.
18. Ibid., 21.

Chapter 3

1. Stephen Kyle, *Beyond Recall* (New York: Hachette, 2000), 222. Stephen Kyle is a pen name used by Barbara Kyle.

2. Adel was prisoner 940 in Guantánamo. Each prisoner was assigned a number at the base and that is how he was known, rather than by his name. The military set up a Web site on Guantánamo that is available to the public and provides continually updated information on operations at the base, www.jtfgtmo.southcom.mil.

3. *Rasul v. Bush*, 542 U.S. 466, 473 (2004).

4. *Hamdi v. Rumsfeld*, 542 U.S. 507, 525 (2004).

5. United States Constitution, Article I, Sec. 9, Cl. 2.

6. A brief history of habeas corpus replete with references can be found in the Supplemental Brief Amici Curiae of British and American Habeas Scholars Listed Herein in Support of Petitioners Addressing Section 1005 of the Detainee Treatment Act of 2005, authored by Professor Jonathan Hafetz in the United States Court of Appeals for the District of Columbia in *Al Odah v. United States*, No. 055095–05–5116.

7. The history of the Center for Constitutional Rights, its involvement in the Guantánamo litigation, stories of some of the prisoners, and the pleadings and briefs filed in the cases can be found on the CCR Web site, www.CCR-NY.org.

8. The litigation on behalf of the Kuwaitis has proceeded under the name *Al Odah v. Bush et al.* The original case number in the United States District Court in the District of Columbia was 02–828. The first decision dismissing the case is cited as *Al Odah v. Bush*, 321 F. Supp. 2d 1134 (DDC 2002). All of the court opinions in this and the cases of the other prisoners are in the public record and available through the courts and on the Internet through a number of Web sites, including www.supremecourt.gov, www.supct.law.cornell.edu, and www.juristlaw.pitt.edu.

9. Michael Kinsley, "The Right's Kind of Activism," *Washington Post*, November 14, 2004, B7, provides an interesting comment on complaints about "judicial activism."

10. A comprehensive study on state prisoner habeas corpus litigation, "Final Technical Report: Habeas Litigation in U.S. District Courts," conducted by Nancy King, and Fred Cheesman, and Brian Ostrom of the National Center for State Courts, can be found at the Vanderbilt University Law School Web site, http://law.vanderbilt.edu/article-search. The statistics for Oregon are compiled by the author's office.

11. *Clark v. Martinez*, 543 U.S. 371 (2005).

12. *Chaman v. Bush et al.*, No. 050887.

13. The Department of Defense Web site, www.defenselink.mil/news/detainees, includes a section on the prisoners in Guantánamo. The memoranda establishing the Combatant Status Review Tribunals and Administrative Review Boards, revising the procedures, and numerous news releases are available on that site. The Wolfowitz memorandum is available at www.defenselink.mil/news/jul2004/d20040707review.pdf. All of the documents discussed in the Supreme and Circuit Court decisions cited in these notes also contain descriptions of, and often verbatim quotes from,

the documents. The ARB process had actually been set up before the CSRT process. This is discussed on page 166.

14. Ibid.

Chapter 4

1. William Vollmann, *Europe Central* (New york: Viking, 2005), 22.
2. See author's note on page 331.
3. A history of religious freedom in the colonies can be found in Edwin S. Gaustad and Leigh Schmidt, *The Religious History of America: The Heart of the American Story from Colonial Times to Today* (New York: HarperOne, 2004).
4. The internment of Japanese Americans was authorized by Executive Order 9066, issued by President Franklin D. Roosevelt on February 19, 1942. A photo history of several of the internment camps can be seen at the Web site of the Willard Marriott Library at the University of Utah, www.lib.utah.edu/spc/photo/9066/9066.htm.
5. The Amache internment camp was located in Colorado. Governor Ralph L. Carr of Colorado spoke against the internment of the "yellow peril." See www.colorado.gov/dpa/doit/archives/govs/carr.html.
6. Jennifer Thompson, "I Was Certain but I Was Wrong," op-ed, *New York Times*, June 18, 2000.

Chapter 5

1. In 2003, long after Adel had left LDI, it was designated as an entity that provided logistical and financial support to mujahideen in the Afghanistan/Pakistan area, www.treas.gov/office/enforcment.
2. The WAMY UK home page is at www.wamy.co.uk.
3. The Revival of Islamic Heritage Society conducted charitable operations in Afghanistan and Pakistan but was suspected of supporting terrorist groups and was designated as a supporter of terrorist organizations by the Treasury Department in January 2002, www.treas.gov/office/enforcement.
4. Documentation on WAMY charitable activities can be found in exhibit 3 to the Motion for Summary Judgment filed in *Hamad v. Bush et al.* The Senate Judiciary Committee received testimony about WAMY, its relationship with the government of Saudi Arabia, and concerns about some of its activities on September 10, 2003, www.senate.gov/testimony.cfm.
5. Carlotta Gall, "Threats and Responses: Prisoners; Military Investigating Death of Afghan in Custody," *New York Times*, March 4, 2003. Ms. Gall and David Rhode followed up on the story a year and a half later when an army sergeant was charged with assault and other crimes in the beatings. "New Charges Raise Questions on Abuse at Abu Ghraib," *New York Times*, September 17, 2004.

6. Hekmatyar became prime minister in March 1993 after reaching a truce with President Burhanuddin Rabbani. "Afghans Appear Close to Peace," *New York Times*, March 4, 1993; "Bitter Epilogue in Afghanistan," *New York Times*, January 27, 1994.

7. *Miranda v. Arizona*, 384 U.S. 436 (1966).

8. Senator Patrick Leahy put together a time line of the memos discussing torture, http://leahy.senate.gov/press/200406/062204c.html. CooperativeResearch.org provides several time lines with synopses of most of the torture memos, www.cooperativeresearch.org/timeline.jsp?timeline-torture,_rendition,_and_other_abuses_against_captives_in_iraq,_afghanistan,_and_elsewhere_978. Another time line with links to some of the documents is available at http://lawofwar.org/torture_memos_analysis.htm. Karen J. Greenberg and Joshua L. Dratel, *The Torture Papers* (New York: Cambridge University Press, 2005), includes many of the relevant legal memoranda in full. Michael Otterman's *American Torture* (London: Pluto Press, 2007) places treatment of the prisoners at Guantánamo and Abu Ghraib in historical context.

9. Geneva Convention III, Art. 3.

10. The text is available at www.humanrightsfirst.org/us_law/etn/gonzales/memos_dir/memo_20020126_Powell_WH%20.pdf and www.why-war.com/files/text.

11. The February 7 memorandum is available from the White House Archive, www.pegc.us/archive/white_house/bush_memo.20020207.ed.pdf.

12. Greenberg and Dratel, *Torture Papers,* 218 ff.

13. Barton Gellman and Jo Becker, "Pushing the Envelope on Presidential Power," *Washington Post*, June 25, 2007.

Chapter 6

1. When we reread this 1967 court opinion in the office during our Guantánamo work, Bryan Lessley commented, "This, as we know, from the man who, as governor of California during World War II, supported the internment of Americans of Japanese descent for national security reasons irrespective of whether there was any evidence against them. I guess he learned as he grew older and wiser, as we all should."

2. *The 9/11 Commission Report: Final Report of the National Commission on Terrorist Attacks Upon the United States* (New York: Norton, 2004), chap 9, p. 28, also www.9-11commission.gov/report/911Report_Ch9.pdf (p 28).

3. The letter can be found at http://www.stanford.edu/group/King/frequentdocs/birmingham.pdf.

4. Gene Weingarten, "Getting Bush's Goat: A primer on priorities," *Washington Post*, July 18, 2004, W13.

5. The full text is available at www.whitehouse.gov/news/releases/2001/09/20010911–16.html.

6. A thorough discussion of the issues can be found in Jacob K. Javits and Winslow T. Wheeler, "The War Powers of the President and Congress," *New York University Law Review* 57, no. 4 (October 1982): 848.

7. The War Powers Resolution, Pub. L. No. 93–148, 87 Stat. 555 (November 7, 1973), codified at 50 USC 1341–1348; John Hart Ely, "Suppose Congress Wanted a War Powers Act That Worked," *Columbia Law Review* 88, no. 7 (November 1988): 1379.

8. The full text of the AUMF is available at the White House Web site, www.whitehouse.gov/news/releases/2002/10/20021002-2.html.

9. The full text of the speech is available at www.whitehouse.gov/news/releases/2001/09/20010920-8.html.

10. A brief history of the phrase "war on terror" can be found at http://en.wikipedia.org/wiki/war_on_terrorism. That history is taken from David C. Rapoport, "The Four Waves of Rebel Terror and September 11," *Anthropoetics* 8, no. 1 (Spring/Summer 2002), www.anthropoetics.ucla.edu/apo801/terror.htm#n16.

11. www.time.com/time/covers/1101010924?wosama.html. A number of recent books deal in depth with Bin Laden's pre-9/11 history in Afghanistan, including Lawrence Wright, *The Looming Tower: Al Qaeda and the Road to 9/11* (New York: Knopf, 2006), and Steve Coll, *Ghost Wars: The Secret History of the CIA, Afghanistan, and Bin Laden, from the Soviet Invasion to September 10, 2001* (New York: Penguin Press, 2004).

12. "Clinton Defends Military Strikes," BBC News, August 20, 1998, http://news.bbc.co.uk/2/hi/africa/155252.stm.

13. "Timeline: The Fall of Kabul," *Guardian Unlimited*, November 13, 2001, www.guardian.co.uk/waronterror/story/0,,592745,00.html.

14. The full text is available at www.whitehouse.gov/news/releases/2001/11/20011113-27.html.

15. "Timeline on the Fall of Kabul."

16. Mark Denbeaux et al., "Report on Guantánamo Detainees: A Profile of 517 Detainees through Analysis of Department of Defense Data," Seton Hall University School of Law, February 2006, 23–25, http://law.shu.edu/news/Guantánamo_report_final_2_08_06.pdf.

17. Ibid. See also www.psywarrior.com/afghanleaf40.html.

18. Ibid.

19. A transcript of the briefings is available at www.defenselink.mil/transcripts/transcript.aspx?transcriptid=2696 and www.defenselink.mil/transcripts/transcript.aspx?transcriptid=2320.

20. See chapter 5, note 8. The subsequent quotes from the memos also come from these sources.

21. See generally William L. Westermann, *The Slave Systems of Greek and Roman Antiquity* (Philadelphia: American Philosophical Society, 1955).

22. Thomas L. Friedman, "From George W. to George W.," *New York Times*, March 24, 2005, quoting David Hackett Fischer, *Washington's Crossing* (New York: Oxford University Press, 2003); John McCain, *Faith of My Fathers: A Family Memoir* (New York: Harper, 2000).

23. Susskind, *One Percent Doctrine*, 62.

24. Eric Schmitt, "Inquiry Ordered into Reports of Prisoner Abuse," *New York Times*, January 17, 2004.

25. Army investigations into prisoner abuse resulted in two reports: A three-part report known as the Fay-Jones Report, is available at http://fl1.findlaw.com/news.
findlaw.com/hdocs/docs/dod/fay82504rpt.pdf. "Article 15-6 investigation of the
800th Military Brigade," also known as the Taguba Report, is available at www.
npr.org/iraq/2004/prison_abuse_report.pdf. Secretary of Defense Rumsfeld's testimony
before Congress regarding prisoner abuse at Abu Ghraib is available at www.defenselink.
mil/speeches/speech.aspx?speechid=118.

26. Josh White, "Abu Ghraib Tactics Were First Used at Guantánamo," *Washington Post*,
July 14, 2005, A01.

27. Joseph C. Wilson IV, "What I Didn't Find in Africa," op-ed, *New York Times*, July 6,
2003; Scott Shane, "Private Spy and Public Spouse Live at Center of Leak Case,"
New York Times, July 5, 2005.

28. The facts about the Uighurs set out in the following pages were all presented to
the United States Court of Appeals for the District of Columbia by Sabin Willett,
Susan Baker Manning, and their team of lawyers at Bingham McCutcheon LLP in
pleadings filed on behalf of their Uighur clients in the cases captioned *Parhat et al.
v. Rumsfeld et al.*, No. 07-1397, and *Mahnut v. Gates*, No. 06-1066. Both pleadings
are fully footnoted to source material.

29. http://christianactionforisrael.org/antiholo/evian/evian.html

30. www.Nizkor.org.ftp.cgi/places/ftp.py?places//USA/conspiracy.004; Fritz Liebreich,
*Britain's Naval and Political Reaction to the Illegal Immigration of Jews to Palestine,
1945–1948*, (New York: Routledge Press, 2004), 183–184.

31. www.narrow-gate.net/jeffking/archives/002665.html

32. Charlie Savage, "Freed from Guantánamo, Five Face Danger in Albania," *Boston
Globe*, May 18, 2006.

Chapter 7

1. The facts about the bombings are based on reports in U.S. and Spanish news media.
Additional references are provided only for direct quotes. The primary sources are
"Madrid Attacks Timeline," http://news.bbc.co.uk/2/hi/europe/3504912.stm; "Timeline: Madrid Investigation," http://news.bbc.co.uk/2/hi/europe/3597885.stm; Tim
Golden, "Bombings in Madrid: The Investigation," *New York Times*, March 15, 16,
17, 2004; "Madrid Train Station Blast Kills 190," www.foxnews.com/story/0,2933,
113887,00.html.

2. Jerome Socolovsky and Tony Jefferies, "Four Terrible Minutes," *Scotsman*, March 12,
2004.

3. Ibid.

4. Elaine Sciolino, "Bombings in Madrid: The Attack; 10 Bombs Shatter Trains in
Madrid, Killing 192," *New York Times*, March 12, 2004.

5. "Madrid Witness 'Spotted Bombers,'" BBC News, July 6, 2004, http://news.bbc.co.uk/
2/hi/europe/3869055.stm.

6. Tim Golden, Douglas Jehl, and David Johnston, "Bombing in Madrid: The Investigation; Spanish Officials Divided on Whom to Blame for Train Attacks: Basques or Islamists," *New York Times*, March 13, 2004.

7. "Blair's Talks with Spain's New PM," BBC News, March 15, 2004, http://news.bbc.co.uk/2/hi/uk_news/politics/3512076.stm.

8. "US Chides Spain for Iraq Pull-Out," BBC News, April 20, 2004, available at http://news.bbc.co.uk/2/hi/middle_east/3640459.stm.

9. BBC News, "Timeline: Madrid Investigation, " http://news.bbc.co.uk/1/hi/world/europe/3597885.stm.

10. Dr. John Thornton, "Setting Standards in the Comparison and Identification," presentation at the 84th Annual Training Conference of the California IAI, Laughlin, Nevada, May 9, 2000, www.latent-prints.com/Thornton.htm.

Chapter 8

1. A description of the task forces can be found at www.fbi.gov/page2/dec04/jttf120114.htm

2. The DOJ stresses their success at prevention in "Fact Sheet: Department of Justice Anti-Terrorism Efforts Since Sept. 11, 2001," www.usdoj.gov/opa/pr/2006/September/06_opa_590.html. Contrast this with "U.S. Campaign Produces Few Convictions on Terrorism Charges: Statistics Often Count Lesser Crimes," *Washington Post*, June 12, 2005, A01.

3. Information about canvassing of Muslim neighborhoods in 2001 and again in 2004 is available on the ACLU Web site, www.aclu.org/safefree/general/18508prs20040805.html.

4. Jim Redden, "Thief or Terror Leader," *Portland Tribune*, July 9, 2004. All of the information about Mr. Steitiye is derived from public documents.

5. *United States v. Steitiye*, 01 Cr 00396, D. Or. The affidavit in support of a search warrant that was issued on October 17, 2001, is the third item in the public docket. The Stipulation of Facts submitted by the parties is number 44 in the clerk's record. The second indictment against Mr. Steitiye was filed under case number 02 Cr 00006. A Stipulaton is number 22 in the clerk's record; the government's sentencing memoranda are numbers 24 and 25.

6. An overview of Berkowitz's case can be found at www.crimelibrary.com/serial_killers/notorious/berkowitz/letter_1.html.

7. *United States v. Steitiye*, Memorandum in Support of Motion to Suppress, 02 Cr 0006, clerk's record no. 6.

8. Ibid., Stipulations, 02 Cr 0006 clerk's record no. 22; Mark Larabee, "Man Sentenced for Crimes, Not Hamas Beliefs," *Oregonian*, September 19, 2002.

9. Redden, "Thief or Terror Leader."

10. Jim Parker, John Becker, and Mahealani Richardson, KGW-TV, December 11, 2001, www.oregonlive.com/special/terror/index.ssf?/special/oregonian/terror/091902.html.

11. *United States v. Steitiye*, Cr 01–396, Memorandum in Support of Motion to Suppress, 8, and transcript of hearing, April 1, 2002, 44–50.

12. *Johnson v. United States*, 333 U.S. 10, 14 (1948).

13. Sherry L. Colb, "Why Get a Warrant? The President's Admission that He Authorized Warrantless Domestic Surveillance," December 28, 2005, http://writ.lp.findlaw.com/colb/20051228.html.

14. *United States v. Steitiye.*

15. Mark Larabee and Shelby Oppel, "Agent Discovers Traces of TNT in Bag Linked to Islamic Leader," *Oregonian*, September 10, 2002.

16. Timothy Egan, "Muslim Held After Bags Failed Check Is Denied Bail," *New York Times*, September 11, 2002.

17. The pleadings in *United States v. Kariye*, 02 Cr 00366, are available from the United States District Court; Mark Larabee et al., "Islamic Center Imam Released," *Oregonian*, October 12, 2002.

18. "Explosive Residue Tests on Kariye's Luggage Thrown Out," KATU News, September 23, 2002, www://katu.com/printstory.asp?ID=50479.

19. The account of the sentencing is based on the author's observations in the courtroom and Jim Redden, "Judge, Task Force Clash Over Sentence," *Portland Tribune*, September 20, 2002.

20. "Explosive Residue Tests on Kariye's Luggage."

21. Shelby Oppel, "Faith Leaders: Muslim's Civil Liberties Erode," *Oregonian*, September 29, 2002.

22. http://archives.cnn.com/2002/US/West/10/04/ashcroft.transcript/.

23. Ibid. The case against the Portland Six, and eventually the Portland Seven when Maher Hawash was added to the indictment, was brought under case number 02 Cr 00399 in the United States District Court for the District of Oregon. Except as otherwise noted, the facts about the case and the people charged in the indictment are taken from the court files.

24. Ford's and the others' stories can be pieced together from some of the court documents and was set out in Julie Sullivan, "Terror Case Stuns Those Who Know Suspects," *Oregonian*, October 6, 2002.

25. Mark Larabee, "'Portland 7' Pair Due in Court," *Oregonian*, September 18, 2003; Mark Larabee, "FBI Offers Reward for Man Suspected of Aiding al-Qaida," *Oregonian*, March 25, 2003.

26. Maxine Bernstein, "FBI Informant's Life Took on New Façade," *Oregonian*, October 31, 2002.

27. Defendant Battle's Memorandum of Law in Support of Motion to Suppress Foreign Intelligence Surveillance Evidence, *United States v. Battle, et al.* (Cr 02–399 JO, No. 275).

28. Mark Larabee and Les Zaitz, "FBI, Joint Terrorism Agents Search Home in Hillsboro," *Oregonian*, March 21, 2003.

29. Ibid.

30. Les Zaitz and Mark Larabee, "Terror Case Draws Two Starkly Different Portraits of Hawash," *Oregonian*, May 11, 2003.

31. Mark Larabee, "Bail Denied for Arab American Being Held as Material Witness," *Oregonian*, April 5, 2003.

32. Mark Larabee, "Friends Rally to Free Hillsboro Man in Federal Custody," *Oregonian*, April 4, 2003.

33. Rachel Swarns, "Muslims Protest Monthlong Detention Without a Charge," *New York Times*, April 20, 2003; "Friends of Arab-American Protest his Detention," CNN, April 4, 2003.

34. The indictment and pleadings in Hawash's case are found under the same case number as the Portland Six, 02 Cr 00399. See note 23.

35. "Muslims Protest at the Oregonian," *Oregonian*, June 20, 2003.

36. Deborah Howlett, "The Two Sides of One Law, the Two Lives of One Man," *Star-Ledger*, July 24, 2005.

37. Zaitz and Larabee, "Terror Case Draws Two Starkly Different Portraits."

38. Ibid.

39. *United States v. Battle*, 02 Cr 00399, transcript of proceedings November 24, 2003, 43–44.

40. Ibid., 18, 24.

41. The transcript of the sentencing is publicly available at the court, *United States v. Hawash*, 02 Cr 00399; Noelle Crombi, "Portland 7 Figure Gets 7 Years for Taliban Aid," *Oregonian*, February 10, 2004.

42. "Prosecutors Say Portland Seven Figure Is Dead, Move to Drop Case," *Oregonian*, June 23, 2004.

43. *United States v. Steitiye*, 04 Cr 00110. The facts in the next paragraphs are derived from the records in the case.

Chapter 9

1. January 1, 1972 Message for the Day of Peace.

2. John Ware, "UK 'Hosted Controversial Cleric,'" *BBC News*, July 11, 2006, http://news.bbc.co.uk/2/hi/uk_news/politics/5168104.stm; "Egypt's Muslim Brotherhood Wins Seats," *USA Today*, November 27, 2005.

3. Ahmed Rashid provides a brief history of the Soviet entanglement in Afghanistan in *Taliban* (New Haven: Yale University Press, 2000), Chap. 1.

4. The Office of Foreign Asset Control, www.treas.gov/offices/enforcement/ofac/.

5. Mark Mazzetti, "C.I.A. Lays Out Errors It Made Before Sept. 11," *New York Times*, August 22, 2007.

6. http://news.bbc.co.uk/2/hi/americas/5321986.stm.

7. See chapter 5, note 7.

8. See author's note on page 331. Federal defender staff brought back documentation of the hospital's operations and connections with the Afghan governments and United Nations Organizations. Those documents were presented to the courts in

Washington, DC, as exhibits in support of the pleadings filed on Mr. Hamad's behalf.

9. David Rose and Gaby Hinsliff, "US Guards 'Filmed Beatings' at Terror Camp," *Observer*, May 16, 2004.

10. See chapter 6, note 16.

11. The dissenting major sat on forty-nine CSRTs. His name remains sealed. The declaration William Teesdale prepared reporting his statement available in the pleadings filed in Adel's DTA case and from www.scotusblog.com. See page 315.

Chapter 10

1. Esmeralda Bermudez, "Soldier felt Army was the key to college, tried to get to Iraq," *Oregonian*, July 31, 2004.

2. Tim Golden, "The Battle for Guantánamo," *New York Times*, September 17, 2006.

3. Ibid.; Carol Leonnig, "More Join Guantánamo Hunger Strike," *Washington Post*, September 13, 2005, A03; www.prisoner345.net/sami-al-haj is a Web site supporting journalist Sami al-haj, one of the Sudanese hunger strikers; "Release Guantánamo Cameraman, Journalists Urge U.S.," Reuters UK, September 24, 2007.

4. The Scotusblog, http://scotusblog.com, has detailed analysis of the *Rasul* decision and much of the Guantánamo litigation with jump cites to original documents. It is a handy reference.

Chapter 11

1. Darrow made this statement in arguing to the jury while defending William Lloyd on charges of advocating the overthrow of the government in 1920 during the era of the Palmer raids. Quoted in Ron Christenson, *Political Trials in History* (Piscataway, NJ: Transaction Publishers, 1991).

2. A history of the community can be found in Roland Reisley, *Usonia New York* (Princeton, NJ: Princeton Architectural Press, 2001).

3. Thousands of aliens suspected of subversive beliefs or activities were deported in raids conducted under the direction of Attorney General Palmer at the end of 1919 and beginning of 1920. A catalog of books and articles on what became known as the Palmer Raids can be found on the Chicago History Museum Web site www.chicagohistory.org/static_media/pdf/historyfair_palmer_raid.pdf.

4. http://historylink.org/essays/output.cfm?file_id_5372. Wikipedia has an extensive entry on the strikes discussed in this and the following paragraphs, with annotations, http://en.wikipedia/May_Day_Riots_of_1919.

5. Marjorie Hunter, "Lawyers Promise Kennedy Aid in Easing Race Unrest," *New York Times*, June 22, 1963, 1.

6. Fred Hechinger, "Education; Now Harvard—The Place Where It Couldn't Happen," *New York Times,* April 13, 1969, E13; "Columbia Halting Work on Its Gym; Suspends Classes; But Students Remain in Five Seized Buildings," *New York Times,* April 26, 1968, 1.

7. Harry Schwarz, "Dubček and the End of the 'Prague Spring,'" *New York Times,* June 1, 1970, 34.

8. Daniel Walker, *Rights in Conflict* (New York: Dutton, 1968). A brief description of the report can be found in "Chicago Examined: Anatomy of a 'Police Riot,'" *Time,* December 6, 1968. See also Michael Kilian, "Walker Report Seen as Weapon for Daley Foes," *Chicago Tribune,* December 9, 1968, 1.

9. A popular account of the convention can be found in Norman Mailer, *Miami and the Siege of Chicago* (New York: World Publishing, 1968).

Chapter 12

1. The FBI's Freedom of Information Act Web site, http://foia.fbi.gov, has a number of interesting documents in pdf format, including a section on "surveillance and harassment" of King in the "Report of the Department of Justice Task Force to Review the FBI Martin Luther King, Jr., Security and Assassination Investigations," 113–132 (January 11, 1977), available at http://foia.fbi.gov/foiaindex/king.htm.

2. Nick Budnick, "Snitch Slapped," *Wilamette Week,* January 22, 2003, tells the sordid tale of the informer in *United States v. Barron.*

3. A brief account of LeGrand's crimes can be found in Joseph P. Fried, "A Job Description Contradicted by Killings," *New York Times,* September 1, 2002.

4. As Supreme Court Justice Sutherland wrote, "the United States Attorney is the representative not of an ordinary party to a controversy, but of a sovereignty whose obligation to govern impartially is as compelling as its obligation to govern at all; and whose interest, therefore, in a criminal prosecution is not that it shall win a case, but that justice shall be done." *Berger v. United States,* 295 U.S. 78.88 (1935).

5. Yee later wrote about his experiences. James Yee, *For God and Country* (New York: PublicAffairs, 2005).

Chapter 13

1. Engraving on the wall outside Judge Jones' courtroom.

2. The District Court of Oregon Historical Society Oral History Project published an oral history of Judge Jones in 2007. It provides significant insights into his career. Oral history interview with Robert E. Jones, Robert E. Jones papers, Mss 1814, Oregon Historical Society Research Library.

3. *Oregon v. Ashcroft*, 192 F. Supp. 2d 1077 (D. Or. 2002). Judge Jones's decision was upheld by the Supreme Court under the name *Gonzales v. Oregon*, 546 U.S. 243 (2006).

4. Transcript, *In re Federal Grand Jury 03–01*, 04–9071 (D. Or. May 10, 2004), 2.

5. Ibid., 7–8.

6. Ibid., 8

7. "A Nation at War: Courts; Ashcroft Is Criticized for Remarks About Witness in Terror-Cell Case," *New York Times*, April 19, 2003.

8. Robert E. Pierre, "Judge Rebukes Ashcroft for Gag Violation," *Washington Post*, December 17, 2003.

9. *Brady v. Maryland*, 373 U.S. 83 (1963).

10. Danny Hakim, "Judge Reverses Convictions in Detroit 'Terrorism' Case," *New York Times*, September 3, 2004; Peter Slevin, "Detroit 'Sleeper Cell' Prosecutor Faces Probe," *Washington Post*, November 20, 2005, A03.

11. Transcript, *In re Federal Grand Jury 03–01*, 33.

12. Ibid., 27.

Chapter 14

1. *Agreement Between the United States and Cuba for the Lease of Lands for Coaling and Naval Stations*; *February 23, 1903*, available at the Web site of the Avalon Project at Yale Law School, www.yale.edu/lawweb/avalon/diplomacy/cuba/cuba002.htm; *Treaty Between the United States of America and Cuba*; *May 29, 1934*, available at www.yale.edu/lawweb/avalon/diplomacy/cuba/cuba001.htm; "A Nation Challenged: Guantánamo Bay; In Cuba, Muted Acceptance Greets Presence of Prisoners," *New York Times*, January 14, 2002.

2. Larry Rohter, "U.S. Starts the Return of Haitians From Guantánamo," *New York Times*, January 7, 1995.

3. Tim Golden, "Military Taking a Tougher Line With Detainees," *New York Times*, December 16, 2006.

4. See chapter 6, note 16.

5. Moazzam Begg and Victoria Brittain, *Enemy Combatant: My Imprisonment at Guantánamo, Bagram, and Kandahar* (New York: New Press, 2006). Rasul's and Iqbal's stories are summarized in "Britons Allege Guantánamo Abuse," BBC News, August 4, 2004, http://news.bbc.co.uk/2/hi/americas/3533804.stm, and the entire 131-page report, "Detention in Afghanistan and Guantánamo Bay," can be found at www.ccr-ny.org/v2/legal/september_11th/docs/Guantánamo_composite_statement_FINAL. pdf.

6. Human Rights Watch has numerous articles and reports on detainee abuse, http://hrw.org/doc/?t=usa_torture; the Amnesty International report, "Cruel and Inhuman: Conditions of isolation for detainees at Guantánamo Bay," is available at http://web.amnesty.org/library/index/engAMR510512007. British journalist Andy Worthington published summaries of the stories of nearly all of the detainees who

are, or have been, in Guantánamo. *The Guantánamo Files: The Stories of 759 Detainees in America's Illegal Prison* (London: Pluto Press, 2007).

7. Joseph Felter and Jarret Brachman, CTC Report, "An Assessment of 516 CSRT Unclassified Summaries," July 25, 2007, www.ctc.usma.edu/csrt/default.asp.

8. Justice Sandra Day O'Connor stated flatly, "Indefinite detention for the purpose of interrogation is not authorized." *Hamdi v. Rumsfeld*, 542 U.S. at 521.

9. See chapter 5, notes 8–13. The administration's memos are also available at www .humanrightsfirst.org/us_law/etn/gov_rep/gov_memo_intlaw.htm. Although Addington does not appear as an author on any of the memos, his role in shaping the August 1, 2002 memo, as well as his secretive and influential role in the administration, was reported by Douglas Jehl and Tim Golden, "In Cheney's New Chief, a Bureaucratic Master," *New York Times*, November 2, 2005.

10. The executive summary is available from the Department of Defense, www. defenselink.mil/news/Jul2005/d20050714report.pdf. The December 2, 2002, memo is available at www.humanrightsfirst.org/us_law/etn/pdf/dod-memos-120202.pdf.

11. ACLU's complaint in *Ali et al. v. Rumsfeld*, United States District Court for the District of Columbia, 05-cv-1377 (TFH), www.aclu.org/images/general/asset_upload _file600_23378.pdf.

12. Rumsfeld's April 16, 2003, memo is available at www.humanrightsfirst.org/us_law/ etn/gonzales/memos_dir/mem_20030416_Rum_IntTec.pdf.

13. "Report on Torture and Cruel, Inhuman, and Degrading Treatment of Prisoners at Guantánamo Bay, Cuba" (New York: Center for Constitutional Rights, July 2006).

14. The ACLU has an entire section of torture-related documents obtained through FOIA, www.aclu.org/safefree/torture/torturefoia.html. Documents specific to the FBI are at www.aclu.org/safefree/torture/27807lgl20070102.html and www.aclu.org/ safefree/torture/27918lgl20070110.html.

15. www.aclu.org/projects/foiasearch/pdf/DOJFBI003362.pdf (sexual rubbing and simulated menstrual blood) and www.aclu.org/projects/foiasearch/pdf/DOD055781.pdf (perfume and touching).

16. See note 13.

17. Adam Zagorin and Michael Duffy, "Inside the Interrogation of Detainee 063," *Time*, June 12, 2005.

18. Shailagh Murray, "Durbin Apologizes for Remarks on Abuse," *Washington Post*, June 22, 2005, A06.

19. "Vice President Dick Cheney Talks With Sean Hannity," Fox News, June 14, 2005, www.foxnews.com/story/0,2933,159469,00.html.

20. See note 14, at http://action.aclu.org/torturefoia/released/022306/2715.pdf.

21. Jacobs also provided an interview to MSNBC, "Is Torture an Effective Anti-Terror Tactic? As Subject Becomes Hot Topic, Analyst Jacobs Discusses His Experiences," November 7, 2005, www.msnbc.msn.com/id/9958544/.

22. See chapter 6, note 26.

23. Sgt. Sara Wood, "DOD Identifies Guantánamo Detainee Suicides," American Forces Press Service, June 12, 2006, www.defenselink.mil/news/newsarticle.aspx?id=16072.

24. James Risen and Tim Golden, "Three Prisoners Commit Suicide at Guantánamo," *New York Times*, June 11, 2006.

25. Richard Norton-Taylor, "Asymmetric Warfare," *Guardian*, October 3, 2001.

26. The number of strikers was said to be 86 in June 2006. Tim Golden, "Guantánamo Detainees Stage Hunger Strike," *New York Times*, April 9, 2007. For a detainee's description of the insertion of the feeding tube, see note 11.

27. Neil A. Lewis, "Red Cross President Plans Visit to Washington on Question of Detainees' Treatment," *New York Times*, December 1, 2004.

28. One of the many times the president has made this statement was in a press conference with Japanese Prime Minister Koizumi on June 29, 2006. www.whitehouse. gov/news/releases/2006/06/20060629-3.html. Statements of the president, vice president, and Press Secretary Scott McClellan from 2005 are compiled at http: //hypocrisyandlies.blogspot.com/2006/02/facts-about-Guantánamo-bay-that-white. html.

Chapter 15

1. Justice William J. Brennan, Jr., "Reason, Passion, and the Progress of the Law," The Forty-Second Annual Benjamin N. Cardoza Lecture, September 17, 1987.

2. Hamdi's story is detailed in *Hamdi v. Rumsfeld*, 542 U.S. at 511–513.

3. Respondent's Response to, and Motion to Dismiss, the Petition for a Writ of Habeas Corpus at 6–13, *Hamdi v. Rumsfeld*, District Court for the Eastern District of Virginia, 2:02cv439, CR-25, http://notablecases.vaed.uscourts.gov/2:02–cv-00439/ docs/69820/0.pdf.

4. Department of Defense Detainee Transfer announcements keep a running tally, www.defenselink.mil/releases/release.aspx?releaseid=11368.

5. Neil A. Lewis, "Taliban Detainee Is Depressed, Lawyer Says," *New York Times*, December 18, 2003.

6. Brief for Respondent at 53, *Rasul v. Bush*, 542 U.S. 466 (2004) (No. 03–334), www. jenner.com/files/tbl_s69NewsDocumentOrder/FileUpload500/170/respondent_brief. pdf.

7. Respondent's Motion to Dismiss Petitioner's First Amended Petition for Writ of Habeas Corpus at 26, *Rasul v. Bush*, District Court for the District of Columbia, 02cv0299, www.ccr-ny.org/v2/legal/september_11th/docs/GovernmentResponseToRasulPetition. pdf.

8. Department of Defense, "Transfer of British Detainees Complete," news release, March 9, 2004, www.defenselink.mil/releases/release.aspx?releaseid=7113.

9. *Korematsu v. United States*, 323 U.S. 214 (1944). Also see Eric Paul Fournier, "Of Civil Wrongs and Rights: The Fred Korematsu Story," *PBS-POV*, Public Broadcasting System, March 1, 2002.

10. Korematsu's amicus brief, www.ccr-ny.org/v2/legal/september_11th/docs/RasulFred KorematsuSCamicus.pdf.

11. Justice Stevens emphasized that "'[A]t its historical core, the writ of habeas corpus has served as a means of reviewing the legality of Executive detention, and it is in that context that its protections have been strongest.'" *Rasul v. Bush*, 542 U.S. 466 at 474 (2004) (quoting *INS v. St. Cyr*, 533 U.S. 289, 301 (2001)).

12. *Handi v. Rumsfeld*, 542 U.S. at 525.

13. "Whatever the general merits of the view that war silences law or modulates its voice, that view has no place in the interpretation and application of a Constitution designed precisely to confront war and, in a manner that accords with democratic principles, to accommodate it." Ibid., at 579 (Scalia, J., dissenting).

14. Eric Lichtblau, "U.S., Bowing to Court, to Free 'Enemy Combatant'," *New York Times*, September 23, 2004.

15. *Padilla v. Hanft*, No. 2:04–2221–26AJ (D.S.C. February 28, 2005), www.pegc.us/archive/Padilla_v_Hanft/opinion_20050227.pdf.

16. Linda Greenhouse, "Justices Let U.S. Transfer Padilla to Civilian Custody," *New York Times*, January 5, 2006.

17. *Padilla v. Hanft*, No. 05–6396, slip op. at 8 (4th Cir. 2005) (order denying request to transfer petitioner from military to civilian custody), http://pacer.ca4.uscourts.gov/opinion.pdf/056396R1.P.pd.

18. *Hanft v. Padilla*, 546 U.S.126 S. Ct. 978 (2006).

19. Abby Goodnough and Scott Shane, "Padilla Is Guilty on All Charges in Terror Trial," *New York Times*, August 17, 2007.

20. Reference to the notice is on the DOD Web site, www.defenselink.mil/news/newsarticle.aspx?id=25730.

21. The notice is available at www.defenselink.mil/news/Dec2004/d20041209HN.pdf.

22. www.defenselink.mil/news/Jul2004/d20040707review.pdf.

23. The May 11 memorandum that established the ARBs can be found in the appendix to the *Al Odah* petition for certiorari at page 189, at http://ccr-ny.org/v2/legal/docs/AlOdah_CertPetition_FinalAppendix.pdf. The July 29 memorandum can be found at http://www.defenselink.mil/newsJul20040730comb.pdf

24. "Tribunals Begin for Guantánamo Detainees," July 30, 2004, www.defenselink.mil/news/newsarticle.aspx?id=25611; "Guantánamo Detainees Notified of Rights; Tribunals to Begin Soon," July 16, 2004, www.defenselink.mil/news/newsarticle.aspx?id=25698.

25. www.defenselink.mil/transcripts/transcript.aspx?transcriptid=2504.

26. The charges included attacking civilians, attacking civilian objects, murder by an unprivileged belligerent, destruction of property by an unprivileged belligerent, and terrorism. See www.defenselink.mil/news/newsarticle.aspx?id=27263.

27. *Hamdan v. Rumsfeld*, 126 S.Ct. 2749, 2760–2761 (2006).

28. A consolidation order referencing the government's motion was entered on August 17, 2004 in a series of cases still captioned *Rasul et al. v. Bush et al.*, 02 CV 0299, and *Khalid v. United States*, 02 CV 0828.

29. The resolution of consolidation is available at the district court Web site, www.dcd.uscourts.gov/GuantánamoResolution.pdf.

30. A brief biography of Judge Green is available at www.dcd.uscourts.gov/joyce-green-bio.html.

31. Response to Petitions for Writ of Habeas Corpus and Motion to Dismiss or for Judgment as a Matter of Law and Memorandum in Support, *In re Guantánamo Detainees*, 355 F. Supp. 2d 443 (D.D.C. 2005) (No. 02–cv-0299), www.pegc.us/archive/In_re_Gitmo/20041004_motion_to_dismiss.pdf.

32. Information on CCR's fight for John Does is available at www.ccr-ny.org/v2/legal/september_11th/sept11Article.asp?ObjID=qyqztHoIf8&Content=549.

33. A brief biography of Gordon England is available at www.defenselink.mil/bios/biographydetail.aspx?biographyid=47.

34. The letter was attached as an exhibit to the declaration of CCR Attorney Barbara Olshansky in support of the John Doe petition and is referenced at www.ccr-ny.org/v2/legal/september_11th/docs/DoeZ_v_Bush_Olshansky_Declaration.pdf.

35. Tim Golden, "Naming Names at Gitmo," *New York Times*, October 21, 2007.

36. A short biography of Olshansky can be found at www.law.stanford.edu/publications/stanford_lawyer/issues/74/LawyeroftheYear.html.

37. Golden, "Naming Names at Gitmo."

38. A brief biography of Judge Leon can be found at www.dcd.uscourts.gov/leon-bio.html.

39. *Khalid v. Bush*, 355 F. Supp. 311 (D.D.C. January 21, 2005).

40. *In re Guantánamo Detainees*, 355 F. Supp. 2d 443 (D.D.C. 2005).

41. Ibid. (February 3, 2005, order granting stay), www.pegc.us/archive/In_re_Gitmo/order_JHG_20050203.pdf.

42. *Hamdan v. Rumsfeld*, 344 F. Supp.2d 152 (D.D.C. 2004).

43. *Rumsfeld v. Hamdan*, 415 F. 3d 33 (D.C. Cir. 2005).

Chapter 16

1. Judge Learned Hand, address delivered in 1951; quoted in Elizabeth Frost-Knappman and David S. Shrager eds., *The Quotable Lawyer* (New York: Facts on File, 1986).

2. A compelling account of Gideon's story and its importance can be found in Anthony Lewis, *Gideon's Trumpet* (New York: Vintage Books, 1989).

3. Ibid., 10.

4. The Supreme Court's opinion discusses the importance of defense counsel in our Constitutional scheme. *Gideon v. Wainwright*, 372 U.S. 335 (1963).

5. The history of the meetings held in the wake of the decision in *Rasul* is set out in the Emergency Motion to Modify Order of August 17, 2004 filed in *Al Odah*, www.pegc.us/archive/Al_Odah_vs_US/al-odah_emerg_motion_20040915.pdf.

6. See chapter 15, note 34.

7. Ibid.

8. This is the same Protective Order applied in each of my office's cases and is available at www.pegc.us/archive/In_re_Gitmo/prot_order_JHG_amend_20041108.pdf.

9. www.ccr-ny.org/v2/reports/report.asp?ObjID=UsyAjyJ428&Content=599.

10. A brief biography of Judge Kay is available at www.dcd.uscourts.gov/kay-bio.html.

11. "McCain statement on detainee amendments," October 5, 2005, http://mccain.senate.gov/press_office/view_article.cfm?id=135.

12. The full text of the DTA, Public Law 109–148, 119 Stat. 2739, is available at www.pegc.us/detainee_act_2005.html. A brief history of the DTA can be found at "Recent Developments: Detainee Treatment Act of 2005," *Harvard Human Rights Journal* 19 (Spring 2006): 257.

13. The significance and use of "signing statements" is discussed in Arsalan M. Suleman, "Recent Developments," *Harvard Human Rights Journal* 19 (Spring 2006): 257, 263, n32; available at www.law.harvard.edu/students/orgs/hrj/iss19/suleman.shtml.

14. Ibid. n33. The signing statement is available at whitehouse.gov/news/releases/2005/12/20051230-8/html.

15. The motion to dismiss Hamdan's Supreme Court case is available at www.pegc.us/archive/Hamdan_v_Rumsfeld/SC_gov_DTA_mot_to_dismiss_20060112.pdf. It is typical.

16. The notice filed in Adel's habeas case appears as number 26 in the docket.

17. The amicus brief Steve Sady and the author filed is available at http://home.gci.net/~fpda/Library/amicus_brief_re_Guantánamo_detainees.pdf.

18. The main briefs in Hamdan's case are available at www.hamdanvrumsfeld.com/briefs. The transcript of the oral argument is available at www.supremecourtus.gov/oral_arguments/argument_transcripts/05–184.pdf.

19. Ibid.

20. The amicus briefs can be found at www.hamdanvrumsfeld.com/briefs.

21. Jess Bravin, "White House Will Reverse Policy, Ban Evidence Elicited by Torture," *Wall Street Journal*, March 22, 2006.

22. Jackie Northam, "Guantánamo Commander Prepares to Leave Post," NPR, March 14, 2006, www.npr.org/templates/story/story.php?storyId=5280165.

23. The government's motion is available at www.pegc.us/archive/Qassim/CAD_gov_em_mot_to_dismiss_20060505.pdf; "Albania Takes Guantánamo Uighurs," BBC News, May 6, 2006, http://news.bbc.co.uk/2/hi/americas/4979466.stm.

24. *Hamdan v. Rumsfeld*, 126 S. CT. 2749 (2006).

25. The text of the memorandum of July 7, 2006, is available at www.slate.com/id/2145592/entry/2145593/; also see Mark Mazzetti and Kate Zernike, "White House Says Terror Detainees Hold Basic Rights," *New York Times*, July 12, 2006.

Chapter 17

1. Executive Order Establishing the Office of Homeland Security and the Homeland Security Council, October 8, 2001, www.whitehouse.gov/news/releases/2001/10/20011008-2.html.

2. Homeland Security Act of 2002, Pub. L. No. 107–296, 116 Stat. 2135 (November 25, 2002).

3. USA PATRIOT Act, Pub. L.107–56, 115 Stat. 272 (October 26, 2001). A summary of the Patriot Act can be found at the ACLU Web site, www.aclu.org/safefree/ resources/17343res20031114.html.

4. 50 USC §§1801–11, 1821–29, 1841–46, 1861–62. A discussion of the FISA can be found in Americo R. Cinquegrana, "The Walls (and Wires) Have Ears: The Background and First Ten Years of the Foreign Intelligence Surveillance Act of 1978," *University of Pennsylvania Law Review* 137 (January 1989): 793–828.

5. John Podesta, "USA Patriot Act: The Good, the Bad, and the Sunset," *Human Rights Magazine* (Winter 2002).

6. President's radio address, December 17, 2005, www.whitehouse.gov/news/releases/ 2005/12/20051217.html.

7. The attorney general made these remarks in a speech at the University of North Carolina at Chapel Hill on September 12, 2006. Lisa Hoppenjans, "Ashcroft Defends the Patriot Act," *News & Observer*, September 13, 2006, www.newsobserver.com/ 161/story/485733.html.

8. A running tally of anti–Patriot Act resolutions can be found at www.bordc.org/ list.php?sortAlpha=1; also see http://action.aclu.org/reformthepatriotact/resolutions. html.

9. James Risen and Eric Lichtblau, "Bush Lets U.S. Spy on Callers Without Courts," *New York Times*, December 16, 2005.

10. A Review of the Federal Bureau of Investigation's Use of National Security Letters, Office of the Inspector General (March 2007), www.usdoj.gov/oig/special/index. htm.

11. Julie Hirschfield Davis, "Lawmakers Warn FBI Over Spy Power Abuse," *Washington Post*, March 21, 2007.

12. Adam Clymer, "Surveillance Rules Are Needed to Save Privacy, Senators Say," *New York Times*, August 2, 2002.

13. The text of the speech is available at http://edition.cnn.com/TRANSCRIPTS/0407/ 08/se.01.html.

14. Numerous volumes have been written about the impact on our society of the informers of the McCarthy era of the late 1940s and early 1950s when concern about communist infiltration in our government, trade unions, Hollywood, and the media was at its height. A number of books are discussed at http://writing.upenn.edu/ ~afilreis/50s/navasky-social-costs.html.

15. Robert W. Poole and James J. Carafano wrote a thorough report for the Heritage Society with jump cites to multiple government studies of airport screening problems, "Time to Rethink Airport Security," July 26, 2006, available at www.heritage .org/Research/HomelandSecurity/bg1955.cfm. See also, Robert O'Harrow and Scott Higham, "TSA Airport Security Contract Examined for Fraud," *Washington Post*, July 1, 2005, A07.

Chapter 18

1. See author's note on page 331.
2. Formal immunity under federal law is defined in 18 U.S.C. §§ 6002–03. The need for an independent source for evidence that was the subject of immunized testimony was discussed in *Kastigar v. United States*, 406 U.S. 441 (1972).
3. A summary of the law of double jeopardy can be found in Timothy Cone, "Double Jeopardy, Post-*Blakely*," *American Criminal Law Review* 41, no. 4 (Fall 2004).
4. The notice and list can be found at No.17 of the clerk's record in the grand jury matter.
5. *United States v. Bernal Obeso*, 989 F.2d 331, 333 (9th Cir. 1993).

Chapter 19

1. The in chambers and in court quotes in the first half of this chapter are found in the transcript of proceedings of May 17, 2004.
2. Eddie Barnes, "Cover-up, Conspiracy, and the Lockerbie Bomb Connection," *Scotsman*, February 19, 2006, http://news.scotsman.com/politics.cfm?id=258742006; Marcello Mega and Rajeev Syal, "Errors Put Wrong Man in Jail, Says Fingerprint Specialist," Electronic Telegraph, August 26, 2001, www.innocent.org.uk/misc/fingerprints_bayle.html.
3. Kelly Pyrek, *Forensic Science Under Siege: The Challenges of Forensic Laboratories and the Medico-legal Investigation System* (Elsevier Academic Press, 2007), 260–261; W. Jerry Chisum and Brent E. Turvey, *Crime Reconstruction* (Elsevier Academic Press, 2006), 551, 552, 570.
4. Years later, Brandon told me he has no recollection that Chris and I told him about our conversation with Moses—he thought that we had been as surprised as he was when we heard Moses's analysis in the courtroom.
5. See author's note on page 331. The quotes and description of the court proceedings from this point in the chapter to the end are found in the transcript of proceedings of May 19, 2004.

Chapter 21

1. ANSO can be accessed at www.afgnso.org/.
2. See author's note on page 331. The full tapes of the interviews were submitted as court exhibits to the district and circuit courts in Adel's case. Excerpts can be found on the Project Hamad Web site, http://projecthamad.org, and the federal defender Web site, http://or.fd.org/gtmo.html.
3. The tapes of the interviews conducted on behalf of Nazar Gul were submitted to the district court in his habeas corpus case, *Gul v. Bush et al.*, No. 05 CV 888. Ex-

cerpts of some of the interviews are available at the federal defender Web site, http://or.fd.org/gtmo.html.

4. The statements obtained on behalf of Al Ginco were submitted as exhibits in both the district and circuit courts under case numbers 05 CV 1310 and 07–1090. Al Ginco's plight has been described in a number of newspaper articles. See, e.g., Tim Golden, "Expecting U.S. Help, Sent to Guantánamo," *New York Times*, October 15, 2006.

Chapter 22

1. See Author's Note. Transcript of proceedings of May 20, 2004.
2. Tomas A. Tizon, "U.S. Frees Oregon Lawyer Held in Madrid Bombings," *Los Angeles Times*, May 21, 2004, A-21.
3. AP, "Spanish Cops: Fingerprints on Madrid Bomb Bag Traced to Algerian," May 20, 2004, www.foxnews.com/story/0,2933,120518,00.html.
4. Sarah Kershaw and Eric Lichtblau, "Questions About Evidence in U.S. Arrest in Bombing," *New York Times*, May 22, 2004, A14.
5. Noelle Crombie and Les Zaitz, "FBI Apologizes to Mayfield," *Oregonian*, May 25, 2004, A1.
6. The press conference was taped and videotaped by a number of media outlets as well as by the staff of the federal defender office. The quotes are taken from the federal defender tapes.
7. FBI press release, "Statement on Brandon Mayfield Case," May 24, 2004, www.fbi.gov/pressrel/pressrel04/mayfield052404.htm.
8. The motion to dismiss is number 32 in the clerk's record of the grand jury matter.
9. Tomas A. Tizon, "FBI Ignored Spain's Doubt on Fingerprint," *Los Angeles Times*, May 26, 2004, A-16.
10. Les Zaitz, "FBI Case Against Oregon Lawyer Built on Blurry Fingerprint, Logic," *Oregonian*, May 30, 2004.
11. Bayle's report is number 42 in clerk's record of the grand jury matter.
12. The front-page story ran on June 5, 2004, and included a photograph of Brandon looking out my office window at the county jail where he had been housed. Sarah Kershaw, "Spain and U.S. at Odds on Mistaken Terror Arrest," *New York Times*, June 5, 2004 A1.
13. The transcript of the hearing, Senator Feingold's remarks, and Attorney General Ashcroft's testimony are available at http://judiciary.senate.gov/hearing.cfm?id=1212. Oversight: Terrorism and Other Topics: Hearing before the Senate Judiciary Committee, June 8, 2004.

Chapter 23

1. The question attributed to former Secretary of Transportation Raymond Donovan was asked again in the context of the unsubstantiated charges brought against Guan-

tánamo Army Chaplain James Yee. Lawrence Aaron, "Will Charges Haunt Army Chaplain?" *The Record* , March 26, 2004.

2. Robert B. Stacey, "Report on the Erroneous Fingerprint Individualization in the Madrid Train Bombing Case," *International Journal of Evidence and Proof* 9, no. 2 (March 2005): 132–47.

3. The case came up in a series of stories and editorials in the newspapers and meetings in town halls across the country. Editorial, *New York Times*, July 4, 2004; Robyn Sumner, "All the Fear That's Fit to Print," *St. Petersburg Times*, June 6, 2004; David Heath, "U.S. Loses Faith in Fingerprints," *Seattle Times*, reprinted in the *Wichita Eagle*, June 13, 2004, 3A.

4. Representative Conyers's staff provided the author a copy of the letter.

5. Ibid.; Fine, 1.

6. Many of the documents in the civil suit *Mayfield et al. v. United States of America*, Cv. 04-1427, are publicly available. Judge Aiken's opinion finding portions of the Patriot Act unconstitutional is available at www.ord.uscourts.gov/rulings/04-cv-1427Opinion.pdf.

7. The opinion is cited hereafter as Aiken Decision with page references to the court-generated document.

8. Before the reports were published, Chris Schatz and I wrote a summary of our work on Brandon's case, "A Multitude of Errors," for the *Champion*, the magazine of the National Association of Criminal Defense Lawyers, September/October 2004.

9. Stacey, "Report on the Erroneous Fingerprint," 6.

10. Fine, 29–31.

11. Ibid., 31; Concise Statement of Material Fact in Support of Defendants Werder, Green, and Weiner's Motion to Dismiss, Exhibit 2–Declaration of Terry Green, *Mayfield v. United States*, No. 04-1427 CR-33, 2–3.

12. Fine, 30–31.

13. Ibid.,144.

14. Ibid.

15. Ibid., 32–33; Stacey, "Report on the Erroneous Fingerprint," 6.

16. David Heath, "Bungled Fingerprint Exposes Problems at FBI," *Seattle Times*, June 7, 2004.

17. Fine, 33.

18. Stacey, "Report on the Erroneous Fingerprint," 5–6.

19. Ibid., 6.

20. Fine, 33.

21. See note 11.

22. Aiken Decision, 6.

23. Fine, 34–35.

24. Ibid., 37.

25. David Sarasohn, "The Patriot Act on Trial," *Nation*, September 26, 2005.

26. Fine, 178, 237–40.

27. Ibid., 238.

28. Ibid.

29. Ibid., 239.

30. Ibid., 240.

31. Ibid., 34.

32. Ibid.

33. Ibid., 37.

34. Ibid., 38–39.

35. The annual reports of the Department of Justice to Congress on the activities of the Foreign Intelligence Surveillance Court are available at http://www.fas.org/irp/agency/doj/fisa/2006rept.pdf.

36. This was the first time in its history that the Foreign Intelligence Appeals Court met. The governments brief on the case is available at www.fas.org/irp/agency/doj/fisa/092502sup.html. The decision in *In re Sealed Case*, No. 02-001 is available at www.fas.org/irp/agency/doj/fisa/fiscr111802.pdf.

37. Ibid., Under 50 U.S.C. 1804, the attorney general may order electronic surveillance, and under 50 U.S.C., he may order physical searches without a judicial warrant.

38. Fine, 39.

39. Ibid., 48–50.

40. Ibid. 49–50.

41. Aiken decision, 23.

42. Fine, 43, 50.

43. Ibid., 53.

44. Ibid., 52.

45. Ibid., 60–63.

46. Ibid., 43–50.

47. Ibid., 60.

48. Ibid., 60–61.

49. Ibid., 62n36.

50. Human Rights Watch and the ACLU, "Witness to Abuse: Human Rights Abuses under the Material Witness Law since September 11," vol. 17, no. 2 (G), June 2005, www.aclu.org/FilesPDFs/materialwitnessreport.pdf.

51. The opinion is available at www.aclu.org/images/asset_upload_file543_26814.pdf.

52. Stacey, "Report on the Erroneous Fingerprint," 6.

53. Ibid.

54. Ibid., 3.

55. Aiken Decision, 9.

56. The text of the letter is included in the inspector general's report, Fine, 51.

57. Jennifer Anderson, "Portland Raises Ruckus with Task Force Demands," *Portland Tribune*, March 25, 2005, 1.

58. The ACLU has compiled reports of domestic political interference. A series of studies and press releases are available at www.aclu.org/search/search_wrap.html?account=436ac9516921&q=jttf+political+interference and www.aclu.org/safefree/general/17513prs20050422.html.

59. Ben Jacklet, "The Secret Watchers," *Portland Tribune*, September 13, 2002.

60. Beeson's remarks can be found at www.aclu-or.org/site/PageServer?pagename= Leg_localgovnmt_pjttf.

61. "A Review of the Federal Bureau of Investigation's Use of National Security Letters," March 2007, available at http://www.usdoj.gov/oig/special/s0703b/final.pdf.

62. The settlement was filed with the court on November 29, 2006. Aiken Decision, 4.

63. A transcript of the hearing testimony is available at www.washingtonpost.com/wp-dyn/articles/A28081–2005Apr5.html.

64. Fine, 221–36.

65. Ibid., 230.

66. Aiken Decision, 43–44.

Chapter 24

1. The text of Judge Hand's address delivered on May 21, 1944 in New York City is available on the Web site of the National Association of Criminal Defense Lawyers, www.nacdl.org/public.nsf/ENews/2002e67?opendocument.

2. The text of the president's remarks is available at http://www.whitehouse.gov/news/releases/2006/09/20060906-3.html.

3. See author's note on page 331.

4. Military Commissions Act of 2006, Pub. L. No. 109-366, 120 Stat. 2600 (October 17, 2006), enacting a new Chapter 47A of title 10 of the United States Code, http://frwebgate. access.gpo.gov/cgi-bin/getdoc.cgi?dbname=109_cong_bills&docid=f:s3930enr.txt. pdf.

5. Section 7 of the MCA provides, "No court, justice, or judge shall have jurisdiction to hear or consider an application for a writ of habeas corpus filed by or on behalf of an alien detained by the United States who has been properly detained as an enemy combatant or is awaiting such determination."

6. Charles Babbington and Jonathan Wiseman, "Senate Approves Detainee Bill Backed by Bush," *Washington Post*, September 29, 2006.

7. A history of the legislation with references is available at www.ccr-ny.org/v2/gac/learnmore/Docs/MCA%20Summary.pdf.

8. A transcript of the speech is available at www.whitehouse.gov/news/releases/2006/09/20060906-3.html.

9. 18 U.S.C. 2241.

10. Mark Landler, "12 Detainees Sue Rumsfeld, Citing Abuse," *New York Times*, November 15, 2006.

11. See chapter 16, note 17.

12. "Faces of Guantánamo" is available at www.ccr-ny.org/v2/reports/docs/faces_of_ Guantánamo.pdf.

13. E.g., Michael J. Sniffen, "U.S. Jails Man Once Tortured by Taliban," *USA Today*, October 21, 2006.

14. Project Hamad can be reached at http://projecthamad.org/. The project is still going strong reporting on Adel's case. A number of the people who have joined have written to Adel in Guantánamo. We know that some of the letters have gotten through because Adel shared his pleasure at receiving mail on my visit in September 2007.

15. Tim Golden, "Detainee Memo Created Divide in White House," *New York Times*, October 1, 2006.

16. A brief biography of Sweigart can be found at http://en.wikipedia.org/wiki/Frank_ Sweigart.

Chapter 25

1. Sabin Willett, habeas counsel for a number of the Uighurs and normally a bankruptcy lawyer, was so appalled at the conditions he found in December that he filed a declaration with the court challenging what he had seen. No action was taken, and in February 2007, things boiled over in Camp 5 with a boycott and hunger strike by the prisoners.

2. Darfur is a western province of Sudan where conflict has existed between the more nomadic Arab tribes and more settled African tribes for centuries. In recent years, as a result of drought conditions, geopolitical concerns, and the policies of the Sudanese government the region has suffered a tremendous human rights tragedy. A brief history of the conflict is available at from the BBC at http://news .bbc.co.uk/2/hi/africa/3496731.stm. In an effort to curb the conflict and deaths in Darfur, the United Nations and the United States imposed sanctions against Sudan in 2004 and 2007. See The United Nations and Darfur Factsheet, available at www.un.org/News/dh/infocus/sudan/fact_sheet.pdf; Whitehouse Factsheet: Fighting Genocide in Darfur, available at www.whitehouse.gov/news/releases/2007/05/ 20070529–2.html.

3. Donna Miles, "New Guantánamo Camp to Pave Way for Future Detention Ops," www.defenselink.mil/news/newsarticle.aspx?id=16280.

4. Tim Golden, "Military Taking a Tougher Line With Detainees," *New York Times*, December 16, 2006.

5. As of November 2007, the video had been viewed ninety-four thousand times on You Tube, with countless additional viewings on other sites. It remains available at www.youtube.com/watch?v=D5E3w7ME6Fs as well as on the Project Hamad Web site.

6. Carol Rosenberg and Lesley Clark, "Global Protesters Decry Guantánamo," *Miami Herald*, January 12, 2007, 1.

7. Stimson's comment was made during a radio interview with Federal News Radio. The audio is available at www.federalnewsradio.com/?sid=1029671&nid=318.

8. Robert L. Pollock, "The Gitmo High Life," *Wall Street Journal*, January 12, 2007.

9. Neil A. Lewis, "Official Attacks Top Law Firms Over Detainees," *New York Times*, January 13, 2007.

10. This was not the first time the government had kicked someone off the base. Mavish Khan, the interpreter we used for our Pashto-speaking Afghan clients, along with most of the habeas counsel, had been banned from the base in the spring of 2006 for photographs and an article she wrote about her visits to Guantánamo for the *Washington Post*. It had taken months and a great deal of patient negotiating before she was allowed back.

11. *Boumediene v. Bush*, 476 F.3d 981 (D.C. Cir. 2007), opinion available at http://pacer.cadc.uscourts.gov/docs/common/opinions/200702/05-5062b.pdf.

12. The second video has not drawn as many viewers on YouTube, only eleven thousand. It remains available at www.youtube.com/watch?v=qKhWShfhyyg and on the Project Hamad Web site.

13. Thom Shanker and David E. Sanger, "New to Job, Gates Argued for Closing Guantánamo," *New York Times*, March 23, 2007.

14. See generally, Australian Attorney General Fact Sheet on David Hicks, www.ag.gov.au/agd/www/MinisterRuddockhome.nsf/Page/RWPA97FEFD2043253A7CA 257283000 E9A8E; Josh White, "Australian's Guilty Plea Is First at Guantánamo," *Washington Post*, March 27, 2007, A01.

15. *Boumediene v. Bush*, No. 06-1195, and *Al Odah v. Bush*, No. 06-1196, 549 U.S. __ (April 2, 2007), decisions available at www.supremecourtus.gov/opinions/06pdf/06-1195Stevens.pdf.

Chapter 26

1. Information on Sami Al Haj can be found in Clive Stafford Smith, *Eight O'Clock Ferry to the Windward Side* (New York: NationBooks, 2007). A summary of Sami's story can be found on the Web site of the Committee to Protect Journalists, www.cpj.org/Briefings/2006/DA_fall_06/prisoner/prisoner.html.

2. See author's note on page 331.

3. The pleadings and orders in Bismullah and Parhat's cases, numbers 06-1197 and 06-1397, are in the public record in their case files. Some of the material is available at www.scotusblog.com/movabletype/archives/BismullahDecision.pdf (July 20 opinion), http://jurist.law.pitt.edu/pdf/bismullahpoproposal.pdf (protective order on counsel access), and www.scotusblog.com/wp/wp-content/uploads/2007/10/bismullahorder.pdf (opinion denying rehearing).

4. The Defense Department announced Errachidi's release in late April 2007, www.defenselink.mil/releases/release.aspx?releaseid=10788. His story is covered in Sean O'Neill, "Chef Who Was Held on False Claims Vanishes into Morocco," Timesonline, April 28, 2007, www.timesonline.co.uk/tol/news/uk/article1717582.ece. The Carter Center then began to weigh in for Adel with phone calls and letters to their contacts in the State Department.

5. Before the conflict in Darfur took center stage, Sudan had been racked by a civil war between the predominantly Arab and Muslim north and predominantly Chris-

tian and African south for twenty years. A Comprehensive Peace Agreement was signed in 2005 that stopped the fighting and divided power between the two factions. Under the agreement the northerners are dominant but cabinet posts are divided between the two groups. The United Nations Mission in Sudan Web site contains a brief history of the conflict and links to many of the peace documents, www.unmis.org/English/cpa.htm.

6. The situation in Darfur has generated intense interest and commentary, with numerous groups and individuals calling it genocide. See, for example, http://kristof. blogs.nytimes.com/2007/03/22/ann-curry-in-darfur/.

Chapter 27

1. The May 7, 2007, OARDEC Instruction 5241.1 was filed as an exhibit in *Bismullah v. Gates*, No. 06-1197, and the instruction is available at www.defenselink.mil/news/May2007/New%20Evidence%20Instruction.pdf.

2. White House press release, President Bush Discusses Genocide in Darfur, Implements Sanctions, May 29, 2007, www.whitehouse.gov/news/releases/2007/05/20070529.html.

3. Press release, Senator Bill Nelson, "Sudan Closing Doors to Scrutiny," May 9, 2007, http://billnelson.senate.gov/news/details.cfm?id=273894&.

4. Frank Lockwood, "Carter Calls Bush Administration Worst Ever," *Arkansas Democrat-Gazette*, May 19, 2007.

5. "An Exit Strategy for Guantánamo," editorial, *New York Times*, May 3, 2007.

6. Leahy's remarks are available at http://judiciary.senate.gov/member_statement. cfm?id=2785&wit_id=2629.

7. Jeff Zeleny, "Democrats Hope to Expand Rights at Guantánamo," *New York Times*, June 6, 2007.

8. Helene Cooper and William Glaberson, "At White House, Renewed Debate on Guantánamo," *New York Times*, June 23, 2007.

9. See S.Amdt. 2351 at www.govtrack.us/congress/bill.xpd?bill=h110-2669&tab= amendments.

10. See chapter 26, note 3.

11. Carol Rosenberg, "Guantánamo Chief Backs off Limits on Habeas Corpus Visits," *Miami Herald*, May 4, 2007. More information on the protective order issues is available on the Jurist Law Web site, http://jurist.law.pitt.edu/paperchase/2007_05_05_ indexarch.php#8422080341783380009.

12. The McGarrah declarartion is available at www.pegc.us/archive/Bismullah_v_Gates/ gov_mot_20070601_McGarrah.pdf.

13. Abraham's first declaration is available at www.scotusblog.com/movabletype/ archives/Al%20Odah%20reply%206-22-07.pdf.

14. The Supreme Court order is available at www.supremecourtus.gov/orders/courtorders/ 062907pzor.pdf. *Boumediene v. Bush*, 476 F.3d 981 (D.C. Cir. 2007), *cert. granted* (U.S. June 29, 2007) (No. 06-1195).

15. William Glaberson, "Supreme Court to Hear Guantánamo Detainees' Case," *New York Times*, June 29, 2007.

16. Lists of briefs and links to view them can be found at www.abanet.org/publiced/preview/briefs/home.html, in the 2007–08 section under "Al Odah v. United States" and "Boumediene v. Bush."

17. The prisoners themselves could still see only the unclassified information. The July 20, 2007 decision, *Bismullah v. Gates*, 501 F.3d 178 (D.C. Cir. 2007), is available at www.scotusblog.com/movabletype/archives/DC%20Circuit%20ruling%207-20-07.pdf.

18. See chapter 26, note 3, Respondent's Petition for Rehearing and Suggestion for Rehearing En Banc. The pleadings the government filed in Adel's cases are cross-referenced to the directors' statements. In the near future, the pleadings should be available at www.pegc.us/archive/ in the Bismullah or Parhat folders. A discussion on the pleadings can be found in "Detainees seek to block rehearing," September 26, 2007, www.scotusblog.com/wp/uncategorized/detainees-seek-to-block-rehearing/.

19. *Bismullah v. Gates*, 501 F.3d___ (D.C. Cir. October 3, 2007) (No. 06-1197), http://pacer.cadc.uscourts.gov/docs/common/opinions/200710/06–1197b.pdf.

20. See author's note on page 331. The declaration is available at www.scotusblog.com/wp/wp-content/uploads/2007/10/hamad-declaration-10-5-07.pdf. A summary of the issues is available from Lyle Denniston at Scotusblog, www.scotusblog.com/wp/uncategorized/a-new-critique-of-pentagon-detainee-panels/#more-5935.

21. The heavily censored document for Adel, ISN 940, listed as Adel Hussein Hassan is available at www.dod.mil/pubs/foi/detainees/csrt_arb/index.html, p. 625 of the records for Administrative Review Boards in 2005.

22. The U.S. government has never provided the author this information or confirmed its existence even though William saw it in the Sudanese embassy.

Chapter 28

1. The statement has variously been attributed to Curran, Thomas Jefferson, Patrick Henry, and Wendell Phillips. Suzy Platt (ed.), *Respectfully Quoted: A Dictionary of Quotations* (Washington, DC: Library of Congress, 1989), nos. 1054 and 1073; available online at www.Bartleby.com/73/. See also www.heartland.org/Article.cfm?artId=10714.

2. *United States v. Detwiler*, 338 F. Supp. 2d 1166 (D. Or. 2004).

3. In the fall of 2007, we were able to download portions of the ARB held on Gul in 2006 and read the references to our investigation, www.dod.mil/pubs/foi/detainees/csrt_arb/index.html, p. 513 of the records for Administrative Review Boards for 2006 under the name Nazargul Chaman.

4. As of the publication of this book, the limited efforts we have been able to make to help Amin Ullah through his family, tribal leaders, and human rights groups have not won him his freedom from the Policharki prison in Kabul.

5. Although a hearing was ordered at the end of August 2007, as of the publication of this book, the government will not tell us if it was held, and Al Ginco remains in Guantánamo.

Postcript

1. *ACLU et al. v. NSA*, Case no. 06-cv-10204 (August 17, 2006)
2. See author's note. Lieutenant Colonel Abraham's second declaration is an exhibit to our November 13 filing.

Index